THINKING PSYCHOLOGICALLY
ABOUT CHILDREN WHO ARE LOOKED
AFTER AND ADOPTED

THINKING PSYCHOLOGICALLY ABOUT CHILDREN WHO ARE LOOKED AFTER AND ADOPTED

Space for Reflection

Edited by

Kim S. Golding
Helen R. Dent
Ruth Nissim
Liz Stott

John Wiley & Sons, Ltd

Other Wiley Editorial Offices

John Wiley & Sons Inc., 111 River Street, Hoboken, NJ 07030, USA

Jossey-Bass, 989 Market Street, San Francisco, CA 94103-1741, USA

Wiley-VCH Verlag GmbH, Boschstr. 12, D-69469 Weinheim, Germany

John Wiley & Sons Australia Ltd, 42 McDougall Street, Milton, Queensland 4064, Australia

John Wiley & Sons (Asia) Pte Ltd, 2 Clementi Loop #02-01, Jin Xing Distripark, Singapore 129809

John Wiley & Sons Canada Ltd, 22 Worcester Road, Etobicoke, Ontario, Canada M9W 1L1

Wiley also publishes its books in a variety of electronic formats. Some content that appears
in print may not be available in electronic books.

Library of Congress Cataloging-in-Publication Data

Thinking psychologically about children who are looked after and adopted : space for
   reflection / edited by Kim S. Golding . . . [et al.].
      p.   cm.
   Includes bibliographical references and index.
   ISBN-13: 978-0-470-09200-2 (cloth : alk. paper),   ISBN-10: 0-470-09200-9 (cloth : alk. paper)
   ISBN-13: 978-0-470-09201-9 (pbk. : alk. paper),   ISBN-10: 0-470-09201-7 (pbk. : alk. paper)
   1. Children – Institutional care – Psychological aspects.   2. Foster home care – Psychological
aspects.   3. Adoption – Psychological aspects.
   I. Golding, Kim S.
HV862.T48   2006
155.44'5 – dc22   2005026867

British Library Cataloguing in Publication Data

A catalogue record for this book is available from the British Library

ISBN-13 978-0-470-09200-2 (hbk) 978-0-470-09201-9 (pbk)
ISBN-10 0-470-09200-9 (hbk) 0-470-09201-7 (pbk)

Typeset in 10/12pt Palatino by TechBooks, New Delhi, India
Printed and bound in Great Britain by TJ International Ltd, Padstow, Cornwall
This book is printed on acid-free paper responsibly manufactured from sustainable forestry
in which at least two trees are planted for each one used for paper production.

We would like to dedicate this book to our families of origin and our families of creation from whom we have learned so much.

A special thank you to:

Chris, Alex and Deborah
Roger, Benedict, Joscelin and Maximilian
Peter
Pat, Ben, Aoife and Lewie

who helped to create the space for us to write this book

CONTENTS

ABOUT THE EDITORS

Kim S. Golding, BSC (Hons), MSc (Clinical Psychology), DClinPsy
Kim is a chartered clinical psychologist, employed by Wyre Forest Primary Care Trust in Worcestershire, providing clinical leadership for the Integrated Service for Looked After Children (ISL). She was part of a small group who developed the Primary Care and Support Team (now part of ISL). The team provides support and training for foster, adoptive and residential carers. Kim has a longstanding interest in parenting, and collaborating with parents or carers to develop their parenting skills tailored to the particular needs of the children they are caring for. Within ISL she has developed a group for foster carers based on attachment theory, and has carried out research exploring the use of the consultation service. Kim coordinated a national network for clinical psychologists working with looked after and adopted children for a number of years. Additional to her clinical work Kim was, for 15 years, an associate lecturer for the Open University teaching Introduction to Psychology and Child Development.

Contact details: Integrated Service for Looked After Children, The Pines, Bilford Road, Worcester, WR3 8PU.
Email: kim.golding@tiscali.co.uk

Helen R. Dent, BA (Hons), MPhil, PhD
Helen is a chartered clinical and forensic psychologist, currently employed as Programme Director of the Doctorate in Clinical Psychology at the Universities of Staffordshire and Keele. Her previous post was Consultant Clinical Psychologist in an Inter-Agency team with children looked after by the local authority. She is continuing her work in this area, and has a contract with North Staffordshire Combined Healthcare NHS trust as Honorary Consultant Clinical Psychologist. She is particularly interested in strategic and systemic interventions, and in neuropsychological development. Prior to training as a clinical psychologist at the Institute of Psychiatry, Helen gained a PhD from the University of Nottingham, for which she carried out pioneering research into children as witnesses. She has held various academic and clinical

appointments and has edited three previous books, including *Children as Witnesses* (1992) with Rhona Flin, published by John Wiley & Sons.

Contact details: Shropshire and Staffordshire Clinical Psychology Training Programme, Faculty of Health and Sciences, Staffordshire University, Mellor Building, College Road, Stoke-on-Trent ST4 2DE.

Email: helen.dent@staffs.ac.uk

Ruth Nissim, BA (Hons,) MEd, PhD

Ruth is a consultant clinical psychologist and UKCP registered family therapist who has been in practice since qualifying in 1977. Since the early 1980s she has specialized in children living away from home in substitute families and in residential care. She has worked in all three agencies: Education, Social Services and the NHS, as well as for a private adoption agency. Since taking early retirement Ruth has worked on a freelance basis with a particular focus on supporting adoptive families. In 1999 she completed a research doctorate looking at the outcomes for children placed in adoptive or foster families longer-term.

Contact details: Dores Cottage, 17, High St, Finstock, Oxon OX7 3DA.

Liz Stott, MSc (Hons), MSc (Clinical Psychology)

Liz is a chartered clinical psychologist who has been working with children for the past 16 years. She has worked in both residential adolescent units and outpatient CAMHS before taking up specific posts to work with looked after children and their carers. She is interested in systemic and psychodynamic approaches to consultation and uses these ideas to inform practice when working with larger organizations such as Social Services, smaller organizations such as children's homes and also in consultation with carers. She is currently employed by Partnership Trust in Gloucestershire.

Contact details: The Child and Adolescent Mental Health Service, Delancey Hospital, Charlton Lane, Cheltenham, Glos GL53 9DU.

Email: liz@patnliz.eclipse.co.uk

CONTRIBUTORS

Sharon Brown   Since qualifying as a general nurse over 20 years ago, Sharon has added Midwifery, Family Planning, Health Promotion and Sexual Health training to her portfolio. She has a wide range of experience but more recently has specialized in working for local authorities as a health coordinator for children looked after in residential and foster care.

Contact details: Centre for Health, St John's Campus, Tiffield, Northants, NN12 8AA.

Email: ShaBrown@northamptonshire.gov.uk

Ann Courtney   Ann originally trained as a social worker, specializing in adoption and fostering. She qualified as a Play Therapist at the University of York in 1997 and now works as a Play Therapist in the Midlands and lectures and supervises on the Play Therapy course at York.

Contact details: University of York, Department of Social Work and Social Policy.

Email: ac47@york.ac.uk

Jane Foulkes   Jane initially trained as a social worker/probation officer. She worked in probation for several years before setting up as an independent therapist and trainer specializing in trauma and attachment.

Contact details: C/O ISL, The Pines, Bilford Road, Worcester, Worcs WR3 8PU.

Email: jane@bjfoulkes.fsnet.co.uk

Catherine Hamilton-Giachritsis   Catherine is a chartered forensic psychologist and senior lecturer at the University of Birmingham. Previously she worked in Birmingham Social Services Psychology Department, undertaking assessments of families where there was considered to be a risk to children or assessing the needs of children and adolescents in such families.

Contact details: Centre for Forensic and Family Psychology, School of Psychology, University of Birmingham, Edgbaston, Birmingham B15 2TT.

Email: C.Hamilton.1@Bham.ac.uk

Helen Hill Helen is an education professional with considerable experience as a middle school teacher, subject coordinator, pastoral head of year, special needs coordinator and deputy head. For the last five years she has been the manager of a multi-agency team of education and Social Services professionals which supports the education of looked after children in Worcestershire.

Contact details: ISL, The Pines, Bilford Road, Worcester, WR3 8PU.
Email: HHill@worcestershire.gov.uk

Julie Hudson Julie is a consultant clinical psychologist who has worked in a range of Child and Adolescent Mental Health Services for 20 years. Since 2000, she has worked in Bath, in a joint Health and Social Services post, developing consultative and therapeutic services for children who are looked after, and for adopted children and their families.

Contact details: LOCATE, Child and Family Therapy Services, 24 Combe Park, BA1 3NR.
Email: julie.hudson@awp.nhs.uk

Anne Peake Anne has worked as an educational psychologist since 1976 for Education and Social Services in Liverpool, London Borough of Haringey and now in Oxfordshire, in a specialist post for looked after children. Her main area of professional interest is in Child Protection.

Contact details: Educational Psychology Service, 44, Church Green, Witney, Oxon OX28 4AW.
Email: anne.peake@oxfordshire.gov.uk

Jenny Stevenson Jenny is a chartered clinical psychologist with over 20 years' experience of working with children, young people and their families in the NHS, Education and Local Authority settings. Jenny is currently in independent practice, working mainly in the Family Courts.

Contact details: 7, Chad Road, Edgbaston, Birmingham B15 3EN.
Email: jennystevenson@aol.com

FOREWORD

To be cared for by substitute parents or residential workers represents a breakdown in the natural order of things. That such a radical change of caregiver is necessary indicates a failure of the child's biological parenting. Thus, not only do placed children suffer a primary loss, invariably they will also have experienced poor quality care, including abuse and neglect. Children develop a range of psychological and behavioural strategies in their attempts to survive these early hostile and helpless caregiving environments. However, these adaptive strategies generally impair their psychological development and lead to a range of behavioural problems. Therefore the premise underpinning children's removal is to ensure their safety and sponsor developmental recovery by placing them with new, protective and emotionally available carers.

It is certainly the case that a change of carer represents the most radical, and potentially most effective child care intervention. But many of these children have survived their original ordeals by learning not to trust carers. Their emotional needs are great. Their behaviours can be difficult, and many children tax even the most relaxed and sensitive of carers. Many also experience problems at school. They underachieve. They find relationships with peers stressful. Recognizing the hurt and damage suffered by more and more placed children and the challenge faced by new carers, child health and welfare professionals accept the need to provide a range of expert support and advisory services. If children are to recover, they have to experience the benefits of long-term, stable and sensitive caregiving. Yet in many cases, it is the children's needs and problems that threaten the placement and the emotional availability of the new parents and carers. It is the job of child health and welfare experts to help carers to understand and connect with their children, and to help children to trust and feel safe with their carers. These are worthy though difficult objectives, but if they are achieved children's lives can be transformed.

Assessing the needs of placed children requires an understanding of developmental psychology and its application. It is therefore logical that policies and practices that affect children who are placed in adoptive, foster or residential care should include the knowledge and expertise of clinical child psychologists. A growing band of professional psychologists are now beginning to take a particular interest in the needs of placed children. The present book brings together the wisdom, experience and expertise of such a group. In timely fashion they not only describe and explain the nature and purpose of their skills, but also provide insights into the world of placed children that will be of great interest and benefit to parents, carers, child care and health workers, teachers and policy makers.

Recognizing the different ways in which early adversity can affect children, the contributors consider the therapeutic and vital support implications for adopters and foster carers, residential workers and educationalists, placement agencies, and the professional networks that gather to help children and their parents. As they write about their work, we gain a fascinating insight into what psychologists do, the way they think, and how they can help this group of children. An appreciation of the special contribution that psychologists can make in helping to develop more comprehensive services for adopted and fostered children should create responses that are both more coherent and integrated.

In the following pages we are treated to descriptions of the techniques and theoretical approaches used by clinicians, a range of innovative practices, and accounts of a psychological perspective made accessible to the rest of the professional and parenting network. As the authors emphasize, key to effective support and practice is interprofessional respect and understanding. By laying their clinical cards so clearly and honestly on the table, readers of this book will not only learn a lot about what psychologists do and what they contribute, they will also develop a fuller understanding of the very particular needs of that special group of children no longer able to live with their families of origin. For this pioneering and extremely valuable compilation, the editors and contributors are to be heartily congratulated.

David Howe
University of East Anglia
Norwich

PREFACE

Much rhetoric around services for children and families proposes joined-up working. The importance of inter-agency working has been discussed for at least the last two decades, and behind this rhetoric there is good will and real endeavours to deliver services in this way. Yet within this seamless, joined-up working many cracks still exist. The tragic death of Victoria Climbié (Laming, 2003) demonstrated to all of us how deep within these cracks some children are. Although receiving services, the children are often not benefiting from a holistic understanding of their needs or from interventions tailored to meet their unique circumstances. These are groups of children who have many needs similar to the population of children and families in general. Yet their particular experience also means that they have special needs, requiring enhanced as well as mainstream services.

This book aims to make psychological thinking for looked after and adopted children accessible. It is our belief that psychological thinking can help services and individuals to reflect upon the needs of the children and young people. This can lead to meaningful and truly joined-up services. While this will include consideration of psychological therapies and interventions, the focus will be much broader, helping others to apply a psychological analysis to this field both at the level of the individual child and carer and at the more complex level of networks and agencies.

Over the years there has been much debate, and much written about what psychology is and what we mean by psychological understanding. Writing this book has led us to revisit these old discussions. We remember the divisions between those viewing psychology as an understanding of mental life – what is going on within the mind – and of those whose focus was on behaviour, of what we see in front of us. We remember arguments about models, theories and perspectives. What distinguishes these and how are they constructed? All of this seems important to us but we find some of these distinctions arbitrary and limiting. Psychological thinking doesn't always offer answers but it does offer us ways of organizing what we see and what we feel. It allows us to hold a range of perspectives in mind and bring these to the real-life situations that we face. In this way we understand people a little better and we have a more rigorous basis for this understanding. This, however, doesn't completely capture what we had in mind when writing this book.

What, we wonder, is the role of psychological thinking in the therapy room, within the classroom, as part of the assessment process, during consultation, support or training? Can psychological thinking move us forward, towards healing, towards resilience? As we think about it we realize that for us the most important role for psychological thinking is the creation of a reflective space. Time to learn from each other. Of course there is a role for psychological theory, for models, and for perspectives, but these alone will not provide the answers. It is what we do within the space that will move us forward, together, on a journey of psychological understanding. Within this book we offer our contribution to the reflective space that lies between us. So, let us think about the children and young people who are at the heart of this book:

Tracey woke up with an awful jolt. Where was she? She didn't recognize the room and the voices on the landing outside were those of strangers. As she gradually came to, she started to remember the nightmare of yesterday. Her adoptive parents had finally said, ''That's enough'' and had phoned Social Services. The social worker had tried to talk them into letting her stay but they'd stuck to their guns. She'd got into the social worker's car and been driven into the night. They arrived at 'an emergency foster placement'. She remembered storming into this strange room and flopping down on to the bed in tears, lying awake for hours and then finally dropping off to sleep.

Someone was tapping on the door, calling her name and telling her the taxi was coming to take her to school. God, she looked a right mess. She hadn't undressed and had refused to wear the nightie the foster mum had given her. She'd been given a towel and stuff but right now she didn't feel like having a shower. She didn't know who she'd meet on the landing and anyway she didn't care if she did smell.

As soon as she got out of the taxi the kids crowded around her. She felt like hitting them but only swore instead. She hadn't got the right things with her and she hadn't done her homework. All morning the teachers were getting at her. Everything had happened so quickly that the teachers hadn't caught up with why she wasn't prepared. She was glad when her social worker turned up. 'We've called an emergency meeting,' she said, 'your parents are refusing to have you home and you can't go back to the family you stayed with last night. They haven't got a bed spare.' She wondered what was going to happen to her but didn't ask. She could see that there were no answers.

When she walked into the meeting, she'd already decided not to talk. Her dad was there but not her mum. He kept saying that she couldn't go home.

> The social worker couldn't persuade him to change his mind. There was talk of her going to a children's home while they looked for a foster family. She could tell that her dad was upset but he still didn't give in. Tracey was finding it hard to concentrate. Suddenly she heard them talking about finding other family members to look after her. This made her feel excited and scared. She'd been secretly thinking about her first mum for ages but hadn't said anything. Maybe she would be able to live with her again! Tracey didn't follow the rest of the conversation as a decision was made for her to go to the children's home while options were considered. As it was still only lunchtime, the social worker decided to take her back to school.
>
> All the kids crowded around her again, wanting to know what was happening. In the end she snapped and lashed out at someone. 'I'm 13 years old, my life is a mess and nobody cares', she thought as the teacher ran towards her.

The starting point for many of those interested in developing and delivering services for looked after and adopted children has been the now well-rehearsed litany of poor outcomes that various studies have highlighted. This fictional story provides a glimpse into the reality behind such facts and figures. Like Tracey, this group of children and young people have complex needs often following early histories in which they experienced extensive abuse and neglect. All of the children have experienced separation from their families of origin and often multiple moves within the care system as well. The impact of these experiences upon the children's health, education and emotional well-being is now well recognized.

In 1996 a well-cited study in Oxfordshire drew attention to the mental health needs of children 'in care'. Ninety-six per cent of children living within residential care and 57% of children living in foster care were found to have significant mental health problems (McCann et al., 1996). A national survey of the mental health of looked after children conducted more recently confirms these findings. Just under a half of all looked after children can be diagnosed with at least one psychiatric disorder. In addition, two-thirds of looked after children have recognized special educational needs, and a similar number were reported to be at least a year behind in intellectual development (Meltzer, 2003).

In the 1960s, Schecter et al. (1964) reported on the increased mental health needs of adopted children compared to the general population. Since these studies the changing face of adoption can only have increased the likelihood of the children experiencing difficulties. Within the UK changes in family planning practices and tolerance and benefits for single motherhood means that the process of adoption has changed. It has become much less about placing an infant with a childless couple, and more about finding a new home for an older child. The population of adopted children is therefore, to a large degree, drawn from the same population as looked after children. Thus the background experience, and the reasons for no longer living with their family of origin can be the same. For children adopted from overseas there are equally painful issues of loss of country, culture, and early institutionalization to contend with. Adoption is seen as a successful solution for these children and studies have demonstrated higher levels of emotional security, sense of belonging and general well-being than children living in long-term foster care (Triseliotis, 2002). Despite this the disruption rate for adoptive placements remains high, reported at between 10 and 16%. These children demonstrate an increased likelihood of psychiatric and behaviour difficulties compared to the general population (Barth & Miller, 2000).

Therefore children living in residential, foster and adoptive care are likely to have a greater need for health, education and social care support than children within the general population. During the 1990s there has been a growing recognition that health and education needs cannot necessarily be met exclusively by mainstream services. These agencies will need to work together and with Social Services and the voluntary sector to provide comprehensive services for children and families.

There is an increasing willingness to place the needs of children looked after, and adopted, on the national and political agenda. The Adoption and Children Act (DFES, 2002) places a duty on local authorities to provide a range of adoption support services. This guidance specifically states that adoption support services should not be seen in isolation from mainstream services. This has been followed by the publication of *Every Child Matters, Change for Children* (DFES, 2004a), the Children Act 2004 (DFES, 2004b) and the *National Service Framework for Children* (DOH, 2004). All of these highlight the need for increased services for looked after and adopted children. The importance placed on inter-agency working is perhaps most clearly stated in the requirement of local authorities to establish Children's Trusts. Guidance aimed specifically at the development of services for looked after children recognizes the importance of multi-agency planning, assessment and support in order to increase choice and quality of placements, to reduce the use of out-of-authority placements and to increase access to activities and opportunities (DFES, 2005).

Parallel with this has been a growing interest in, and development of, psychological services for looked after and adopted children. Until this century the children were most commonly offered the same services as other children, with little attention being given to their unique experiences. Psychologists are now becoming increasingly involved in the development of services tailored to the needs of looked after and adopted children. There is increasing recognition that health and education services can be inaccessible and that psychological services need to be designed and delivered in a way that is different from traditional services (see Golding et al., 2004).

There are, however, dangers here. As a scarce resource, psychologists can be over-valued for what they have to offer. As they are flattered into the role of expert it can appear that they know much while others know nothing. Myths of the psychologist able to 'fix the child' then become embedded into services. Psychologists don't have all the answers, but it is our suggestion, by writing this book, that psychological thinking does have something different to offer. A psychological perspective can enrich understanding and guide the interventions and support being offered.

This book is an attempt to provide that different perspective. This alone will not make life different for children and young people, but it is our belief that, when combined with the expertise of all those working in this field, we can move forward together with hope. Our aim is to reflect on psychological thinking in relation to the special needs of the children and their carers and to explore how this has influenced the development of practice.

We begin the book with a chapter that discusses the importance of listening to those we are serving and explores how psychological thinking can help these important voices to be heard. We consider the range of voices that are trying to be heard illustrated with the voices of the children, and their families.

In Part I we map out the territory. Chapter 2 provides an overview, setting the scene for the ensuing chapters. It considers the importance and necessity of inter-agency working, taking into account the different perspectives of all concerned. The onion model presented in this chapter is a visual representation of the complexity of this area. It highlights the need for multi-levels of working and the importance of managing this complexity. The following chapters consider how a psychological perspective can help us to think about and intervene with the education, and health needs of the child.

Part II moves on to consider the context for helping children to change and develop. Chapter 5 considers the role of the psychologist in the assessment of the looked after child, with a particular focus on assessment within a court arena. The following chapters discuss the way in which psychological perspectives can inform consultation and training with carers and other professionals involved in the care of the child. It also provides an exploration of how optimal environments can be provided within residential care.

Part III opens the door on therapeutic interventions. Informed by research, practice and psychological theory, it explores how interventions can be developed or adapted for looked after and adopted children, young people and their families and carers.

Although this book covers a wide range of topics exploring the helpfulness of a psychological perspective that can inform understanding and interventions, we are aware that this is by no means comprehensive. We acknowledge the areas that have been covered sparsely or not at all. We have not done justice to the cultural and diverse needs of children and families nor to helping the child with learning disabilities. Physical health is covered in less depth than mental health and the educational needs of the children are explored in one chapter only. However, our hope is that all professionals and carers involved in the care and education of looked after and adopted children will find food for thought here. Psychological understanding and interventions can often lie behind a veil of myth and mystique. We hope that we have been able to draw aside this veil, demonstrating how psychological thinking can help in the task of reaching between the cracks to the children and young people attempting to grow and thrive there.

KSG
HRD
RN
ES

REFERENCES

Barth, R.P. & Miller, J.M. (2000) Building effective post-adoption services: What is the empirical foundation? *Family Relations*, **49**(4), 447–456.

DOH (2004) *National Service Framework for Children, Young People and Maternity Services*. London: TSO.

DFES (2002) *Adoption and Children Act 2002*. London: TSO.

DFES (2004a) *Every Child Matters, Change for Children*. London: TSO.

DFES (2004b) *Children Act 2004*. London: TSO.

DFES (2005) Commissioning placements and services for looked after children and children with special educational needs and disabilities in residential placements. http://www.everychildmatters.gov.uk/key-documents/

Golding, K., Taylor, J., Thorp, D., Berger, M. & Stevenson, J. (2004) *Briefing Paper: Looked After Children: Improving the Psychological Well-being of Children in the Care of the Looked After System. A guide for clinical psychologists working with or considering the development of psychological services for looked after children and their carers*. Produced by Faculty for Children and Young People of the Division of Clinical Psychology. British Psychological Society, January.

Laming, Lord (2003) *The Victoria Climbié Enquiry*. London: TSO.

McCann, J.B., James, A., Wilson, S. & Dunn, G. (1996) Prevalence of psychiatric disorders in young people in the care system. *British Medical Journal*, **313**, 1529–1530.

Meltzer, H., Gatward, R., Corbin, T., Goodman, R. & Ford, T. (2003) *The Mental Health of Young People Looked After by Local Authorities in England*. London: TSO.

Schechter, M., Carlson, P.V., Simmons, J.Q. & Work, H.H. (1964) Emotional problems in the adoptee. *Archives of General Psychiatry*, **10**, 37–46. [In D.M. Brodzinsky & M.D. Schechter (Eds) (1990) *The Psychology of Adoption*. Oxford/New York: Oxford University Press.]

Triseliotis, J. (2002) Long-term foster care or adoption? The evidence examined. *Child and Family Social Work*, **7**, 23–33.

Notes About the Book

1. Throughout this book case examples have been described to illustrate and enliven the discussion. To protect the confidentiality of individual children, carers or professionals, these case examples are composite and drawn from a number of similar examples known to the authors. Names and autobiographical details have been altered in every case.
2. After some thought we have chosen to observe the current terminology used to describe looked after children and adopted children. However, we think it is important to acknowledge that the children are children first and foremost and their 'looked after' or 'adopted' status is secondary.

ACKNOWLEDGEMENTS

We have learned most from the children, carers and colleagues with whom we have worked. We would especially like to thank all the young people and carers whose voices we have included in the book. Very special thanks go to Caroline for her insightful thoughts about living in foster care and to Kerry for sharing her poems with us. Thanks also to Tricia Skuse for sharing her research with us.

Others we would like to mention by name are Dan Hughes for inspirational training and for helpful comments; Wendy Picken for help in developing ideas; Mary Williams, Angie Hart and Lisa Cogley for helpful comments on chapters; Elisabeth Epps and Natalie Lowndes for practical help; Jenni Randall whose 30 years of residential experience and excellent library on this topic proved invaluable; Peter Bramley for reading and commenting on drafts, but also for behind the scenes support which made the editorial collaboration work so well; Jenny Sprince, Fiona Brodie, Tess Docherty, Andrew Lister, Hilary Burgess, Moira Keyes and Mary Holba for support and helpful comments.

There are inevitably more people than we can include, who have made a contribution to the creation of this book. To those we have not specifically mentioned here, we give our sincere thanks.

David Howe deserves a special mention for his tireless peer review of all the chapters and for his encouragement for the project.

We all owe a great debt of gratitude to our families who have provided the space for us to reflect, create and write; to each other for endless hours of discussion, critical appraisal and reading drafts; to Ruth and Peter for their fabulous hospitality in Dores Cottage during editorial weekends; and to Kim for being an amazingly talented and hard-working senior editor. Without her dedication, some of us would have fallen by the wayside! At the outset Kim was the only one who knew us all and the process of getting to know each other's work, of understanding, accepting and learning from our differences has been one of the highlights of the whole experience. We believe that the book as a whole has benefited greatly from this process.

BEING HEARD: LISTENING TO THE VOICES OF YOUNG PEOPLE, AND THEIR FAMILIES

Kim S. Golding, Helen R. Dent, Ruth Nissim and Liz Stott

> Upon rereading my old diaries I realized how hard foster care was and what a detrimental effect it had on me at that time. Before my first foster placement broke down I thought foster care was a relatively positive experience, apart from the usual problem of occasionally feeling a bit awkward around the family, but when my foster care placement did break down literally overnight I realized why some young people in care do have the problems they do. I became very defensive and was determined to never let anyone ever hurt me ever again. I developed a very hard exterior to protect me at that time.
>
> (Caroline Cuckston, 2004, p. 24)

Historically the voice of the person receiving services has been overlooked. The welfare tradition in the UK has its roots in the Victorian moral imperative to help the disadvantaged and those less fortunate. This moral stance did not expect or actively elicit a voice from the 'grateful poor'. This was further reinforced by the strong role the Christian Church took in rescuing lost souls and guiding the sinners back onto paths of righteousness. The guidance of a wise God who knew best did not leave a lot of room for alternative perspectives.

It is only very recently that procedural or legal frameworks have been set up to ensure that there is user involvement in the development and delivery of

Thinking Psychologically About Children Who Are Looked After and Adopted
Edited by K.S. Golding, H.R. Dent, R. Nissim and L. Stott.
Copyright © 2006 John Wiley & Sons, Ltd.

services. This has extended into the provision of services for children. Within child protection services, for example, there is now considerable focus on involving the child and parent. This policy development has in turn become enshrined in law. Thus the Children Act 1989 (DOH, 1989) identified the need for collective responsibility in the care and protection of children. This act, for the first time, placed emphasis on a partnership between local authorities and families. It placed the wishes of parents and children as central within decision making, only to be over-ridden in exceptional circumstances through a court process (Hill, 1999). This same focus is present within a number of acts, for example, in proceedings for adoption via the Adoption Act (DOH, 1976) and in divorce involving children via the Family Law Act (DOH, 1996). More recently *Every Child Matters, Change for Children* (DFES, 2004a) clearly sets out the need to ensure that children and young people are listened to and that they are involved in the design and delivery of services. This is followed through in the Children Act 2004 (DFES, 2004b), which sets out the establishment of a children's commissioner, part of whose duty is to involve children in the provision of services and to promote the awareness of the views of children. In particular, the children's commissioner is tasked with involving children who do not otherwise have adequate means by which they can make their needs known. Guidance to support the programme of change outlined in *Every Child Matters* includes advice about commissioning placements and services for looked after children. This sets out as a key principle that 'mechanisms should be in place to enable the views of children in placements and using services to be taken into account' (DFES, 2005, p. 9).

Within the United Nations Convention on the rights of the child, Article 12 states the right of capable children to express their views freely in all matters affecting them (United Nations, 1989). Foster children have not been overlooked in this process. The 10th article of the Bill of Rights of Foster Children 1973 states that the foster child should receive high-quality child welfare services, including involvement in major decisions that affect his or her life. This article also highlights the need to involve the natural parents in decision making (see Martin, 2000), while the UK joint working party on foster care (NFCA, 1999) set out as a central principle a partnership approach to foster care – embracing parents, carers, social work services and the children themselves. Similarly, *Promoting the Health of Looked After Children* (DOH, 2002) emphasizes consultation and involvement with children and young people and the front-line staff delivering services to them.

The National Service Framework for children, young people and maternity services (DOH, 2004) has been developed to improve health and social care services, organized around the needs of the children and their families. These standards require services to involve children, young people and their parents in planning. Again there is particular emphasis on listening to the views of users both in relation to individual care that is being provided and in the development of local services. Particular attention is given to hearing from those who are often excluded.

Thus it is clear that there is increasing awareness of the principle of hearing the voice of the recipient of services. Having a principle, even one that is enshrined in law, however does not ensure good practice. A study by the Joseph Rowntree Foundation concludes that, at an individual level, children and young people are still not being properly consulted about decisions that affect their lives (Stuart & Baines, 2004). Thomas (2005) has compared the responses of local authority childcare managers to a postal survey carried out during 1997/8 and repeated in 2004. He concludes that there have been significant changes in the engagement of children and young people in the provision of services. This, however, only represents a changed culture in some areas. There is still some way to go in the development of a process for taking a child's view into account.

Moving from principle to practice, especially in the complex area of looked after and adopted children, is not likely to be straightforward. For example, what is the relative importance of the child's and the parent's views when these are not in accord? How do you best listen to the voice of the child without compromising the needs of the carer? There are also tensions between the child's right to participate in decisions and the right to have his or her welfare protected (Schofield, 2005). At what point do you override the requests of the child because it is deemed unsafe or clearly against his or her interests, when a child's wish is to return to what is considered an unsafe home, for example. What is the process whereby the child is listened to, heard and also protected? The fact that these questions are being asked and actively considered indicates the progress that has been made in this area. However, there is some considerable way to go if services are truly to be developed around the expressed wishes of child, carer and parent.

Jennifer is 12 years old and is voluntarily accommodated. She is living in a residential unit. Over the years she has had several returns home, none of which has been successful. Jennifer has been left feeling rejected but still desperately wanting to live at home. At a recent review Jennifer's father has once again said that he wants Jennifer home. Jennifer is very excited about this and wants it to happen immediately. Jennifer's key worker is very concerned about this, envisaging another breakdown in the future and worried about the impact of this on Jennifer's mental health. A decision is made for Jennifer to go home the following week. Two weeks later Jennifer is returned to care. She is in a distressed state and engaging in self-harming behaviour. Could this process have been managed differently? A slower process of working towards returning home might be helpful. This would allow time to work with Dad and Jennifer about how to make this return home more successful or for them to find an alternative way of having a stronger relationship that didn't end in rejection. Their wishes for reunion could be heard while also hearing the voice of the carer and the fears being expressed. This could have allowed everyone to be heard with an eventual plan that did not have such damaging repercussions for Jennifer or her Dad.

WHAT DO WE KNOW ABOUT THE VIEWS OF CHILDREN, YOUNG PEOPLE AND THEIR CARERS?

There is a growing literature on user views within adult services (e.g. Campbell, 1999; Pilgrim & Hitchman, 1999; Chambers et al., 2003). This, in turn, has led to attention being focused on child services. Thus children have been asked for their perceptions of services provided by child guidance clinics (Ross & Egan, 2004), of mental health services (Laws, 1998; Leon, 1999), of services for young people (Franklin & Madge, 2000) and of play therapy services (Carroll, 2002). Similarly, children's perceptions of therapeutic change have been sought (De La Cruz, 2002; Jessie, 1999).

Seeking children's views about the process of adoption, fostering or residential care is an important part of understanding the needs and wishes of children, but until recently research has been scarce.

An exception to this is the Who Cares? Trust. In 1992 it commissioned a survey of 626 looked after children and followed this up with a larger survey of the views of 2,000 looked after children in the UK (Shaw, 1998). This wide-ranging questionnaire survey obtained views on many aspects of being in care, including lifestyle, education, health, emotional well-being and leaving care. Some of the key findings were that:

- entry into care can be traumatic and needs to be better thought out and resourced;
- only 57% could state with certainty that they had a care plan;
- education was improved by being in care except that many of those regularly attending school reported never receiving homework or not having a quiet place and resources to do it;

- the health education needs of under 11s (e.g. body changes, sex) were not generally being met; despite receiving helpful advice on health, many were still putting their health at risk;
- many reported loneliness, isolation and lack of support;
- foster care generally appeared to be more successful in all respects than residential units, with the important exception that children in foster care were less protected by knowledge of their rights, e.g. complaints procedures, awareness of the need/right to have a care plan;
- there was a much higher incidence of risk taking in residential care – smoking, drugs, alcohol – and poorer educational attainments.

Thomas et al. (1999) reported on a study of adopted children that provides invaluable guidance for helping children with the process of being adopted and the continuing difficulties of contact, stigmatization and bullying. While this study is rich in providing a window on the voice of the child, the children interviewed were all successfully integrated into their families. The voice of the child troubled within an adoptive family, or who has suffered adoption breakdown, is missing.

More recently there has been increased interest in nationally relevant studies that seek to ascertain the views of children about the care system. For example, Skuse and Ward (2003) conducted a study of children's views when they were living within the looked after system, and after they had left. Dance and Rushton (2005) report on the Maudsley follow-up study of children joining foster or adoptive families in middle childhood. These studies reveal that children can be settled and positive about their experience although Dance and Rushton (2005) point out that it can take a considerable length of time to feel settled. The small sample size and difficulties in recruiting children, especially those experiencing placement disruption, make it difficult to generalize these findings.

The Commission of Social Care Inspection has produced a series of reports following consultation with children (see www.csci.org.uk). At the time of writing, the CSCI is reporting on findings from the children's audit of inspections. These are visits made to children's homes and boarding schools to talk to the children shortly after inspections have been conducted (Morgan, 2005). The CSCI has also surveyed foster children alongside foster carers and birth parents (in Collier, 2005). Children like having a sense of belonging, being cared about, stability and feeling safe. They are equally clear in wanting improved monitoring of residential units and foster placements, better communication between professionals, and keeping the same social worker. Children want action to be taken, not just talking and listening.

Research that explored children's views in the UK is mirrored by similar research in America. The National Survey of Child and Adolescent Well-Being included 316 children living in foster, residential or kinship care. These children report satisfaction with their placement and feel close to their carers, with children living in residential care being least satisfied. The ambivalence the children experience, however, is expressed through their desire for more family contact and their wish to live with their biological mothers (Chapman et al., 2004).

There is therefore a range of research studies that provide the child with a voice (Box 1.1). These will help to guide the future development of services for children who are looked after or adopted.

BOX 1.1   THE VOICE OF THE LOOKED AFTER CHILD

- 'Foster parents should not work all day because they don't have any time for the children.'
- 'I personally have been helped a great deal with all my school work by the assistant teacher who works with children in care.'
- 'People don't understand how much anger is inside me.'
- 'You're given a time to talk in Key Working, but what if you want to talk at other times? You're told, "Not right now, we're too busy with paperwork."'
- 'My foster parents have treated me differently to their own children, which I don't think is fair.'
- 'Social workers seem to think they own you, and make all the decisions about your life.'
- 'I think social services need to spend more money on important things, e.g. keeping children in care after they are 16.'

(Reproduced from Shaw (1998) by permission of the Who Cares? Trust)

When carrying out such studies special efforts are needed to hear the voices of children living within minority groups. These children can be especially affected by problems of exclusion, discrimination and stereotyping. They need opportunities to express their views separate from, as well as being part of, studies talking to children.

The Worcestershire Children's Fund commissioned a research study exploring the impact of a range of projects on the children, their families and communities. This contained a separate report concerning the impact on minority groups, including children from minority ethnic groups, children with learning disabilities and young carers. Through talking to the children and their families, the differing needs and experiences stemming from social, cultural or practical issues were apparent (Cooper & Cooper, 2004). Children from such minority groups, living within the looked after system, can be doubly disadvantaged. Studies will need to make special efforts to include these children and to provide them with a separate voice.

While there is a small but growing literature reporting on the perceptions of children, there is little research or guidance about how to best use the views once they are expressed (Maguire et al., 2001). The studies are seen as providing powerful messages for practitioners and decision makers, but more research studies are needed on how these messages can be successfully listened to and whether the services that develop as a consequence are then perceived more positively.

There is also less information about how to listen and use the voices of multiple families and the children and young people. Guidance, especially about how to develop services around the differing views of children, their carers and their families of origin, is lacking.

> No matter how much support you get in foster care, be it from social workers, foster carers or psychologists, you still feel alone as there is no one definite to turn to. Other young people would have their parents. From my experience this sense of lack of belonging was reinforced by statements such as 'do you still want to live here?', and examples of normal teenage behaviour, e.g. 'if the untidy room doesn't stop then you'll have to go'.
>
> (Caroline Cuckston, 2004, p. 24)

PROVIDING SERVICES THAT LISTEN TO THE VOICES OF CARERS AND PARENTS

Services can be set up in a way that either gives a voice to those who are at the receiving end or prescribes the service for them. Traditionally the NHS/medical model of intervention is one of experts treating patients. Patients place their trust in the professional and until relatively recently did not expect to be asked for their views.

Often psychological services for children and families have moved away from this expert model, preferring to adopt more collaborative approaches to intervention. This approach places more emphasis on working in partnership and thus provides a greater scope for eliciting and listening to the views of those receiving the service.

Collaborative practice is not, however, without its difficulties. Psychologists and other professionals providing a service are often invited to take charge and be in control rather than working collaboratively. Expectations and limited resources can reduce the time made available for really listening to the child and family and fully involving them in planning assessment and interventions. Allowing the child, young person or carer to have a clear voice means that sufficient time needs to be made available for them to talk and be listened to and that careful attention is given to how the individual or family can be empowered to be full partners within the design and delivery of interventions.

Golding (2004) describes some of the difficulties of partnership working within a consultation service for foster carers. While the carers were given considerable opportunity to input into the consultation there was a perception that telling their story was all that was expected from them. A perception of the psychologist as expert offering answers, rather than having expertise that offers a different perspective, may limit the amount of collaborative problem solving that can take place.

A consultation for residential carers and social workers concerned about a 15-year-old boy demonstrating challenging behaviour is memorable as an example of non-collaborative practice. During the first hour the consultees were very involved in describing the young person, considering his early experience and relating their attempts and difficulties in helping the young person settle and develop relationships. The psychologist listened to this discussion and then prepared to provide some psychological understanding that she felt might be helpful for the consultees to reflect upon. At this point all discussion ended as the consultees in unison picked up their pens and paper to write down the 'answers' they were anticipating. This effectively ended any collaborative thinking that might have taken place.

Considerable effort is needed to use the consultation as a collaborative process, which acknowledges and uses the expertise of all those attending (see Chapter 6).

Collaborative working becomes even more complex when we consider that listening to carers can involve listening to multiple families. These multiple families include 'parents' who are also professionals as in foster and residential carers, parents who have lost their parenting role and parents who, by adopting a child, have to be mindful of and maintain some connection with a family of origin. Listening to all these voices can be a daunting and at times painful task. The family of origin can be uncomfortable to listen to. It involves listening to their pain and to their distrust of professionals. The substitute carers may struggle to cope with the pain of what has happened to their child and the emotion they feel towards the original family. Hearing and including all these voices is important if ultimately everyone is to work together to meet the needs of the child.

Additionally there can be a tension between the child's needs and the family of origin's needs. Different professionals can be pulled in different directions. It is important that networks work together so that multiple voices can be heard and sensibly acted upon (see Chapter 2 and Box 1.2).

BOX 1.2 THE VOICE OF THE FOSTER CARER

- 'Fostering is a very challenging job that requires immense patience and understanding. It is a good job. However it can at times be extremely up-setting to everyone involved. Fostering is a job that is in desperate need of support!'
- 'Nothing can prepare you for the impact fostering will have on your emotions, your family life, and your attitudes and values.'
- 'Never believe that by providing a good home and love it stops all the prob-lems.'
- 'We were informed of our foster child's problems and the desperate need for therapy and then none was offered.'
- 'The fact that people listened and acknowledged the problems – this dra-matically reduced my feelings of isolation and also the feelings of frustration that I had been experiencing.'
- 'Support is most useful; in many cases I feel it prevents the breakdown of placements. I'm no longer banging my head on a brick wall.'

(Foster Carers, Worcester, UK, personal communication)

LISTENING TO MULTIPLE VOICES

Issues of trust mostly arise from foster placement instability. Therefore adults are normally not the answer to your problems but the cause. Combined with this general mistrust of adults, strangers are also an object of mistrust. This especially applies to young people who have had a number of placement breakdowns.

(Caroline Cuckston, 2004, p. 25)

Looked After Children and Carers

Being looked after inevitably means multiple and sometimes traumatic expe-rience of families. Children or young people will have experienced decisions being made by others. Often they lack understanding of why these decisions are viewed as being in their best interests. Thus these individuals will be disempowered and will lack trust in others. Listening to these children and young people will take time and patience. Careful thought needs to be given to the place of the interview, the attitude of the interviewer and the meaning of questions being asked, always being mindful of previous experience. The young person's race, culture and family experience will need to be taken into account while a good understanding of the individual child's current developmental ability will need to inform the interview process. Attention will need to be given to the power relationship between the adult and the child and care taken to create conditions within which the child's views are validated and treated with respect (Del Busso, 2004). Tools are being developed to aid this process. For example the *My Turn to Talk* guides help children to understand how decisions are made and help them to give their views and make their own decisions (Lanyon & Sinclair, 2005a, 2005b).

Foster and residential carers often report feeling undervalued and unsupported (Warren, 1999). This in turn can lead to feelings of disempowerment affecting the ability of the carers to contribute effectively to the planning and delivery of services or to decision making around the child in their care. Additionally, services under pressure to find and maintain placements for children can fail to involve carers in planning, with little reflection about the needs of the child (Kelly, 1995). Many carers stop fostering because they feel undervalued, unsupported and feel that others have little interest in them as people (Bebbington & Miles, 1990; Strover, 1996/1997). Good levels of support, training and a willingness to listen to what carers have to say can, on the other hand, provide services with a valuable resource on the needs of looked after children. This means finding time and space to consult with carers, being willing to listen to their views and to include their ideas within inter-agency discussions about the care of a child or about service planning and development. When this is done carers can feel listened to, understood and valued, and the services can benefit from the wealth of experience they have to offer (Golding, 2004). Good-quality training for carers can also lead to feelings of empowerment and an improved ability to express views within network meetings. Thus attendance at a group for carers of children with attachment difficulties led to carers feeling that they had a better understanding of the children they were caring for. They reflected that this in turn helped them to cope better in meetings because they now knew what they were talking about. Having previously struggled to get their points across they now felt confidence in what they were saying (Golding & Picken, 2004).

The fathers in foster and adoptive families can be overlooked especially when combining parenting with being the main wage earner. Evening groups and special efforts to include them will be needed. A failure to include fathers can prove detrimental.

A psychologist worked closely with a foster mother to develop a placement for Candice, a very troubled young girl. They met regularly to review progress and plan ways that the carer could offer a therapeutic placement for the child. This went well, and for the first time Candice started to trust and allow another person to nurture her. As time went on Candice became more and more needy and preoccupied with maintaining the undivided attention of the carer. The carer was determined to persevere and the psychologist supported her. However the increasing concerns of the foster father were overlooked. He was worried about the effect on his wife of this intense emotional involvement, and also concerned that their own children were not getting the attention they needed. As he became increasingly concerned Candice sensed a new rejection. Her behaviour quickly escalated to the point that the placement broke down. Listening to the father's concerns and fully involving him in planning and developing the placement might have led to a different, less tragic outcome.

Birth Families

Within the network of looked after and adopted children arguably the most disempowered of all are the birth families. These families are not accustomed to having a voice, and frequently mistrust the professionals. Finding ways to fully listen to these families can present a complex challenge. If birth families are to be given a voice then issues of blame and lack of trust need to be confronted and resolved. These families are likely to have longstanding feelings of shame and worthlessness and will often have rigid defences in place as protection against hopelessness and despair. They may thus deny, minimize or distort information in order to protect themselves against the pain of not being good enough to look after their child (Kagan, 1996). The interviewer needs to be prepared to spend time with the family, to work with them as they currently feel and to explore what has led to the removal of their child. These families will only be able to have a voice if interviewers are not only prepared to recognize and acknowledge the struggles and competencies within the family, but are also prepared to build trust and slowly engage the family in communicating their feelings and views (Kagan, 1996). Issues of differences between interviewer and family need to be acknowledged and efforts made to remove the barrier that this can create. A good understanding of class, cultural and religious difference will be essential and time will be needed to provide an interviewing environment that helps the family to feel at ease and know that their views are valued.

Hearing the voices of fathers can present some particular difficulties. As birth fathers can be more inaccessible, especially when they are not currently living with the mother, special efforts may be needed to find and give these fathers a voice. This may involve visiting them in prison, in new homes and making a special effort to keep them involved in the life of the child.

> Lisa at age 6 was nearing the completion of her adoption. She had experienced extensive physical abuse from her father earlier in her life, and all contact had ceased a number of years previously. However the father was now 'pestering' the social worker who, having removed the child from her family of origin, was finding this extremely difficult. An independent worker agreed to meet with the father. She found a man who recognized that he was to blame for what had happened, but longed for some continuing link to his daughter. He was finding it hard to remember what she looked like, or to imagine where she now was. It was agreed that this father could have a contemporary photograph of Lisa in her new home, but which would not identify where she was geographically. He was satisfied with this and did not want to pursue any further contact. This photograph was important to the father. As Lisa grew older and needed to make sense of her life story, she would have the knowledge that her father valued her enough to want a photograph of her.

Family group conferencing has developed as one way of ensuring that families have a voice when plans are made for their children. This promotes collaboration between professionals and families. Originally developed in New Zealand as a way of offering a more relevant and respectful service to the Maori Community, this type of conferencing spread rapidly across the whole population. These conferences proved so successful that they became a legal requirement as set out in the Children, Young People and Families Act 1989 (NZ). (See Morris & Maxwell, 1998; Ryburn, 1993.) The conferences occur in several stages:

- *Stage 1* – A coordinator invites the extended family and close friends (including the child and child advocate if he or she wishes to be involved) to a family group conference. The coordinator reflects the culture and race of the family, and works closely with the family to set up the meeting.
- *Stage 2* – The relevant professionals share information, views, and answer any questions raised by the family.
- *Stage 3* – The professionals then withdraw leaving the family to make a plan to meet their child's needs.
- *Stage 4* – Once the family have agreed a plan the professionals rejoin the meeting and agree any necessary involvement and monitoring arrangements.

Family group conferencing has been used within the UK (Lawrence & Wiffin, 2002) and is promoted by the Family Rights Group who write: 'Family group conferences put families in charge of the decision making; the process strengthens families and respects and affirms each family's unique cultural experience' (www.frg.org.uk).

Adopted Children and Parents

These families may be less disempowered than birth or foster families and may advocate strongly for their needs. Adoptive families can also be well supported by local support groups and nationally through organizations such as Adoption UK. However, the adoption process itself can be disempowering and its impact should not be underestimated. The relationship with the adoption agency and the decision-making process – often on top of infertility problems and coupled with the extent to which the family can feel at the mercy of the child's previous experience and heredity – can all be powerful factors in creating feelings of powerlessness (Hartman & Laird, 1990).

As adoption becomes the solution of choice for so many children who cannot live within their family of origin, the recruitment of sufficient adoptive families is problematic. There is therefore a growing inclusion of less conventional families as potential adoptive families. Gay couples and single carers, for example, are more likely to be considered more favourably than previously. These families remain marginalized however, as recruitment is usually based on need rather than recognition of what they have to offer. These families are still most likely to be recruited for the children who are most difficult to place, e.g. children with severe disability or older children demonstrating challenging behaviour. This highlights how disempowered these families remain. Only when services are organized around what families have to offer children rather than around societal assumptions about what constitutes a family, will the more marginalized adoptive families have a strong voice in the development of services.

While adopted children have a strong voice via their parents, there is a risk that they may not be heard in their own right either by their parents or by the system. The average age of adoption is $4\frac{1}{2}$ years old with many children spending 13 months in placement before the adoption is finalized. Thus children are moving into their adoptive homes on average at the age of 3 years (Hart & Luckock, 2004). While infant adoptions are much less common in the UK they are still found in inter-country adoptions. Adopted children are therefore usually too young to give informed consent with regard to decisions being made about where they should live. Additionally a desire to be a 'normal' family can mean that the child is silenced around issues about the family of origin and early experience (Hartman & Laird, 1990). Ongoing contact between the child and the family of origin can also be a topic that is difficult to discuss. Contact is set at the point of adoption, most typically in the form of letterbox contact. The changing needs of the child or the family of origin over time can be overlooked, especially when contact makes parents feel uncomfortable or anxious.

The adoption support services regulations published in 2003 following the Adoption and Children Act 2002 (DFES, 2002) are helping to create a specialized forum for adoptive families to get help with issues particular to adoption, thus ensuring that adoptive families are being heard. This is not without its problems, however. In particular the involvement of parents in the planning and delivery of these services appears to be lacking (Hart & Luckock, 2004). These authors suggest that: '. . . adoptive status seems to marginalize those affected in relation to the new participation rights of other vulnerable groups. Arguably, this is a good example of discrimination against minority groups' (p. 69).

If the voice of the adoptive parent is marginalized, it could be argued that the voice of the child is even more so (Box 1.3). This imbalance can be addressed through interventions with the child and family.

A couple had adopted two brothers now aged 7 and 9 years and were struggling with the behaviour of the older brother, Nathan. The younger brother, Thomas, on the other hand, was very good and compliant. At the time of the referral there was a lot of concern that this adoption would break down. The adoptive parents had put a lot of energy into getting 'help' for their eldest adopted son, but neither boy had been asked how he felt about his new family. When the psychologist did talk to them she found that both children could articulate concerns about their new family and fears that the adoption might break down. Thomas was dealing with this by being very compliant. Nathan, on the other hand, wanted to test out the fear that they were about to be rejected and pushed his adoptive parents to their limit with his behaviour. Neither child could express his concerns. Thomas was torn between loyalty to Nathan and loyalty to his adoptive parents. He didn't talk about this as he endeavoured to maintain his parents' belief that he had no problems. Nathan, on the other hand, had a good understanding of the pain his adoptive parents experienced in not having biological children. 'The trouble is that we are not their children and they are not our parents.' However his difficult behaviour meant that his adoptive parents did not appreciate this understanding. Talking with the psychologist allowed the children to find their voices separate from their adoptive parents and to be supported in being heard by them.

BOX 1.3   THE VOICE OF THE ADOPTED CHILD

- 'I didn't want to move. I wanted to stay with my foster family 'cause I'd moved around so much.'
- 'I wanted a family that would take care of me and not leave me alone. And when I want them, they always come and feed me properly and look after me, and be kind.'
- 'I can remember that night when my social worker came over and we were all watching telly and she said "I've found a new mummy and daddy for you." I don't know why but I burst into tears. . . . I think it was the shock really.'
- 'I felt sad when I left my family. The feeling was like having a solid block of ice inside me . . . when all the ice has melted I will be ready for a new family.'
- 'Like sometimes when we see my birth mum you feel that you need to cry when you leave her and things, but you hold it in to be brave for everyone else . . . I mean it's OK if you get used to holding your tears in, if you know you're going to see your mum again'
- '. . .' cause I never, ever heard from my dad and I really wanted to but I just don't know where to start. I've never talked to mum about it. But I really do want to get and meet my dad as well.'
- 'I wanted to go to court to watch everything being finalized. . . . Seeing like the case being closed . . . the book shut on it really. Feeling of triumph . . . watching them close the book . . . knowing that nothing else was going to happen. It was just going to be ordinary life from now on.'

(Reproduced from Thomas et al. (1999) by permission of BAAF)

Other Voices from the Network

Many workers are trying to help these multiple voices to be heard. While they are at some remove from the day-to-day experience of the children and their carers, it none the less has a significant emotional impact upon them. If all voices are to be heard, this needs to be acknowledged. For workers to be genuine partners in the journey these children and carers take, they need to enter emotionally as well as intellectually into the network around the child. In this way our voices can all be heard and together we can find the way ahead.

PROVIDING SERVICES THAT LISTEN TO THE VOICE OF CHILDREN AND YOUNG PEOPLE

Another reason why cognitive therapies are not very successful is that young people in care are more heavily involved with professionals, e.g. social workers, than other people. They may go through the same questions about how they are feeling a lot more than other young people, yet still they feel like no action is being taken. In their eyes adults have failed them again. This negativity causes some foster children to clam up, and refuse to talk. Not because they are refusing help, but because they feel uncomfortable, nervous or at times think that the psychologist cannot help them as most adults have previously given up on them. They therefore end up concluding that they're beyond the professional's help. The classic teenage line: 'you don't understand me!'

(Caroline Cuckston, 2004, p. 25)

The earlier part of this chapter focused on the importance of collaborative partnerships between the adult and the intervener. In this section consideration will be given to communication with children and how this can lead to their involvement in expressing wishes and feelings and thus their involvement in service development and delivery.

Child Development Theory

Developmental research can provide important guidance about the developmental stage of children and therefore what their likely level of understanding and ability to communicate will be. For example, a lot is known about the child's developing ability to take the perspective of another. Piaget highlighted how children move from an egocentric stage of understanding when they can only take a view from their own perspective to one in which, as adolescents, they are able to take multiple perspectives (e.g. Piaget, 1973). The importance of the social context within which this development occurs has been emphasized by many authors (see, e.g., Perret-Clermont et al., 2004). This, in turn, has led to increasing awareness of the importance of good early relationships. Children with early experience of dysfunctional parenting and separation from their parents are likely to have poorer perspective-taking abilities. Questions that involve taking another's perspective may therefore cause the child some difficulty.

Children who have experienced adversity within their family can have difficulties in thinking, in naming and understanding their feelings and in exercising autonomy. These difficulties will interact, making it difficult for them to understand and communicate their wishes and desires. A good understanding of a child's developmental strengths and difficulties is essential to help the child to communicate and to make sense of the communication (Schofield, 2005).

The development of a sense of self is another very important part of a child's development. This is critically dependent upon interactions with others (e.g. Mead, 1934), and is therefore susceptible to the impact of early relationships. A good understanding of children's sense of self, and their ability to reflect upon and express their own opinions separate from those of others, will be important for the interviewer. For example, has the child had his or her own thoughts and feelings validated allowing the formation of a concept of self as separate from others able to hold views that are different? Imagine the difficulties for a child who has grown up within an enmeshed relationship with a mother. The mother has encouraged the child to hold views and opinions that are hers and not the child's. When asked within an interview about this view, the child is most likely to borrow the views of the mother and present these as his or her own.

It is important to remember that while age guidelines might be helpful to understand the child's developmental abilities, these will need to be adapted to the individual child. Children who have grown up within abusive environments are likely to have more developmental difficulties than those who have experienced more optimal environments. Children will have learned ways to interact with adults that have helped them to survive early, difficult experiences. They can, for example, present as developmentally immature or with pseudomaturity. In both cases a good understanding of children and their cognitive ability will be important for successful interviewing.

Finkelhor and Kendall-Tackett (1997) suggest that children who have experienced early adversity may have different problems that can interfere with their ability to communicate at different developmental stages. Thus toddlers may be either excessively clingy with their carers, or indiscriminate in their affection with relative strangers. They may also be excessively fearful and may demonstrate behavioural difficulties. School-aged children can be aggressive and oppositional, or dissociative and withdrawn. They may have poor self-esteem that interferes with their confidence in talking to the adult and they can show extreme anxiety and fear, sometimes accompanied by post-traumatic stress symptoms. As the child grows older these difficulties can become combined with feelings of depression, worthlessness, self-blame and a deepening lack of trust in adults. In addition, all of these children may have had previous experience of police and social care systems that further decrease their willingness to engage with the adult.

These brief examples therefore highlight the importance of a good understanding of child development and a good ability to apply this understanding to the individual child (see also Zweirs & Morrissette, 1999). Schofield (2005) provides a developmental model to aid hearing the voice of the child within family placement decision making. This model emphasizes the complex transactional and psychosocial nature of development, which needs to be understood in order to make sense of the child's communications. She high-lights the importance of understanding children's development and how dif-ferent areas of development interact with each other and with the children's early experience of abuse and neglect. Listening to the child is a process of understanding the child's experience, developmental ability and view of the world.

Communicating with Children

Successful communication with children and young people has been a topic of study especially in the use of children as witnesses (Jones, 2003), but also for interviewing children generally (Zweirs & Morrissette, 1999; Aldridge & Wood 1998). This research can be usefully applied to help looked after or adopted children to have a voice in the services they receive.

An awareness of children's assumptions based on past experience of talking to adults is critical to successful communication (Poole & Lamb, 1998). These assumptions can influence the answers that children will give. For example, children may expect that:

- the adult will be the expert;
- the adult already knows the answers to questions;
- every question must be answered;
- they can't answer with 'I don't know';
- each question will have a right or wrong answer;
- an arbitrary answer will be better than no answer;
- if a question is repeated the previous answer must be wrong and a different or right answer is required.

Interviewers need to spend time helping children to understand that these assumptions do not apply. They will need help to seek clarification when they do not understand something and to realize that their views and feelings are important. It can be helpful to talk about a neutral topic of interest to the child initially to model that the child is expert within the interview (Finkelhor & Kendall-Tackett, 1997).

Assessing stage of language development will be critical when using language-based interviews. The child can be confused by complex language, and will have difficulties understanding when the adult uses words that are not in the child's vocabulary. In turn, the adult communicator needs to be familiar with the language rules of the child and especially how these change with age (Thomas et al., 1999). The first language of the child also needs to be taken into account. It is self-evident that children are likely to cope better if interviewed in their first language. However, in the process of learning a new language, children can become less fluent in their first language. This is especially so when the second language is the dominant language away from home or if they are discouraged from using their first language (Zweirs & Morrissette, 1999).

There is a large amount of research about the use of questions with children that has informed the use of interviews with child witnesses (see Jones, 2003; Zweirs & Morrissette, 1999). This can be useful to consider when helping children to express their wishes and feelings, and while it cautions against the use of leading questions and the problem of 'why' questions that tend to be perceived as blaming, it argues for the helpfulness of open questions and the general importance of using language that is simple, clear and avoids the need for a child to understand at a level that, for him or her, is too advanced.

Children can be more highly suggestible than adults and this needs to be held in mind during an interview (see Jones, 2003). For example, children are not as good as adults in understanding the source of information they possess. They find it more difficult to distinguish their own experience from that related to them by another or from their imagined experiences. An expressed wish to go home, for example, could be based on a fantasized expectation of what home would now be like. This may have arisen from a conversation they have had with a birth parent who has told them that they should come home or from a thought out wish based on recent experience with the family. Children may also more easily defer to an adult's opinion, feeling that they should accept the implicit knowledge of the adult. The adult interviewer needs to be aware of conversations that the children have had with others and also with themselves that may influence their responses. An interviewer should be especially careful not to express his or her own judgements or values in order to get a true picture of the child's wishes and feelings.

Guidance is available in how to structure interviews to help children to communicate their wishes and feelings (Finkelhor & Kendall-Tackett, 1997; Thomas et al., 1999). For example, a child will be helped by:

- having a familiar, supporting adult;
- time being taken to explain the reasons for the interview;
- allowing the child to be involved in when and how the interview will take place;
- proceeding at the child's pace with short interviews, and structured breaks;
- good eye contact that can help with attention difficulties;
- allowing sufficient time to build rapport;
- tolerance for the need to test the trustworthiness of the interviewer;
- being aware of body language, as the child may be vigilant for signs of disapproval or disinterest from the interviewer;

- following the child when he or she jumps around, taking opportunities to explore further as these arise;
- tolerating silences, don't rush the child and avoid interruptions.

The child will also be able to recognize feigned interest from the adult. The interviewer needs to be genuinely interested and to be able to convey this interest and show an understanding of what the child has told them.

The process of interviewing children needs careful thought. Children and young people need careful preparation with opportunities to find out about the adults they will be meeting and to ask questions about the reason for the interview. Explaining and practising ground rules is important, and the interviewer has the responsibility to engage the children's interests and place the children at their ease. Attention needs to be given to issues of confidentiality, ensuring that children understand what will happen to the information they are sharing. Thomas et al. (1999) also found that giving children the power to influence important aspects of the interview was crucial in helping them to be heard. They advise allowing children plenty of opportunities to ask questions, helping children to express their fears about the interview, and being aware of the possible impact of emotional distress on their understanding. Additionally, they have found that children can be helped to communicate by the use of props such as games, cards, books and videos. Creative ways of engaging a child's interest and finding developmentally meaningful ways for the child to communicate can mean that even very young children can be enabled to express their views. For example, Clark and Statham (2005) have developed a mosaic approach, which uses a range of verbal and visual tools to help the interviewer to understand the perspective of preschool children. These creative techniques are potentially useful for the older child with cognitive or emotional difficulties.

Nissim (1999) found that children were helped to express their views when provided with a structure. She interviewed children of 6 years and older by offering them a series of statements with which they could agree or disagree on a five-point scale (yes definitely, yes mostly, sort of, not really, and definitely not). In this way children could comment on a range of subjects such as:

- I'm getting on ok at school.
- I would like to be adopted and not just fostered by this family.
- I would rather be living in a children's home.
- Nobody listens to what I think in this family.
- I get upset easily over contact.

And a final overall statement:

- I think that all in all I have been successful in this family.

In this way, the children reported on a range of views, some of which correlated with the actual outcome for the child. For example, children who reported behaviour problems, continuing attachment to previous carers, difficulties with contact with family of origin, wanting to live elsewhere and negative relationships with their current carers were more likely to have unsuccessful placement outcomes. The children therefore were enabled to communicate by a method that meant that they didn't have to say anything out loud, and that was less affected by their relationship with the interviewer. They also had something to keep at the end of their interview.

PUTTING RESEARCH AND PSYCHOLOGICAL UNDERSTANDING INTO PRACTICE

> Young people in care have very little control about where they are living, family problems and who will be the next person staying with them. But in the sessions with the psychologist I think it is very important for the young person to be in control if possible. If the young person sets the agenda, then the problems that he or she wants to sort out, or issues he or she wants to raise and feels comfortable talking about, can be looked at, which not only helps the young person but also builds trust.
>
> (Caroline Cuckston, 2004, p. 25)

Having good communication with the child or young person is, of course, only half of the process of hearing the voice of the child. Thought is also needed about how to act on what is heard. This has been explored within the 'Investing in Children' project. The authors write:

> Investing in Children seeks to create opportunities for children and young people to assert their right to have a say in decisions that affect them. Furthermore, it is concerned to ensure that their voices are heard, that having a say is not an end in itself, and that making an effective contribution to dialogue needs to be understood as part of a political process leading to change.
>
> (Cairns & Brannan, 2005, p. 79)

This project, while demonstrating some noticeable successes in helping children to be heard, has found that it is easier to help young people to articulate their experience than to effect and sustain changes in services or in attitudes.

Del Busso (2004) suggests that only when children are involved in how their feedback is used within service planning will the process be empowering. Without this additional process the evaluation can become merely 'lip service' carried out to satisfy research and service agendas rather than as a means to improve services in line with the expressed needs of children.

Services need a process to listen to children and also a framework within which they can actively use these contributions. This may be to allow the children some influence in their own experience of services and in decisions being made on their behalf. It may also allow the children to influence service development and evaluation more widely.

A number of self-completion satisfaction questionnaires have been developed for children. These include questionnaires that can be used with preschool children as well as for school-aged children (see Hennessy, 1999). In addition to structured questionnaires, qualitative and semi-structured interview methods can also be used, and have been recommended as a means of empowering others to share their views. Such interviews can allow children to talk about their experiences in their own words. This in turn can powerfully convey to the child that his or her view is valued and will be listened to (Del Busso, 2004). It is important that mechanisms are in place to ensure that the child's views are elicited, to record these views and to feed them back to the relevant people.

Consideration will need to be given to the degree to which the child is involved. This does not need to be all or nothing but may lie within a continuum model of involvement (e.g., see Hart, 1992). The child may be consulted or informed at one end or may be allowed to initiate and direct services at the other. The optimum level of involvement is likely to vary in different areas of practice and for different children.

Maguire et al. (2001) suggest that the following questions could usefully inform the process of involving children and young people in service planning and development:

- Is there a forum in the service for discussing how children's views may be sought?
- Is there a clear rationale about what views are to be sought and in relation to what particular innovations?
- Is it clear what the status of any views elicited will be? (For example: For information? For action?)
- What will be the process when a decision is made to act in a way that is contrary to the views or wishes of the child?

For children who are looked after there are added dimensions of complexity in obtaining and acting on their views. Not only are there more voices that might be added to the child's when making decisions, but also the decisions being made can be very complex. In addition, issues of power imbalance are even more salient for this population of children and young people. Frequently their previous experience has been of severe disempowerment with adults, and their expectations are commonly that adults are untrustworthy making them reluctant to engage in the process of evaluation (Del Busso, 2004).

A balance is needed between the voice of the child, the views of the parents/carers and the views of professionals as to what is in the best interest of the child (Maguire et al., 2001). It is important that the child is heard but this should not be to the point that the adult defaults on his or her own responsibility. The children's views are not an alternative for thinking about what is in the best interest of the child.

An example can be given to explore this further. The issue of what degree of contact looked after children should be having with their birth family is not an easy one to get right. There is a danger that different voices become dominant in the decision-making process such that balanced decisions are not reached. Additionally the children's desire for contact may be acted on against their best interests when this contact continues to be damaging to them. The process of hearing children and meeting their needs can be complex. If it can be safely done it may be possible to listen to the child's desire for contact while helping him or her to come to terms with the reality of contact. A way forward can then be found towards an optimal level of contact that is not harmful.

Ryan, a 12-year-old boy living in a children's home, is requesting contact with his mother. She is currently living in a filthy, chaotic house and continues to struggle with alcohol use. She would not or could not come to the home to see Ryan. The social worker is not happy for this contact to occur, as he wants to protect the child from further trauma and abandonment. The psychologist works with the social worker and residential social worker to plan a series of four safe contacts. Ryan will be accompanied for the first visit, and for further visits if he wants this.

These visits occurred as planned. Ryan was accompanied for the first two visits. He then had two unaccompanied visits but with the residential social worker on standby to pick him up if he phoned. On both these occasions he came back early. At his next review Ryan decided that he wanted no further contact. He had seen the reality of life with his mum and was now ready to move on with his own life. By listening to Ryan the professionals didn't protect him from the pain of contact with his mother but instead supported him to test out his fantasy of what life with mum would be like. Ryan could then come to terms with this and move on rather than remaining stuck with a longing for something that was unattainable and resentment of those he perceived as denying it to him.

Figure 1.1 illustrates a process whereby the child's views can be listened to and acted upon. In taking into account the wishes and views of the child an understanding of how these views have arisen is needed. The child's

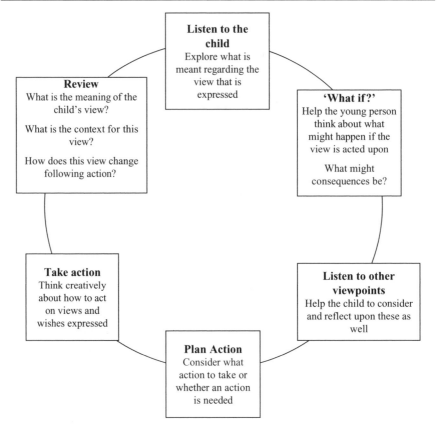

Figure 1.1   A model for listening to the voice of the child

history may be useful to aid this understanding. It is important not just to listen to what is expressed but also to really understand what is intended. It is then possible to work with the child to explore what he or she is expressing. The child or young person can be helped to think about the consequences of the request, and a 'what if' game can be played to explore whether this is really what he or she wants. It is also important to consider alternative viewpoints, and thinking alongside other people can help the process of reflection.

It is important to listen to the child's views even if these views cannot be practically acted upon. The process of helping the child to understand this might be sufficient to help him or her to feel heard (Figure 1.1). Creative solutions to meet a wish within existing resources might be needed. There can be a need to advocate for better resources while working with 'the art of the possible'. It is also important not to get stuck on being unable to deliver an ideal action, thus constraining any action.

Finally it is necessary to review and adjust these actions, as they are experienced. Having been listened to, the child's experience of the wishes being acted upon can lead to reflection and an adjustment on what he or she would like to communicate.

> Young people in care however do find it hard to ask for help. Some may have been used to or had to become independent, and therefore it is hard to accept the help offered around them. But this may also be a good way to build trust, as if more help is offered through hard times then the young people will realize that the adult will not give up on them.
>
> (Caroline Cuckston, 2004, p. 26)

AWARENESS OF RACE, CULTURE, RELIGION

To successfully hear the voice of the child or carer (Box 1.4), awareness of racial and cultural differences is central. Language and cultural differences may be subtle but if not taken into account can jeopardize the process. (For a fuller consideration of issues of race and ethnicity, see Goldstein & Spencer, 2000, or Richards & Ince, 2000.)

Good collaborative working will allow the family members to be expert on their own culture, with help also coming from interpreters and those who are well acquainted with the culture.

The interviewer needs to be aware of different cultural practices. (For example: What is the meaning of direct and averted gaze? Who in the family would be expected to speak and who to be silent? Whether a male or female interviewer would be preferred.) It is also important not to rely on stereotypical information but to explore the meaning of race and culture for the individual being interviewed (Finkelhor & Kendall-Tackett, 1997). It may be that different aspects of the culture may have different levels of salience. For example, religious faith may be very important to one Jewish family but of less importance to another family while they still observe many of the cultural rituals. It is also important that professionals be aware of their own assumptions about religions. There is a danger that the thinking of professionals may become organized around their own assumptions rather than what the other person is saying to them.

BOX 1.4   THE VOICE OF THE CHILD

- 'My foster parents are white and I love them very much and I would die for them, but increasingly as you get older you realize how alienated you are.'
- 'I ended up with a white family at 9 years old because I specifically requested it. My social worker was fine about it. It made life easier for her . . . and it made my life easier. Today I struggle to reconcile living with a white family. I think my biggest regret is that I wasn't with a black family.'

(Reproduced from Richards & Ince (2000) by permission of the Family Rights Group)

Similarly status differences need to be carefully considered. There is a tendency for the articulate and well educated to be accorded most status. This will be very disempowering for the less articulate and less educated, leading to a danger that their voice will be excluded. Similarly, foster carers can feel of lesser importance within a professional arena. It is important not just to provide an opportunity for these people to express their views but to actively seek ways of enabling them to speak and be heard.

Political correctness, while focusing attention on issues of race and culture, can also get in the way of good communication. Can the fact of ethnic differences make it harder to listen and act? For example, might social workers not investigate the fostering practice of a black foster carer in case they are thought to be racist, despite the communications from a child? Awareness of difference can get in the way of thinking. It is important that multi-cultural and multi-racial networks work together to hear and act on the many voices speaking. This, of course, raises workforce problems, as many minority cultures are under-represented within professions.

In the last few years more effort has been made to hear the voice of the child from black and ethnic minority communities. For example, studies have highlighted the difficulties that these children can have in accessing mental health services (e.g. NIMHE, 2003; Malek & Joughin, 2004; Young Minds, 2005). This is despite the increased likelihood of mental health difficulties for looked after and adopted children. Within the black and ethnic minority looked after population there will be a population of refugees and asylum seekers. These children are likely to have experienced significant trauma, loss and bereavement. They may struggle more than other children to communicate their needs.

The Minority Voices study has provided a means for young people from black and minority ethnic backgrounds to communicate their views about mental health services. This study included children living within the looked after system. The children highlighted the importance of accessible and culturally aware mental health services. This requires sufficient staff training to ensure that mental health professionals feel confident that they understand and have the skills to work with children from different cultural, religious or ethnic backgrounds. Voluntary organizations can provide a resource for traditional health services, although this can be hampered by problems of short-term funding and lack of communication structures between the two. Innovative ways of informing young people about services available to them are needed, and can include the use of the internet, media, and local faith groups (Young Minds, 2005).

AWARENESS OF DISABILITY

The presence of a disability can be a barrier to both communicating and listening. Interviewers need to be creative in finding ways to enable the person to communicate, and can include non-verbal tools and the use of translators (Zweirs & Morrissette, 1999). As with culture, it is important to recognize the individual's awareness of their disability, using this awareness to circumvent the barriers to communication. Additionally, parents and siblings are often experts at communicating with the child in the family who has a disability (Zweirs & Morrissette, 1999). Those who work in disability services can equally be an important source of knowledge and help. Time and effort will need to be given to finding ways of communicating so that those with a disability are heard rather than excluded. Further advice can be found in a study conducted jointly by the National Children's Bureau and Barnados, which explored the needs of young people with learning disabilities living in foster care (Reed, 1993; see also Box 1.5). This study also highlighted the difficulty the foster carer's own children can experience when a child with a learning disability comes into the carer's home.

BOX 1.5   THE VOICE OF THE BIRTH CHILD

- 'At first I didn't like it, but eventually you get used to it, You get used to having things broken so it doesn't bother you so much. I like helping most of the time because he is fun to be with.'
- 'The thing I find difficult is the arguments that are caused by X's behaviour. . . . When X is constantly bad it upsets my mum and she takes a lot of time trying to sort out the problems, but then has no time for mine.'
- 'I wish I could turn him into a boy like me.'

> • 'First I thought it would be fun.
>   Now some days I wish we hadn't begun.
>   Althought I love them very much.
>   But they can be a pain in the bum'.
>
>   (Reproduced from Reed (1993) by permission of the NCB and Barnados)

CONCLUSION AND THE WAY FORWARD

Finally, from speaking to many people and from personal experience the main message from people who had a bad experience of mental health services was the need for trust. Without this I believe, and probably you believe, the root of the problem can never be solved. Without the immense trust I have with my psychologist, half of my problems would still be in my head and would have taken longer, or probably never, to have been solved.

(Caroline Cuckston, 2004, p. 26)

Caring for children in substitute homes is a process of reconstructing families and the retelling of family stories. These families are formed out of a relationship between children, parents, carers and professionals (Hart & Luckock, 2004). This is as true in residential homes as it is in foster or adoptive homes. The complexity of this process with children whose prior family stories are painful to hear and integrate into new stories means that the families will need continuing and changing professional support and advice. However, there is a danger of imposing this support in a way that disempowers both the family and the child. The family can be left reluctant to ask for help and with a strong need to reveal themselves as capable parents. The reconstruction of families is a process that needs to be shared, with professionals and families working together in mutually supportive and collaborative ways. Hart and Luckock (2004, p. 52) describe this process eloquently in relation to adoptive families: 'The most distinctive aspect of this approach is that it is seen as a joint "practice" bringing together parents and professionals, children, relatives and friends, as collaborating "practitioners" of adoptive family life and its support.'

Listening to and acting on the multiple voices involved in the care of the looked after or adopted child is a complex process, and attention needs to be given to how we get through all these complexities. In particular we all need to search for the middle ground between silencing and ignoring those who are receiving services and being overwhelmed by their voices. Strong frameworks will be needed to listen to and act on the discussions held between all those involved in the care of children, not forgetting the voices of the children themselves.

Taking account of the views of the children or young people requires continuing thought. Sometimes these views will be counter to what is thought to be best for them, and this can lead to rather polarized responses. We might, for example, go with the child's view unreflectively because that is what has been expressed. The child will learn to manipulate to get what he or she wants. Alternatively, we might decide it cannot happen, and by relaying this to the child, the child learns that he or she has no say in what happens. Both of these positions ignore full communication with the child. It is important that we work with the child and his or her communication. Working together can allow a position to be reached with which everyone is comfortable. At the same time the child is learning how to negotiate and how to work through an issue with other people. The child learns to have a voice and to listen to the voices of others. This, of course, is no different to reasonable parenting practice within which there are continuous requests and feedback between parent and child leading to a natural and on-going process of negotiation. It is important that the child's voice is heard within such a normative framework.

To hear the voice of the child, parent or carer properly, adequate time and resources are needed. It is important to have clear processes and procedures that draw on the best of our knowledge about how to communicate and listen and enable us to apply these processes to the individual we are listening to. This requires us to take into account culture, abilities and needs. Psychological thinking can help us to understand what the individual is saying, how to help him or her to say it, and how to use this understanding once gained. It is important not to take a cookbook approach to communicating with others. There are dangers in adopting a process or procedure and using this at the expense of thinking psychologically about each situation in its own right.

The looked after children's review booklet is an example of a process that can be used reflectively or unreflectively. The child completes this booklet prior to the review, usually helped by the carer or social worker. This provides the child with a voice at the review when he or she is not there in person or when it is difficult to speak out within the meeting. An example of unreflective practice would be where the child's wishes are noted and acted on with little discussion or thought. The child asks for more contact, for example, and the review rubber stamps this wish and asks the social worker to arrange the increased contact. Those at the review might hear the child and might use the review process to allow the network to reflect upon this. Thought can be given to the pros and cons of granting the child's wish and a decision can be reached that is in the best interest of the child. Time can also be spent on how to communicate this decision back to the child and how to support the child if the decision is counter to his or her wishes.

To be heard we need a listener, but learning to be a good listener takes time and effort. Psychological thinking can help in this process. In this way young people and their families can influence their own interventions and service planning and delivery. Multiple voices can be heard and reflected upon leading to action that is comfortable for all those involved.

Note: the quotations from Cuckston (2004) are reproduced by permission of the author.

REFERENCES

Aldridge, M. & Wood, J. (1998) *Interviewing Children: A Guide for Child Care and Forensic Practitioners.* New York: John Wiley & Sons.

Bebbington, A. & Miles, J. (1990) The supply of foster families for children in care. *British Journal of Social Work,* **20,** 283–307.

Cairns, L. & Brannan, M. (2005) Promoting the human rights of children and young people. The 'investing in children' experience. *Adoption and Fostering,* **29**(1), 78–87.

Campbell, P. (1999). The service user/survivor movement. In C. Newnes, G. Holmes & C. Dunn (Eds), *This is Madness. A Critical Look at Psychiatry and the Future of Mental Health Services* (pp. 195–209). Ross-on-Wye: PCCS Books.

Carroll, J. (2002) Play therapy: The children's views. *Child and Family Social Work,* **7**(3), 177–187.

Chambers, R., Drinkwater, C. & Boath, E. (2003) *Involving Patients and the Public. How to do it Better.* Abingdon, Oxfordshire: Radcliffe Medical Press.

Chapman, M.V., Wall, A. & Barth, R.P. (2004) Children's voices: The perceptions of children in foster care. *American Journal of Orthopsychiatry,* **74**(3), 293–304.

Clark, A. & Statham, J. (2005) Listening to young children. Experts in their own lives. *Adoption and Fostering,* **29**(1), 45–56.

Collier, F. (2005) News from BAAF. *Adoption and Fostering,* **29**(1), 5–7.

Cooper, M. & Cooper, C. (2004) *Listening to Children's Voices – Impacts on Minority Groups.* Children's Fund www.worcestershire.gov.uk/childrensfund

Cuckston, C. (2004) 'Caroline' BPS, DCP, faculty for children and young people. *Service and Practice Update,* **3**(3), 24–26.

Dance, C. & Rushton, A. (2005) Joining a new family. The views and experiences of young people placed with permanent families during middle childhood. *Adoption and Fostering,* **29**(1), 18–28.

De La Cruz, M.P. (2002) From a child's perspective: How children in family therapy characterize their families and view therapeutic change. *Dissertation Abstracts International, Section A: Humanities and Social Sciences,* **62**(12-A), 4054.

Del Busso, L. (2004) Sharing power in the research process: Interviewing young people in the looked after system. *Clinical Psychology,* **44,** 7–9.

DOH (1976) *Adoption Act 1976.* London: HMSO.

DOH (1989) *Children Act 1989.* London: HMSO.

DOH (1996) *Family Law Act 1996.* London: TSO.

DOH (2002) *Promoting the Health of Looked After Children.* London: TSO.

DOH (2004) *National Service Framework for Children, Young People and Maternity Services.* London: TSO.

DFES (2002) *Adoption and Children Act 2002.* London: TSO.

DFES (2004a) *Every Child Matters, Change for Children.* London: TSO.

DFES (2004b) *Children Act 2004*. London: TSO.

DFES (2005) *Commissioning Placements and Services for Looked After Children and Children with Special Educational Needs and Disabilities in Residential Placements.* http://www.everychildmatters.gov.uk/key-documents/

Finkelhor, D. & Kendall-Tackett, K. (1997). A developmental perspective on the childhood impact of crime, abuse, and violent victimization. In D. Cicchetti & S.L. Toth (Eds), *Developmental Perspectives on Trauma: Theory, Research, and Intervention. Rochester Symposium on Developmental Psychology*, Vol. 8 (pp. 1–32). Rochester, NY: University of Rochester Press.

Franklin, A. & Madge, N. (2000) *In our View: Children, Teenagers and Parents Talk About Services for Young People*. National Children's Bureau.

Golding, K.S. (2004) Providing specialist psychological support to foster carers: A consultation model. *Child and Adolescent Mental Health*, 9(2), 71–76.

Golding, K.S. & Picken, W. (2004) Group work for foster carers caring for children with complex problems. *Adoption and Fostering*, 28(1), 25–37.

Goldstein, B.P. & Spencer, M. (2000) *'Race' and Ethnicity – A Consideration of Issues for Black, Minority Ethnic and White Children in Family Placement*. London: BAAF.

Hart, R. (1992) *Children's Participation, from Tokenism to Citizenship*. UNICEF.

Hart, A. & Luckock, B. (2004) *Developing Adoption Support and Therapy*. London/Philadelphia: Jessica Kingsley Publishers.

Hartman, A. & Laird, J. (1990) Family treatment after adoption: Common themes. In D.M. Brodzinsky & M.D. Schechter (Eds), *The Psychology of Adoption*, (pp. 221–239). New York/Oxford: Oxford University Press.

Hennessy, E. (1999) Children as service evaluators. *Child Psychology and Psychiatry Review*, 4(4), 153–161.

Hill, M. (Ed.) (1999) *Signposts in Fostering. Policy, Practice and Research Issues*. London: BAAF.

Jessie, K.A. (1999) Children's and parents' perceptions of treatment acceptability and treatment response to components of a day treatment program. *Dissertation Abstracts International: Section B: The Sciences and Engineering*, Vol. 59(9-B), Mar. 1999, 5088. US: Univ. Microfilms International.

Jones, D.P.H. (2003) *Communicating with Vulnerable Children: A Guide for Practitioners*. DOH, London: Gaskell, Royal College of Psychiatrists.

Kagan, R. (1996) *Turmoil to Turning Points. Building Hope for Children in Crisis Placements*. New York: W.W. Norton & Co.

Kelly, G. (1995) Foster parents and long term placements: Key findings from a Northern Ireland study. *Children and Society*, 9(2), 19–29.

Lanyon, C. & Sinclair, R. (2005a) *My Turn to Talk. A Guide to Help Young People in Care Aged 12 or Older have a Say about How they are Looked After*. London: NCB.

Lanyon, C. & Sinclair, R. (2005b) *My Turn to Talk. A Guide to Help Young People in Care Aged 11 and Under have a Say about How they are Looked After*. London: NCB.

Lawrence, P. & Wiffin, J. (2002) *Family Group Conferences. Principles and Practice Guidelines*. Ilford, Essex: Barnardo's/Family Rights Group/NCH.

Laws, S. (1998) *Hear Me! Consulting with Young People on Mental Health Issues*. The Mental Health Foundation.

Leon, L. (1999) *Young People Have a Say!* The Mental Health Foundation.

Maguire, P., Wolpert, M., Rowland, A. & Drinkwater, J. (2001) *Position Paper: Promoting User Participation in Clinical Psychology Services for Children and Young People: How to Hear the Voice of the Child*. Special Interest Group (Children and Young People) of the Division of Clinical Psychology, The British Psychological Society. October.

Malek, M. & Joughin, C. (Eds) (2004) *Mental Health Services for Minority Ethnic Children and Adolescents.* London: Jessica Kingsley Publishers.

Martin, J.G. (2000) *Foster Family Care, Theory and Practice.* Boston, MA: Allyn & Bacon.

Mead, G.H. (1934) *Mind, Self and Society.* Chicago: University of Chicago Press.

Morgan, R. (2005) *The Children's View of Inspection. First Report of Children's Audits of Inspection by the Commission for Social Care Inspections.* Newcastle-Upon-Tyne: CSCI.

Morris, A. & Maxwell, G. (1998) Restorative justice in New Zealand: Family group conferences as a case study. *Western Criminology Review* **1**(1). [Online]. Available: http://wcr.sonoma.edu/v1n1/morris.html.

NFCA (1999) *UK Joint Working Party on Foster Care.* London: National Standards for Foster Care.

NIMHE (2003) *Inside Outside: Improving Mental Health Services for Black and Minority Ethnic Communities in England.* London: DOH.

Nissim, R. (1999) *Substitute Family Placement: A Systemic Perspective on Pre-placement Factors, Placement Outcomes and the Relationship Between Them.* Dissertation submitted for the degree of PhD, University of Reading.

Perret-Clermont, A., Carugati, F. & Oates, J. (2004) A socio-cognitive perspective on learning and cognitive development. In J. Oates & A. Grayson (Eds), *Cognitive and Language Development in Children* (pp. 303–332). Oxford: Blackwell Publishing Limited in association with Milton Keynes: The Open University.

Piaget, J. (1973) *The Child's Conception of the World,* trans. by J. Tomlinson & A. Tomlinson. London: Paladin.

Pilgrim, D. & Hitchman, L. (1999). User involvement in mental health service development. In C. Newnes, G. Holmes & C. Dunn (Eds), *This is Madness. A Critical Look at Psychiatry and the Future of Mental Health Services* (pp. 179–194). Ross-on-Wye: PCCS Books.

Poole, D.A. & Lamb, M.E. (1998) *Investigative Interviews of Children: A Guide for Helping Professionals.* Washington, DC: American Psychological Association.

Reed, J.A. (1993) *'We Have Learned a Lot from Them.' A Study of Foster Care for Young People With Learning Disabilities.* National Children's Bureau.

Richards, A. & Ince, L. (2000) *Overcoming the Obstacles, Looked After Children: Quality Services for Black and Minority Ethnic Children and their Families.* London: Family Rights Group.

Ross, N. & Egan, B. (2004) 'What do I have to come here for, I'm not mad?' Children's perceptions of a child guidance clinic. *Clinical Child Psychology and Psychiatry,* **9**(1), 107–115.

Ryburn, M. (1993) A new model for family decision-making in child care and protection. *Early Child Development and Care,* **86**, 1–10.

Schofield, G. (2005) The voice of the child in family placement decision-making. A developmental model. *Adoption and Fostering,* **29**(1), 29–44.

Shaw, C. (1998) *Remember My Messages. The Experiences and Views of 2000 Children in Public Care in the UK.* The Who Cares? Trust.

Skuse, T. & Ward, H. (2003) *Outcomes for Looked After Children: Children's Views of Care and Accommodation.* Interim report to the DOH, Loughborough University: Centre for Child and Family Research. In H. Ward, T. Skuse & E.R. Munro (2005) The best of times, the worst of times. Young people's views of care and accommodation. *Adoption and Fostering,* **29**(1), 8–17.

Strover, A. (1996/1997) How foster parents experience social work with particular reference to placement endings. *Adoption and Fostering,* **20**(4), 29–35.

Stuart, M. & Baines, C. (2004) *Progress on Safeguards for Children Living Away from Home: A Review of Action since the 'People Like Us' Report*. York: Joseph Rowntree Foundation.

Thomas, C., Beckford, V. with Lowe, N. & Murch, M. (1999) *Adopted Children Speaking*. London: BAAF.

Thomas, N. (2005) Has anything really changed? Managers' views of looked after children's participation in 1997 and 2004. *Adoption and Fostering*, 29(1), 67–77.

United Nations (1989) *Convention on the Rights of the Child*. New York: United Nations.

Young Minds (2005) *Minority Voices. Research into what Young People from Black and Minority Ethnic Backgrounds – and the Staff who Work with Them – say about Mental Health Services*. London: Young Minds.

Warren, D. (1999) Setting new national standards for foster care. *Adoption and Fostering*, 23(2), 48–56.

Zweirs, M.L. & Morrissette, P.J. (1999) *Effective Interviewing of Children. A Comprehensive Guide for Counsellors and Human Service Workers*. Philadelphia: Accelerated Development, Taylor & Francis Group.

PART I
MAPPING THE TERRITORY

2

HOLDING IT ALL TOGETHER: CREATING THINKING NETWORKS

Liz Stott

Kirsty sits between her father and foster mother. Sitting opposite are her therapist, teacher and social worker. They all wait for the review to begin.

Kirsty is terrified. She has no idea what will happen at the review. She knows things are bad at her foster home. Her social worker has been talking to her foster mum. She loves her dad and knows he wants to apply to Court so she can go back home. She feels comfortable with her foster mum. She seems to understand but then they argue. She likes her teacher, but things haven't gone well. She has been excluded again. She glances at her therapist. He knows her well but he asks so many questions about things she doesn't want to talk about. She feels confused and angry. 'What is the point in saying anything? They have all decided what is going to happen. Anyway who really knows what they want when they are only 13?'

Kirsty's dad feels apprehensive, he desperately wants his daughter to come home and live with him. How can he convince the meeting that she should come home to him?

Kirsty's foster mum feels despondent. She has tried to give Kirsty boundaries, structure to her day and a real feeling of being cared about. She's worked hard to convince school to take her back, has taken her to her appointments every week to see her therapist. Now the new social worker has encouraged

Thinking Psychologically About Children Who Are Looked After and Adopted
Edited by K.S. Golding, H.R. Dent, R. Nissim and L. Stott.
Copyright © 2006 John Wiley & Sons, Ltd.

contact with her father against her advice. Kirsty's behaviour has got much worse since and now he wants her home. What is the point of these reviews if no one listens?

Kirsty's therapist feels uncomfortable in the same room as Kirsty's father. He's written to the social worker, explaining the danger of reinstating contact, of confusing her, traumatizing her but it has gone ahead. How can he explain how therapy works, that it takes a long time? Kirsty needs stability. Things often get worse before they get better, but he feels under pressure to change things overnight.

Kirsty's social worker feels pleased that Kirsty's dad has come to the review. She has worked very hard to gain his trust and to reinstate contact between himself and Kirsty. She hopes that the foster carer can see that this is a good thing. She knows that he abused Kirsty when she was little, but she really believes that he has changed.

Kirsty's teacher is concerned. Kirsty has been out of mainstream school for two years now. She is bright and has the potential to get good GCSEs but she has become increasingly unsettled and disruptive in the last year. She really can't see how Kirsty will cope in a mainstream secondary school. They can't hold her place in the reintegration service indefinitely. What can they offer?

The chairperson is dreading the review. She has looked at the file and is aware that there are disagreements between all the main agencies. Kirsty has told different things to different people. How can she have any authority over all these professionals to get them to put their differences aside and focus on Kirsty's best interests? What hope does she have when even the Directors of Education, Social Services and Health cannot agree on the way forward for the new Children's Trust within the county?

Aspects of this composite case are probably familiar to many people working within networks set up to support looked after and adopted children. The potential advantage of a multi-agency perspective can be easily over-ridden by the politics between agencies. The potential for confusion and misunderstanding about one another's role is large and can obstruct individuals working together for the best interests of the child.

This chapter will explore the dynamics that can occur in multi-agency networks and the distinctive way these agencies become involved for children who do not remain with their birth families. The focus will be on psychological thinking at the level of the professional networks and systems around the child. Ideas from psychoanalytic, systemic and attachment theory, together with composite cases and agency scenarios, will be used to illustrate the impact of both thinking and unthinking networks on the outcome for the child.

The chapter will conclude with thoughts about the importance of supervision, consultation and further training.

THE ONION MODEL OF POTENTIAL SYSTEMS AROUND THE CHILD

The Onion Model (Figure 2.1) is adopted as the underlying framework within which to examine the various systems involved with looked after and adopted children. It is a non-hierarchical model similar to the ecological model developed by Bronfenbrenner (1977). It provides a visual representation of the

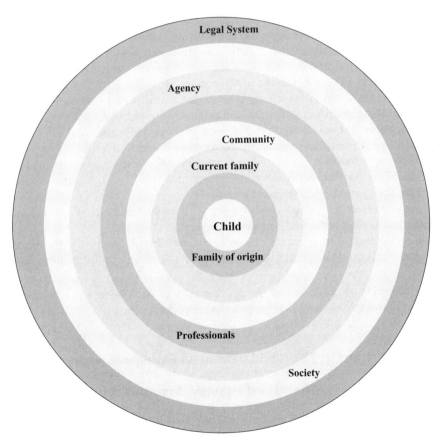

Figure 2.1   Onion model of potential systems around the child

impact of various systems upon each other and, as a result, upon decisions made about the child.

1. The child or young person is at the core of the model. This part represents the children themselves, their sense of self and their understanding of the various worlds around them.
2. The next layer represents the family of origin. This represents the original kinship networks that surrounded looked after and adopted children at birth. This includes the birth parents, full and step-siblings and extended family.
3. The third layer encompasses current family and former carers in both foster families and residential settings. This includes adoptive parents as distinct from the birth parents. This layer includes foster and adoptive siblings and other members of the carers' kinship network.
4. The fourth layer represents the community networks and culture within which the adoptive or foster family are living. It also represents the community into which the child was born and the culture and support of that community in relation to the birth family.
5. The professional network represents the variety of professionals most likely to be involved with a looked after or adopted child.
6. The outer layer represents the agency context. How the local education, health and Social Services organizations are integrated and work together. This includes historic issues and relationships and the beliefs and behaviours that impact upon functioning at a local level. Voluntary organizations are also represented here.
7. Society refers to current views on the welfare system held by central government, the media and society at large.
8. Legal systems represent the outer skin or containing structure of the model. Although these are created by society they also maintain the structure of it.

This model is used to explore the specific roles of each layer and the interactions between these layers of systems around the child.

I and 2. The Child Within its Family of Origin

The 'Good Enough' Scenario

The predominant agencies involved with children design and deliver their services with the assumption that children live within birth families. This assumption also includes ideas about how children will have learned to understand themselves and others within the context of the parenting relationship.

This gradual process of knowing oneself and forming relationships with others begins in the early experiences of relating in the birth family. The parents hold together the varying images or pictures of their child as they come to know them. This is a subjective process but over time parents develop sustaining and differing views of their child. External agencies such as health and education tend to step in and out of family life, predominantly in the role of supporter to the parents. The parents' 'story' of their child changes as the different dimensions and interpretations of their child are recreated and retold in different and at times more objective contexts external to the family system. Ideally parents are able to share their stories in such a way that the experience of being known away from the immediate family becomes mutually pleasurable and exciting, opening new possibilities and horizons. The child is able to move easily and gently between the birth parents and immediate family into his or her local communities and then into school. Despite the increasing involvement of the state in shaping the child, ultimate responsibility and authority clearly remains with the parents and the child continues to move between the main systems of home and school throughout childhood.

The 'Not Good Enough Scenario' and Introduction of Alternative Carers

The experience for a child who is no longer living with his or her birth family is very different. The multitude of internal and external pressures and preoccupations of the birth parents means that it is extremely difficult for them to have 'held the child in mind' even as an infant. These parents are likely to have been preoccupied with their own distress and its management through drugs, alcohol and domestic violence. Selwyn et al.'s (2003) study of children placed for adoption aged 3 and above found that in 90% of cases the early history involved harm or risk of harm to the child from abusive and rejecting parenting. Two-thirds of the mothers had themselves been in care or special schools. Family life characterized by domestic violence was found in nearly all cases and by alcohol and drugs misuse in half of the cases. The baby's neediness and vulnerability is likely to be overwhelming for parents in such circumstances. This is likely to trigger intense unmanageable feelings from the parents' own past. As a result the parents may try to protect themselves by cutting off emotionally from their child. Thus neglect follows. Alternatively the parents may try to wipe out the emotion by attacking or punishing the child. The parents may also struggle to differentiate themselves from their child, having no sense of their child as separate with different needs and wishes. Inevitably the initial story of babyhood will be incoherent and frequently terrifying.

In Kirsty's case her mother, Janet, had a history of being in care herself as a child following rejection by her birth mother. This followed her allegations of sexual abuse by her father. She formed a relationship with Kirsty's father while in care and was pregnant at 16 years with Kirsty's older brother Wayne. She began using heroin and alcohol and this continued through her pregnancies with Donna and then Kirsty herself. The scant records indicate concern from neighbours about Kirsty being left for hours strapped in a buggy in the flat. Health visitors reported concerns about failure to thrive and difficulty accessing the flat to visit. There were some police records of domestic violence between her parents who would periodically split up, with her father leaving the home. A number of different partners moved in and out of the home. Kirsty was moved periodically to stay with her extended family. She didn't attend toddler or playgroups. She was removed from the family at 4 years following physical abuse from her father, and started school three weeks later.

3. Alternative Carers

'The care system fragments people's lives. As a parent myself, my child's life revolves around her welfare, her education, her health, her social activities, everything is there. It's not fragmented into little bits. But that's what the care system did to me.'

(Maggie Lane, in Morris, 2000, p. 23)

For many children such as Kirsty, transitions into alternative care are often abrupt, crisis driven and without clear preparation. Foster carers and adoptive parents rarely have the luxury of a coherent and sustained narrative about the child. The information that is available may be, like Kirsty's, a harrowing and unbearable story, a catalogue of traumatic experiences cumulating in removal from the care of birth parents. The new parents work hard to get to know the child, to create a bearable story with the traumatic fragments they have and with the emotional distress they see before them. Already by virtue of becoming accommodated the child is involved with complex agencies that may know more than the primary carer about the experiences of the child. The child may already be part of the education system or, like Kirsty, enter it all too soon with a far more fragile sense of being known or understood than the average child. This lack of a coherent narrative in itself can lead to confusion. Which person representing which agency knows or understands the child? Who is in the best position to make decisions? This directly impacts on the parenting or 'holding of the child in mind'. The new school may be confused when Kirsty doesn't settle to the rules as expected. They may be confused that the foster parent, unlike their experience with most biological parents, knows little about her.

In the case of adopted children there is usually less ongoing multi-agency involvement. The rights and responsibilities of adoptive parents are clear but the initial influence of birth parents and the sustained narrative attached to this should not be underestimated. Research indicates that many adopted children present to child and adolescent mental health services (CAMHS) at adolescence. Many issues connected with the narrative sustained prior to adoption may interfere with the usual tasks of identity formation and separation in adolescence (Selwyn et al., 2003).

The role of residential care for looked after young people is often seen as a last resort. Alternative family care options have been exhausted or the child's need for therapeutic care is beyond what can be provided locally via outpatient services. The shift system and high staff turnover in traditional Local Authority run homes makes building relationships with both young people and other parenting figures in the child's life an ongoing challenge. Residential staff often feel devalued and unsupported in their role. Despite the desire to make a difference in the lives of looked after children; they often find themselves struggling to address non-school attendance or the beginnings of offending behaviour. Unpublished research looking at residential staff's understanding of their role in relation to looked after children in the South West revealed staff who felt undervalued and overlooked in the system. They wanted to make a difference to young people's lives but struggled with what they saw as children being able to get what they wanted when they wanted it from their social workers (Lister, Haslam, C. & Stott, 1999, personal communication). Research looking at the interface between CAMHS and residential staff found frequent misunderstandings and isolation. This was despite many looked after children being seen by CAMHS and residential staff requesting direct support and supervision from mental health staff (Hatfield et al., 1996).

4. Community

It goes to the heart of the duty all societies owe children – that if parents cannot meet children's needs, then children have a moral claim on the rest of us.
(UNICEF, 1998, p. 259)

Boushel (1994) explores the complexities of the systems around children both within their birth families and within foster families. She looks at protective environments for children, exploring the value attributed to various parts of their world. This involves looking at the value ascribed to the children themselves, the status accorded to the carers, the social interconnectedness of both the children and carers and the extent and quality of the safety nets available. She believes the most effective interventions take account of the varying systems, strengths and stressors in these environments.

In Skuse and Ward's research interviewing children about their experiences in care, many of the children who had positive experiences highlighted material differences, doing better educationally and feeling valued.

> '. . . (The foster carers) were nice. They actually asked what I wanted for tea and asked us what I wanted for this and asked me what I wanted for that, and, it was quite nice. I didn't get ordered to do anything, they would ask me. And she used to bake cakes and quiches on a Saturday. Unless we were going on a day trip. She used to, every Saturday morning without exception, she used to bake a nice chocolate sponge cake, with chocolate icing all over the top. One of the best cakes I've ever tasted.'
> (Gary, in care between ages of 9 and 12 years, in Skuse & Ward, 2003, p. 67)

Other children highlighted the difficulties in making the transition into other communities and families, especially changing schools.

> 'I didn't like not being with my own family and knowing that my carers were not my own family and I hated being far away from my friends and school and family.'
> (Eliza, in care between the ages of 12 and 13 years, in Skuse & Ward, 2003, p. 187)

5. Professional Network

> 'And when they do come they seem to think they know everything when they do come, because they have read your files . . . They don't really know do they, how I have been feeling because they have not been to ask me but then they seem to think they know everything.'
> (Eliza, in care between 12 and 13 years, in Skuse & Ward, 2003, p. 112)

The professional network around looked after and adopted children is often extensive and will at some point have involved a social worker and usually Social Services or voluntary adoption agencies. As part of the legal process of coming into care or being adopted, expert witnesses such as psychologists or child psychiatrists will have assessed many of these children. Some may have had a CAFCASS Guardian appointed. All children currently looked after and adopted will be involved with education services and health services. Some children may also be involved with mental health services. Many young people and their carers will be involved with independent or voluntary agencies such as specialist adoption agencies, support agencies, independent foster care organizations and private children's care homes. Other young people may be involved with probation services. For young people in secondary education, Connexions workers may be involved in helping with transitions beyond school into the world of tertiary education and work.

When Kirsty was first removed into short-term foster care, Social Services applied to Court for a Freeing Order with a view for adoption. Kirsty was assessed by a CAFCASS Guardian who was very impressed by the foster carers and their relationship with Kirsty. She made a strong case for Kirsty to remain with her foster carers. The Courts decided to support the plan for long-term foster care. Social Services had not approved the carers for long-term care and had concerns about this. However the social worker was directed by Court to continue to support the foster placement. Following these differences of opinion the relationship between Social Services and the foster carers broke down. The foster carers felt criticized over their management of Kirsty's behaviour and the social workers felt compromised in their care of Kirsty. The decision to reinstate contact following repeated requests from Kirsty was interpreted by the foster carers as Social Services attempts to return Kirsty to her father. Her father was hopeful of this and actively undermined the foster carers to Kirsty. The current social worker felt strongly that there were insufficient grounds to continue to refuse contact with Kirsty's father, despite the anxieties of the network. Although Kirsty was involved with therapy at the local CAMHS the content of this was kept confidential, which led to the foster carer feeling further excluded from understanding Kirsty. The teachers believed that with proper therapeutic work Kirsty should be contained enough to manage in mainstream school. They questioned why it was taking so long. The therapist himself felt compromised in trying to explain his work to the network and keeping confidentiality of the sessions. He felt every decision to move Kirsty, change her school or reinstate contact had a direct impact on the success of the therapy.

6. Agency

'The culture of children's services needs to be one that enables flexible provision. Resources are very often hidebound in organizational structures which are often vertical with a sort of silo mentality. There's still the residential arm of the department, there's still the fieldwork arm, there's still day services, and there is someone who liaises with health and education. But the crucial issue is where they integrate horizontally, where do they come together to respond to an individual child and family's need? You need to break it all down, so that they can come together in a package in response to individual need.'

(Steve Hart, Social Services Inspector, in Morris, 2000, p. 51)

There is a culture of service delivery based on birth children living with their birth parents and concerns about education on health happening in isolation from one another. Thus adopted and looked after children challenge these agencies to have to work together.

The scenario at Kirsty's multi-agency review can easily be imagined. Those present do not feel particularly good about their input. Everyone is likely to be feeling defensive. In such a public setting it is difficult for those representing the different agencies to admit their limitations. They are more likely to defend their involvement and protect their reputation rather than be free to focus on the true needs of Kirsty. This reflects the challenges of delivering services to children not able to live with their birth families, and occurs most starkly with looked after children.

The primary task of education as an organization is to have an impact on the knowledge and learning of children. The culture in schools is of knowledge-based expertise, with respect for authority. Many looked after and late-adopted children directly challenge this culture. They have difficulties absorbing knowledge due to competing emotional preoccupations. They struggle to manage issues of authority, having had very different experiences with their primary authority figures, namely their birth parents, prior to coming to school. It becomes increasingly difficult for schools to manage their role as educators in the face of such clear challenges to their ability to educate and manage.

Similarly, the primary task of health as an agency is to universally support and promote optimum physical and emotional health. It is apparent from statistics on the physical and emotional well-being of looked after children that many have not received fundamental health services (see McCann, 1996).

As statutory services fail to meet the needs of the children, a proportion of them will go on to develop even more challenging difficulties. For example, looked after children are over-represented among groups of children engaged in offending behaviours, and youth offending teams are set up to reduce such offending behaviour. Treatment is usually only available after an offence takes place and is based upon treatments found to be effective in the general population of offenders. For many looked after young people these services are not particularly effective. Victim empathy work can only be effective if the capacity for empathy is developed. For children struggling with long-term attachment difficulties and high levels of shame such programmes merely reinforce the negative views these young people hold of themselves. This increases the likelihood of re-offending as anger remains with the victim and the system for making the individual feel so bad (see Hughes, 1997). Alternatively, more positive identities such as those held through educational achievement or employment are often difficult to achieve for this group of children. Not surprisingly, looked after children are fifty times more likely to go to prison than a child who has remained with his birth family (Warren, 1999).

As the main statutory agency involved in child protection and the accommodation of looked after children, the role of Social Services is clear. The Children Act 1989 (DOH, 1989) directed Social Services to work in partnership with parents and to maintain the needs of the child as paramount. The least interventionist approach is encouraged, avoiding legal procedure where possible and attempting to work in agreement with parents' wishes. Contact with birth family is inbuilt except where a strong case can be made for it not being in the interests of the child. However, inherent in this is a central paradox. While working in partnership with parents, Social Services workers are expected to maintain the welfare of the child as paramount. It is difficult to work alongside parents who have difficulty holding their children in mind without being unduly influenced in a direction unhelpful to the child. This requires great skill and reflection in order to maintain the delicate balance of interests on both sides.

The ethos or culture within Social Services as an agency is historically based around empowerment and improving the welfare and inclusion of those at the margins of society. It is clearly a needs-based model and so encourages withdrawal of input whenever needs are met or the child is no longer at risk. However a different and conflicting force is also apparent in the form of financial and local council politics. Professionals within Social Services are often under financial pressure to justify their decision-making. This is rarely fully appreciated by professionals from other agencies who are often protected from the financial implications of professional judgements or the overt challenges faced in the Court arena. As a result it is easy for Social Services to become the agency most likely to be scapegoated in the network for continuing to neglect the children's needs.

Taking into account the very different cultures and ideologies of the agencies involved with looked after children, it can be envisaged that the current proposals for the formation of multi-agency Children's Trusts within each county will involve a complex process of coming together (DFES, 2004). The areas already piloting such organizations are reporting success where there were previous good relations between agencies at a local level. Such a coming together of agencies has to be in the interests of looked after and adopted children with complex needs, who desperately need all the 'parents' to be working together. Without clear Government guidance on how to proceed where there are historic rifts between agencies, it is hard to know how these difficulties will be resolved in the best interests of children.

7. Society

'What people forget is, when they get a paper in the morning and it says, child has been raped, child has been abused and they think oh, my God that's really out of order, and then when it comes to children's homes, they forget that's probably why they're in a children's home and they automatically think those children are bad. But half of us are in there, not through our fault, but through the fault of other people.'

(Kay Connolly, in Morris 2000, p. 4)

The experiences of looked after and adopted children with their original carers are at some point deemed unacceptable by society. The decision to remove a child from the birth family is made by social workers as agents of society within the framework of the law. The desire among systems at this point is for the damage to be stopped and the child removed to a better home. Such potential idealization of the alternative family, whether that be foster or adoptive family or a residential home, is held by the agents of change, by their organizations and by society as a whole. This is a defence against the anxiety aroused by removing a child from its own birth family often against the child's will. This polarized thinking creates a context of good and bad, abused and abuser, victim and rescuer with nothing in between. Often looked after children are depicted in the media as either innocent victims of evil parents or as bad children who, despite the opportunities given to them, cannot change because of their family origins. It is at some level easier for the difficulties faced by these children to be blamed on individual pathology or bad families rather than examining the responsibility of society itself in creating environments within which children are abused and neglected by their own parents.

8. Legal Systems

The Children Act 1989 set out to clarify the responsibilities of each of the main agencies with regard to upholding the welfare of the child as paramount. Child protection procedures informed by the Act have become the main forum for inter-agency working. The guidance *Working together under the Children Act 1989* (Home Office et al., 1989) clearly sets out the importance of inter-agency working and collaboration around child protection. This recognizes the value of hearing views from birth parents and the different professionals, representing the main agencies, before taking joint responsibility for the decision reached in the meeting. There is clear recognition of the importance of the process of decision making that ultimately influences the long-term outcome of the conference and sets the scene for future multi-agency working.

More recent child protection tragedies such as the death of Victoria Climbié reveal the fatal mistakes made when rifts between agencies develop, created by unclear accountability, failure to share information, poor coordination and ineffective training. Lord Laming's (DFES, 2003) recommendations highlight the importance of bringing child protection into the realms of universal services for children aimed at improving children's lives as a whole. The Children Act 2004 (DFES, 2004) proposes that there should be cooperation between agencies aimed at improving the well-being of children in the area.

THEORETICAL PERSPECTIVES: CONTAINING THE CHAOS

Systemic and psychoanalytic theory has made valuable contributions to thinking about systems around looked after children, but such thinking often remains inaccessible to professions in other agencies and to the carers involved in the day-to-day care of the children.

Psychodynamic Perspectives

Some of the fundamental ideas of Melanie Klein and Wilfred Bion are very helpful when thinking about relationships at both an individual and an agency level.

Klein (1959) introduced the ideas of splitting and projection. Developmentally, Klein saw splitting as a natural way of managing the strong but opposing feelings of love and hate felt by an infant towards his or her primary object, the mother. These opposing feelings, Klein suggests, are initially focused on the mother's breast. This is the primary source of love and nurturing. When the breast is unavailable, the infant experiences rage and hatred. In order to manage these overwhelmingly opposite and contradictory feelings towards the same object, the infant splits the feelings into good and bad as a form of defence. This leads to the representation of the good and bad breast. In time, and with a mother able to bear these strong feelings attributed to her or projected into her, without retaliation, the baby reaches the 'depressive' position. The baby is able to integrate the conflicting feelings of love and hate and to acknowledge the external reality that this is the same person. The child is then able to hold onto the idea of the mother being an object of both love and hate, lovable and hateful but all the same person. This position stirs up guilt, concern and sadness and there is often a desire to make reparation. Klein believed that until a more integrated depressive position had been reached it was psychologically impossible for true connection and empathic relationships to develop. Canham (2003) argues 'This is the struggle of the depressive position – to reconcile conflicting pictures we have of others and of ourselves. For fostered and adopted children to achieve this requires considerably more psychic work as they have ambivalent feelings in relation to two sets of parents rather than one' (p. 16). For many fostered and adopted children the primitive and persecuting figures of early phantasy life may have been a reality. This makes conceiving of parents as containing good and bad qualities so much harder. Canham makes the point that many birth children have secret unconscious ideas or phantasies that they have been adopted by humble parents but are really the children of royalty. This is a way of coping with disappointments in the relationship with true parents. For the adopted child this is often the reverse and the phantasy wish is to be the birth child of the adopters in order to deny the fact of adoption and the dreadful circumstances of not being wanted.

These ideas can be reflected upon at the level of professional or agency involvement. The danger in inter-agency forums is that there is great potential to split professionals or agencies into good and bad, helpful or neglectful, rescuing or abandoning. This is a way of dealing with the heightened emotion of working with strong and opposing feelings towards the same child or birth parent or carer. The child living away from its birth family may arouse strong feelings of compassion and the desire to rescue, often illustrated by a social worker's desire to offer respite to a foster child or for residential social workers to want to take home, at weekends, a teenager from their unit. The same concerned workers may then feel manipulated and rejecting towards the child who actively rebuffs their attempts to rescue. For example, by making allegations of sexual abuse towards their social worker, or by staying out all night using drugs when the residential worker had pleaded with them to stay and have key work time. It is incredibly difficult for the network to hold its mind and protect thinking space in the face of such non-thinking and acting out of split off projections into various aspects of the network. As Marta Smith candidly reflects, 'close contact with the mental pain, the despair and rejection looked after children experience sucks their carers into the enactment of these states of mind, which the child is unable to contain. Much time is then spent in mopping up after crises and managing while the thinking process is wiped out' (Smith, 2000, pp. 18–19). In order not to wipe out the thinking process it is important that both extremes of feeling – the desire to love, rescue and repair and the desire to hate, abandon and destroy – are acknowledged, tolerated and understood.

The concept of maternal ambivalence is extremely helpful in this respect. Parker (1995) examines the culturally rigid view of mothering in which the good mother is seen as at one with her baby, never resenting it or having anything but loving and positive feelings towards it. Mothers who dislike their babies or resent them are depicted as evil and unnatural by a society unable to take a depressive position in relation to mothering. Parker makes the important point linking Klein's and Bion's thinking that the awareness of ambivalence in mothers actually stimulates their thinking about their relationship with their babies. The position of maternal reverie or preoccupation described by Bion (1962) is, in her view, not just 'free floating attention' but demands an 'exquisite receptiveness' from the mother. Parker believes that the state of reverie involves an active albeit unconscious capacity on the part of the mother to be in touch with her own turbulence and the need to understand her own feelings of both wanting to shut the baby up versus wanting to make it better. If this thinking is extended to inter-agency working it can be envisaged that, to create a state of network, reverie is not just a matter of making space or time but involves an awareness of the ambivalent and opposing feelings apparent in each of the agencies and the professionals represented. Recent developments in attachment theory, particularly the use of adult narratives about childhood, as depicted in the Adult Attachment Interview (Main et al., 1985), have important links with the concept of being in touch with and reflecting upon one's own turbulence in order to be able to fully contain and process the emotion felt in such intense relationships. In terms of working between agencies, it is helpful to think of the effect of the narrative from the agency in relation to the looked after child and how this may have become internalized by the workers themselves.

Contributions from Attachment Theory

Contributions from attachment theory help to illustrate how the beliefs inherent in one person or agency can influence behaviour. Bowlby's clinical findings from his work with boys with behaviour problems in the East End of London led him to look at the relationships between the boys and their mothers (Bowlby, 1988). Descriptions of types of attachment are made in purely behavioural terms, how a child may respond to a primary caregiver once the attachment system has been activated. These descriptions are, however, illustrative of the 'internal working model' or concept children have developed about themselves in relation to their primary caregiver (see Chapter 12). The importance of having a 'secure base' from which to explore is inherent in this model.

Interestingly, Emanuel (2002) has explored the attachment systems of professionals involved with looked after children, specifically social workers. Parallels are drawn between the types of 'attachments' needed by social workers to their managers and agencies and the ability to undertake the task needed with the children. She discusses insecure ambivalent as well as insecure avoidant patterns of involvement with cases where professionals may become over-preoccupied or detached from a case. She draws parallels between the collapse of strategy in babies with disorganized attachments and the 'drift' or paralysis in Social Services systems when faced with contradictory demands from birth parents and looked after children. She uses the metaphor to examine a disorganized state of mind within the care system whereby social workers become paralyzed by the conflicting demands of children, birth parents and their managers. This paralysis is understood as a 'counter transference reaction' whereby the child's feelings are projected or put into the professionals. The professional needs space to reflect in order to avoid re-enactment of these feelings in the form of neglecting the child or allowing the case to 'drift'. The agency and management systems can provide a secure base within which processes to allow these reflections are protected. These thoughts will be further explored later in the chapter.

Systemic Perspectives

In systems thinking, simple linear cause and effect thinking is replaced by circular thinking. Interconnected components of a system have an effect upon each other with no one aspect acting in isolation. Systems therefore need to be examined in context and as a series of interrelated and interconnected parts. Within a network of different agencies it could be seen that no agency acts in isolation from the effects of the other agencies, either consciously or unconsciously.

A consideration of the beliefs and behaviours of various components of the system can increase an understanding of how these influences are communicated (Campbell et al., 1994).

In families this may entail exploring the beliefs of various family members about certain issues and how this influences their behaviour. The narrative or story associated with the issue is made more conscious and explicit. This automatically influences the thinking in the present and creates a space in which such beliefs may be explored or challenged. This then has the potential to influence consequent changes in behaviour.

Changes in behaviour around inter-agency issues can be achieved in the same way. Contributions from psychotherapy and systems thinking can come together to create a space for 'reverie' in the network. The different and opposing beliefs inherent in each agency both about themselves and their own functioning, as well as those of the other agencies and professionals present, can be explored. If this is done in a safe and non-threatening way then there is a chance of creating a space in which thinking between agencies about the true needs of the child can be addressed. Professionals can be more aware of the beliefs they have about their own functioning and that of their organization and about the other organizations present. It is then far more likely that the needs of the looked after child will become the true focus of the network meetings. This in turn avoids an enactment of the dynamics between the agencies, which gets in the way of the main task of thinking about the child.

> '(I wish I could have seen)... someone impartial because everyone has a vested interest somewhere, even the people I met from Social Services.... Just to be able to step away from the situation and deal with it without so much emotion because everyone was just thinking about themselves and I think whilst I was in this situation it was very emotional and I felt pressured to be "happy" within the Social Services. As long as you are happy that's fine. There was an awful lot of pressure because that is what the Social Services are there for. To put you in a position of getting somewhere in life, otherwise you will be on the streets.'
> (Louise, in care between the ages of 16 and 19 years, in Skuse & Ward, 2003, p. 70)

APPLICATIONS OF THEORY TO INTER-AGENCY WORKING

A number of clinicians have written describing the application of such theories to work with networks. One of the earlier papers by Carr examines counter transference reactions experienced by workers in a child abuse team towards families where abuse has occurred (Carr, 1989). A counter transference reaction is one of the main methods of communication within psychotherapy. Carr describes it as 'a process which occurs outside a clinician's awareness, where an intense emotional reaction is elicited by certain characteristics of a family being treated but is fuelled by significant prior experiences' (p. 87). Once clinicians are able to acknowledge and accept their counter transference reactions they are then able to use them as an important source of information about the family being treated. Carr uses Karpman's (1968) Drama Triangle to draw out the different roles in the drama around child protection. The rescuer, victim and persecutor are positioned at each point of the triangle. This is a visual representation of the changing roles that can be taken by the child, family and professional especially at times of high levels of emotion in the network.

In Carr's analysis of the child abuse team in which he worked, he identified five main counter transference reactions. These included a desire to rescue the child, to rescue the parents and to persecute the family. He discusses the likely situations where this may occur. For example, individuals' own histories and motivations for coming into the area of work might increase the likelihood of such reactions. In turn the lack of reflective space in organizations to hold and understand the strong feelings of the different professionals in the team can contribute to the difficulties.

Some of the ideas from workers in the field of organizational consultancy are helpful in this respect. Zagier Roberts (1994) examines the career pathways, client group and work settings chosen by individuals and how these are often influenced by the need to come to terms with unresolved issues from their own past. She makes the point that often agencies attract staff with similar internal needs and with certain types of defences. This leads to the development of collective defences against the anxieties stirred up by the work. For example, individuals may join mental health teams for children as a way of reworking some of their unresolved issues from their own childhood. They may have had to manage a needy parent and thus not been adequately held in mind. Defences to manage this may include being the expert on issues to do with parents and challenging figures in authority that, like their parents, will never be good enough. She warns that the nature of the task of organizations involved with care is often to empathize with their clients. However, the close resemblance to the clients' own unresolved issues from their past continually challenges this capacity. Often defences are created to distance from the pain such as seeing clients as weak, mad and needy and the staff as strong, expert and helpful. Menzies Lyth (1988) talks extensively about the role of defences in her seminal paper on containing anxiety in institutions. She describes the collective distancing of nursing staff from their patients through preoccupation with procedures. This is one way of managing the intense feelings stirred up by being in close contact with dependent adults in pain.

The following example comes from a composite description of an inter-agency project set up for looked after children. It clearly illustrates the difficulties inherent in inter-agency working around looked after children. When the defences created within the different agencies to manage the feelings stirred up by the looked after child cannot be understood in a containing and constructive way, they get acted out via the clinical work.

A new service was being developed for looked after children in an industrial inner city. There was a history of good relations between Health and Social Services. This led to the creation of a joint-funded project offering mental health input to looked after children and their residential and foster carers. A psychologist and family therapist were chosen to set up and deliver the service. Initially there was much enthusiasm on both sides. The mental health staff regularly met with the managers of children's Social Services, and all were very positive about the potential for the service.

As the service got up and running the backdrop changed. Social Services were found to be vastly overspent. Sensing a change in climate, the managers in Social Services left. New management was brought in with a clear task to save money, predominantly by bringing children back into the city from expensive out-of-county placements. The impact of increasingly disturbed and acting out young people moving back into foster and residential care was powerful. The mental health staff picked up a feeling of being overwhelmed and out of their depth from the largely unqualified and overstretched residential staff and foster carers. Their contact with children became increasingly concerning from a mental health perspective, as extreme forms of acting out and self-harm occurred. Being used to an organization such as CAMHS where severity of mental health need led to rapidity of response and allocation of resources, the mental health staff wrote reports and letters of concern to Social Services management. They were met with silence. At the same time Social Services became increasingly dissatisfied with the service, stating it was too costly.

The mental health staff were confused by the sudden change in climate and responded by writing more reports outlining risk and mental health concern. As the concerns about the care of the young people grew, so did the disappointment and disillusionment with the service from both sides. As more unmet needs were identified in the client group, so the carers felt more and more despondent and deprived.

The situation came to a head following one particularly concerning situation when a self-harming boy was moved out of residential care into a bed-sit. The mental health staff felt unable to continue to practise safely and with consultation from their manager withdrew the service. They were left with a strong sense of personal and professional failure and shock at the sudden turn of events. They were unable to comprehend why their reports were ignored and their concerns not heard. They felt guilt at the ending of a service that was so clearly needed and at abandoning clients and their carers traditionally marginalized from mainstream CAMHS services.

There was a need to understand and work through what had happened in a constructive way. An external consultation using a psychodynamic and organizational framework was commissioned.

What became apparent during the course of the consultation was that the professionals within the new service had taken on an 'idealized parent' position aiming to fill the neglect both in the system and in the children themselves. They could be seen as part of a 'better off' family of health, not having to cope with the financial constraints of 'the less well off family' of Social Services. Inevitably the phantasy of the perfect parent could not be maintained. Parallels can be drawn with children who often experience a 'honeymoon period' with new carers, before the problems begin to be displayed. To some extent the defences used by mental health staff to manage their emotions were linked with taking an expert position. The consultant was struck by the ambitious way the service had been set up. Two part-time posts, for an extensive inner city population of 3 million, were expected to be both clinically responsible for the children as well as providing support to the staff and carers. When clinical concerns arose about the children this inadvertently became a criticism of the 'parents'. Inevitably Social Services felt criticized about the care they provided, and began to feel unhappy with the service. Rifts in the relationship between the agencies became increasingly apparent, as the culture changed and funding became an issue. Social Services' aim was to survive. Inevitably as more mental health issues were raised it became apparent that more money was needed, not less. Social Services literally could not afford to be consciously aware of what was happening. There was no space for their own concerns to be voiced and, as a result, the mental health staff felt increasingly unprofessional, overwhelmed and anxious. The consultation helped staff to understand their pain and distress at failing the children and how this was shared with staff in Social Services. They were able to appreciate the painful day-to-day issues for Social Services staff and carers working closely with these children. They were able to understand how being unable to communicate concern to those with power to change the situation led to extreme reactions to manage the anxiety, similar to the children in their original birth families. They understood better how residential staff and carers began to give up voicing concern and coped with the anxiety by seeing the children as manipulative or attention seeking. This defended against feeling their emptiness and sense of deprivation. They became more able to empathize with the impossible position in which Social Services as an organization is often placed and how being critical only serves to polarize the agencies further. They were aware of the importance of having a secure organizational base, which validated and supported their concerns so that they didn't feel they were 'losing their minds'.

In working with children who can no longer live with their birth parents it is clear that there is such a desire to idealize potential workers. They become overwhelmed with a never ending need for more. Similarly, it is very flattering for professionals to be put in the position of expert or rescuer but inevitably the pedestal crumbles under the weight of overwhelming expectation.

However, it is not only professionals who are at risk from these projections; carers too can be drawn into these positions. There is a real danger that all the negative, neglectful and abusive feelings are put into the birth parents. This leaves the adoptive, foster or residential parents in the very precarious position of becoming the idealized or perfect parent by the network. Hart and Luckock (2004) make the important point that adoptive families are often subjected to extremes of ambivalence about their position in relation to 'normative family life'. Adoptive family life does not begin with conception and birth; adoptive children often arrive some years later, the average age in 2002 being 4 years 6 months (Hart & Luckock, 2004). Adoptive families may be denigrated and stigmatized for this genetic difference. On the other hand, adoptive families may be idealized, with the parents seen as better than average, having been specifically selected by panels of professionals. Inevitably this cannot be sustained.

Kirsty is typical of many of the looked after children who have not come to the attention of services until a history of traumatic separations and chronic neglect is uncovered. It can be envisioned that Kirsty, in psychoanalytic terms, has been unable to reach a 'depressive position'. In other words, she cannot incorporate both the good and bad aspects of herself and others at the same time. She is unlikely to have ever felt held emotionally and so will have developed defences to cope. When experiencing overwhelming or unmanageable feelings such as hatred or anger she is likely to split these off and project them into others, thus experiencing, for example, an approach by another child as hostile and potentially threatening. She may initially idealize her new carer, denigrating her birth father. Unfortunately the systems around her can encourage this thinking. They may set up new carers and therapists as potential rescuers and perfect idealized parents. Birth families are viewed as bad, abusive and destructive. As a child Kirsty may have coped with an idealized phantasy of a good parent and when confronted with the reality of a 'good enough' parent is devastated. As a way of coping with the crushing disappointment she is forced to spit out or reject this person as bad. This is often played out in Network meetings where professionals and carers collude with the view that previous carers were bad or inexperienced. This almost sets up the next carers to fall into the same trap. They are idealized only to be shot down once reality becomes clear. For a child such as Kirsty, continually replaying the same script within the context of a wider system that is also unable to incorporate good and bad increases the risk of this becoming an internalized concept of herself, as split into good and bad. The over-representation of children with care histories, in adult mental health statistics, particularly understood as 'borderline personalities' needs further consideration. By not acknowledging the ambivalence and splits between agencies in the networks, we are denying these children the opportunity to experience something different.

It is not surprising that the multi-agency review for Kirsty is a difficult experience. She is aware of the different parts of herself she has disclosed to the different parts of the network. The coming together of these in the form of a review is in itself terrifying for her. She believes her love for her father will be wiped out by allegations she has made about what happened in his care. She believes her positive feelings for her foster mother cannot survive her opposing desire to be reunited with her father. Her father says he loves her and wants her home but he is still drinking and has badly neglected her. The painful reality that she was abandoned and hurt in her own father's care is too distressing for them both to acknowledge. Kirsty desperately wants to feel loved and wanted by her father; he in turn wants to make up for all that went wrong in the past. Yet neither of them has been able to truly make sense of what happened in a way that allows them to develop a more realistic relationship. Contact is a continual roller coaster of hope and disappointment with the anger and frustration aimed at others in the network.

Kirsty's social worker wants her to say what she wants in her review. There is a sense of needing certainty when none exists. The teacher longs for a specialist unit within which Kirsty could be contained enough to learn. She faces continual disappointment. Kirsty's therapist yearns for the ideal context for therapy, for stability and containment and continuity. While none exists he remains frustrated by the unobtainable ideal. Similarly, Kirsty's foster carer continually strives to find the key to unlock all that is trapped within Kirsty. She believes there is a wonderful lovable bright child just waiting to be freed. Kirsty, at the centre of all this, is likely to be very aware of the hopes, longings and fantasies held not only by herself but also in the network around her.

Unless the systems around children such as Kirsty become more aware and able to articulate and reflect on these powerful processes it is likely that they will continue to trap these children in a continual frustration of the unobtainable ideal. Bion refers to this as basic assumption mentality, which generates feelings, thoughts and behaviours with the primary aim of defending against a painful or conflictual reality (Bion, 1961).

In this situation there is a collective and unconscious belief in the network that whatever the current problems for Kirsty and the network involved in her care, some event in the future will solve them. For example, the perfect foster carer, a better social worker, proper educational provision within the county, a better therapist, and designated services for looked after children. While, obviously all these are important components, continuous thinking in the future avoids facing the painful reality of the present and that maybe Kirsty's needs can never be fully met. A 'good enough' network that can remain mindful of the middle ground may be more helpful.

THE ROLE OF CONSULTANCY TO THE NETWORK

A more comprehensive discussion about consultancy to networks can be found in Chapter 6 of this book.

Following the review a referral was made to the psychologist in a designated service for looked after children. This requested support to the foster carers who were struggling with Kirsty's behaviour. Initially, a network meeting was called to look at the understanding of Kirsty's difficulties. It was apparent at the outset that there was disagreement and splits within the network. The social worker voiced her concern about the way the foster carers were managing Kirsty. At one point she stated that she felt she may have grounds for removing Kirsty due to their abusive management of her. The teacher spoke clearly about her support for the foster carers who had worked hard to manage Kirsty themselves despite pleas to CAMHS and the psychologist for help. The teacher felt that Kirsty's introduction of contact with her father two years ago had led to all the difficulties within school. She also acknowledged that the transition to secondary school was a difficult time for this contact to have been introduced. The therapist spoke of his frustration that contact had been introduced at a difficult point in the therapy and that he felt compromised in his relationship with Kirsty as a result. The social worker stated clearly that Kirsty had requested contact with her father; it had been denied for six years despite her father's repeated requests. She herself supervised the contact and could see how pleased they were to see each other. The psychologist then met with the carers and Kirsty. Kirsty was challenging although she got on well with her carers. The carers felt strongly that they had been undermined by Social Services and that reinstating contact had had a terrible effect on Kirsty's behaviour.

Bentovim (1980) in Argent (1995) makes important points about decision making around contact. He acknowledges the importance of allowing the birth parents space to 'grieve the fact that they could no longer remain parents in the fullest sense of the word and accept the importance of the new carers to the child' (p. 13).

Renewed contact had had a major impact on the systems around Kirsty. Kirsty herself had felt torn in her loyalty, as if she had to choose between her father and foster mother. For her father, contact had reawakened his hope for his daughter's rightful return to her family. He could not accept her new carers and continuously encouraged Kirsty to challenge their authority.

Bentovim's second point involves the need for support to contain the carers' anxiety that the child will idealize his or her birth family and, as a result, reject them.

> It is very difficult for the foster carers to feel supported by the very agency they feel disapproves of them. They have had previous experience of placement breakdown following contact prior to looking after Kirsty. They are already unconsciously protecting themselves by distancing from Kirsty. For example, they are asking for increased respite care, so that, for the first year they can take a family holiday together without her. Kirsty is hyper-vigilant of any changes in their reaction and also tries to protect herself by being abusive and rejecting in return. The network around Kirsty understands these changes in behaviour in simple linear terms. Kirsty's behaviour has worsened since contact began. Therefore the solution is to stop contact.

The therapist in this case sought an external consultation, as she felt unsure of how to proceed.

> The consultant adopted a psychodynamic perspective, reflecting on the systems surrounding Kirsty. It became apparent that the belief that only a therapeutic community out of county could address Kirsty's needs was getting in the way of the work that was needed. In reality it was highly unlikely that all three agencies would agree to fund such an idea. It was suggested that Kirsty needed a 'therapeutic community' mind within the network. This would allow progress in thinking together to occur, but would require the therapist and psychologist to join with the difficulties faced by the social worker, which included supporting Kirsty's desire for contact, managing her father's unrealistic dreams of her return home, and reassuring the foster carer. Similarly, links were needed between the teachers managing Kirsty and the understanding of her difficulties within her therapy. The idea was to encourage the network to hold together the split off and opposing feelings and dynamics expressed by Kirsty and to think beyond them about what she really needed in order to move on. Instead of the network becoming stuck by acting out these differences particularly via the issue of contact, the consultant encouraged a holding together of the thinking and a joining of forces. The potential effect of this is a much more containing network around Kirsty in which she feels safer in expressing her ambivalent feelings without the fear that they will become acted out in the network and inevitably lead to a breakdown in placement.
>
> Unfortunately this thinking came too late for Kirsty. Her father proceeded with going to Court to apply to revoke the care order. The social worker removed Kirsty from her foster carers, convinced they were being abusive. The

therapist withdrew, feeling it was impossible to proceed therapeutically in such circumstances and the education placement broke down as Kirsty became increasingly violent. All the professionals were left feeling that they had failed Kirsty, and Kirsty was left to experience what she now believed to be the inevitable, that she was unmanageable, unlovable and it was safer never to trust anyone.

IMPORTANT COMPONENTS OF THINKING SYSTEMS: THE WAY FORWARD

One of the likely outcomes of networks that cannot think together is placement breakdown for the child. It is crucially important that cases such as Kirsty's are not forgotten. It obviously makes easier reading and writing to focus on cases where the outcome is successful. However painful for the network, it is important to focus on what went wrong in order to change practice.

The consultation highlighted how easy it was for thinking to be hijacked by splits between agencies as the 'parents' become preoccupied with their own agendas. The social worker became convinced that the foster carers were abusive, the carers were convinced that Social Services wanted to return Kirsty home, the therapist felt compromised in the therapy and withdrew and the psychologist, convinced that the only solution was an out-of-county therapeutic community, was unable to offer the carers the support they needed. This case highlights the very real problems with creating thinking systems when the cultures and agendas between agencies are so diverse. As a result, Kirsty is left, lost within the uncontained network re-evoking her primary experience of not being held in mind.

Garnett (1992) found that only half the children who entered the care system before adolescence left the care system from a stable long-term placement. The potential for a thinking network to be able to make a difference is apparent in the next case example. This boy had many of the characteristics that would predict multiple placement breakdowns. For example, placement breakdown is more likely for older children with complex meaningful attachment to family of origin, problems at school and behaviour problems, specifically acting out behaviours such as violence, running away, the use of drugs and alcohol and criminal behaviour (Nissim, 1999).

John, a 7-year-old boy, had experienced a number of placement breakdowns since coming into care at the age of 4. His current primary school was extremely worried about his disruptive and violent behaviour and the risk of exclusion. John's school had been the most secure place in his life. New foster carers had been found following the breakdown of another placement because of John's violent behaviour. However, they lived some 10 miles from the school. A meeting was held with the network. The social worker agreed to request funding for transport to maintain the school placement. The clinical psychologist from CAMHS agreed to meet regularly with the new carers to look at what had led to previous placement breakdowns and to offer ongoing support. The educational psychologist offered regular weekly meetings to the head teacher to support her in managing staff issues around John's behaviour. The social worker met regularly with John to discuss how he was finding the changes. The clinical psychologist, social worker, and educational psychologist met regularly to discuss concerns from various parts of the network and to think together about how to support John. As a result John managed to continue at his primary school and to stay with his foster carers for what he himself described as his record of five years. In this case it was apparent that the initial motivations of all the professionals were to try to prevent another placement breakdown for John and to try to establish some continuity. This served to unite the network powerfully around a common goal that was only achievable through working together. Systemically it was very apparent that one aspect of the network could not survive without another. This case did not have the complications of the politics and history that Kirsty's case had become so embedded in, and as a result led to a much more positive outcome.

Hart and Luckock (2004) adapt the concept of 'communities of practice' (Wenger et al., 2002) to create a context for supporting adoptive families. Wenger and colleagues define communities of practice as 'groups of people informally bonded together by shared expertise and a passion for joint enterprise'. Hart and Luckock envisage family members, friends and agency workers as practitioners of life in adoption. It is an image of an informal culture of collaboration, which crosses the usual boundaries of language and organization and allows people to 'look afresh at their own assumptions'. Although this idea has been taken from industry, it offers the creation of a different culture of collaborative thinking and reflection, which could provide a helpful framework for the idea of network reverie. Until individuals in the network are freed from the constraints of their organizational culture and belief systems and actually meet together with a common goal that they feel passionately about, it is unlikely that true communities of support around these children can develop. In the following example it can be seen how easily these communities can undermine each other if no reflective space is allowed, and how powerful a collective approach can be.

Pete was removed from his birth mother at 4 years following a chronic history of sexual abuse and intergenerational incest. He was placed in a supportive foster family where he lived for 10 years with his older sister Kate. Following an incident when Kate sexually abused a younger girl at their school, she was removed from the foster family and placed in a specialist centre for young abusers. Pete became increasingly aggressive and challenging and was referred to the local CAMHS team where he began weekly psychotherapy.

The psychotherapist asked the psychologist in the team to support the foster family during the therapy. The psychologist wanted to piece together the various aspects of the story that had led to the original request for help.

The foster carers were distraught at Kate's sudden removal after having lived with them for 10 years. They were afraid that Pete would also be removed. They were increasingly concerned about his level of violence, and worried that they would not be able to cope with Pete as an adolescent. Kate's removal, and the introduction of psychotherapy, led the foster carers to question whether they were 'good enough' to manage Pete. Their fantasy was that the 'experts', the psychotherapist and the specialist centre for Kate, were better at it. They were also unhappy with the school's management of Pete and his sexually inappropriate behaviour.

The psychologist met with the head teacher and staff. The school felt reprimanded by Social Services for not reporting an original incident between Kate and the girl and so felt incompetent and unsupported. As a way of managing the extreme anxiety this caused in the staff team, they isolated Pete from his peers. They confused Pete's behaviour with that of his sister, fearing that a similar incident might occur. Pete was reacting to his isolation and the anxiety of the adults around him by becoming increasingly violent and abusive. He had come to represent all the possible child protection issues in the school. His isolation was not contingent on his actual behaviour but the perceived threat that he represented in the school. By doing this Pete was getting set up to act out. He became increasingly aggressive. If allowed to continue Pete might have acted out the strong projections leading to a major incident. Pete would have been excluded, leading to a fantasy that the child protection threat was removed and the school and its staff could relax again. Social Services' concern about the school's handling of the child protection issues inadvertently isolated the school further from sources of support and increased the chances of it happening again.

It became apparent that the network around Pete had become unable to think in the wake of his sister's sexual abuse and removal to another part of the country.

It is obviously much easier for networks to become thinking systems in a position of 'network reverie', when not experiencing criticism or hostility from other agencies. In the above case it can be seen that while the school and foster family were feeling vulnerable to criticism, and Social Services were seen as the enemy, it was impossible to think together about how best to support Pete.

> The psychologist involved Pete's social worker, the foster carers and the staff in a meeting to focus on a common goal. It was agreed that this goal was helping Pete to manage his angry and upset feelings in a safe way both at home and at school. The outcomes of this meeting were that the social worker liaised with the Social Services' training department to offer a workshop to the school where their concerns about managing child protection issues could be voiced. The psychologist offered space to help the head teacher and key staff to clarify their behaviour management strategies in a clear and supportive way. The psychologist then met with the social worker and foster carers to discuss management of Pete's behaviour at home. Ongoing communication was held between the psychotherapist and psychologist in understanding the meaning of Pete's behaviour in the light of his therapy. Joint meetings were held termly where the staff, head teacher, foster carers and psychologist could exchange ideas about helpful ways to support and manage Pete's outbursts. Not surprisingly, as all the 'parents' got together to think about Pete, his behaviour calmed down. He was able to reach a point where he could make a disclosure. He was the first in his family to clearly name his Aunt in the generations of incest that had occurred.

Luckily as all aspects of the network were open to thinking about Pete it was possible to create more of a community of practice around understanding and managing him which led to a much more constructive outcome.

In cases where the outcome is not in the child's best interests it is useful to stop and reflect upon what may have happened, and try to learn from the experience. This is often difficult to do in supervision within the host organization, and the involvement of a consultant external to the systems can be helpful.

Sprince (2000, 2002) discusses the importance of attending to the network in order to be most helpful to the child. She challenges traditional models of child psychotherapy, working individually behind the closed doors of the therapy room. She introduces the role of consultation to the front-line workers such as foster carers and social workers working with looked after children. However, the complexities of the systems in which consultation may take place should not be underestimated and good supervision and support are essential. Traditionally, psychologists see consultation as part of their role, yet often overlook the impact of the unconscious dynamics involved. It only became clear after the consultation about Kirsty how powerfully the dynamics between the agencies had influenced the decision making. What had been felt to be a professional and impartial decision became in hindsight a re-enactment of the neglect suffered by Kirsty.

Further training, such as that offered at the Tavistock Clinic in London, in studying organizational dynamics is helpful. This can facilitate thinking about the impact of wider systems upon decisions that are made around these children. Good psychoanalytic and systemic supervision can also be invaluable to provide an ongoing forum within which to explore the meaning of the feelings and behaviours experienced by the workers.

As Sprince (2002) explicitly states in her paper on psychoanalytic consultancy to a therapeutic community for traumatized children, 'Anyone who works closely and sensitively with these children will have similar experiences: through the ordinary human mechanisms of empathy and intuition we find ourselves, at certain moments, feeling their feelings and the feelings of their abusers' (p. 148). It is important that networks are encouraged to reflect and think about the strong feelings and dynamics that occur normally and are part of the work, in order to learn from the experience.

The least we can do for these children is to offer them a space for reflective thought rather than to continue the reacting without thinking that has become so familiar from their past.

REFERENCES

Argent, H. (1995) *See You Soon: Contact with Children Looked After by Local Authorities.* London: BAAF.

Bentovim, A. (1980) Psychiatric issues. In M. Adcock & R. White (Eds), *Terminating Parental Contact: An Exploration of Issues Relating to Children in Care.* London: BAAF.

Bion, W. (1961) *Experiences in Groups.* New York: Basic Books.

Bion, W. (1962) *Learning from Experience.* London: Heinemann.

Boushel, M. (1994) The protective environment of children: Towards a framework for anti-oppressive, cross-cultural and cross-national understanding. *British Journal of Social Work,* **24,** 173–190.

Bowlby, J. (1988) *A Secure Base: Clinical Applications of Attachment Theory.* London: Routledge.

Bronfenbrenner, U. (1977) Toward an experimental ecology of human development. *American Psychologist,* **32,** 513–531.

Campbell, D. Coldicott, T. & Kinsella, K. (1994) *Systemic Work with Organizations.* London: Karnac.

Canham, H. (2003) The relevance of the Oedipus myth to fostered and adopted children. *Journal of Child Psychotherapy,* **29**(1), 5–19.

Carr, A. (1989) Countertransference to families where child abuse has occurred. *Journal of Family Therapy,* **11,** 87–97.

DFES (2003) *Every Child Matters*. Government Green Paper. London: TSO.

DFES (2004) *Children Act 2004*. London: TSO.

DOH (1989) *Children Act 1989*. London: TSO.

Emanuel, L. (2002) Deprivation ×3. The contribution of organisational dynamics to the 'triple deprivation' of looked-after children. *Journal of Child Psychotherapy*. **28**(2), 163–179.

Garnett, I. (1992) Leaving care and after. In M. Shaw (1994) *A Bibliography of Family Placement Literature*. London: NCB.

Hart, A. & Luckock, B. (2004) *Developing Adoption Support and Therapy*. London/ Philadelphia: Jessica Kingsley Publishers.

Hatfield, B., Harrington, R. & Mohamad, H. (1996) Staff looking after children in local authority residential units: The interface with child mental health professionals. *Journal of Adolescence*, **19**, 127–139.

Home Office, DOH, DFES, Welsh Office (1989) *Working Together Under the Children Act 1989. A Guide to Arrangements for Inter-agency Co-operation for the Protection of Children from Abuse*. London: TSO.

Hughes, D. (1997) *Facilitating Developmental Attachment*. New Jersey: Jason Aronson.

Karpman, S. (1968) Fairy tales and script drama analysis. *Transactional Analysis Bulletin*, **7**(26), 39–44.

Klein, M. (1959) Our adult world and its roots in infancy. In A.D. Coleman & M. H. Geller (Eds) (1985) *Group Relations Reader 2*. Washington: A.K. Rice Institute series.

Main, M., Kaplan, K. & Cassidy, J. (1985) Security in infancy, childhood and adulthood. A move to the level of representation. [See Growing points of attachment theory and research. In I. Bretherton & E. Waters (Eds), *Monographs of the Society for Research in Child Development*, Vol. 50, pp. 66–104.]

McCann, J. (1996) Prevalence of psychiatric disorders in young people in the care system. *British Medical Journal*, **313**, 1529–1530.

Menzies Lyth, I. (1988) Containing anxiety in institutions. *Selected Essays*, Vol. 1. London: Free Association Books.

Morris, J. (2000) *Having Someone Who Cares? Barriers to Change in the Public Care of Children*. London: National Children's Bureau and Joseph Rowntree Foundation.

Nissim, R. (1999) *Substitute Family Placement: A Systemic Perspective on Pre-placement Factors, Placement Outcomes and the Relationship Between Them*. Dissertation submitted for the degree of PhD, University of Reading.

Parker, R. (1995) *Torn in Two: Experience of Maternal Ambivalence*. London: Virago Press.

Selwyn, J., Sturgess, W., Quinton, D. & Baxter, C. (2003) *Costs and Outcomes of Non-infant Adoptions*. A report to the Department of Health. Bristol: University of Bristol.

Skuse, T. & Ward, H. (2003) *Outcomes for Looked After Children: Children's views of Care and Accommodation*. An Interim Report to the Department of Health. Loughborough University: Centre for Child and Family Research.

Smith, M. (2000) Psychotherapy with 'looked after' children and their carers. *Association of Child Psychotherapy Bulletin*, **106**, 18–20.

Sprince, J. (2000) Towards an integrated network. *Journal of Child Psychotherapy*, **26**(3), 413–444.

Sprince, J. (2002) Developing containment: Psychoanalytic consultancy to a therapeutic community for traumatised children. *Journal of Child Psychotherapy*, **28**(2), 147–161.

United Nations Convention on the Rights of the Child Adopted by the General Assembly of United Nations on 20 November 1989.

UNICEF (1998) *Implementation Handbook for the Convention on the Rights of the Child.* United Nations Children's Fund.

Warren, D. (1999) Setting new national standards for foster care. *Adoption and Fostering,* **23**(2), 48–56.

Wenger, E., McDermott, R. & Snyder, W.M. (2002) *Cultivating Communities of Practice: A Guide to Managing Knowledge.* Boston, MA: Harvard Business School Press.

Zagier Roberts, V. (1994) The self-assigned impossible task. Chapter 12 in A. Obholzer & V. Zagier Roberts (Eds), *The Unconscious at Work: Individual and Organisational Stress in the Human Services.* London: Routledge.

3

THE ZOO OF HUMAN CONSCIOUSNESS: ADVERSITY, BRAIN DEVELOPMENT AND HEALTH

Helen R. Dent with Sharon Brown

One has to be bilingual, switching from the language of neuroscience to the language of experience; from talk of 'brain systems' and 'pathology' to talk of 'hope', 'dread', 'pain', 'joy', 'love', 'loss' and all the other animals, fierce and tame, in the zoo of human consciousness.*

In November 2004, a 14-year-old boy set fire to the hair of an 11-year-old girl. The girl had only just regrown her hair after chemotherapy for a brain tumour (Radio 4, November, 2004). From recent research and scholarship, this chapter attempts to find explanations for such disturbing behaviour and to explore the implications for mental and physical health. There has been no further news report of the boy to provide any reasons for his behaviour, but the chapter will end with some theoretically based hypotheses. Later chapters in this volume will focus on direct and indirect interventions aimed at helping children who

---

*Reproduced from Broks (2003) *Into the Silent Land* (p. 130), by permission of Atlantic Books, London.

Thinking Psychologically About Children Who Are Looked After and Adopted
Edited by K.S. Golding, H.R. Dent, R. Nissim and L. Stott.
Copyright © 2006 John Wiley & Sons, Ltd.

develop emotional and behavioural problems as a result of early ineffective care.

Throughout the chapter, the story of 'Nathan' will be interwoven to illustrate the theory with practical examples.

NEUROLOGICAL DEVELOPMENT

Nathan was born in 1994. His mother, Lisa, was 16 when he was born, and had lived in three different residential units since she was 11. She was pregnant when she left care and went to live in a flat with her boyfriend, Darren. She and Darren met in her last unit. Both of them smoked and drank heavily and were occasional cannabis users.

In the past decade, thanks to modern technologies, research into the developing brain has made great strides forward (for accessible reviews see Gerhardt, 2004; Cairns, 2002, and Glaser, 2000). This has been mapped onto psychological observations and theories of development by various writers (e.g. Fonagy et al., 2002; Siegel, 1996), but most thoroughly by Allan Schore (1994, 2003a, 2003b), an American research scientist and psychotherapist.

Essentially, this research indicates that the human brain is a self-organizing system, and that cognitive and emotional experiences have a physical impact on how the brain develops. Moreover, the relationship between the infant and their primary carer, most often the mother, is fundamental to how the brain grows (Schore, 2003a). This relationship has the most powerful influence at the early stages, with the level of influence gradually declining over childhood as the brain matures. For example, unregulated stress at an early age has been found to have a more profound and damaging impact upon the individual's later ability to regulate emotions and behaviours, than if a similar level of stress has been experienced in later childhood (Essex et al., 2002).

Lisa was erratic in attending to Nathan's needs and often left him crying.

Nevertheless, on an optimistic note there is evidence that the brain will continue to organize itself in the context of a relationship with another self over the lifespan. There are certain periods, notably adolescence, when the brain is undergoing reorganization and is particularly susceptible to the positive influence of a secure attachment (Siegel & Hartzell, 2003). Since adolescents may be accommodated in residential units, it will be important to maximize the opportunities for developing attachments.

One of the important tasks of the self-organizing brain is the development of self-regulatory structures (Schore, 1994), which Fonagy et al. (2002) consider is dependent upon reflective function or mentalization (being aware of and understanding one's own and others' states of mind). They suggest that there is a relationship between the process of attachment and the development of mentalization and that this ability determines self-organization and affects regulation.

> An illustration of the impact of a non-mentalizing stance is an 11-year-old girl who flies into a rage whenever she is told no, or can't have her way. She is unable to think about the explanation, however kindly or sensitively given. She has made progress in emotional regulation ability, but still rages quickly to such triggers, though she can now calm down from these more easily.

Self-regulatory structures will range from regulation of physical states, such as body temperature, to regulation of emotions and behaviours. In the early weeks, a baby has limited control over its own body temperature, so it is vital that this is externally regulated by controlling the room temperature and by adding or removing covers and clothes. As the infant grows his or her body develops temperature regulation mechanisms such as shivering, flushing and sweating, and eventually the awareness of the need and the ability to adjust clothing to control temperature. The caregiver acts as an external physical regulator of temperature and also as an educator to help the child to learn to manage his or her temperature independently: 'put your coat on or you'll be cold', 'you look hot; let's take off your sweater'.

Similarly, with emotional regulation, the infant is initially dependent on adults to control the emotional environment by maintaining an optimal level of stimulation, and to calm and soothe the infant when necessary. If the environment under-stimulates the baby, he or she will get bored and ultimately fail to thrive. In this state, endorphin levels (happy hormone) decrease and cortisol levels (stress hormone) increase. If the environment is over-stimulating, the baby will 'switch off' to protect itself, in an early manifestation of 'dissociation'. Dissociation is a normal response to emotional overload, but if it occurs frequently, it will interfere with learning because, while in this state, the infant is not able to cortically process information and learn or adapt to new experiences. Dissociation can also become a learned automatic response to stress, as indicated by research showing associations between traumatic childhood events and proneness to dissociation (Irwin, 1994; Ogawa et al., 1997).

> When Lisa was tired, or had been drinking, she would ignore Nathan. When she was in a good mood she would play with Nathan, bombarding him with different toys and objects, but she felt angry with him if he started to cry. She would get particularly angry if he wouldn't take his bottle. Nathan learned to cry less and became listless, often staring vacantly at the ceiling.

In either of these situations, the 'good enough' carer will act as an external, physical regulator of the 'emotional' environment; when a baby wakes up crying and hungry the mother will soothe the child before he or she will feed; and as an *empathic* educator to help the child to learn about emotions and how to control them – '. . . it's alright, you don't need to be frightened, I'm here with you', '. . . my, you *are* angry, tell me about it . . . '. The empathy is not optional!

The consequences of inadequate regulation can be extreme, over- or under-heating, and severe under-stimulation resulting in failure to thrive can each be crucial. Extreme over-stimulation can prevent normal learning and development of the brain, for example, resulting in a lack of awareness of different emotions and a consequent inability to name and control them. Regulation is therefore an important mechanism for survival. Self-regulation is, to a large extent, learned from the carer. Emotional self-regulation will be most effectively learned from a carer who is able, consistently, to regulate external stimulation and soothe internal distress.

Children who become looked after or adopted do so because their birth families are unable to care for them effectively. Clinical experience and research indicate that many of these children's parents have not been able to regulate their emotions well enough, and that the difficulties they experience stem from the consequences of this early deprivation. The research of Lewis and colleagues (in press) indicates that young children in foster care often show signs of physiological, behavioural and emotional dysregulation, such as atypical production of cortisol across the day. This is a serious indication of malfunction in a major regulatory system, which in adults is associated with PTSD and psychopathy (Yehuda et al., 2001) and depression and anxiety (Plotsky et al., 1998). Children in foster care have also been found to have greater problems with regulating such behaviours as sleeping and eating (Dozier et al., 2002), and greater difficulties in regulating emotions (Rutter, 2000) than comparison children. Children in adoptive care are over-represented in Child and Adolescent Mental Health Services (Quinton et al., 1998) in which most referrals concern problems with regulating behaviour or emotions.

Nathan was first taken into care, to a foster home, when he was 4 months old. His father Darren, had been shaking him, and the health visitor was concerned that Lisa could not protect him.

SOCIAL AND EMOTIONAL DEVELOPMENT

The area of the brain that links to subcortical structures and regulates socio-emotional functioning is called the orbitofrontal cortex. It has links to cortical sensory and motor systems as well as subcortical limbic and autonomic centres. The mature orbitofrontal area acts as an executive control function for the right cortex, which modulates affect, non-verbal communication and unconscious processes (Schore, 2003a).

The orbitofrontal cortex does not function at birth, but develops links with limbic structures over the first year of life and undergoes further maturation in the second year of life, as the toddler begins to regulate his or her own affect (see Schore, 2003b). This maturation is experience-dependent. Two linked experiences that particularly affect maturation at this stage are 'dyadic shame' and 'disruption–repair transactions' (Schore, 2003a). These are part of the normal socialization process. Indeed, Schore (1994) argues that shame is the essential emotion that facilitates parents' socialization of their toddler, as they work to inhibit pleasurable but socially unacceptable behaviours such as throwing food.

Dyadic shame may also be part of the survival mechanism for infants as they become mobile. They will first experience it between 7 and 15 months, perhaps when reprimanded by the carer for reaching to touch a hot object or for running off in the street. Enjoyment of exploratory behaviour is sharply disrupted, and the humiliation of shame will flood their consciousness, acting as a 'punishment' for the risky behaviour that provoked it. In this way, the carer is helping to keep the child safe from that particular risk now and in the future.

If the carers are sufficiently sensitive to the children's needs, the experience of shame will normally be followed by 'disruption–repair', mending the breaks in the harmonious relationship. The carers will reassure the toddlers that they are not angry with them, but only concerned for their safety, and will overtly demonstrate their love with a smile, hug or other positive behaviour.

> Nathan returned to live with his mum when he was 6 months old and Darren had moved out of the flat. She managed better until Nathan started toddling. At first she was quite patient, but when he kept on not doing as she asked, she shouted at him and then started shutting him in his room, once for a few hours.

If disruption- or relationship-repair does not happen, the child will be left with a feeling of pervasive shame that he or she has done something wrong, that it is his or her fault and that he or she is bad. This may become an enduring belief if the carer fails too often to reassure the child after a shame experience, and will have a profound impact upon the growing child's self-esteem and self-confidence. One observational study found that mothers of 11- to 17-month-old toddlers expressed a prohibition on average every nine minutes (Power & Chapieski, 1986), which provides many opportunities for the empathic bonding of relationship-repair or, conversely, many occasions for the damaging impact of remaining in shame.

Shame and being ashamed are often confused. Shame is the internally focused, humiliating feeling of being worthless; it arises between 7 and 15 months, prior to language development and is therefore pre-verbal. Being ashamed is related to guilt, and can be externally focused and involve empathy for others; it is considered to develop from about 3 years of age, when language is established. Shame is a more primitive emotion generated by the subcortical brain, during which cortical processing does not appear to happen. Guilt and being ashamed can develop if adequate disruption-repair occurs after shame, allowing the event to be cognitively processed.

A child may cope with remaining in shame in various ways, but often by becoming angry and aggressive. Anger is a strong emotion that can mask the painful experience of shame. Anger is also a very rewarding behaviour. It induces strong reactions in others, and tends to be self-perpetuating. The child's ability to recognize and regulate emotion may also be impaired, so he or she will be less able to control anger than his or her peers. Many children who become looked after or adopted as a result of inadequate care develop this pattern of angry behaviour as a way of coping with the painful internal emotion of pervasive shame. It is often hard to understand and always extremely hard to manage.

> Nathan was again taken into care, to a different foster home when he was $3\frac{1}{2}$ years old, after the health visitor found bruising on his body. His new foster carers found his behaviour puzzling and difficult to manage. He was sometimes very engaging, but would go into unpredictable rages. They also noticed that he sometimes just sat staring into space.

MANAGING PERVASIVE SHAME

Children and young people who suffer from pervasive shame will be particularly sensitive to signs of displeasure in their carers, and to facial expressions of anger or hostility, even if these are unintended or absent. They may see unintended displeasure when foster or adoptive carers unwittingly display behaviours that signalled hostility from earlier abusive carers. When such situations occur, they provide an opportunity to find out about an earlier shame experience and to engage in therapeutic disruption-repair or relationship/interactive-repair (see Chapter 12). Each instance of relationship repair is important, but many experiences will be needed to alter brain patterns concerning worthlessness and to wipe away pervasive shame.

Nathan's foster carers became despondent when, despite their best efforts, he did not seem to be getting any less aggressive. They decided that they were not up to the task of caring for him. Lisa had attended a parenting group and asked to have him home, so he returned to her care for a while.

The following are some general guidelines for intervening with children and young people who experience pervasive shame:

- Provide a nurturing environment in which to address emotional needs.
- Provide a structured environment to manage and contain challenging behaviours.
- Discreetly provide a higher level of supervision to limit risk (e.g. being present in a potentially dangerous area such as the kitchen).
- Respond calmly and consistently to angry or aggressive behaviour.
- Be sensitive to signs of shame – head down, lack of eye contact, rage.
- Empathize with and *mirror* the emotion.
- When calm is achieved, actively repair the relationship by providing reassurance of your care and the child's worth.

Mirroring an emotion is done by responding to children with the same emotional intensity and vitality as they are showing, but without the negative emotion. For example, if a child is screaming angrily, you would reply at the same volume and intensity of tone, perhaps saying, 'I wonder why you're so angry, perhaps you think I don't like you because I asked you to pick up your toys.' As the child responds you can calm him or her by gradually dropping the volume and intensity of your voice. Just as you have 'mirrored' him or her, he or she will 'mirror' you.

NEUROLOGICAL DEVELOPMENT AND ATTACHMENT THEORY

Various psychological theories, including those of Erikson, Klein, Piaget, Skinner and Winnicott (see Harris & Butterworth, 2002; or Schaffer, 1996; for an overview) attempt to explain and describe childhood development. One of the most helpful explanations of the cognitive and emotional development of looked after and adopted children is John Bowlby's Attachment Theory (1969, 1973, 1980).

Attachment theory focuses on the importance of a child's relationship with the primary carer. It provides a framework for understanding what happens when this relationship is not 'good enough', and gives an explanation of children's emotions and challenging behaviours when their needs have not been met (see Chapter 12 in this book; Howe et al., 1999; Hughes, 1997).

Schore (1994, 2003b) draws attention to parallels between neurological development and important stages in attachment behaviour. This provides both evidence to support the theory and a deeper explanation of the cognitive and emotional experiences accompanying insecure or disorganized attachment. For example, between the ages of 7 and 15 months, patterns of attachment behaviour are being established (Bowlby, 1969) and myelination (insulating nerves to increase efficiency of conduction of information) of limbic and cortical association areas in the brain is taking place (Kinney et al., 1988).

Schore (1994) argues that the neurological correlate of the psychological processes in attachment theory is the regulation of socio-emotional processes. He suggests that in each category of secure and insecure attachment, the infant's socio-emotional development can be understood in terms of the primary carer's type of inability to maintain an optimal level of arousal in the infant.

> When Nathan 'challenged' Lisa by not doing as she asked, she felt frightened and out of control, then angry. It evoked pre-verbal memories of her own abusive childhood experiences. Instead of being calm and firm with Nathan, thereby containing his emotions, she escalated his level of emotion with her anger.

Other research also supports this notion; for example, children who are hospitalized for 'failure to thrive' experience detrimental effects upon their cognitive development (Singer & Fagan, 1984). More recently research has linked failure to thrive and poverty with adverse effects on cognitive development in children who are not hospitalized (Mackner et al., 2003). The same research shows that early intervention such as Head Start programmes can ameliorate the effect, but does not seem to reduce it completely.

> Following Lisa's parenting group, she had a better idea about how to manage Nathan. Unfortunately, he had become extremely hard to manage, and she was struggling with very limited support and resources, in a poky flat with little money. Nathan's social worker had too high a caseload to monitor him closely. Lisa started leaving him on his own when she couldn't cope, and after a few months he was taken into care again.

NEUROLOGICAL DEVELOPMENT AND HEALTH

Factors that adversely affect neurobiological and socio-emotional development, such as family and neighbourhood violence, poverty, homelessness, poor pre-natal care, pre-natal infection, pre-natal maternal substance abuse, parental mental illness, neglect and abuse are commonly found in the lives of children who become looked after or adopted both in the USA (Zlotnick et al., 1998; Curtis, 1999) and in the UK (Iwaniec, 1995; Buchanan, 1996; Ward, 2000). These factors have a direct impact on the mental, social and physical health of the individual (e.g. neglect causing physical illness).

The same factors will also have an indirect impact upon health, through the adverse impact upon brain development of early adversity (e.g. neglect causing the brain to be deficient in regulation strategies, resulting in substance abuse or poor anger management). Problems in the areas of mental, social and physical health for people who have experienced neglect or abuse in early life may be understood in terms of the way in which the brain has developed as a direct result of this adversity (Van der Kolk, 1996) (see Figure 3.1).

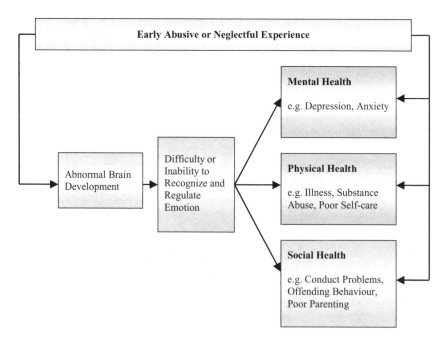

Figure 3.1   The multiple impact of early adversity upon mental, physical and social health

It is common to have different explanations, understanding and interventions for 'symptoms' in each of these areas: for example, infection and medicine for physical illness; emotional trauma and psychotherapy for mental illness; personality disorder and prison for crime. However, if these mainstream explanations and interventions are ineffective, it is possible that early experience may underpin the presenting problems (see Taylor & Rogers, 2005). The next three sections explore the relationship between early adversity and health and the implications for intervention.

MENTAL HEALTH

Just as early abuse or neglect is a common precursor to coming into care, emotional and behavioural difficulties are more prevalent in looked after children than in their peers (McCann et al., 1996; Dimigen et al., 1999; Richardson & Joughin, 2000; Quinton & Murray, 2002; Blower et al., 2004). McCann and colleagues (1996) found that of 134 young people aged 13–17 years in the care system in Oxfordshire:

- 67% had significant psychiatric symptoms;
- 96% of those in residential units had significant psychiatric symptoms;
- 15% of a comparison group had significant psychiatric symptoms.

Dimigen et al. (1999) found that over 50% of their sample of 89 children entering care in Glasgow had 'elevated' or 'very elevated' symptoms of depression using the Devereux scales of mental disorders, compared with the expected population norm of below 20%. Allen et al. (2000) found in their sample of 160 children entering Baltimore City Department of Social Services foster care, that levels of depression were significantly higher than published norms as measured by the Children's Depression Inventory. These researchers, from different sides of the Atlantic, call for a much quicker response by health services to the mental health need that their research has identified.

Sue Gerhardt's recent book, *Why Love Matters* (2004), eloquently and accessibly explains in depth the links between early abusive care, neurological development and subsequent emotional and behavioural difficulties.

There is less documented evidence of a greater level of emotional and behavioural difficulties in adopted children, which is not surprising since they are often removed from their families of origin earlier, and have more stable lives, once adopted, than do most looked after children. Nevertheless, they are over-represented in referrals to Child and Adolescent Mental Health Services (CAMHS) (Quinton et al., 1998) and experience emotional difficulties in their teens over and above 'normal' teenage angst (Verrier, 2000).

For looked after children there is evidence that having fewer placements is associated with better adjustment and outcomes (Kelly & Gilligan, 2000; Martin, 2000). Jackson and Thomas (1999) discuss the harmful effects of instability, and argue that children should not be moved because of resources, but equally should not be maintained in unsuitable placements. This is consistent with research that has identified the role of secure attachments in the development of and the healing from psychological disorder (e.g. Kaniuk. et al., 2004).

'SOCIAL' HEALTH

Social health in this context is considered to be behaviours that affect other people, including family members, friends, acquaintances and strangers. The types of difficulties experienced (and complained about) most commonly are difficulties with relationships, including parenting, challenging behaviours (also known as conduct and oppositional disorders and ADHD) and criminal or offending behaviours. Dimigen and colleagues (1999) found that over 60% of the children in their sample had 'elevated' or 'very elevated' symptoms of conduct disorder. When challenging behaviour is more closely examined, there is often an underlying issue of control.

> When Nathan is asked to tidy up his toys, someone else is in control, and that is scary. When his mum was in control, she didn't keep him at the right temperature, she didn't soothe him when he was over-stimulated or scared, and she frightened and hurt him. So Nathan developed a way of managing to feel safe by taking control of his life away from his mum and other carers. Anger helps him to be in control of other people and it masks the underlying fear and humiliation he suffers. So, when asked to tidy his toys he takes control by refusing to comply, and becomes more and more angry in his refusal until he has 'won'. The 'fierce animals' in his consciousness have taken control.

Unfortunately, being in control does not wipe away the underlying feeling of worthlessness; rather the opposite, as it blocks the experience of being nurtured by a carer who takes appropriate control, the experience of being so valued by a carer that they reliably prioritize your needs over their own.

Being close to a carer is a terrifying experience for children whose carers have actively harmed them. When children are afraid, the natural instinct is to turn to the primary caregiver, but when that caregiver is the source of the fear, the child is placed in an impossible spiral (see Figure 3.2).

When the caregiver cannot be relied upon to provide safety, the child will learn to take control of the situation, rather than rely on the carer for protection

EXPERIENCES FEAR

APPROACHES CARER

Figure 3.2   Fear–approach spiral

and nurture. Being in control will become associated with feeling safe, and being out of control will be associated with fear and chaos. Children who have suffered from this type of care cope by forming many superficial relationships to meet their need for attachment. They are often charming to strangers and new acquaintances who find it hard to believe accounts of their bad behaviour. They settle quickly into new placements, but after a few weeks or months become difficult to manage, partly through fear of the increasing attachment, in which they must relinquish control to the new carer. However, avoiding intimacy prevents the child from learning that close relationships can be supportive. It also interferes with learning that difficulties in relationships can be repaired and that people are not either all good or all bad:

- Children need to be helped to form appropriate trusting relationships.
- Carers need to understand the nature of the barriers to developing these relationships.
- Carers particularly need support themselves during this phase.

The consequences of failing in this endeavour will be impairment in experiencing empathy for others. This may result in using people, moving from relationship to relationship, or seeing individuals as all good or all bad, with accompanying emotional pain for all involved. Such relationships appear to be at the heart of borderline personality disorders (Bandelow et al., 2005), psychosis (see Read et al., 2003) and serial offending (Ireland et al., 2003; Myers et al., 2005), so the costs of failure may be very high.

Even when the child learns to trust his or her new carers, the difficulties are not all over. This unaccustomed feeling of security and safety is often accompanied by an increase in challenging behaviour that can be perplexing and hurtful to carers. It is vital to support carers at this time, to prevent placement breakdown and the loss of the important gains made so far. A helpful explanation of this deterioration in behaviour is that the child is now able to safely process his or her previous abusive experiences, which have until now needed to be blocked from conscious awareness. Research into the neuropsychological sequelae of trauma has shown that an important element in healthy recovery is the ability to process memories cognitively so that they can be appropriately stored. In this way they appear not to interfere with everyday functioning (see, e.g., Siegel & Hartzell, 2003; Grunert et al., 2003).

- Carers need to be prepared for the possibility of children's behaviour getting worse when they become more secure in their placement.
- Carers need to understand the importance of this phase of recovery.
- Carers need continuous reminders of this (it's easy to forget in the stress of the moment).
- Carers need practical support in helping them to cope with these difficult times.

Children who do not get help with their social health will sadly pass this on to their own children, through the same process that they themselves suffered, i.e. early care that is not 'good enough'. As a parent the child will become afraid and withdraw when he or she is not in control of his or her baby, the baby will respond by being more demanding, which will exacerbate his or her fear. Without help, the relationship will have little or no attunement and the baby will develop an insecure attachment pattern. This will be unrewarding to the mother who needs and craves unconditional love, and she will withdraw further from her baby, perhaps actively punishing it for its failure to meet her needs. Early intervention at ante-natal and post-natal clinics can help the mother to develop a positive spiral of behaviour with her baby such that both their needs are more likely to be met (see Gerhardt, Ch. 9, 2004; and Brisch, 2002, provides some case studies of such interventions). People who are able to sustain long-term relationships with stable partners are also more likely to parent their own children successfully.

MANAGING CHALLENGING BEHAVIOURS

There is a growing understanding of the approaches that are and are not likely to be effective with children who have received seriously inadequate or abusive early care (Delaney, 1998; Howe & Fearnley, 1999; Hughes, 1997). When children are actively angry or still obviously in shame, they are not processing information cognitively because the brain is dominated by more primitive subcortical processes. This means that children need to have extreme emotion soothed or contained before they can learn from behavioural or cognitive strategies how to change their behaviours or regulate their emotional states. Hughes (1997) describes how, when children are angry or in shame, there is a window of opportunity to explore the abusive events that lie behind the current emotion. This can be therapeutic if it helps children to understand why they behaved as they did, that this was a normal reaction to their previous 'care', and that it is no longer needed in the current home. Hughes (1997) recommends maintaining strict boundaries with appropriate 'consequences', but stresses the need for this to be done with a high level of empathy. At a neurological level, the empathy will be helping the child to remain sufficiently regulated to process the implementation of the boundary at a cognitive level, and thus be able to learn from it.

Carers need good support to enable them to provide consistent boundaries and nurturing in the face of constant challenge. It is important that they receive compatible advice and support from professionals who come together for consultation meetings and work to a jointly constructed care plan.

Nathan was given a new social worker who had attended intensive training workshops on working with children with attachment difficulties. She found foster carers for him who understood and were willing to work with such children. She also worked in collaboration with a clinical psychologist in the Looked After Children team to set up regular consultation meetings with the other professionals who work with Nathan, to support the foster carers. With this support, Nathan's new carers were able to put into practice the strategies they had learned and to calmly and firmly persist in helping Nathan to comply with the normal rules of their home, and to engage in relationship repair each time.

At first, this had adverse effects on his behaviour at school. However, having the designated teacher for looked after children from his school at the consultation meetings helped the school to understand this and gave them complementary strategies to manage his behaviour. With school and home singing from the same hymn sheet, Nathan's behaviour improved gradually over the year. Each instance of relationship repair helped to build Nathan's self-esteem and his confidence noticeably improved. He became particularly proud of being able to control his temper in the playground. The school acknowledged and rewarded his achievement by presenting him with an end-of-year certificate for 'The pupil who has made the most progress over the year'.

Nathan's efforts were further rewarded by his foster carers deciding that they would like to adopt him.

PHYSICAL HEALTH

Low self-esteem, difficulties in recognizing or regulating emotion, and other psychological consequences of early disadvantage are related to the development of health problems and risky health behaviours prevalent in looked after children, such as poor nutrition, unhealthy lifestyle, dental problems, early sexual activity and early pregnancy, prostitution, smoking and alcohol abuse, self-harm and suicide attempts (Jackson et al., 2000; Williams et al., 2001). A survey by the Who Cares? Trust shows that 40% of children under 11 felt that they had not received enough health information and advice, and around half of those in children's homes and secure units considered that they put their health at risk in some way (Shaw, 1998).

Traditional interventions through education and health promotion need to take account of the underlying problems to help to ensure effectiveness in the content and delivery of their messages. Initial engagement with the young person will be primary and will need to involve building an appropriate, trusting relationship, within which to build self-esteem and security. The relevance and comprehensibility of any teaching materials need to be considered. The extent to which the young person understands consequences and has the ability to plan ahead will need to be factored in to both the message and the solution – for example, spelling out the relationship between sex and pregnancy and discussion of how to ensure that contraception is in place when needed. Two related areas of sexual health and substance misuse are discussed in more detail in the next section, to explore how this model fits.

Sexual Health

The arena of sexual health is an important one for children and young people who have suffered neglect or abuse or who have significantly insecure attachments to their primary carers. It is well documented that children and young adults who have been in care are particularly likely to engage in early and risky sexual activity (Corlyon & McGuire, 1999; Stock et al., 1997). This may occur for many reasons, which are likely to be complex and interrelated, for example:

- a desire to experience longed for warmth and closeness;
- a way of buying friendship or love;
- to blot out emotional pain;
- being in a victim role;
- being unable to say 'no' because of the power of early grooming prior to sexual abuse;
- diminished ability to regulate emotion and control impulses;
- impaired planning ability or assertiveness (re contraception);

- to get pregnant and have a baby to love who will return this love unconditionally;
- to get money;
- to avoid punishment.

A major 'risk' of early sexual activity is pregnancy. Biehal and colleagues (1995) found that half of a sample of young women leaving care became mothers within a period of 18–24 months and Corlyon & McGuire (1999) suggest that looked after young people appear to be keener to have children than young people who are not looked after. Related research shows that girls who have a history of sexual abuse have a greater desire to conceive than girls without abuse histories (Elders & Albert, 1998). A common thread in both these populations may be the desire to have someone to love and be loved unconditionally. Sadly, this aim is often thwarted as our main learning experience for parenting comes from our own experience of being parented. We are particularly likely to do what was done to us in pressured or stressful situations when the ability to think is impaired.

It is important to remember, too, that being sexually active does not always go hand in hand with good knowledge about sex. In a survey of young people in care commissioned by the Who Cares? Trust, one young person said, 'I would like to know more about drugs, safe sex and boys' (Shaw, 1998, p. 43). There is evidence that greater levels of knowledge about sex are correlated with later onset of sexual activity. Boys who become fathers in their early teenage years are likely to have lived with neither or only one of their natural parents, and in families where discussion of sex was difficult or did not take place (Home Office, 1998).

Safer sex education and advice needs to encompass all these factors and explore the individual's reasons for early or risky sexual activity in order to be effective (Chambers et al., 2000). It also needs to focus on self-esteem, impulse control, understanding consequences, assertiveness and the ability to plan ahead.

Prostitution

Young people in care, especially in residential units, are particularly vulnerable to prostitution, and it is important to know the warning signs.

Sara Swann (2000) has campaigned for prostitution to be relabelled as child abuse and for customers to be called paedophiles and prosecuted as such. In her research she has found that some Local Authorities are unaware of this activity in their area and she has developed workshops to help to raise awareness. She has identified warning signs for prostitution, including:

- having a boyfriend more than 5 years older;
- regularly being taken out 'socially' to other towns or cities;
- staying out overnight;
- receiving expensive gifts.

Swann's (2000) research into the common patterns for grooming girls and young women into prostitution indicate that it begins as an exploitation of the huge need to be special to someone. It is no coincidence that girls in residential units are particularly targeted. The grooming quickly degenerates into brutal and frightening coercion, not free choice, often using addictive drugs. Since prostitution is illegal in the UK, girls are afraid to ask for help or do not know who to turn to. Being out of control and at the mercy of an abusive adult is a repetition of earlier abuse that may lead to a feeling of helplessness.

Important preventative steps that need to be taken are:

- the development of secure supportive relationships between carers and young people to help to fulfil the need for close attachments;
- education for all carers, social workers and other professionals about the real nature of prostitution as child abuse;
- knowledge of local prevalence;
- knowledge of warning signs;
- liaison with other professionals and agencies, particularly the police.

Smoking, Alcohol and Drugs

As indicated above, there is a strong link between drug use and prostitution, yet there are usually separate teams for working with drug abuse, who are not also experts in risky sexual behaviours. *Promoting the Health of Looked After Children* (DOH, 2002) recommends joint commissioning, planning and delivery by Social Services and the NHS of some services. They particularly emphasize contraception and sexual health services, and young people's drug services.

Research indicates that looked after children start substance abuse earlier and are greater consumers than young people in the general population (Ward, 1998). Their reasons for drinking have an emphasis on coping with stressful or traumatic life events (Honess et al., 2000). Since research also indicates that early stress, trauma and insecure attachments diminish an individual's neurological and emotional capacity to manage current stress (Schore, 2003a), interventions that focus on sustaining secure attachments to caregivers and providing structure and support in all areas of life, are likely to be most effective.

> Nathan was adopted by his foster carers and until he was 11 years old they experienced relatively few problems. However, when he started secondary school, he found it hard to organise himself to be at the right place for each lesson. He also found the work much harder as the teachers did not know him and he received less support than if he were identified as a 'looked after child'. He didn't want to admit this to his parents, and started to become angry and resentful as he felt out of control of his life once more. He stopped working in lessons, misbehaved and became friends with two boys who were both living in a residential unit. They brought cigarettes and cans of lager into school, and shared them with Nathan at lunchtime. At first Nathan's parents didn't notice as they were distracted by his adoptive grandmother having been diagnosed with cancer. Because Nathan was adopted and not on a list of 'looked after children', school staff were not alert to the possibility that he may experience difficulties.

Education, health promotion and the provision of opportunities for promoting healthy behaviours in all areas of life are obviously important, but helping the most troubled young people to take care of their health will need to begin with forming trusting relationships, exploring underlying reasons for low self-esteem and poor self-care and targeting interventions appropriately.

NEW SERVICES TO MEET THE NEEDS OF LOOKED AFTER AND ADOPTED CHILDREN

Other reasons why coming into care does not produce better health outcomes may be connected to the fragmentation of services concerning some of the more common health challenges facing looked after children, for example, CAMHS, Drug Abuse Teams, and professionals working with sexual health, teenage pregnancy and prostitution. Many of these challenges are a result of emotional problems and are a way of managing or masking psychological pain. Services that are designed to work with looked after and adopted children can develop expertise in these areas so that the 'whole person' can be worked with, and the root cause of the child's problems can be addressed.

One way forward would be to limit the number of professionals involved with a young person, by linking social care, health and educational services for children in special circumstances, as recommended in the Children Act 2004 (DFES, 2004a), and the National Service Framework for Children (DOH, 2004). This would help to promote healthy attachments between the young person and a few trusted adults in his or her life.

Over the past four to six years, specialist services for looked after children have been developed in different parts of the UK. Some examples of these are the Children Looked After Mental Health Service (CLAMHS) in the South London and Maudsley NHS Trust, the Primary Care and Support Team (PCST), now part of the Integrated Service for Looked After Children in Worcestershire, the Behaviour Resource Service (BRS) in Southampton (Kelly et al., 2003) and the ROSTA Project in Liverpool (see Golding et al., 2004). These teams have been created out of a recognition that it is not currently easy or possible to prioritize children looked after in a generic service for the psychological needs of all children. It is important to provide a dedicated service in order to begin to reduce the large gulf between the health needs of children who are looked after by the Local Authority and those who are looked after by their own parents. Legislation, including *Working Together* (DOH et al., 1999), *Quality Protects* (DOH, 1998), *Promoting the Health of Looked After Children* (DOH, 2002), *Every Child Matters* (DFES, 2003), *Next Steps* (DFES, 2004c), *Every Child Matters, Change for Children* (DFES, 2004b) and the development of the *National Service Framework for Children* (DOH, 2004) have been important catalysts for these initiatives, partly by encouraging Primary Care Trusts (PCTs) to provide much needed extra resources to this group of service users.

One innovative model of service delivery for the holistic health needs of looked after children has been developed in Northamptonshire and is described in detail in the next section.

NORTHAMPTONSHIRE CENTRE FOR HEALTH FOR LOOKED AFTER CHILDREN

Northamptonshire Social Services Department and 'Quality Protects' initiatives provided an opportunity to consider delivering health services for looked after children in a flexible and innovative way. The Centre for Health was opened in summer 2001 and created an ideal opportunity to create a central base for looked after children and to develop health services for the complex health needs of this group.

There is evidence that some children in special circumstances have poorer access to mainstream services. For example, children living in domestic violence refuges often find it hard to access services, and a third of looked after children do not have an annual dental check (DOH, 2004). As a result of poor access to mainstream services, looked after children may require specialist knowledge and input into their health care.

The Centre for Health was designed to fulfil these requirements by providing a flexible health service. The concept of the Centre for Health was developed to provide mobile health services to increase access for looked after children to health providers. The team of nurses, psychologists and youth workers use imaginative and flexible models of working to address the historical problems of poor access; for example, to consider reasons why young people do not attend appointments, such as venue, time of day and even their mood on the day. The practical organization of the service is based on the belief that a completely flexible approach makes eventual engagement with the service more likely to happen. An element of the success of this flexible model is that young people are able to see evidence of perseverance by the health provider. This all serves to challenge the issues of poor self-esteem and self-worth beliefs held by this group of young people. Another example of flexibility is a mobile sexual health service where contraception and sexual health trained nurses see young people in their homes, keep records of when their contraception is due and take the service to them.

The specialist skills currently offered directly by the team are summarized in Figure 3.3.

Northamptonshire Centre for Health Partnership with Primary Care Trusts (PCTs)

To achieve any real improvement for the health outcomes of looked after children, it is crucial that their health agenda becomes part of the improvement plans for PCTs. This is recognized and encouraged by the government through inclusion of services for looked after children in performance indicators for PCTs. The Health Coordinators work closely with community health services to increase access for looked after children by attending team meetings for health visitors, school nurses, GPs and voluntary agencies to increase awareness of the specific health needs of this client group, as well as giving advice and information on how to engage looked after children. There are three PCTs in the county, one of which has recently developed a service for looked after children. The team consists of a designated nurse, designated doctor (consultant community paediatrician) and an administrative clerk. The community paediatrician undertakes the initial health assessment, and school nurses or health visitors carry out subsequent health assessments. It is anticipated that this model will be used by other PCTs within the county.

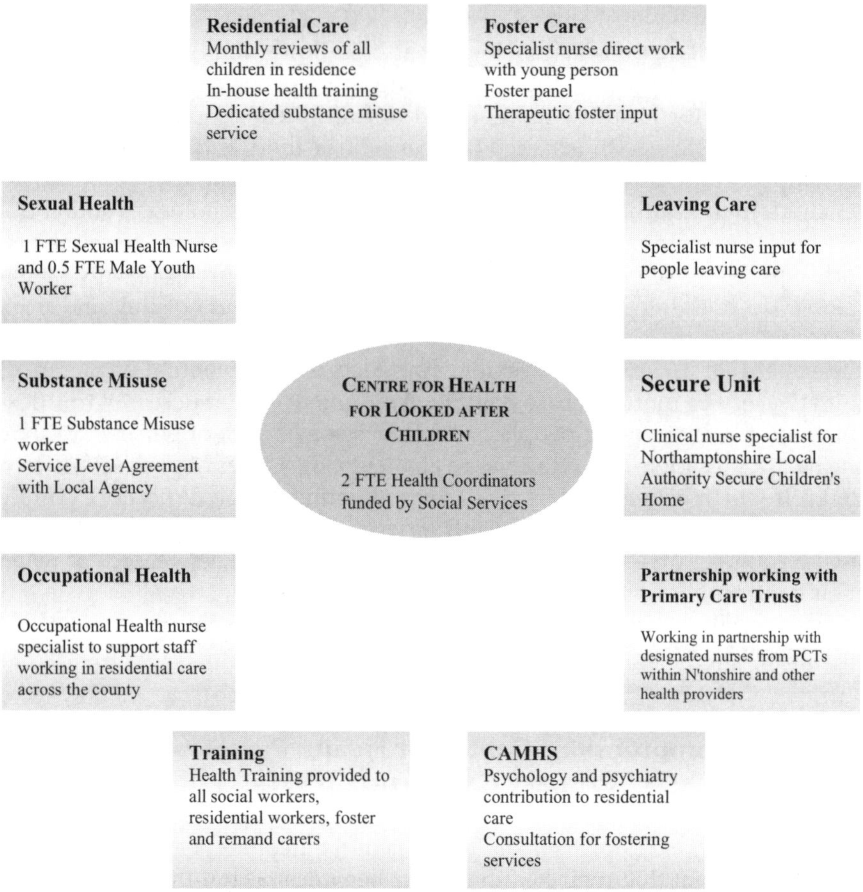

Residential Care
Monthly reviews of all
children in residence
In-house health training
Dedicated substance misuse
service

Foster Care
Specialist nurse direct work
with young person
Foster panel
Therapeutic foster input

Sexual Health
1 FTE Sexual Health Nurse
and 0.5 FTE Male Youth
Worker

Leaving Care
Specialist nurse input for
people leaving care

Substance Misuse
1 FTE Substance Misuse
worker
Service Level Agreement
with Local Agency

**CENTRE FOR HEALTH
FOR LOOKED AFTER
CHILDREN**

2 FTE Health Coordinators
funded by Social Services

Secure Unit
Clinical nurse specialist for
Northamptonshire Local
Authority Secure Children's
Home

Occupational Health
Occupational Health nurse
specialist to support staff
working in residential care
across the county

**Partnership working with
Primary Care Trusts**
Working in partnership with
designated nurses from PCTs
within N'tonshire and other
health providers

Training
Health Training provided to
all social workers,
residential workers, foster
and remand carers

CAMHS
Psychology and psychiatry
contribution to residential
care
Consultation for fostering
services

Figure 3.3   Services offered by the Northamptonshire Centre for Health

Northamptonshire Centre for Health Training Agenda

Training is seen as one of the keystones of the service. As this service is placed within the Social Services this gives the health professionals an unusual insight into the difficulties experienced by colleagues. Health training is delivered and specifically tailored to the needs of social work colleagues, residential carers and foster carers. Several training events are provided throughout the year, including:

● sex and relationships;
● contraception;

- substance misuse;
- mental health.

Many of the training programmes are focused on skilled carers working directly with the young people they look after, because often they are the people with the existing relationships. It also has benefits in the other directions, by bringing a social-work perspective to colleagues in health, where there seems to be limited understanding regarding the specificity of the complex health needs of this group of children and young people. An example of this is raising the awareness of the inability of young people who are looked after to take their own health seriously (no surprise, when their lives may be in chaos).

Success Factors of the Northamptonshire Centre for Health

The success of this service is dependent on several factors:

- Staff having a 'can-do' attitude, which is essential when using this model.
- Good relationships between the Centre for Health team and colleagues in the NHS and Social Services.
- A consistent health team that stays involved with children irrespective of placement moves.
- Dedicated funds from Social Services.

There are, however, some outstanding factors that need to be considered:

- There is no evidence yet to support an *actual* improvement in the life chances of looked after children due to this model.
- The service is largely dependent on the dynamics of the team and the dedication and skills of individual team members.

Crucially, structures need to be developed with health providers for services that are not dependent on personal relationships with individuals. One way to address these issues and to take the service forward may be to develop Service Level Agreements between the agencies involved.

USING EXISTING SERVICES DIFFERENTLY

Another approach to the 'failure of the corporate parent to advocate for health' (Mather et al., 2000) has been to help existing services to meet these needs by providing education and training about the needs of children who have suffered early disadvantage. Some initiatives have included training nurses in basic counselling skills and in more specialized therapeutic approaches that can be used to enhance their work, for example during health checks. With appropriate supervision this can be an effective strategy, as young people do not always want specialist psychotherapy. Being referred to CAMHS is often seen as yet another stigma, which can be avoided. Other advantages of training nurses include:

- Building upon the foundations of an existing trusting relationship, rather than passing the child on to yet another professional.
- There are more nurses than psychologists and mental health workers.
- Not pathologizing what may be normal reactions to abnormal circumstances.
- Not conveying the implicit message that the young person's emotional issues are so dreadful that only a mental health professional could bear to listen (Hunter, 2001).

Professionals who are not mental health specialists may also be able to help a young person through the various stages of pre-contemplation and contemplation of the need to change (Prochaska & DiClemente, 1982) by using Miller and Rollnick's (1991) motivational interviewing strategies. This approach was first developed with people who abuse alcohol and incorporates elements of Rogerian counselling (Rogers, 1951) such as acceptance and empathy, in order to help individuals to reach their own understanding of their need for help or desire to change.

INFORMED CONSENT

Even in an ideal situation, issues around consent can arise which make it difficult for health professionals to deliver appropriate care. This is more common in mental health settings, but can arise in physical health too, as in the following case:

> Kylie, an 11-year-old girl, who had been severely abused and neglected by her alcoholic father, and who had a great fear of anyone seeing any part of her body, sustained a serious injury to her hand and refused treatment. She was taken to A&E but objected so violently to being there that her social worker had to be called to help to calm her down and take her away. She refused all treatment

for a week despite clear indications that it was needed. Medical staff became concerned that if her hand did not heal it may have to be amputated. This produced discussion among the professionals concerning the relative damage of forcing her to have treatment, versus the responsibility to ensure that she reached adulthood without avoidable disability. Kylie's father was involved in an emergency consultation meeting, following which he persuaded her to receive treatment.

In this situation, the relevant adults were willing and able to give the time immediately to attend a consultation meeting in which they discussed their concerns with Kylie and her father. This was more easily accomplished because the professionals were employed in a dedicated service for looked after children. In other circumstances, health care professionals may have decided early on that Kylie was not capable of making a rational decision, and have forced her to receive treatment. Baldwin (2001) has stated that the capacity for rational decision making requires:

- that children can express a preference;
- that they can understand and appreciate the situation;
- and that they can reach a reasonable decision and positive outcome.

The criterion for judging the third point is often effectively whether the child's decision is in accordance with the professional's view, since there tends to be a narrow perspective on what constitutes a reasonable decision and positive outcome. Children who have psychological or emotional difficulties are commonly thought to lack the necessary capacity for rational decision making that is required for informed consent. This is not necessarily the case, and even if the adult has to overrule the child's wishes, this can be done in a caring and respectful manner. If consent is not sought, the child may experience the situation as another instance of not being listened to, and an opportunity to learn to trust adults will be lost.

The factor that made a difference for Kylie was the professionals working together. Their cohesiveness and lack of coercion gave her grounds for believing they had her best interests in mind, and that they could be trusted. This will pave the way for Kylie to trust professionals in the future. There are many barriers to multi-professional and multi-agency working, which have been discussed in Chapter 2 of this book, but the problems are not insurmountable and it is important to overcome the obstacles in order to make a difference to the lives of vulnerable and disadvantaged children.

CONCLUSIONS AND THE WAY FORWARD

There is a rapidly growing body of evidence from neurological and psychological research that the brain develops differently in adverse circumstances such as severe and enduring abuse or neglect. This affects the ability to understand and regulate emotion, to empathize with others and to behave in a socially acceptable manner. In effect a hidden disability is created, which manifests itself as 'naughtiness', 'nastiness' and 'indifference'. Such terms imply volition, but these children do not have the luxury of choice. Without help they are unable to behave differently. This hidden disability impacts upon mental, social and emotional health, and often results in poor life outcomes. However, this trend can be reversed with appropriately skilled staff and carers.

Research into the underlying needs of looked after and adopted children suggests that long-term benefit is most likely to occur through supportive and nurturing relationships, which are most likely to develop if the young person has a smaller number of carers and professionals to relate to. Conveniently, other strands of evidence (e.g. Hill & Thompson, 2003) and policy documents (e.g. Laming Report, 2003; DOH, 2004; DFES, 2004a) indicate that it is vital for services and agencies to work together, sharing information and developing joint care plans. If 'working together' reduces the number of professionals who have face-to-face contact with each child in substitute care, a double benefit will occur. With greater understanding of the issues and dedicated services, there is a real chance that the outcomes for looked after children could improve by the end of this decade.

For this to happen, changes will need to take place at many levels in the context surrounding the child (see the Onion Model in Chapter 2), for example:

- *Legislation* – Reduce child poverty; provide structures to support and encourage parenting; increase funding for services for children.
- *Society and agency* – Value children, parents and those who work with children.
- *Professional network* – Early intervention; universal services focusing on parent–child bonding such as the Oxford Parent Infant Project (Gerhardt, 2004) and the Sunderland Infant Programme (Svanberg, 2005); early removal of children from homes that are not good enough; improved inter-agency working; increased understanding of effective interventions.
- *Community* – Improve work/life balance and care more for each other.
- *Carers* – Resolve own psychological issues; implement therapeutic caring.
- *Family of origin* – Spend time with children; notice and praise the positives;
- *Child* – Talk to someone who'll listen – parent, teacher, carer, professional, Childline, friend.

The chapter began with the news report of a 14-year-old boy who had set fire to the recently regrown hair of an 11-year-old girl. Why he did this may never come into the public domain, but on the basis of research reported in this chapter it is possible to speculate. For such an extreme act of aggression against a vulnerable, younger girl, it is almost certain that he had experienced serious abuse or neglect as a very young child to the extent that he had failed to develop the ability to regulate or control his emotions and the capacity for empathy, which would have aroused his protective instincts. If no one had protected him as a child, he may have felt extreme resentment against a girl whom everyone else was caring for and rejoicing over her recovery. When she had no hair, perhaps he saw her as another outsider like himself and was angry with her for 'deserting' him when her hair grew back. Perhaps the dashed hope of this perceived alliance was sufficient to make him re-experience the shame of not being good enough. And perhaps the unbearable pain of this shame made him want to annihilate the cause of it – the hair that had grown back.

Greater understanding of what drives such challenging behaviour will enable services to be more closely tailored to meet children's needs.

REFERENCES

Allen, E., Combs-Orme, T., McCarter, R. & Grossman, L. (2000) Self-reported depressive symptoms in school-age children at the time of entry into foster care. *Ambulatory Child Health*, **6**, 45–57.

Baldwin, S. (2001). When 'No' means 'Yes': Informed consent themes with children and teenagers. In C. Newnes, G. Holmes & C. Dunn (Eds), *This is Madness Too. Critical Perspectives on Mental Health Services*. Ross on Wye: PCCS Books.

Bandelow, B., Krause, J., Wedekind, D., Broocks, A., Hajak, G. & Ruther, E. (2005) Early traumatic life events, parental attitudes, family history and birth risk factors in patients with borderline personality disorder and healthy controls. *Psychiatry Research*, **134**(2), 169–179.

Biehal, N., Clayden, J., Stein, M. & Wade, J. (1995) *Moving On: Young People and Leaving Care Schemes*. London: HMSO.

Blower, A., Addo, A., Hodgson, J., Lamington, L. & Towlson, K. (2004) Mental health of 'looked after' children: A needs assessment. *Clinical Child Psychology and Psychiatry*, **9**(1), 117–129.

Bowlby, J. (1969) *Attachment and Loss. Vol. 1. Attachment*. New York: Basic Books.

Bowlby, J. (1973) *Attachment and Loss. Vol. 2. Separation, Anxiety and Anger*. New York: Basic Books.

Bowlby, J. (1980) *Attachment and Loss. Vol. 3. Loss, Sadness and Depression*. New York: Basic Books.

Brisch, K.H. (2002) *Treating Attachment Disorders From Theory to Therapy*. English Edition. New York: The Guilford Press.

Broks, P. (2003) *Into the Silent Land*. London: Atlantic Books.

Buchanan, A. (1996) *Cycles of Child Maltreatment: Facts, Fallacies and Interventions*. Chichester: John Wiley & Sons.

Cairns, K. (2002) *Attachment, Trauma and Resilience. Therapeutic Caring for Children*. London: BAAF.

Chambers, R., Wakely, G. & Chambers, S. (2000) *Tackling Teenage Pregnancy: Sex, Culture and Needs*. Oxford: Radcliffe Medical Press.

Corlyon, J. & McGuire, C. (1999) *Pregnancy and Parenthood: The Views and Experiences of Young People in Public Care*. London; National Children's Bureau.

Curtis, P.A. (1999) The chronic nature of the foster care crisis. In P.A. Curtis, G. Dale & J.C. Kendall (Eds), *The Foster Care Crisis: Translating Research into Policy and Practice*. Lincoln, NE: University of Nebraska Press.

Delaney, R.J. (1998) *Fostering Changes. Treating Attachment-Disordered Foster Children*. Oklahoma City: Wood & Barnes Publishing.

DOH, Home office & DFES (1999) *Working Together to Safeguard Children*. London: TSO.

DOH (1998) *Quality Protects: Transforming Children's Services: The Government's Objectives for Children's Social Services*. London: TSO.

DOH (2002) *Promoting the Health of Looked After Children*. London: TSO.

DOH (2004) *National Service Framework for Children, Young People and Maternity Services*. London: TSO.

DFES (2003) *Every Child Matters*, The Green Paper. London: TSO.

DFES (2004a) *Children Act 2004* London: TSO.

DFES (2004b) *Every Child Matters, Change for Children*. London: TSO.

DFES (2004c) Every Child Matters: *Next Steps*. London: TSO.

Dimigen, G., Del Priore, C., Butler, S., Evans, S., Ferguson, I. & Swan, M. (1999) Psychiatric disorder among children at time of entering local authority care: Questionnaire survey. *British Medical Journal*, **319**, 675.

Dozier, M., Dozier, D. & Manni, M. (2002) Attachment and bio-behavioural catch-up: The ABCs of helping foster infants cope with early adversity. *Zero to Three Bulletin*, **22**, 7–13.

Elders, M.J. & Albert, A.E. (1998) Adolescent pregnancy and sexual abuse. *Journal of the American Medical Association*, **280**(7), 648–649.

Essex, M.J., Klein, M.H., Cho, E. & Kalin, N.H. (2002) Maternal stress beginning in infancy may sensitise children to later stress exposure: Effects on cortisol and behaviour. *Biological Psychiatry*, **52**, 776–784.

Fonagy, P., Gergely, G., Jurist, E.L. & Target, M. (2002) *Affect Regulation, Mentalisation and the Development of the Self*. New York: Other Press.

Gerhardt, S. (2004) *Why Love Matters. How Affection Shapes a Baby's Brain*. Hove and New York: Brunner–Routledge.

Golding, K., Taylor, J., Thorp, D., Berger, M. & Stevenson, J. (2004) Briefing Paper: *Looked After Children: Improving the Psychological Well-being of Children in the Care of the Looked After System. A Guide for Clinical Psychologists Working with or Considering the Development of Psychological Services for Looked After Children and their Carers*. Produced by Faculty for Children and Young People of the Division of Clinical Psychology, British Psychological Society, January. Appendix IV. Models of existing practice, January, pp. 28–31.

Glaser, D. (2000) Child abuse and neglect and the brain – A review. *Journal of Child Psychology and Psychiatry*, **41**(1), 97–116.

Grunert, B.K., Smucker, M.R., Weis, J.M. & Rusch, M.D. (2003) When prolonged exposure falls: Adding an imagery-based cognitive restructuring component in the treatment of industrial accident victims suffering from PTSD. *Cognitive and Behavioural Practice*, **10**(4), 333–346.

Harris, M & Butterworth, G. (2002) *Developmental Psychology: A Student's Handbook*. Hove: Psychology Press.

Hill, C. & Thompson, M. (2003) Mental and physical health co-morbidity in looked after children. *Clinical Child Psychology and Psychiatry*, **8**(3), 315–321.

Home Office. (1998) *Supporting Families: A Consultation Document*. London: TSO.

Honess, T., Seymour, L. & Webster, R. (2000) *The Social Contexts of Underage Drinking*. London: Home Office.

Howe, D., Brandon, M., Hinings, D. & Schofield, G. (1999) *Attachment Theory, Child Maltreatment and Family Support. A Practice and Assessment Model*. Basingstoke: Macmillan.

Howe, D. & Fearnley, S. (1999) Disorders of attachment and attachment therapy. *Adoption and Fostering*, **23**(2), 19–30.

Hughes, D. (1997) *Facilitating Developmental Attachment: The Road to Emotional Recovery and Behavioural Change in Foster and Adopted Children*. Northvale, NJ: Aronson.

Hunter, M. (2001) *Psychotherapy with Young People in Care*. Hove, East Sussex: Brunner–Routledge.

Ireland, C.A., Naylor, K. & Wilks-Riley, F. (2003) Personality disorder and psychopathy: Facing challenges in sex offender group treatment. *Forensic Update*, **75** (October), 31–36.

Irwin, H.J. (1994) Proneness to dissociation and traumatic childhood events. *Journal of Nervous and Mental Disease*, **182**, 456–460.

Iwaniec, D. (1995) *The Emotionally Abused and Neglected Child*. Chichester: John Wiley & Sons.

Jackson, S. & Thomas, N. (1999) *On the Move Again? What Works in Creating Stability for Looked After Children*. Barnardos.

Jackson, S., Williams, J., Maddocks, A., Love, A., Cheung, W. & Hutchings, H. (2000) *The Health Needs and Health Care of School Aged Children Looked After by Local Authorities*. Final Report to the Wales Office of Research and Development for Health and Social Care.

Kaniuk, J., Steele, M. & Hodges, J. (2004) Report on a longitudinal research project, exploring the development of attachments between older, hard-to-place children and their adopters over the first two years of placement. *Adoption and Fostering*, **28**(2), 61–67.

Kelly, C., Allan, S., Roscoe, P. & Herrick, E. (2003) The mental health needs of looked after children: An integrated multi-agency model of care. *Clinical Child Psychology and Psychiatry*, **8**(3), 323–335.

Kelly, G. & Gilligan, R. (2000) *Issues in Foster Care*. London: Jessica Kingsley.

Kinney, H.C., Brody, B.A., Kloman, A.S. & Gilles, F.H. (1988) Sequence of central nervous system myelination in human infancy: II. Patterns of myelination in autopsied infants. *Journal of Neuropathology and Experimental Neurology*, **47**, 217–234.

Laming, H. (2003) *The Victoria Climbié Inquiry: Report by Lord Laming*. Cm. 5730. London: TSO.

Lewis, E., Dozier, M., Knights, M. & Maier, M. (in press) Intervening with foster infants' caregivers: Attachment and biobehavioural catch-up. In R.E. Lee (Ed.), *Handbook of Relational Therapy for Foster Children and their Families*. Washington, DC: Child Welfare League of America.

Mackner, L.M., Black, M.M. & Starr, R.H. (2003) Cognitive development of children in poverty with failure to thrive: A prospective study through age 6. *Journal of Child Psychology and Psychiatry*, **44**(5), 743–751.

Martin, J.G. (2000) *Foster Family Care, Theory and Practice*. Boston: Allyn & Bacon.

Mather, M., Batty, D. & Payne, H. (2000) *Doctors for Children in Public Care*. London: BAAF.

McCann, J., James, A., Wilson, S. & Dunn, G. (1996) Prevalence of psychiatric disorders in young people in the care system. *British Medical Journal*, **313**, 1529–1530.

Miller, W.R. & Rollnick, S. (1991) *Motivational Interviewing: Preparing People to Change Addictive Behaviour*. New York: Guilford Press.

Myers, W.C., Gooch, E. & Meloy, J.R. (2005) The role of psychopathy and sexuality in a female serial killer. *Journal of Forensic Sciences*, **50**(3), 652–657.

Ogawa, J.R., Sroufe, L.A., Weinfield, N.S., Carlson, E.A. & Egeland, B. (1997) Development and the fragmented self: Longitudinal study of dissociative symptomatology in a non-clinical sample. *Development and Psychopathology*, **9**, 855–879.

Plotsky, P.M., Owens, M.J. & Nemeroff, C.B. (1998) Psychoneuroendochrinology of depression: Hypothalamic-pituitary-adrenal axis. *Psychiatric Clinics of North America*, **21**, 293–307.

Power, T.G. & Chapieski, M.L. (1986) Child rearing and impulse control in toddlers: A naturalistic investigation. *Developmental Psychology*, **22**, 271–275.

Prochaska, J.O. & DiClemente, E.C. (1982) Transtheoretical therapy: Toward a more integrative model of change. *Psychotherapy: Theory, Research and Practice*, **20**, 161–173.

Quinton, D. & Murray, C. (2002) Assessing emotional and behavioural development in children looked after away from home. In H. Ward & W. Rose (Eds), *Approaches to Needs Assessment in Children's Services*. London: Jessica Kingsley.

Quinton, D., Rushton, A., Dance, C. & Mayes, D. (1998) *Joining New Families: A Study of Adoption and Fostering in Middle Childhood*. Chichester: John Wiley & Sons.

Read, J., Agar, K., Argyle, N. & Aderhold, V. (2003) Sexual and physical abuse during childhood and adulthood as predictors of hallucinations, delusions and thought disorder. *Psychological Psychotherapy: Theory, Research and Practice*, **76**, 11–22.

Richardson, J. & Joughin, C. (2000) *The Mental Health Needs of Looked After Children*. London: Royal College of Psychiatrists/Gaskell.

Rogers, C.R. (1951) *Client-centred Therapy*. New York: Houghton Mifflin.

Rutter, M. (2000) Children in substitute care: Some conceptual considerations and research implications. *Children and Youth Services Review. Special Issue: Child Welfare Research for the 21st century*, **22**, 685–703.

Schaffer, H.R. (1996) *Social Development*. Oxford: Blackwell.

Schore, A. (1994) *Affect Regulation and the Origin of the Self*. Hillsdale, NJ: Lawrence Erlbaum.

Schore, A. (2003a) *Affect Dysregulation and Disorders of the Self*. New York: Norton.

Schore, A. (2003b) *Affect Regulation and the Repair of the Self*. New York: Norton.

Shaw, C. (1998) *Remember My Messages. The Experiences and Views of 2000 Children in Public Care in the UK*. London: The Who Cares? Trust.

Siegel, D. J. (1996) *The Developing Mind. How Relationships and the Brain Interact to Shape who we Are*. New York: Guilford Press.

Siegel, D.J. & Hartzell, M. (2003) *Parenting from the Inside Out*. New York: Tarcher/Putnam.

Singer, L.T. & Fagan, J.F. (1984) Cognitive development in the failure to thrive infant: A three year longitudinal study. *Journal of Pediatric Psychology*, **9**, 263–283.

Stock, J.L., Bell, M.A., Boyer, D.K. & Connell, F.A. (1997) Adolescent pregnancy and sexual risk taking among sexually abused girls. *Family Planning Perspectives*, **29**(5), 200–203 and 227.

Svanberg, P.O. (2005) *Promoting attachment security in primary prevention using video feed-back: The Sunderland Infant Programme*. Submitted for publication, April 2005.

Swann, S. (2000) *Safeguarding Children Involved in Prostitution*. DOH.

Taylor, E. & Rogers, J.W. (2005) Practitioner review: Early adversity and developmental disorders. *Journal of Child Psychology and Psychiatry,* **46**(5), 451–467.

Van der Kolk, B.A. (1996) The body keeps the score: Approaches to the psychobiology of post traumatic stress disorder. In B.A. Van der Kolk, A.C. McFarlane & L. Weisaeth (Eds), *Traumatic Stress: The Effects of Overwhelming Experience on Mind, Body and Society.* New York: Guilford Press.

Verrier, N. (2000) *The Primal Wound.* Baltimore: Gateway Press.

Ward, J. (1998) Substance use among young people looked after by social services. *Drugs: Education, Prevention & Policy,* **5**(3), 257–267.

Ward, H. (2000) Poverty and family cohesion. In J. Bradshaw & R. Sainsbury (Eds), *Getting the Measure of Poverty: The Early Legacy of Seebohm Rowntree.* Aldershot: Ashgate.

Williams, J., Jackson, S., Maddocks, A., Cheung, W.Y., Love, A. & Hutchings, H. (2001) Case-control study of the health of those looked after by local authorities. *Archives of Diseases in Childhood,* **85**, 280–285.

Yehuda, R., Halligan, S.L. & Grossman, R. (2001) Childhood trauma and risk for PTSD: Relationship to intergenerational effects of trauma, parental PTSD and cortisol excretion. *Development and Psychopathology,* **13**, 733–753.

Zlotnick, C., Kronstadt, D. & Klee, L. (1998) Foster care children and family homelessness. *American Journal of Public Health,* **88**(9), 1368–1370.

4

'LIKE HIGHLY POLISHED MIRRORS': EDUCATIONAL PSYCHOLOGY AND SUPPORT FOR THE EDUCATION OF LOOKED AFTER AND ADOPTED CHILDREN

Anne Peake

We have all had the experience of looking into a highly polished mirror and finding that we are surprised, and probably disappointed, by what we see. We see age lines and blemishes that we suspected were there, but would rather ignore. Much the same happens when we look into the education of looked after and adopted children. Like highly polished mirrors, we see through the children's experiences, the lines and blemishes in our education system. Looked after children have endured early disadvantage, many have been abused and they have the disruption of being in care. Adopted children, whilst now having the stability of a permanent family often share similar early experiences. The consequences of all this can leave them at odds with the education system. Education is largely based on the assumption that most children are able, willing, and supported, to take up education opportunities. The experiences of looked after and adopted children undermine their capacities and disrupt their opportunities. Working as a psychologist to support

Thinking Psychologically About Children Who Are Looked After and Adopted
Edited by K.S. Golding, H.R. Dent, R. Nissim and L. Stott.
Copyright © 2006 John Wiley & Sons, Ltd.

their education means that one looks at the effects of time and history on individual children and at the blemishes that become sore testing points in our system of providing for their education.

Looked after and adopted children are in the first instance children like any others, but our picture of them needs to be sharper. Ages, stages, and abilities or disabilities range in all children, but for children with poor early experience and disrupted care there are additional complexities. From the moment of birth the foundation for the children's capacity to benefit from a learning environment is being laid. However early and however brief, the experience of adversity will have consequences for the child's cognitive development. This means that there are likely to be difficulties in thinking and reasoning, planning and organization. In spite of improvements in their care circumstances, these early developmental foundation stones may be insufficient to bear the weight of subsequent educational opportunities. The fact that the children have been separated from their families of origin further contributes to developmental difficulties. This in turn undermines their capacity to benefit from educational opportunities. The consequences of this early start are far reaching, influencing the children and young people throughout their educational experience and into adulthood.

In addition to all the normal educational challenges these children can become preoccupied with issues of identity, where they belong, and whether they are good enough. This can further undermine their prospects of success at school. These struggles can, however, become translated into challenging behaviour or can remain hidden from view.

> 'The only person I talk to is my teddy bear.'
>
> (Susan aged 10 years)

This chapter will consider the impact of the experience of looked after and adopted children on their ability to benefit from education. The role of psychological support to improve the children's capacity to benefit from education will be explored.

THE IMPACT OF EXPERIENCE ON THE ABILITY TO BENEFIT FROM EDUCATION

> 'I think at school they just didn't understand what being in care was. I think they still thought of it as orphanages, or something, you know what I mean. Their idea was like, Oliver Twist. And it was not like that, so they had just different ideas of care at school. The teachers as well, I think.'
>
> (Menna, in Skuse & Ward, 2003)

If we are going to peer into these highly polished mirrors, then it is useful to remind ourselves about the core of the children's disruption. When we are clear about this, we are better able to imagine the pain it causes and plan sensitively.

Children in the looked after system can often experience numerous, and often unplanned moves of home. Disrupted schooling and disruptions in care placements are two major contributory factors accounting for their low educational achievements. Garnett (1994) noted that only 27% of children remained in the same placement during their stay in care, half the children had two placement changes and a quarter had at least four changes. Most significant of all is the finding of Evans (2003) that 34% of all children in care moved home within the final six months of statutory schooling. This is quite different from children living with their families of origin, where a change of home or school is unlikely in the final two years of secondary schooling.

For adopted children the move from their families of origin can involve changes of home and school. While the move to an adoptive home holds the promise of more stability, there are significant adaptations that need to be made. Crucially the child has to adapt to a change in family style, a change in neighbourhood and often an increase in expectations. Typically adoptive parents are likely to have been successful when they were at school. It is not unusual for their experience of education, which can be significantly different from the experience of their adoptive child, to influence their aspirations for their child. The much longed for adopted child becomes a focus for their love and hopes, sometimes in ways that can be challenging for the child. Loving parents may be disappointed that, in spite of their best efforts, the child continues to struggle with education. This is also likely to be linked to issues of emerging identity and self-esteem but these may get hidden behind apparent school difficulties such as completing homework and working with peers.

The move from their family of origin for whatever reason disrupts the children's sense of who they are. The process by which a child leaves his or her family has its own impact, and the reactions of each child will be different. When siblings are separated the links between children are disrupted by time and distance, and it will take hard work on the part of carers and professionals to establish contact. This can contribute to restoring some sense of kinship for the children. Moves can mean a break with extended family members, friends, neighbours and the local community. All this undermines the child's sense of security and social well-being, which in turn, will impact on the child's capacity to successfully attend and benefit from the educational and social experience of school.

Only the children know the real details of their histories, but they often do not have the insight to recount these histories, even to themselves. Their histories have shaped their personalities, learning styles, behaviours and their worldviews. It is this we see in school. Some placements are so short term that neither the child nor the carers invest in a continuous, dependable relationship. For some children much needed work on early experiences may be postponed until a more permanent placement is found. This can leave the child, the carers and teachers struggling to understand the meaning of what has happened. Children may need this work to be done to assess their difficulties and enhance their understanding; otherwise wrong assumptions can be made about the child's capacity to achieve emotional literacy. Children in long-term foster care, and even more so in adoptive homes, have a greater sense of permanence. However, for older children, moving into these homes typically means a change of school. Adults unfamiliar with the children are put in the position of helping them to make sense of their experience.

The moves of placement for a child rarely coincide with the common entry points to school. Generally children share the start in reception class, the move to junior school, or secondary school transfer. Any changes of school are difficult, but for the child who has moved to a new placement necessitating a change of school, this is rarely a shared experience. He or she has to cope with the reasons that prompted the move while trying to fit into a family or placement, and this may be on top of several previous moves of school or time out of school. The change of school can plunge a child into a setting in a highly visible way. The child feels like an intruder, and at worst is treated as one. There may be complexities of relationships within the child's placement. There can be a balance to be struck between the children in the home. There can be biological children/grandchildren, siblings and other foster children, all of whom need to establish relationships. The needs of black and ethnic minority children may not be adequately provided for, which then adds to the extent to which these children feel that they can't get the praise and recognition they need so much.

Given children's experiences of disrupted care, they all need individual care and support. Lack of continuity in school will, however, have undermined their progress, leaving them less able to make relationships with teachers or to trust in their guidance. Mistrust then acts as a barrier to the enjoyment of school and educational success. Some of the children may have identified special educational needs, and there may be other barriers to providing effectively for their needs. The moves of placement and school lead to difficulties in assessment, effective inter-agency liaison and good understanding of a child's behaviour. Carers may need help to understand all the child's special educational needs, access the appropriate professional help, and secure resources to support the child in school. What can be even more difficult is when a child has had adverse early experiences, moves of placement/school, and has unidentified special educational needs. If too much is made of the child's disrupted childhood, the recognition of the real extent of the child's special educational needs can be at best delayed, and at worst overlooked completely. Difficulties are attributed to the child's history. Managing the impact of a disrupted childhood may cloud the picture of the child's difficulties. Disruptions in school and care placements can lead to information being lost, or it might be collected but interpreted differently by adults charged with the responsibility for making decisions about the child. Unlike parents who care for a child from birth, there is no one person who can trace the history of a child, and his or her strengths and difficulties.

When children have had a lack of continuity in care and schooling, it can be particularly difficult for them to make and sustain relationships with peers. They have to make new friends more frequently than their peers, despite low self-esteem and limited social skills consequent to the disruptions they have endured. This all leaves the child at a disadvantage. Friendships provide positive regard, which enhances self-esteem, possibilities for play and shared activities. They promote engagement and the building of social skills. Friends have opportunities to share thoughts and feelings, leading to trust and reciprocity in social settings.

Parents can do much to promote friendships for children. They provide secure attachment in early childhood, promote age appropriate and varied play opportunities, and supervise and support children's friendships. There is a lack of continuity in such parental support for many children in the looked after system, and, ironically, this occurs when they need to make friends more frequently. Adopted children have the benefit of more continuous parental support. However low self-esteem, emotional immaturity and deficits in social skills mean that they cannot always benefit from this support. Peer groups can have both positive and negative influences on a child. Like other children, children in care experience bullying, racial abuse and isolation, all of which compound their difficulties and detract from their self-esteem still further. The importance of friendship increases as children grow older, and this is at its most significant in adolescence, a time of great change for all children. The most common correlate with peer rejection is aggression. Rejection over time can lead to problems of truancy, law breaking and mental health. When we think about the numbers of adolescents in the looked after system who have to cope with moves of home or school, we see very clearly how problems with friendships can undermine their self-esteem and coping strategies. The risk of longer-term adjustment difficulties is high.

The children come to school from a variety of home bases. These include family or kinship care, varieties of foster care (short-term, long-term, respite care), adoptive families, and varieties of residential care (small group homes, residential provision with or without education, boarding schools, special schools, assessment centres and secure units). Each of these home settings adds its own layer of complexity to the aim that the children should be willing, able and supported to take up the opportunities of education. Home/school liaison is important and needs careful planning for any child. For children in the looked after system, these home bases place greater demands on the carers and teachers of the children. For example, planning home/school liaison for a secondary school age child who lives in a small group home needs careful thought between subject teachers and carers. Home/school links need to be flexible to cope with the shift working patterns of residential social work staff.

Adopted children can be virtually invisible within schools. While their history shares many of the facets of disruption experienced by looked after children, the circumstance of their adoption can obscure them from view. Most importantly, schools are not always aware of the child's adoptive history. Their adoptive parents are frequently childless. They have sought adoption as it provides them with opportunities to make a commitment to a child. They are parents with the means to support children independent from local authority funding. After careful preparation, the children are placed with them, their surnames are changed and the family works hard to understand and provide for them. The hope is always that this is the beginning of a 'happy ever after' story for all involved. Some adoptive families need ongoing support, as the children can struggle with what they know of their history, which can have effects on their self-esteem and worldview. In addition, difficulties that are constitutionally based can emerge and everyone concerned then needs the support of further assessment and intervention. Without the markers of an allocated social worker, looked after children reviews, and Personal Education Plans (PEPs), they can be invisible in education settings.

Christopher is 7 years old and has recently been adopted. He has started at a new school near to his family. His teacher finds it difficult to manage him in the classroom. She complains that he can't concentrate, does little work, and is very attention seeking. He can't play with other children in the playground as he seems to provoke arguments. The school decides to ask for additional resources to provide him with one-to-one support. The educational psychologist sees Christopher in class and on his own. She feels Christopher is very bright, but the work in class is being presented in a way that fails to engage him. His teacher notices what he does wrong in her wish to help him behave well. The work of the psychologist focuses on helping the teacher to understand how Christopher is dealing with the change in his life. They discuss the ways in which his school experiences can build his self-esteem and teach him the social skills he needs to make and sustain friendships.

THE CONTRIBUTION OF THE EDUCATIONAL PSYCHOLOGIST

Wherever we look, looked after and adopted children are in the full range of school settings: playgroups, nurseries, primary schools, secondary schools, special schools, pupil referral units, and out of school. If we are to be truly inclusive in meeting the educational needs of these children then we all need to be working to promote schools that are experienced in and committed to meeting individual needs (NFER, 2003). It is to this common purpose that psychologists, particularly educational psychologists, have so much to contribute. They are the one education support service that provides a regular service to all schools.

Educational psychologists are ideally placed to look into the highly polished mirrors and make something of what they see. The task is not simply to see the children more clearly, but to see how their history and experiences, the burdens of disruption that they carry, and the variety of settings from which they attend our schools, affect their educational opportunities. In this way they are in a position to promote their education and enhance their experiences in school. The particular contributions of educational psychologists are based on their training and sphere of work in an education system that serves all children. This system needs to improve to serve children in the looked after system, and many children who are adopted. Educational psychologists have an in-depth training that focuses on children's development, learning, and behaviour. They have detailed knowledge of and experience in the different types of school settings and systems, together with a unique insight into the process of teaching. This is gained by an understanding of the theory of education and their own experiences of practice. This is further developed by their ongoing work with teachers. The practice of educational psychology depends on the ability to work at all levels in the system, which include:

- The development of policy and practice guidelines in education.
- Multi-agency working with colleagues from different disciplines and departments (for example, education social workers, school nurses, specialist teachers, and health professionals).
- Systemic work, whereby from a position of influence in the system, it is possible to see what is problematic and have the time and energy to work for changes to the system.
- Casework for individual children – work that can be highly complex.

NATIONAL AND LOCAL GOVERNMENT POLICY

A closer look at National and Local Government policy informs the contributions of the psychologist. The Government's long-term policy objective is to ensure that every child in care is able to fulfil his or her potential.

The work of the Social Exclusion Unit (2003) has examined the barriers that prevent children in the looked after system achieving their educational potential. This has highlighted specific areas of action to improve their life chances:

- children in the looked after system should experience greater stability, so that they do not have to move home or school as often as has been the case previously;
- children need less time out of school and longer time in education.

To achieve this they need:

- help with school admissions;
- better access to education with more support to help them to attend school regularly and stay on after the age of 16;
- help with schoolwork by being given more individually tailored support backed by more training for teachers and social workers;
- help from home to support them in their schoolwork, and this can be achieved by giving carers better training in children's education;
- improved health and well-being, with teachers, social care staff, health workers and carers all working together in the interests of the children.

The Green Paper *Every Child Matters* issued by the Department for Education and Skills was the Government's response to the Public Enquiry into the death of Victoria Climbié. What was so helpful about Lord Laming's recommendations was that he made it clear that child protection cannot be separated from policies to improve children's lives as a whole. Proposals were made to combine the development of an overall framework for universal children's services with a need for targeted services to protect vulnerable children (DFES, 2003). This has culminated in the programme of change described in *Every Child Matters, Change for Children* (DFES, 2004a). *Every Child Matters, Change For Children in Schools* (DFES, 2004b) explains the contribution schools will make. This includes guidance for supporting children with complex needs and promoting the educational achievement of looked after children. It also guides the development of local protocols for hard to place children.

The Department of Health commented that 'the single most important indicator of children's life chances is educational attainment' (DOH/DFES, 2000). This has led to a priority being placed on the educational achievements of looked after children. The Social Exclusion Unit (2003) has established and reviews targets for the education of looked after children. The Public Service Agreement aims to improve the life chances for children by substantially narrowing the gap between the educational attainment and participation of children in care and that of their peers by 2006.

Example of targets:

- The achievements of 11 year olds in English and Maths should be at least 60% as good as those of their peers.
- The proportion of looked after children leaving school without having sat a GCSE equivalent exam is no more than 10%.
- The proportion of looked after children aged 16 who get qualifications of five GCSEs graded A to C should be greater than 15%.

The notion of 'corporate parenting' has been established. It means that the whole Local Authority, not just the Social Service Department, has a responsibility to act as a corporate parent for children in care and to provide the kind of loyal support that any good parents would give to their children. This notion has proved to be a potent driving force in securing a positive direction for the children. Scrutiny shows us some of the flaws in the concept of corporate parenting. Most children have one or two parents, with additional parent figures for children with step-parents. Children in the looked after system have nominally many corporate parents: carers, social workers, teachers, support workers, psychologists, etc. While all are now charged with the notion of acting as a corporate parent should, most have the responsibilities this brings, but none of the powers. Decision-making powers remain where they always were. So, for example, in schools, teachers are faced with the consequences for children of social work decisions to which they may or may not agree.

Local Authority policy is developing a view of adopted children. Recent guidelines have prescribed that Local Authorities will provide services to all concerned in adoption and post-adoption (The Adoption Support Services Regulations (DOH, 2003), under The Adoption and Children Act (DFES, 2002)). In the spirit of *Every Child Matters*, this previously invisible group is getting recognition, which leads on to the provision of services for the children and their parents. Adopted parents want to be parents like everyone else, and so, in a way, have subscribed to this invisibility. For some, there is a need for services that are supportive and empower them as parents, but provide interventions beyond the resources of the family. Further legislation is likely to follow and this will extend the tasks of social workers and teachers to support adopted children and their families.

TARGETS FOR THE EDUCATION OF CHILDREN IN THE LOOKED AFTER SYSTEM

Tracy was first referred when she was in primary school. She was not making progress in basic literacy and numeracy, and her behaviour was challenging. Social Services were involved because of Child Protection concerns. An educational assessment revealed that she had learning difficulties. Despite extra support in class protected by a Statement of Special Educational Needs, her move to secondary school was disastrous. She wouldn't work, she argued with peers and adults alike, and worryingly she began to leave the school premises. After one outburst, she was excluded, and she then refused to return. A move to a Special School provided opportunities for small group teaching geared to her learning difficulties and a programme of work designed to boost her self-esteem and develop her social skills. This proved to be just what she needed. She attended school every day, made some friends and gained eight Certificates of Educational Achievement.

So were Government targets met?

How can psychologists act as corporate parents and contribute to Government targets, set to improve the life chances for looked after children?

Contributions can include:

- The most basic and important contribution a psychologist can make is with regard to the collection of data. The training of a psychologist in research techniques and statistical analysis has much to offer to the clouds of data that sometimes obscure our view of the children. Children need care for different reasons at different points in their life, and for varying lengths of time. These movements of children are difficult to track, and few if any authorities do so in a way that ensures that all children get the services they need. Psychologists can combine their understanding of data collection with their familiarity with school and agency systems to contribute to the way data is collected.
- There has been a national complication to this data collection. This is with regard to the children placed out of county because they have complex needs that have not been met by their local services. The fact that their parents have had difficulties and their childhood has been disrupted can often mean that they were not brought to the attention of school services early enough. This may be because there was no parental support for such intervention. Alternatively, concerns about the child's well-being can influence

the perception of difficulties in school, and these may be attributed to difficulties at home. Interventions may be postponed until the home situation improves. At worst the children are overlooked. The fact that the children are placed away from home and out of county adds to their sense of dislocation and to their vulnerability. We also know from child abuse enquiries that where agencies fail to protect, a common feature is that the child or family has moved around (Reder et al., 1993). It has been difficult to get good reliable information and prompt services. For out of county children an additional barrier to achievement can be the divide of 'their children' and 'our services'. The Belonging Regulation, Circular 1/96 (DFES, 2005), determine the local authority area to which children belong for the purpose of claims relating to inter-authority recoupment. Children who are placed out of county have the most complex needs, which have not been met by local services. It is also common for them to have had the additional disadvantage of moves of placement and school, prior to the decision to place them out of county. Some will have Statements of Special Educational Need and some will not. It may well be the complexity of their needs and the number of their moves that has denied them prompt services. Psychologists can make a significant contribution by prioritizing the need for all children placed out of county to have a named educational psychologist, responsible for monitoring the education provision for them. Psychologists can contribute to ensuring that the complexity of children's situations does not become an additional barrier to services.

• Children who are placed out of county evidence an assumption that the child, who can't be managed in-county, can be managed in a placement elsewhere. While there are specialized placements that do meet complex needs and psychologists often contribute to making these placements special, there is a duty on behalf of all Local Authorities to ensure that this is the case. What we know from our understanding of systems and our casework is that some of the placements are rather less able to manage the child than had been hoped at the point of placement. Given the huge amounts of money involved in paying for specialist placements out of county, and the fact that the staff in the placements are perhaps less likely to be drawing the attention of the placing authority to difficulties they are having in meeting a child's needs, there is a clear role for psychologists to play a part in evaluating what specialist placements have to offer in terms of the quality of the education provided.

• As mentioned earlier, educational psychologists spend the majority of their time working with teachers and schools. Experience and in-service training can provide insights into the barriers to achievement for looked after children. It is vital that psychologists have the time and support they need for individual casework. Services need to prioritize referrals of children in the looked after system, and this can be done in a variety of ways:

– Having regular contact with designated teachers responsible for monitoring the education of the looked after children.
– Providing prompt consultation when difficulties arise.
– Identifying children who need an assessment of their educational difficulties. Ensuring that they get a full assessment, which considers a variety of hypotheses for their difficulties, and using this to provide teachers and carers with advice and support.
– Contributing to Personal Education Plans. Making suggestions for positive achievable targets, which can be systematically reviewed, to aid measures of a child's progress.

In these ways casework can promote stability, time in school, help with schoolwork, support for carers to support school, and joint working to promote health and well-being.

● While the Public Service Agreement with regard to targets of achievement has focused educational endeavours on behalf of looked after children, there is much that psychologists can say with regard to the choice of targets. Psychologists are needed to help teachers find effective ways to achieve the targets, to challenge the suitability of these targets for some children, and to advise on alternative measures of success. In the case example featuring Tracy, Government targets were not met. Despite a variety of measures of success, there is no credit to the Local Authority. What this highlights is that measures follow traditional views of educational success, not real stories. So Tracy's hard-won gains are obscured in the final picture of the achievements of children in the looked after system. Psychologists can advise on value-added measures whereby targets for improvement test children against themselves, rather than against a peer group population.

● An understanding of life cycles can promote the understanding and implementation of 'life-long learning' for looked after children. This involves working with colleagues outside the school systems in further education, workplace schemes and community education so that children have more time and opportunities to improve their life chances.

'Criminal . . . That's what I will be . . . I was born into it, I have never been any other way.'

(Ryan 15 years)

We need systems and support to challenge Ryan's view of his future.

SPECIALIST SERVICES FOR CHILDREN IN THE LOOKED AFTER SYSTEM

'I would never have got my education had I not gone into care...I wouldn't have got any at all...I don't think I would have got any other GCSEs because the school that I was in down here was rubbish basically.'

(Lisa, in Skuse & Ward, 2003)

One of the key proposals in *Every Child Matters* gave Local Authorities a new duty to promote the educational achievement of looked after children and young people. Other proposals refined this aim. These include the development of integrated teams of health and education professionals, social workers, and connexions advisers, based in and around schools and Children's Centres. Added to this is a workforce reform package that aims to make working with children an attractive career. The aim is to improve the skills and effectiveness of the children's workforce. This has led to the establishment in Local Authorities of teams dedicated to improving the education of children in the looked after system. Some of these teams also have a focus on children who have been adopted, although dedicated services to these children are less well established. Two organizational models have been established. The first is a discrete model, with a dedicated team responsible for a range of functions such as monitoring and direct services. This model works best to ensure that there are adequate advocates for, and focused attention on, the education of the children. The second, an 'inclusive' approach, involves a smaller number of people coordinating responses and maintaining an overview of interventions. The direct services and functions such as monitoring are embedded in the mainstream system. Experience suggests that this model works best in authorities where there is a strong tradition of inclusive education.

These teams are part of a wider picture where schools have identified governors with responsibility for looked after children. Each Local Authority has a lead elected member for the children. Educational psychologists can contribute much to these dedicated teams in the following ways:

- They are experienced in assessment techniques and can adapt these to the complexities of individual children's situations. Psychologists also know about the limitations of assessment techniques and can work to prevent assessments that set children at a disadvantage – for example, when measures are inappropriate for children from different ethnic groups.
- Their familiarity with the range of school support services and their experiences of working alongside them can provide a helpful overview of

the management of resources to support children and their teachers and
schools.

- Their familiarity with local schools as part of a regular delivery of service
  provides an insight into local complexities and possible levels of resistance.
  This can move forward the promotion of educational chances for looked
  after children.
- Their experience of delivering INSET to teachers can provide a way of improving the responses of staff generally, and of designated teachers specifically, to the challenges these children present in schools. An example of
  such work can be found in a booklet produced for teachers in schools
  on 'attachment and the consequences of disrupted childhood' (Bannell &
  Peake, 2004). Alongside specific advice for individual class teachers, the authors have produced some guiding principles for all teachers with regard
  to support for looked after children. The emphasis is on developing insights, working in partnership with carers and using psychology to inform
  everyday practice in schools. (See Appendix 4.1.)
- Educational psychologists are positioned in services that deliver ideas and
  support to a whole range of children. They need to maintain a balance between a systemic and a casework approach. As a case worker one always
  has to be dealing in the here and now, with the need to be pragmatic. Casework is time consuming. It can be hard to see long-term goals for numbers
  of children when one is faced with huge and overwhelming short-term
  issues for individual children. Yet the balance between casework and systemic work needs to be held. Children in the looked after system form one of
  the most disadvantaged groups in the system. It is clear that their predica-
  ments challenge the educational systems we have in place for children
  generally. A systemic approach seeks to deal with the challenges to a system that is currently good for the many. In this way it can be amended and
  altered to also cater for the few. Systems tend to homeostasis and so when
  change is muted, there can often be resistance. This can be uncomfortable,
  particularly when workers are advocates for the disadvantaged and powerless in the system. As part of generic services, educational psychologists
  can contribute to holding that balance. One way is to use a consultation
  model to provide prompt input and advice when difficulties arise. (See
  Appendix 4.2.)
- Psychologists can bring their knowledge and experience of psychology
  and education to the task of improving the skills and effectiveness of the
  children's workforce. In addition to INSET delivery to teachers, educational
  psychologists can provide a service to carers of children. Psychologists can
  develop models of work aimed at providing some regular and reliable
  support for carers with regard to the education of the children in their
  care. Carers can feel overwhelmed by the task of supporting the education

of the child for whom they care. In some instances, the Local Authority will be asking them to provide a higher level of support than they have previously offered. This aims to raise the achievements of the children, in some instances to a level beyond the achievements of the foster carer themselves.

Models of work would be most useful if based on the following principles:

- It is helpful if carers can meet and get to know an educational psychologist who can help them, before a particular crisis arises with regard to an individual child.
- Carers benefit from having more information about how schools work, how children with special needs are assessed and supported in school, what resources there are for children in school, and the ways to measure the successes of children in school. Carers may themselves need advocates, if they are to support the education of children in their care.
- It is more empowering to carers, and a more economic use of psychologists' time, to provide some support in group settings. While there will be occasions when a more individual approach is needed, this can be better negotiated on the basis of familiarity and mutual understanding.
- The content of work by psychologists with carers could touch on the following: learning more about schools; discussing difficulties children can have in school; providing information about how children's special educational needs are addressed; informing carers about education support professionals/agencies and ways to access them; providing a forum for an early identification of children with specific difficulties who may need services to prevent a breakdown in school; sharing strategies for managing difficulties at home in terms of support for education; and establishing a channel of communication between carers and the education department.

Specialist services could also be considered for adoptive children and their parents. Adoptive parents offer their children a permanent home and do not depend on State financial support. They are usually financially secure and have themselves been successful in school. They want to prioritize the education of their child from a position of knowledge of schools and resources. They want to be proactive in maximizing their children's chances in school. A joint parent/professional forum in which education is a standing item to which psychologists contribute, could be an ideal way to provide information, share ideas and work in partnership, with what is often a very informed and dynamic parent group.

DESIGNATED TEACHERS

'I had one child from when she was 5 years old 'til she was 10. She went to the local school. They didn't know what had hit them at first. The special needs teacher helped me a lot by listening, listening is very important.'

(Rosalie – Foster Carer)

It is Government policy that every school should have a designated teacher to act on behalf of looked after children. As key workers, designated teachers are people who should also peer into the highly polished mirrors provided by looked after and adopted children in education. Their role is seen as one that should be flexible to meet local needs. They advocate for children in care within the school, in school partnerships, with support agencies and with the Local Education Authority. They monitor the progress of the individual children in care in the school. They provide information and advice to other staff on the needs and experiences of looked after children. Many useful initiatives have grown up around these three functions and there is much that psychologists can do to work with designated teachers.

The creation of designated teachers in every school has clearly placed the education of looked after children on the main school agenda. It has meant that there is a member of staff in school who is aware of which pupils are in the looked after system and has the brief to advocate on their behalf. The designated teacher role ensures that there is continuity in the support of the children. This would be less possible when they are supported by changing class teachers each year in primary school and by changes of subject teacher, form tutor, and heads of year in secondary schools. They provide a point of contact and continuity for psychologists wanting to work for greater stability in the education of the children. This can be most clearly seen at the point of secondary school transfer. Moving from primary to secondary school is a difficult move for any pupil. Children are moving from the familiarity of one teacher every day for a year to a much larger school setting. The children have to adapt to changes of teacher as many as six or eight times a day. There are expectations of increased work output, homework and more independent learning. This move is important educationally, but it actually affects many aspects of children's lives. The time the family gets up in the morning is often earlier to fit in with longer journey times. There are changing demands for uniform including PE kit, science overall, cookery apron, etc. There are changes to the contact between home and school (Peake, 2004). Bearing in mind the experiences of looked after children, it is clear how difficult this transition can be. The establishment of designated teachers has created a point of contact between primary and secondary schools and for other professionals. This can lead to more effective information sharing. Joint planning can lead to increased stability, more time in schools, and more targeted support for schoolwork.

Educational psychologists can work with designated teachers to support them in their task of monitoring the progress and performance of the looked after child. This joint work can lead to initiatives to promote basic skills, plan individual support, and proactively use support services on behalf of the child. Psychologists can advise with regard to assessment techniques, education planning, and strategies for managing behaviour. The designated teacher liaises with staff who have day-to-day contact with the child. The educational psychologist provides casework, advice on systems in school, and liaison with fellow professionals in the wider professional network. The combined work of these two roles can be powerful.

The establishment of designated teacher posts in every school has allowed a build-up of expertise within the school with regard to the education of looked after children. This has the helpful benefits of there being a key person who can advise staff in school on a day-to-day basis, and who can provide insights and training with regard to looked after children. Work by designated teachers with whole staff groups can lead to a variety of initiatives such as mentoring for individual pupils, and revision support (The Who Cares? Trust, 2003). Out-of-school activity groups can be set up to offer children opportunities for success. For example, these could enable access to computerized learning such as SAM learning which provides exam practice and associated revision.

When one examines the role of the designated teacher in a highly polished mirror, there are blemishes that can adversely affect the usefulness of the role. The majority of schools now have a designated teacher for looked after children. Much depends on the nature of the appointment. They can be the head teacher, the deputy head teacher, the inclusion coordinator, the special educational needs coordinator, the designated teacher for child protection; and some are several of these in one person. How well this works depends on the type of school, the level at which the post is pitched in the school's organization, and the resources and support given to the post. A view of practice shows us that, in small village schools, it can be the head teacher, who also has responsibility for some teaching, the work for special needs in the school, child protection and mending the boiler! This heady combination of roles can effectively undermine the profile of the education of looked after children in the school. In sharp contrast, in a large secondary school, there can be as many as 25 children in the looked after system. These children present complex difficulties, and involve school staff in a plethora of liaison networks. The designated teacher can become overwhelmed by the complex and often competing needs of these children who challenge the system. It can then be extremely difficult to combine the roles of teaching and advocacy. Some schools allow non-contact time for designated teachers to fulfil their roles. However, there is no clear requirement for schools to do so. What is more there is no gauge by which to establish the need for non-contact time. Educational psychologists, with knowledge of children in the looked after system, can advise on the establishment of these posts.

Designated teachers need time for the following:

- To attend training covering all aspects of the care system, the impact of care on education, legal responsibilities and associated guidance.
- To secure and read background information about individual pupils so that responses in school can be sensitively planned to provide more effective support.
- To work with colleagues on their staff group to provide an informed and consistent approach to helping each child in care.
- To contact key professionals in the wider network to ensure integrated team work on behalf of children.
- To organize meetings and complete the inevitable paperwork needed to prepare Personal Education Plans (PEPs). This leads to effective planning and delivery of services to the children to raise their educational achievements.
- To liaise with carers and provide, when needed, insights into the needs of the child in education and how best the child can be supported at home.

Without appropriate amounts of non-contact time, much of the above is at best flawed and at worst neglected. Even a simple gauge for non-contact time, for example half an hour per looked after child per week, would provide a sharper focus for the demands of such a post. For a primary school with two looked after children the designated teacher would need an hour of non-contact time each week. For the busy secondary school with 25 looked after children, two days a week of non-contact time would be needed.

There remain further blemishes in this picture. Teachers who are invited to take up the additional responsibility of designated teacher are, surprisingly, offered no pay incentive to do so. There is no established recognition of the demands of the post, such as additional seniority. Yet the post demands that a teacher take a lead role on behalf of the most disadvantaged and complex children in the system.

There are instances where the system fails completely when the designated teacher:

- is insufficiently senior in the school system to be effective;
- leaves the school and is replaced by a 'pressed volunteer' who will need to work immediately on behalf of the looked after children and may, however, have to wait for training or at worst have any training needs overlooked;

- has few or no additional resources;
- is placed in a position of irreconcilably conflicting roles – for example, a head teacher who has to balance the needs of the school as a whole for calm routines and good order, with the support needed for a child seriously challenging the school system.

As psychologists we have much to say with regard to how such posts could be more effective in terms of allocation of time, pay, training, status and support.

SPECIAL HELP FOR ADOPTED CHILDREN

A parent/professional partnership is needed to help staff to recognize the needs of adopted children. Not all adopted children have specific needs; however, it is likely that at some level they will be affected by the knowledge of their adoption. They will be even more affected emotionally if they have been subjected to physical, sexual or emotional abuse or extreme neglect prior to being adopted. More and more children will have lived with birth parents, extended family members and a number of foster carers, before coming to live with their adoptive parents. So, like looked after children, they may have difficulties building secure relationships and learning to trust. These difficulties can lead to difficult behaviours, which are visible in school, although the reasons for the behaviours are not visible. While the child may not understand this behaviour, we do know that there are some common possible reasons. These can include:

- An every day incident, which may trigger subconscious memories that may feel overwhelming to the child.
- The child's behaviours may make sense if seen as an effort to control the environment and the people in it. This may be a reaction to a previous lack of control and a need for boundaries and security.
- The child's mind may be preoccupied with being in a family and learning to trust to the extent that it will take time before he or she can focus on schoolwork, and especially on homework!
- All children who are adopted have experienced loss, so for them, change has deep-rooted meanings. This may be related to feelings of being out of control, and extreme insecurity.
- Many adopted children have low self-esteem, which means that they are sensitive to failure that confirms their view of themselves. They can also be indiscriminate in seeking affection and approval.

● Some adoptive children may have difficulties telling the truth. What has happened to them means that universal truths of parentage and love have been betrayed.

Psychologists with insight into adoption can work with adoptive parents to provide advice for teachers (Oxfordshire LEA, 2004). (See Appendix 4.3.)

PERSONAL EDUCATION PLANS

It is a requirement that children in the looked after system have Personal Education Plans (PEPs). The idea came from the *Guidance on the Education of Children and Young People in Care* (DOH/DFES, 2000). They are a vehicle for joint working to effectively plan a child's education. These Plans are commonly written following a meeting, which includes the child, his or her carers, and all relevant professionals. This includes the social worker, designated teacher or other teacher, and anyone providing individual support. Personal Education Plans ensure access to services and support, contribute to stability, minimize disruption and broken schooling, signal particular and special needs, establish clear goals, and act as a record of progress and achievement. These meetings should 'add value' to the education of a child in the looked after system. The meeting is a chance to discuss and underline the importance of education. It should be focused and not anecdotal. The views of the young person should be viewed as important and part of the PEP. The adults supporting the young person should hold high expectations even when the child cannot hold them personally. The meetings should be held at six-monthly intervals. In addition it is important that meetings are held at key times and at times of transition (changes of care placement or school transition: infant to junior, primary to secondary, Key Stage 3 to Key Stage 4, school leaving to post-16 education/employment). The value of Personal Education Plans cannot be overstated. Their value and importance lies in that:

● they are a vehicle for communication with school staff and other agencies;
● they can enable schools to clarify plans for children;
● they provide an opportunity to gain and act upon children's views;
● children want adults who play a role in planning their lives to talk to each other – the PEP meeting is one place to do this.
● a well-recorded PEP can become an added component of life story work, done with the child to develop understanding and insight into his or her experiences;

- it is a means of ensuring that educational provision goes beyond merely making the school place available for a child;
- the PEPs can provide children with routes to achieving their ambitions and future plans;
- the meetings can be an opportunity for social workers to be seen as positively involved in a child's future;
- the PEPs can be written in ways that are mindful of fragile care placements and helpful to those placements.

These are important meetings from which good documentation must flow. Educational psychologists have well-established expertise in assessment, choosing targets, monitoring progress, liaising with other professionals, and listening to children. Their work in managing a Code of Practice, which involves a staged approach to the support of children with special educational needs in schools, makes them uniquely placed to advise on Personal Education Plans. The preparation of a PEP is an important process rather than an event or a piece of paper. Thus PEPs are based on individual education planning, the voice of the child and joint agency consultation – Social and Health Care and Education. This is a process that is not always easy to manage. While the consultation is between two or more departments, the extent to which it represents joined-up thinking has some inbuilt limitations. In addition there can be difficulties around the interface between PEPs and other documentation with regard to educational planning: for example Individual Education Plans for children with special educational needs and Pastoral Support Plans for children with the need for specific interventions to manage their behaviours. Educational psychologists who provide regular services to schools can aid the designated teacher and child's social worker in managing the interface between these processes and documents. Careful management of this interface will ensure that, should major difficulties arise, the storm winds will not blow the paperwork in a way that obscures our view of the education of the child. Educational psychologists with their theoretical roots in an understanding of the power of rewards, have much to contribute to ensuring that PEPs are not only about educational planning but also about the celebration of achievement.

LEAVING SCHOOL/CARE

'When you are moving to a flat they drum in your head that as soon as you turn sixteen or as soon as you leave care you go into a flat and you need to get yourself a job, as there's no time for college and you basically need to get a job to support yourself. That is what is drummed into you.'

(Gill, in Skuse & Ward, 2003, p. 26)

Schools have a great deal to offer to children in the looked after system. They offer:

- opportunities to learn to make relationships with peers and adults, and particularly to make and retain friendships;
- a place away from the experiences of the past and the closeness of family life, a neutral ground away from painful areas;
- a world where the child can assume a meaningful role in a predictable, child-centred environment;
- daily contact with concerned adults who model an interest in learning, development and problem solving;
- routines and structures in which to build personal confidence and social skills;
- structured learning geared to provide experiences of success and to build self-esteem;
- an introduction to what is hopefully life-long learning, interests and hobbies;
- a system that has support agencies and networks that can be used to provide counselling and support for personal problems;
- opportunities and achievements, which are a gateway to adult life and the world of employment.

It is a huge step to leave school, but for children in the looked after system, it is a transition that sets them at further disadvantage. Demographic studies show that children who live in families are continuing to live with their parents for longer. Pressures of the cost of buying a home, shortages of social housing and debts incurred in post-16 education are often cited as contributing to this trend. For looked after children who don't have the security of a stable parental home, leaving school and getting an entry into further education or employment is much more difficult. They face this, as the further transition of leaving care also looms. Looked after children are more likely to have under-achieved in school, less likely to go on to further education or training and more likely to be unemployed. Sinclair and Gibbs (1996) found that 50% of 16 year olds leaving care in their sample were unemployed, compared to a national mean of 18%. While the introduction of the Connexions Service has done much to begin to address leaving school, and entering employment, children in the looked after system are at a clear disadvantage. Pressures on resources mean that they move into independent living much earlier than their peers. Any limitations in the amount of preparation they received compound their earlier disadvantages. This then is reflected in the fact that children who were in the looked after system are over-represented in those groups which lack educational qualifications; are unemployed, live in poverty, have unsettled relationships and present with mental health difficulties. This bleak picture tells us that, at the time such children are leaving school, education support agencies and particularly educational psychologists are scaling down their input when they should be doing the opposite in the interests of children in care. This is an under-developed area of psychologist endeavour. Possibilities include:

- Continuing psychologist input and support to looked after and adopted children post-16 years.
- Ensuring that the service does not diminish in further education for those who need it.
- Contributing to liaison between services in ways that support young people who have had disrupted childhoods and have complex needs. Currently the divide between children's services and those for adults is unclear and at times cavernous.

As 'corporate parents' psychologists can look to see that the needs of those with a history of being in care are literally 'looked after', on leaving school.

CONCLUSION AND THE WAY FORWARD

Children in the looked after system form one of the most disadvantaged groups in society. When we look into their experiences in education, it is like looking into highly polished mirrors. We see much that is familiar, but we are also probably surprised and disappointed by what we see. We see the lines and blemishes in the education system. Much is being done to improve the educational achievements of the children. We are improving the stability of home and school. Children are spending less time out of, and longer time in school. Children are getting help with schoolwork and there is better training for teachers and carers.

Belatedly there has been recognition of the needs of adopted children. The profile of children coming into adoptive homes has shifted, with a larger number of children having longer histories in care and consequently being older at the point of adoption. It is more likely, therefore, that they will need the kind of services currently provided for looked after children. The capacity of adoptive parents to bring this need to our attention sharpens our focus.

Nevertheless, the picture in education still has flaws. Some targets owe too much to a traditionalist view of education; there are problems of data collection; and there are also shortcomings in meeting the complex needs of the children we move. We need to ensure that designated teachers have the time, resources, and monetary reward for their tasks. Educational psychology services need to prioritize support for the children and contribute to much needed systemic developments. Paperwork should record and enhance the work of support agencies, instead of so often obscuring the view.

Throughout this whole process we must never forget the predicament of the child at the centre of the education experience. We need to remain mindful of the long-term consequences of early adversity and transitions from family of origin and through the care system. For those children who express this through challenging behaviour these difficulties are very clear. We cannot fail to see these children but we must be careful to look beneath the surface to the complexities that are there. Other children will conceal their deepest worries. The danger here is that the professional can overlook these children and fail to understand their hidden needs.

This chapter has reflected the education system in all its complexity, and explored the ways in which it is increasingly working towards meeting the needs of this complex and disadvantaged group of children and young people.

APPENDIX 4.1

Extract from *Attachment and the Consequences of Disrupted Childhood* (Bannell & Peake, 2004)

Guiding Principles – for teachers of all children who have had disrupted childhoods.

1. Ask the parent/carer about the child's experiences and think about the messages the child may have taken from what has happened. Understand that no matter how much you care or you try, you can't put things right and that the child needs help to come to terms with what has happened and that this will take time.
2. The parent/carer lives with the child, and perhaps other children. He or she is a major figure in the child's life. Foster carers are special parents who have been assessed and trained, and have ongoing professional support. They need to be involved by and in school. See yourself as a partner with the parents/carer demonstrating how adults can work together for the child. Find out how the parent/carer and the child manage enquiries

about the child's history and support the child to deal with intrusiveness at school.

3. Value effort as much as achievement and judge a child by his or her own progress not by that of the group. Positively notice the child during a day in a way, which he or she can accept. Provide tangible recognition of success such as praise in a home–school book, a certificate, a comment written on work. Above all make learning interesting and fun.

4. Understand that poor self-esteem and destroyed trust make it hard to build friendships. If you as the teacher demonstrate to the class that you value the child and can cope by positively reframing difficulties, then this provides a powerful model for the other children. Use your classroom routines and management to support the child with peers, providing good supervision and discrete guidance when needed. Help the child use the school to find situations such as sports, teams, clubs, in which to learn to relate to others.

5. Don't assume that all children who have had disrupted childhoods are the same or likely to be difficult. If there are presenting problems, these may or may not be due to past experiences. Be fair in your dealings, the child may be less able to explain than a child who has had no disruptions. Be alert to difficulties, and consider how you can actively involve school support agencies to help you to help the child.

6. Some children have grown up with neglectful/abusive parenting and they have learned to adapt their behaviour in order to survive. Abusive interactions and attachments may be all they have known and work for them while in those relationships. When in the care of sympathetic and supportive adults the new, positive management styles are unfamiliar and may not make much sense. The children may not initially relate to good nurturing; they may be dismissive and rejecting of it. This can leave very well intentioned adults feeling dejected and demoralized. However, it is very important to sustain the nurturing management of the children because by doing so you can help them form positive attachments that will sustain them in the future.

7. Be clear what the concerns are for the child and how the care plans are drawn up. Attend meetings arranged to plan for the child and help to prioritize education as one way of improving the life chances of the child.

8. If the children are looked after make sure you are familiar with the systems that operate to protect them. There is a designated Teacher for looked after children in your school who will take a key role in supporting both you and the children.

(Reproduced by permission of Anne Peake)

APPENDIX 4.2

Extract from protocol for the provision of case consultation meetings (Peake, 2004).

The Reach Up Team Case Consultation Meetings to Address Concerns about Looked After Children

It is proposed that a Professionals' Planning Meeting is called when there are concerns about a child, which adversely affect his or her educational opportunities and progress. It is envisaged that these meetings will be particularly useful with regard to those children who are:

- proving to be difficult to integrate in a mainstream school and/or are at risk of exclusion.
- returning from out-of-county placements.
- in special schools.
- in PRUIS (pupil referral unit/integration service).

The concerns might relate to the child's school and/or home placement. For the meetings to be most useful in terms of preventing school/home placement breakdowns, key professionals in the network of agency support for the child and carer, need to attend.

The aim of the meetings is to provide:

1. Proactive support for front-line workers with children and their carers.
2. An offer of specialist advice with regard to the areas of concern.
3. Information and advice about additional resources for the child in school.
4. An opportunity for an in-depth case consultation geared to avoiding school/home placement breakdown.

Requests for a consultation may well arise from Care Reviews, SEN reviews, discussions around a child's Personal Education Plan (PEP) or on the basis of particular concerns raised by professionals in the local network.

If it is agreed that a Case Consultation meeting should take place, *it is essential that the child's social worker and a key worker from the child's school/education provision attends*. If the social worker and key member of staff from the child's school are not able to attend, then the meeting will not go ahead. Parents/carers are invited. The child/young person is not included in the meeting, as the emphasis is on professional planning. The views of the child are best represented in the meeting by those who know the child, given that there can be a large number of people attending.

The Reach Up Team will provide a core of workers to attend these meetings with a view to providing information, advice and support. These workers are:

- Health Liaison Nurse
- Educational Psychologist
- Behaviour Support Service
- Education Social Worker
- PRUIS specialist for looked after children
- Assistant Education Officer.

The venue for the consultations is flexible and it is envisaged that in the first instance, if possible, it should be held in the child's school.

The aim is to provide an in-depth case consultation to address the areas of concern and draw an action plan to support the child in education and with the carer. Consultations are likely to take up $1\frac{1}{2}$ to 2 hours. If professionals are unable to attend on time and remain in the meeting until it ends, then we ask that the meeting is not disturbed.

All consultations will be written up, together with the action plan, and circulated to those present and other key professionals nominated by the meeting. For the purposes of monitoring and evaluation, copies will also be sent to the Development Officer, The Reach Up Team. Professionals requesting a consultation will be asked after an interval of three months to provide feedback about the usefulness of the service. This will be used to inform and improve practice.

(Reproduced by permission of Anne Peake)

APPENDIX 4.3

Extract from *Adoptive Parents Leaflet* (Oxfordshire LEA, 2004)

What Teachers can Do to Help

We realize that you will already do many of these!

Be Accepting of Adoption

Families have changed over the years. Teachers can do a great deal if they can set a tone of acceptance for a range of family structures and especially adoption. They can demonstrate this by including adoption when they talk about families, inherited characteristics, and care for children. The school could recognize the importance of 'Adoption Day'. The child and family may have their own special days, such as the day the adoption went through.

Use the term 'birth' parents rather than 'natural' or 'real' parents – which can seem to imply that adoptive parents are, by comparison, unnatural or unreal.

Reinforce the Sense of Belonging and Acceptance

Children who are adopted have had experiences of breaks in building secure relationships. Teachers can help the child by promoting his or her feelings of being accepted and belonging. One way would be to greet the child by name in the morning and try hard to end each day on a positive note.

Build Self-esteem

Give positive, low key, genuine praise. Don't be put off by a negative reaction to it or it being rejected – you can be sure it is needed and the child does appreciate it.

Check the Curriculum

Some work will identify the child as different, e.g. work on family histories, family trees, Mother's/Father's days, baby photos, biographies, family holidays. It will help to discuss the curriculum with the parents beforehand, so that they can prepare the child in a way that is comfortable for them. Listening to the parents helps the teacher to be sensitive to the particular issues for an adopted child.

Organization

Don't 'nag' the child about organization; you could help by providing strategies to enable the child to be more organized and more able to take increased responsibility. The child will be helped by clear, consistent, classroom routines, simple displays of prompts, and having more time available for the child to learn to be organized.

Be Creative in your Discipline

Set small achievable targets. When the child shows signs of difficulties, step in and give the child strategies and a 'safe space' to regain self-control before it is lost. Conventional systems, e.g. star charts, are often ineffective, as rewards need to be immediate and not cumulative.

Anticipate/be Aware of Signs of Bullying

Teachers may overhear intrusive questions being asked by peers. Talk to the family about whether there is a story the family and child uses to deal with unwelcome questions. The teacher can step in to help the child being questioned, in much the same way as for issues such as divorce, race, etc. Adopted children's feelings about their families are at the core of their being. They will need help to protect that core.

Use Space Sensitively

Avoid placing children in confined spaces against their will, e.g. an office with the door closed, but offer secure spaces to sit in if the child feels anxious. Some children may even need to 'build' round themselves with cushions, etc.

Homework

Managing children to do homework is a skill all parents have to learn. Be understanding and talk to the parent about homework. Homework can be a real issue, which increases the pressures at home. Homework needs to be clearly set, achievable for the child and aid learning.

Talk to the Families – Keep Lines of Communication Open

The family may have adopted the child and been brought suddenly into contact with schools. They will need information about school systems so that they can support their child. Adoptive parents feel different to other parents: they are dealing with much more than just bringing up a child. They are dealing with instant parenthood, perhaps the placement of more than one child – children with competing needs, and perhaps a less established support network for them as parents. Teachers need to know from the family whether there are confidentiality issues that could be breached by using the child's birth family name on class lists, displays or photographs of the child published outside the classroom.

Ask for Support when you Need it

Tell the family if you need more information or guidance. Agree with them how you can get this. When children are first placed they will have a social worker. You could talk to the social worker or consult with the post-adoption worker.

(Reproduced by permission of Anne Peake)

REFERENCES

Bannell, C. & Peake, A. (2004) *Attachment and the Consequences of Disrupted Childhood.* Oxfordshire Local Education Authority.

DFES (2002) *Adoption and Children Act 2002.* London: TSO.

DFES (2003) *Every Child Matters.* Government Green Paper. London: TSO.

DFES (2004a) *Every Child Matters, Change for Children.* London: TSO.

DFES (2004b) *Every Child Matters, Change for Children in Schools.* TSO.

DFES (2005) *Notification of Out-of-Authority Placements for Looked After Children.* Circular LAC 2005. DFES.

DOH/DFES (2000) *Guidance on the Education of Children and Young People in Public Care.* London: DOH/DFES.

DOH (2003) *Adoption Support Services (Local Authorities) (England) Regulations.* London: TSO.

Evans, R. (2003) Equality and the education of children looked after by the state. *International Journal of Human Rights*, 7(1), 58–86.

Garnett, L. (1994) *Education of Children Looked After.* Humberside SSD & Education Dept.

NFER (2003) *Education Protects – The Role of the School in Supporting the Education of Children in the Looked After System.* Ten Policy Briefing 43/03. DFES.

Oxfordshire LEA (2004) *Adoptive Parents Leaflet: The Adopted Child in School.* Oxfordshire Local Education Authority.

Peake, A. (2004) *Moving on to Secondary School: A Handbook for Parents/Carers.* Oxfordshire Educational Psychology Service in conjunction with the Reach Up Team. Oxfordshire Local Education Authority.

Reder, P., Duncan, S. & Gray, M. (1993) *Beyond Blame. Child Abuse Tragedies Revisited.* London: Routledge.

Sinclair, I. & Gibbs, I. (1996) *Quality of Care in Children's Homes.* University of York.

Skuse, T. & Ward, H. (2003) *Outcomes for Looked After Children: Children's Views of Care and Accommodation.* An interim report for the DOH. Loughborough University: Centre for Child and Family Research.

Social Exclusion Unit (2003) *A Better Education for Children in Care.* Office of the Deputy Prime Minister.

The Who Cares? Trust (2003) *Education Matters – For Everyone Working with Children in the Looked After System.* London: The Who Cares? Trust.

ADDENDUM TO PART I

SUPPORTING THE LOOKED AFTER CHILD IN SCHOOL: A CASE EXAMPLE

Helen Hill

The Integrated Service for Looked After Children (ISL) provides additional support to ensure that looked after children living in Worcestershire gain maximum benefits from educational opportunities, health care and social care. This has developed through the linking of two existing services. The carer support team is a multi-agency service set up to promote inter-agency working through holistic and collaborative interventions. The aim is to maximize placement stability through the provision of advice and guidance to carers and the network. This helps to raise awareness and increases understanding. The education support team is a flexible, rapid response support service for looked after children in all key stages who have an urgent or severe need for support to prevent exclusion or to raise achievement. The following case example illustrates how the education support team can provide enhanced support to a child struggling within school and to the network of professionals trying to help the child. The focus here is on the help that can be provided to the child in the school setting. This support would typically be embedded within a comprehensive package of support for the carers and professionals that constitute the network around the child, and complements the training and awareness raising that is provided by ISL across the agencies.

Thinking Psychologically About Children Who Are Looked After and Adopted
Edited by K.S. Golding, H.R. Dent, R. Nissim and L. Stott.
Copyright © 2006 John Wiley & Sons, Ltd.

Kerry, a girl in foster care aged 10, was referred to the Integrated Service for Looked after Children (ISL) because her teachers were struggling to manage her behaviour. She was in Year 6 in a primary school and had been on roll for 6 weeks. During that time her attendance had been very poor (below 30%) and when in class she had been unwilling to join in, either orally or with written work. She was uncommunicative and withdrawn for most of the time but occasionally there had been outbursts of violent behaviour in which Kerry had appeared to be out of control, and considerable damage had been done to school property. The school had not been able to identify any particular trigger for these outbursts and were considering warning Kerry and her carer that any recurrence would result in a fixed term exclusion. A referral had also been made to the Education Welfare Service.

The ISL support teacher contacted the network of professionals involved with Kerry in order to gather information about her history. Kerry had experienced both severe neglect and physical abuse from her birth parents and had been placed with three different foster carers prior to her current placement. Little could be established about her educational history as she had not attended regularly for many years and no assessments had been carried out. Kerry was not on the Special Needs Code of Practice. Records from previous schools were skimpy and no Personal Education Plan had been completed. Kerry was the eldest of three children and had acted as carer for her younger siblings. Foster placements together with her siblings had broken down and Kerry had now been placed on her own in a private foster placement far away from her original home. The placement was going well and Kerry appeared to be becoming very attached to her new carers. Difficulties were occurring each morning however, and Kerry was crying and refusing to go to school in spite of her carers' best efforts. The daily morning battle was proving exhausting for the carers and this, together with Kerry's non-attendance at school, was putting the placement at risk. The support teacher also talked to Kerry who expressed the view that she hated school and didn't see why she had to go. She also mentioned the coming SAT exams and said that she would definitely not be taking these. She said that she would, however, be prepared to work on a one-to-one basis with the support teacher in order to explore her feelings about school.

An individualized 8-week Support Plan was put in place for Kerry with the following desired outcomes:

1. To increase Kerry's school attendance by at least 50%.
2. To introduce Kerry to the Protective Behaviours approach in order to help her to recognize her feelings and to develop strategies to feel safe.

Kerry followed an 8-week course of one-to-one sessions with the support teacher for one hour each week. These sessions all took place at school and focused on helping Kerry to recognize her own early warning signs, which indicated that she was becoming anxious. Kerry learned that everyone has the right to feel safe and that when she was feeling anxious or unsafe, she could adopt a range of strategies to help herself. She also learned that while feelings are feelings, behaviour is a choice with a consequence. The ISL support teacher worked with a core group of school staff in order to raise their awareness of the losses and trauma experienced by Kerry both before and since entering the looked after system and the effect of these on her behaviour. The Protective Behaviours approach was explained and her support needs were reframed in the light of her emotional needs. The Protective Behaviours approach is a practical approach to help people to feel safe. 'It is a process which encourages self-empowerment and brings with it the skills to avoid being victimized' (www.protectivebehaviours.co.uk).

Additional support was needed to help to reduce her levels of emotional distress when separating from her carer and also to help her to manage her feelings of anxiety and lack of control while in school. Kerry's difficulty in trusting others and her fear of failure in the classroom were recognized as inhibiting her learning. The class teacher implemented a 'time out system' for her to use and Kerry also identified a number of 'safe' people and places in school, which could be used for support when she felt she needed it. Kerry's carer supported her with literacy at home and Kerry also took part in a small daily literacy support group at school led by a teaching assistant funded by ISL. Kerry's carer brought her right into the school each morning where she was greeted and supported immediately by a teaching assistant, only entering the class when she felt ready and able to do so. At the review it was noted that Kerry's attendance had improved dramatically during this period (to 80%) and her reduced feelings of stress and ability to choose more appropriate behaviour was evident, with only two minor outbursts during the 8-week period. Her progress in class had been outstanding, especially in literacy. Looking at Kerry's needs from a psychological perspective had been helpful to the school staff, who felt that they had gained an understanding of some of the reasons behind Kerry's behaviour and were now able to devise a range of strategies to support her. She was moved to School Action Plus on the special needs code of practice, so that external agencies would continue to support her, and an Individual Education Plan was completed. A request for the involvement of the educational psychologist was made, in recognition of the fact that Kerry's additional support needs were unlikely to be short term.

A further 8-week Support Plan was implemented in which the sessions with the support teacher were reduced to fortnightly and were more focused on

Kerry's social needs with another child of Kerry's choice joining in each time. The school put a lunchtime support package together for a group of children, including Kerry, who needed additional support with social skills. The daily literacy sessions with the teaching assistant continued and Kerry agreed to work towards sitting her SAT tests in English and Maths. The decision was made for her not to sit the Science SAT test because there were so many gaps in her knowledge. At the review it was noted that the desired outcomes of this second plan had been met; Kerry's attendance had increased to 95%, and her behaviour was much improved. There was evidence to show that Kerry was now able to recognize her own feelings and choose more appropriate behaviour. She was more confident in class and had started to build a friendship group. Her social worker attended this review and a Personal Education Plan was completed. The placement was no longer felt to be at risk.

This period of intensive support from ISL helped the network of professionals to offer consistent support to Kerry both at school and in her placement. By the end of this intervention a better understanding had been gained about her additional emotional needs and good working relationships had been established between professionals. Appropriate educational support systems were in place and an agreement was made for ISL to continue to monitor Kerry and to include her and her carer in a project to support all looked after children sitting their SATs later in the year.

PART II
CREATING A CONTEXT FOR CHANGE

5

A SNAPSHOT IN TIME: THE ROLE OF PSYCHOLOGICAL ASSESSMENT OF CHILDREN AND YOUNG PEOPLE IN THE COURT SYSTEM

Jenny Stevenson and Catherine Hamilton-Giachritsis

Many children looked after or adopted will at some point have been the subject of a formal Court process. This chapter aims to demystify what often appears to happen behind closed doors to the exclusion of many carers and professionals who work closely with these children. It explores the role of a psychologist as expert witness in the Court procedure and looks at what should be asked and expected of psychologists in such roles. It emphasizes good practice in gathering sources of information widely, not only from children themselves but from their families, carers and the network of professionals and agencies around them.

Assessment is a fundamental component of psychological thinking and should create the context for further action rather than being seen as an end in itself. It is important that a formal Court assessment is seen as part of a much wider process involving the day-to-day interactions with a child and the surrounding systems. Although the impact of the Court process upon the networks around the child can be significant, good practice in the Court process can be inclusive and embrace the expertise of significant others involved

Thinking Psychologically About Children Who Are Looked After and Adopted
Edited by K.S. Golding, H.R. Dent, R. Nissim and L. Stott.
Copyright © 2006 John Wiley & Sons, Ltd.

in the day-to-day care of the child. It is important that those involved with the welfare of the child have a good understanding of the child, as well as realization that the assessment of any child in the Court arena is fortunately both permeable and welcoming of pertinent views and assessments of the child from comprehensive external sources.

HISTORICAL CONTEXT

Academic and applied psychologists have been concerned with the development, assessment and treatment of children. However, traditionally this has tended to exclude some of the most vulnerable children in society – those who no longer reside with a biological or adoptive parent but who are placed in the care of the Local Authority, either in residential or family-based foster placements. More recently, this imbalance has been addressed through a policy of placing looked after children in priority services provided by Social Care and Health and CAMHS services, although it will probably take the best part of a decade for services to have an automatic inclusive policy for looked after children and adolescents.

The use of psychologists in the courtroom began to occur in the late 1890s and early 1900s, focusing initially on eyewitness testimony (Thomas-Peter & Warren, 1998). This was formalized by The Civil Evidence Act 1972, which first allowed evidence to be introduced in civil proceedings by any expert qualified in the subject-matter concerned. Since then, there has been an increase in medical, psychological and psychiatric evidence in relevant cases (pers. comm., Andrew McFarlane, QC). However, it is only much more recently that a role was perceived for psychologists in child custody cases (Pfeifer, 1999; Samra-Grewal, 1999), child care proceedings or with children looked after by the Local Authority. While many psychologists came to this indirectly via traditional clinical psychology roles in the Health Service, this situation is beginning to change with the rise of forensic psychology and the employment of psychologists within Social Services Departments.

ASSESSMENT OF LOOKED AFTER CHILDREN AND ADOLESCENTS

Psychologists working with looked after children are asked to assess children and young people in two contexts:

- Assessments of therapeutic need (non-Court driven)
- Assessments in care proceedings in Court where key issues are the best outcome for the child in terms of future placement, as well as future contact issues with birth family members and other significant adults.

However, it is also the case that child care assessments pertaining to Court proceedings often include instructions to assess the child's therapeutic needs and thus the former often incorporate the latter. This chapter will focus on a Court-based process with the assumption that there will be commonalities between a Court-based assessment and an assessment of therapeutic need. It will highlight what should be asked of a psychologist in this context and what should be expected from his or her contribution.

MODELS, THEORIES AND RESEARCH

Theoretical Frameworks

Although working within the wider remits of the legislation outlined below, psychologists are less constrained by a professional and legal framework than their social work colleagues. For example, they have few statutory obligations. In addition, psychologists are not encouraged or expected to follow a specifically prescribed format for a psychological assessment and therefore assessment approaches are generally theoretically dependent, and their content may be highly idiosyncratic depending on the psychologist's training, theoretical orientation and professional experiences. A report is likely to have a slightly different focus depending on the theoretical perspective adopted by the instructed psychologist. Hence, it is important to have a brief understanding of the main theoretical frameworks.

However, despite differing theoretical approaches, almost all psychologists adopt a scientific-practitioner model (Drabick & Goldfried, 2000), which includes comprehensive data collection and the development of robust hypotheses and formulations based on objective information and data obtained. Hypotheses at this early stage are not only wide-ranging but often contradictory, with an explicit avoidance of pre-emptive conclusions. The purpose is to test out objectively these differing hypotheses, utilizing the information to adapt and amend existing assumptions or hypotheses. Over time, this process should lead to informed decision making.

Traditionally, psychiatry has tended to take a medical model approach to assessment presuming an underlying biological basis and the use of medication to relieve symptoms. In contrast, psychology can be divided into five main theoretical perspectives with subordinate theories within them: psychoanalytic/psychodynamic; humanistic/phenomenological; cognitive-behavioural; attachment; and systemic theories. In order to best illustrate the various frameworks and how these may impact on the psychological report, it may be useful to consider a particular case and outline formulations from each theoretical perspective.

Emma is a 5-year-old Caucasian child presenting with behavioural problems at home and in school, diabetes and with early queries about an autistic spectrum disorder. Her early childhood experiences included witnessing adult domestic violence, accompanied by maternal mental and physical health difficulties. Having had several foster care breakdowns, the core question was whether Emma would be beneficially placed via permanency and adoption or via long-term foster care. Another key issue was whether she should be placed with her 8-year-old sister or whether they would continue to benefit from separate placements.

Psychoanalytic/Psychodynamic Theories

This school (e.g. Freud, Jung, Klein, Anna Freud) focused on internal mechanisms – Freud's Id, Ego and Superego theoretical structure – with an emphasis on the psychosexual theory of development (see Burton & Davey, 2003, for an overview). A focus on the unconscious, alongside drives and instincts, by Freud attacked the dominance of and exclusive interest in the conscious mind. Freud, who has become a highly controversial figure, was to his credit the first well-known psychological theorist to emphasize the developmental aspects of personality and, in particular, to stress the decisive role of infancy and childhood in laying the foundations of the basic character structure of the individual. Key summaries of Freud's theory can be found in Freud (1923), Freud (1938) and Anna Freud (1965).

Increasing interest in object relation theories led to more focus on developmental issues and more concern with relationships: classical object relations theorists consider that the individual's *raison d'être* is the strive for autonomy and the over-arching principle of reason – although individuals may be flawed in some respects, they are able to overcome such flaws and become 'fairly decent' (Akhtar, 1992). Klein (1932, 1959, and see Chapter 2 in this volume), for instance, considered that mental structures arose out of a variety of internal objects (essentially fantasies about people in the infant's life), which changed in character in unconscious fantasies as the infant progressed through childhood. Later developments focused on the importance of defence mechanisms, such as denial, repression, displacement and projection, which allow the conscious mind to function reasonably in everyday settings (e.g. Anna Freud, 1970).

A psychological assessment based on this framework would try to identify the defence mechanisms an individual (adult or child) had put in place. Looked after children with damaging backgrounds and disturbed behaviour, such as Emma, may demonstrate strong features of regression and denial.

Emma had returned to a state of bed-wetting and thumb-sucking (both signs of regression), as well as her denial of any problematic behaviour despite the evidence of previous placements being disrupted. She rationalized her behaviour as 'the man inside my head told me to do it'.

Attachment Theory

John Bowlby (1951, 1953) broke away from the psychoanalytic framework and tradition of focusing on child sexuality, but emphasized that our early relationship experiences defined later emotional and cognitive development in adulthood. The provision of consistent, sensitive and responsive caretaking for the child ensures the formation of early secure relationships – attachments where caregivers represent the 'secure base' (Bowlby, 1988). Via the secure relationship, the child internalizes representations of appropriate close relationships (the early 'internal working models', Bretherton, 1999), and develops a sense of self-worth. Bowlby (1988) was convinced that differences in the security of the infant/child–caregiver attachment would have a long-term impact in terms of self-awareness and later intimate relationships, as well as being the key to psychological disturbance.

Looked after children have frequently experienced disrupted family relationships, alongside numerous placement moves. Insecure attachments are sadly relatively common. Thus, attachment theory is a particularly relevant theoretical framework for the assessment of looked after children and adolescents. It is likely to underpin many commissioned psychological assessments.

Insecurity of attachment is broken into three categories for the child – avoidant/dismissive, preoccupied/ambivalent and disorganized. Avoidant/dismissively attached children are best described as inhibited, both behaviourally and in the expression of feelings. These children are often viewed as subdued, independent and self-sufficient. Unwilling to rely on others, they have learned not to make undue demands upon others and, although they may have become expert in suppressing feelings, paradoxically they are seen as being self-occupying, often busily absorbed in play, school tasks and so forth. Avoidant attachment is associated with rejecting and/or intrusive over-involvement by the parent/carer (Morton & Browne, 1998).

In contrast, preoccupied/ambivalent children are described as being at the mercy of their emotions. Their early experiences have taught them that others may well be unavailable or inconsistent in availability. Therefore, the child employs a strategy of maximizing proximity and involvement of the caregiver via expressed emotions and behaviours. For example, this child maintains caregiver attention through shouting, whingeing, clingy behaviour and tantrums.

Children are preoccupied with whether others will consistently attend, evince interest or involvement in them; these children are often overwhelmed by separations or even the prospect of separations. They are dominated by emotions and, in contrast to the avoidant/dismissive child, have no surplus psychic energy to devote to exploration or cognitions. An ambivalent pattern is commonly associated with parental withdrawal, under-involvement and/or inconsistency (Morton & Browne, 1998).

Disorganized attachment is characterized by contradictory behaviour patterns: incomplete actions, stereotypic movements and approach/avoidance behaviours simultaneously executed. The child is in a paradox as the caregiver, whose proximity represents a 'comfort zone', is also a frightening and/or frightened figure. Essentially these children's attachment strategies fail and collapse (Main & Solomon, 1990). Children who have experienced abusive childhoods may well demonstrate disorganized attachment features and a minority may suffer from Reactive Attachment Disorder (Van Ijzendoorn & Bakermans-Kranenburg, 2003). Generally, 'disorganized' children do not view themselves as worthy of care and have limited expectations of others' availability for them and interest in them.

Key summaries of attachment theorists can be found in Bowlby (1969, 1973, 1980, 1988), Ainsworth (1989, 1990), Ainsworth and Bowlby (1991), Main and Solomon (1990), Main and Hesse (1990) and Cassidy and Shaver (1999). See also Chapter 12 in this volume.

> As a result of psychological and emotional unavailability, Emma was not provided with appropriate consistent and sensitive caregiving and was unable to form necessary secure attachments in infancy and early childhood. Frequent relocations and multiple new caregivers have additionally compounded her distorted internal working models of relationships, based on conflict and violence. This has led to Emma having a poor perception of her self-worth, a lack of trust in others and therefore difficulty developing close relationships. Thus, her present disturbed behaviour is likely to continue without appropriate stability and support.

Humanistic, Phenomenological and Existential Theories

Kelly, Maslow and Rogers (Kelly, 1955; Maslow, 1973; Rogers, 1961, 1969, 1978) are the best-known representatives of this school. In all these theories, the self is seen as central and each individual has a unique perspective on life that cannot be fully understood by any other. Humanistic theory followed and differed fundamentally from behaviourist and psychodynamic theories, in that the focus is on optimal functioning of an individual rather than psychopathology of an individual (see McLeod 2003 for a review). Thus, the focus of therapy is to assist individuals to be the best they can be (self-actualise), rather than focusing on mental ill-health.

Likewise, existentialism–phenomenologism suggests that the constant task facing individuals is to come to terms with life, the world and oneself (i.e. create a self and find meaning) on physical, social, psychological and spiritual dimensions (Van Deurzen, 2002; see Spinelli, 2003 for a review). Sudden exposure to vulnerability may trigger a sense of extreme anxiety (Van Deurzen, 2002). Thus, existentialism would argue that psychopathology results when an event or series of events occur that challenge the individual's belief that the world is a safe, predictable place. A child who has experienced an abusive and/or neglectful childhood would therefore have a fragile sense of self, and difficulty in perceiving the world as a safe, secure place and others as trustworthy. A psychological assessment based on this theoretical framework would focus on identifying physical, social, psychological and spiritual goals and fears (Van Deurzen, 2002).

> Emma had learned that the world is unpredictable and frightening, and her damaged close relationships have resulted in a poor sense of self-worth and self-esteem where others have not seen her as worthy of appropriate care. With her basic needs (such as basic physical and emotional care – 'psychological') often unmet, her focus would be on an attempt to have these met and therefore there was little opportunity to address additional needs (such as identity, status and self-worth – social and spiritual).

Cognitive-Behavioural Theory

Beck (1976) and other proponents (Clark & Fairburn, 1997; Persons, 1989) further developed traditional behavioural and social learning approaches (Bandura, 1977), emphasizing the importance of a cognitive component in learning and behaviour.

Beck and colleagues developed the concept of the link between thoughts, emotions and behaviour, such that the interpretation of a situation by an individual is more important in determining emotions and response than is the situation itself (Beck, 1995; Beck et al., 1990). For example, a young girl may be asked to consider how she would feel if her teacher was going to speak to her mother if (a) she had been 'naughty' that day (the implication being she might become anxious that her mother would be told and would be cross with her) and (b) she had won a prize that day (the implication being that she would be happy for her mother to be told because she would be pleased).

The cognitive–behavioural approach is perhaps the most formulaic of current theories, with many proposed models (e.g. Beck, 1995; Padesky & Greenberger, 1995; Persons, 1989; Gilbert, 1984). However, each model is based on determining early experiences, the development of negative automatic thoughts, underlying assumptions (if... then...) and core beliefs about self, others and the world (the cognitive triad).

Individuals' core beliefs are likely to have served a useful function in a 'risk' situation (e.g. abuse) and, as such, are functional at that point in time. However, the persistence of these core beliefs in other, non-risky, situations becomes increasingly dysfunctional. Looked after children struggle to adapt their previously functional beliefs (protecting them in risky situations) and they may even attempt to re-create a situation where their beliefs are accurate because this is psychologically more comfortable. Thus, when new experiences are unable to modify existing cognitions (e.g. everyone hates me) and negative core beliefs (e.g. I am worthless), psychopathology frequently results.

A psychological assessment based on this theoretical perspective would aim to identify the automatic thoughts, underlying assumptions and core beliefs.

> Emma had negative early experiences that are likely to have led to the development of cognitive distortions (e.g. 'no one wants me', 'everyone thinks I am bad'). In turn this leads to the development of 'rules for living', i.e. underlying assumptions (e.g. if I hurt others first then they can't hurt me; people will only care for me when I am naughty) and core beliefs (e.g. I am worthless, I am unlovable). Thus, she acts out behaviourally to test the commitment of her carers to her, despite her behaviour resulting in increasingly frequent placement breakdowns and a further escalation of her troubled and troublesome behaviours.

Systemic Theory

While there are a number of different schools of systemic therapy (see Bor & Legg, 2003; Burnham, 1986; Street & Dryden, 1988), overall they are defined by consideration of the individual within the wider system: e.g. family, friends, community, culture, nation and world (e.g. Bronfenbrenner, 1979). Ideally, each system is in perfect equilibrium and therefore disequilibrium within the system would signify damage and distress. It is the interactions and relationships with others that define the individual and a formulation of difficulties could not consider an individual in isolation. Circular rather than linear models of causality and interrelationships are used to explain the origins and maintenance of a system's difficulties (Burnham, 1986).

A psychological assessment using this framework would take a wider per-spective than most other theories, focusing beyond the individual. Common assessment strategies would involve asking about relationships from a num-ber of sources (Bor & Legg, 2003), an eco-map for the individual (Hartman, 1978) and a detailed genogram (Bailey & Simeonsson, 1988).

> Emma's formulation would focus on her relationships with her parents, her sibling, other significant adults (e.g. extended family), her friends, her relation-ships with teachers and peers at school, her role in the community as a child in care, her relationships with professionals as both a looked after child (e.g. social workers) and a child with physical disabilities (e.g. health professionals). For example, the presenting problem of domestic violence would be linked to possible previous cycles of family violence in the parents' families of origin as children and the current family cycles created by those parents/individuals. Emma's 'difficulties' are socially defined by her parents, teachers and perhaps professionals. They also reflect the dysfunctional interactions between herself and her mother, which are then further reflected in Emma's negative inter-actions with others. Emma's father has grown up in a family where violence was a usual form of conflict resolution and this pattern has been repeated and augmented in his adult relationships.

Integrative Approaches

Despite the apparent differences among the above approaches, it is notable that formulations from the different perspectives rest upon several common-alities. It could be argued that the differences are lingual and perhaps reflect slight differences in emphasis, while the core elements bear a striking resem-blance. One of the most notable developments in recent years has been the rise of integrative practice and formulation within psychological practice. In-deed, there is an increasing trend towards both integration of theories and the eclectic approach of skills and techniques (Hollanders, 2000; Palmer & Woolfe, 2000), as a means of encouraging 'an attitude of openness and ex-ploration...unrestrained by the limitations imposed by adherence to one particular approach or theory' (Arkowitz, 1991, p. 1, cited by Hollanders, 2003).

There is awareness that a drive towards an integrative approach may result in loose hypotheses and, in turn, interventions that lack a robust research base, yet currently it is accepted that this approach will have more advantages than disadvantages. Consistent with this attempted integration, most assessment frameworks for children and adolescents within the literature are based on cognitive-behavioural and attachment perspectives, yet consider the child's perspective and the child as part of their wider environment (e.g. Graham, 1998; Spence et al., 2000). Thus, perhaps best practice in assessments of looked after children and adolescents will reflect an eclectic approach encompassing factors and dimensions from all five models.

LITERATURE ON ASSESSMENT OF CHILDREN AND YOUNG PEOPLE

There is relatively little literature on the assessment of looked after children and young people and much of this tends to be practically based and aimed specifically at social work practice (e.g. *Framework for the Assessment of Children in Need and their Families*, DOH et al., 2000). Some key texts for psychologists and psychiatrists working more generally in the area of parenting assessments for children involved with social services include Gopfert et al. (1996), McNeish et al. (2002), Reder et al. (2000) and Reder and Lucey (1995). One reason for the dearth of literature in the area might be that assessments of children and young people in child care proceedings fall between the forensic psychology literature that tends to focus on offenders more than victims and the child development psychology literature that tends to focus on stages of development in non-clinical populations.

Therefore, psychologists in child care proceedings rely on textbooks describing general assessments of children and adolescents (e.g. Gumbiner, 2003; Lidz, 2003) as well as more specific sources. For example, in relation to contact, adoption/fostering issues and placement of siblings, sources would include the attachment literature (e.g. journals: *Adoption and Fostering; Child Abuse and Neglect; Attachment and Human Development*; books: Cassidy & Shaver, 1999; Crittenden & Claussen, 2000).

A BEST PRACTICE MODEL FOR ASSESSMENT OF LOOKED AFTER CHILDREN AND ADOLESCENTS

One difficulty in discussing a best practice model is the lack of agreement between practitioners as to what might constitute an assessment and whether it is appropriate for the same clinician to provide the treatment component as well. One school of thought argues that treatment recommendations should be provided by the same assessing clinician to ensure availability of treatment and continuity of engagement. In contrast, others believe that this would involve a conflict of interests, particularly if provided on a private consulting basis. In addition, it could be argued that the nature of an assessment of a child's therapeutic needs within a broader framework of decisions about placement is not the same as a brief assessment as part of a formulation of therapeutic need. Such engagement issues need to be addressed at the outset of any psychological assessment.

Legal Framework

One of the key roles for psychologists in assessing looked after children involved in a Court process, be it a custody dispute or child care proceedings,* is to ensure that the Court is aware of the child's needs based on relevant developmental and attachment literature (Covell, 1999). In addition, attention should be paid both to the Children Act (DOH, 1989) where the interests of the child are paramount, and the slightly different balance afforded by the Human Rights Act 2000, where the rights of the child are balanced with the rights of the parent (with the child being placed in priority if those rights conflict). In particular, Articles 8 (the right to family life) and 6 (the right to a fair trial) are applied to child care proceedings. Furthermore, most UN countries have signed up to the *Convention on the Rights of the Child* (United Nations, 1989), which also promotes the best interests of the child, with the parent seen as having responsibilities to fulfil those rights (Covell, 1999).

Setting Considerations

Alongside decisions about who to meet with, it is also important to consider the setting, what questions should be asked by whom, what information is required, how the assessment might be undertaken and what other professionals should expect from the report.

The key features to consider prior to the onset of any psychological assessment are:

- The reason for and purpose of psychological assessment.
- How the psychological assessment will map onto the other components of the multidisciplinary assessments.
- Necessary prior information and documents to be made available to the psychologist.
- Time frames.

---

*Custody cases are private civil matters, whereas child care proceedings are public law involving statutory agencies and address a wider remit.

To ensure the assessment is most beneficial to the child and to the Court process, clarity is required in terms of why the psychologist has been approached, what the psychologist is being asked to assess and what will be done with the information when obtained. It is also necessary to avoid duplication of work by different professionals – there is often confusion as to the respective roles of the CAFCASS guardians (formerly the Guardian ad Litem), social worker and psychologist. For example, the social worker (as usually the first point of contact) is typically engaged in a broad family-based assessment underpinned by the *Framework for the Assessment of Children and Need and their Families* (DOH et al., 2000). In turn, the psychologist is more appropriately focused on complex family dynamics, detailed personality analysis, complex attachment issues, rigorous hypothesis testing and models of risk/risk assessment. Furthermore, whereas social workers have to comply with statutory obligations, psychologists are classed as 'Expert Witnesses' and as such are entitled to provide an opinion to the Court on the basis of their area of expertise, rather than a restriction to present facts. The CAFCASS Guardian, as the child's advocate, summarizes all assessments and information (including the psychologist's) and makes specific recommendations within the legal framework.

A tension often arises for practitioners in terms of realistic time frames. A Court-driven process will demand a completed assessment and report within a very short interval. Indeed, the new Protocol being tested in certain regions due to be rolled out nationally in 2005/2006 demands a time scale of 40 weeks from the start of all assessments and professional involvement to completion at court (Home Office, 2003). However, this may well conflict with a needs-driven assessment for a child where a lengthier process allowing for the testing-out of informed hypotheses may result in a much more comprehensive assessment. Theoretically, assessment is always an ongoing process rather than a one-off event, but practice dictates the need for realistic time scales so decisions can be made about a child's future.

What Questions should be Asked of the Psychologist and by Whom?

Increasingly in child care proceedings for looked after children and adolescents, the psychologist is jointly instructed by all parties involved in the proceedings (e.g. solicitor for each parent, solicitor for the Local Authority and solicitor for the child). This is seen as best practice and is recommended by the American Psychological Association in terms of custody evaluations (APA, 1994) and acknowledged as increasingly common by the British Psychological

Society (BPS, 2004). In other cases where a psychologist is required to undertake a non-Court requested assessment of a looked after child, it is likely to be a social worker who requests the work and would therefore generate the questions to be answered by the assessment.

The first issue is to determine the type of psychologist to be instructed. Most psychologists working in the child care arena have a forensic or clinical psychology background, with educational psychologists more likely to address educational issues and provision. A broad distinction between forensic and clinical psychologists is that the former might be more involved in issues of risk and the latter in issues of child mental health. It should be noted, however, that there is considerable overlap and it is necessary to consider an individual clinician's experience and areas of expertise.

The first point to note is that to answer effectively the questions about a looked after child or adolescent in child care proceedings, the assessment will almost certainly need to include assessment of the parent/carer(s). Thus, typical questions asked of the psychologist relate to both the child/adolescent and the parent(s). In our experience these tend to include some or all of the following examples:

- Requests for an individual, comprehensive assessment of each parent, e.g.:
  - What is the level of cognitive functioning of this adult and likely implication for his or her ability to parent?
  - Does this adult demonstrate any psychological difficulties or mental health issues that would adversely affect parenting capacity?
  - Does this adult's use of alcohol or other substances, currently or in the past, have relevance for their parenting capacity?
  - Does this adult's history of relationships, with particular reference to violence, have any relevant link with his or her current functioning within his or her intimate relationship?
  - Does this adult's difficulty in the control of anger have current relevance?
  - Is it possible to assess the likely impact on the family unit of the forthcoming baby?
- Requests for an individual comprehensive assessment of a looked after child tend to focus on developmental, emotional, educational, psychological and social issues that are likely to have been affected by the child's previous experiences, possible removal from the family of origin and out of home placements. For example:
  - What is the level of cognitive functioning of this child? It is anticipated that this will include psychometric testing.
  - What is this child's level of emotional and social functioning within the family and external to the family?

- What is the likely impact of this child's previous childhood experiences?
- Is the child developmentally delayed? If yes, to what can the delay be attributed and what support is required?
- Is this child under-achieving in the school context? If so, can the likely causation of this be established?
- What is the nature of this child's relationships and attachments?
- If the decision is made to place this child in alternative provision, should this child be placed with siblings or separately?
- If the decision is made to place this child in alternative provision, what should be the contact between child and family members and/or significant others?
- What are the likely therapeutic requirements for this child with likely time scales and potential outcomes?

Some 'Dos' and 'Don'ts' of Instructions

It is not unknown to receive three to four closely typed pages of instructions. However, a 'scatter-gun' approach is not useful in that it does not allow the psychologist to concentrate on the important areas for consideration. In practice, it often hides the fact that there has been very little prior assessment work done with a family, such as, the Local Authority's Core Assessment of family members which should be a key document in the background documents provided to the psychologist.

If there is doubt about some instructions for the psychologist, it is good practice for the lead solicitor in the case to provide draft instructions to the psychologist, explain the nature of the queries from other parties and seek the psychologist's opinion prior to finalizing the instructions.

Overall, parents should be given every opportunity to demonstrate their ability to parent their child(ren) because it is in the best interests of the child(ren) to be raised with their biological parents wherever possible. However, a balance must be found between giving parents this opportunity and expecting them to undertake numerous assessments ('assessment shopping') in instances where previous assessments have produced negative findings in relation to the parents. In these circumstances, repeat assessments by other expert witnesses are sometimes sought in an attempt to rectify this, which may be unfair both in terms of raising false expectations in the parents and forcing a crucial delay in the decision making, with children frequently left in limbo. This is most frequently seen in cases of fabricated illness (previously known as Munchausen's Syndrome by Proxy) with examples of up to 20 experts being instructed in one matter. However, it is acknowledged that this is a difficult balance to meet.

What Information should the Psychologist be Provided with Prior to or During Assessment?

Alongside the receipt of the instruction letters, accompanying documentation should include medical records for the parents and child(ren), prior reports (e.g. social services, health agencies, education, residential assessments), statements (e.g. foster carers, contact supervisors) and criminal records of parents and/or adolescents. These should be regularly updated with any new documents, such as inter-agency reports, as the assessment proceeds. It is acknowledged that there are often difficulties in obtaining these reports but it is an essential part of any psychological assessment.

How would a Psychologist Undertake the Assessment?

The Best Practice model in assessment is to obtain information from numerous sources in order to cross-check and critically examine all data. This is a time-consuming exercise and there is inevitable tension between a comprehensive assessment and the time constraints of the child and the Court. Nonetheless, a robust professional assessment is required to ensure that the best interests of the child are met. There are five common sources of information:

- *Clinical interview* – The approach taken is likely to depend on the assessing psychologist's theoretical perspective, as well as the aims of the assessment and specific instructions.
- *Self-report* – This is one of the most important aspects of any assessment allowing the parent and child the opportunity to provide their own narrative.
- *Psychometrics* – Psychologists are uniquely placed to administer and interpret psychometric tests having been specifically trained in the analysis and interpretation of these tests. As such, many remain 'closed' and should not be used by other professionals, but can be a beneficial addition to assessment if interpreted in light of other information. Best Practice indicates that psychometric tests should always be considered as only one source of information, rather than the definitive answer.
- *Corroborative information* – Routine sources of information about the looked after child/adolescent will include:
  - Parents and relatives
  - Foster carers
  - Education (teachers, school nurses, education welfare, SENCO)
  - Social Services/Social Care and Health – day and residential staff

- Health (health visitors, paediatricians, physiotherapists, speech thera-
pists, psychologists)
- Police
- Voluntary agencies (e.g., NSPCC, Surestart).

● *Observation* – Observation of the looked after child can take place in school, at the foster carers, during contact with the parent(s) or in other community settings. It allows comparison of the child in interaction with adults and peers in different settings. Observation of parents is made in clinical interview, as well as at contact sessions and meetings.

Ethical Issues in a Psychological Assessment

The ethical issues of assessing both children/young people and adults (particularly vulnerable adults such as those with a learning disability) are complex and an in-depth analysis is beyond the scope of this chapter. Some key issues are briefly outlined below, but the following articles/sources are recommended to the reader: the British Psychological Society *Code of Conduct* (BPS, 2000); Thomas-Peter and Warren (1998) for a review of the responsibilities of forensic psychologists working with adults.

Informed Consent

The legal situation is that the parent gives consent in relation to the assessment of the looked after child (or Local Authority in 'loco parentis'). In reality, just as would be done with an adult, time should be spent explaining to the child or adolescent what a psychologist is, why he or she has been asked to see a psychologist, what the psychologist will do and that subsequently a report will be written. This allows the child the opportunity to consent and forms the basis for the establishment of a good rapport. In addition, increasing numbers of looked after children in puberty and adolescence are being separately represented in Court proceedings and are directly instructing their own solicitor, thereby giving their own consent to proceedings.

Confidentiality

This is an important issue to address with a looked after child. The child needs to be very clear that what he or she says to the psychologist cannot (in these circumstances) remain confidential because the assessment is Court-driven and a report will be required. Our experience is that many looked after children are very well aware that blanket confidentiality cannot be assured due to their involvement with so many professionals.

Testing Procedures

It is essential to use tests appropriate to the age, cultural background, ability of the child or adolescent and the instructions provided. Best Practice would also include an explanation to the child of the purpose of the test and its relevance to his or her particular circumstances.

Practical Considerations

Deciding on appropriate places to meet with looked after children can be a difficult issue and may change from case to case. Consideration should be paid to issues such as familiarity, child's preference, disability, place of contact, safety and attitude of parents.

Race and Culture

It is extremely important that race and cultural considerations are given sufficient weight in any child or adolescent assessment. As before, it goes beyond the remit of this chapter to discuss in detail, but the reader is referred to Gopaul-McNicol and Brice-Baker (1997) and McGoldrick et al. (1996). One further point to make is that, while professionals are sometimes unclear about appropriate norms and practices, all countries (with the exception of the USA) have signed the UN *Convention on the Rights of the Child* and this is a cross-cultural standard applying to the care of all children, be it with biological or substitute carers.

WHAT SHOULD A PSYCHOLOGIST ASSESS?

Using any of the approaches outlined above, there are a number of common areas psychologists are likely to address when taking a background history. These include intrapersonal, interpersonal, environmental, educational and health factors. For full references for the psychometric assessments mentioned in this section, see Appendix 5.1.

Family History and Relationships

Childhood relationships with parents, siblings, extended family, foster carers, peers and teachers are usually key areas. When assessing parents, it would also be necessary to consider relationships in adulthood within the family, romantically and with children. In particular, it is important to look for recurring themes in relationship styles, such as their fundamental way of interacting with the world or serial relationships involving violence.

As well as interview, self-report and other sources of information, assessment of relationships may be via standardized tests (e.g. Bene–Anthony Family Relations Test) or via more projective tests (e.g. Thematic Apperception Test*). It may also be useful to consider the child's attachments via informal methods such as Attachment Story Stem techniques and qualitative methods such as drawings of the child's perceived family/families (Fury et al., 1997; Veltman & Browne, 2001, 2002, 2003).

Cognitive Functioning

This is typically assessed via the administration of a relevant intelligence test, which the psychologist is uniquely qualified to administer and interpret. There are a number of intelligence tests in widespread use that are well standardized and vary according to the age of the child. The most well known, however, is the Wechsler Intelligence Scale for Children (WISC). There are also tests that avoid cultural bias such as the Leiter International Performance Scale. This does not require language and is designed for use with children who may be cognitively delayed, non-speaking or have English only as an additional language.

School Performance and Presentation

There are numerous measures used in school settings to help with assessments of children. The Conners Rating Scales (short and long form) can be used by teachers and foster carers to rate difficulties and problem behaviours in children with an age range of 3 to 17 years. In addition, the Conners Parent Rating Scale provides views of the child from a variety of sources. The Strengths and Difficulties Questionnaire is also in increasing use in schools and with parents and/or alternative carers. The Devereux Behavior Rating Scales are often used to monitor progress with children aged 5–12 or 13–18 years during specific educational interventions.

When assessing a looked after child, we consider it particularly important to assess the child *in situ* in school, taking the opportunity to discuss the child with relevant staff. Directly sourced data is infinitely richer than information obtained via a remote standardized questionnaire returned through the

---

*The Children's Apperception Test is for younger children, aged 3–10 years.

post by school personnel. Along with information about the child's attainments and behaviours in school, this is a rich source of information about the presence or absence of the child's peer friendships and social networks.

Medical/Physical History

Children in the care system often have histories of frequent moves, and information may therefore be fragmented and sparse. We consider it vital that the child's medical records are accessed (usually from the relevant General Practitioner via the lead solicitor) as this is often a comprehensive continuous record of the child's locations, schools and homes as well as past medical history. It is also a vital aspect in terms of future planning for the child, from the more simple information of whether the child has indeed suffered common childhood illnesses and has necessary immunizations through to considerations of HIV status and future implications or genetically endowed illnesses in the birth family such as Parkinson's, etc. However, psychologists have a responsibility to ensure that they use the information respectfully and ethically, including only summaries of issues that are directly relevant to the issues in hand as stated by the instructions.

Sexuality

This may be a specific aspect of the psychologist's instructions if a child has been previously sexually abused and/or the child is demonstrating inappropriately sexualized behaviours. The child may find direct discussion difficult – these children have often been 'silenced' in some way – and thus the psychologist may use methods such as play, artwork, collages, story-telling techniques and poetry. Some people use customized worksheets with sentence completion items and may suggest an ongoing journal or diary if the child can cope with written material.

Even if it is not included specifically within the psychologist's remit, the evidence currently is that many adult male rapists, paedophiles and adults with sexual perversions reveal in interviews that they were first perpetrating sexual abuse by their early teens (Elliott, et al., 1995). There is meagre evidence in relation to the adolescent female population and, as a society, we still remain reluctant to countenance the possibility of female perpetrators of sexual abuse (Saradjian & Hanks, 1996). It behoves any clinician therefore to assess the child's sexual history and to be vigilant regarding any atypical presentations or interests.

Forensic History

All details should be sought of any cautions and charges, not merely relying on convictions, thereby providing a more accurate profile of any criminal activity over time. Psychologists would note the known link between early conduct disorders and antisocial behaviours with later delinquency and possible adult criminality (Luntz & Widom, 1994; Lynam, 1996). Unfortunately, it is known that many looked after children become involved in criminal activities from an early age.

Self-assessment

There is a variety of standardized tests in use in this area, many of them focused on specific clinical/personality factors. The Self-Image Profiles come in two age groups: 7–11 years and 12–16 years. This test also usefully provides a measure of Self-Esteem as well as a short, simple questionnaire ('What I am Like') that provides ratings on perceived competences such as social acceptance, physical appearance and behavioural conduct. This is a particularly relevant test for looked after children, given the likely impact of their early experiences. A further self-report measure that is widely used is the Adolescent Coping Scale. This has both a long and a short version, both of which focus on numerous coping strategies, as well as providing information about reactions in possible scenarios.

Psychological Profile

This is perhaps one of the key areas expected from others reading a psychological report. Although the profile will be developed from all sources of information, there may be particular dimensions that the psychologist wishes to address via certain instruments. These areas may include depression (e.g. Child Depression Inventory), post-traumatic stress (e.g. Trauma Symptom Checklist for Children), anxiety (e.g. Beck Anxiety Inventory for Children) and general difficulties in living (e.g. Impact of Events Scale). Again, unfortunately, these are all highly relevant for the looked after children population. There are also personality tests for use with adolescents, such as the Minnesota Multiphasic Personality Inventory for Adolescents (age range 14–18 years) and the Millon Adolescent Personality Inventory (age range 13–19).

The psychologist is also likely to conduct direct interviews and will consider critical dimensions for looked after children and adolescents such as risk-taking behaviours, self-harming behaviours, substance misuse, school refusal and truancy, self-esteem measures, the ability to self-soothe, disinhibited behaviours and a capacity for self-regulation alongside proven self-controls. In terms of interpersonal skills, the psychologist is likely to focus on the child's/adolescent's capacity for empathy and sensitivity, social networking or withdrawal, enduring or volatile short-term relationships, distorted attributions and expectations in relation to others, and any indicators of aggression, overdependency, avoidance, etc.

The psychological profile usually comprises all test results and interview data in association with corroborative information from other sources; this is distilled and interpreted to provide the psychological formulation in respect of the child's psychological presentation.

However, it is also worth reiterating that, despite the array of psychometric tests available and more informal methods using questionnaires and brief screening tools, the information obtained from them should always be corroborated and contextualized with clinical information obtained from a variety of sources. George Kelly, the guru of Personal Construct Theory, when asked what tests he might recommend, said that it was 'always good just to ask the person – you never know, they might just tell you!' (1955).

Specific Issues

When assessing looked after children and adolescents, there are also a number of other factors that must be taken into account, particularly when providing an opinion on issues such as future placements, movement and contact. These include:

- Age
- Physical and intellectual disabilities (developmental legacy)
- Cultural issues
- Mental health
- Attachment
- Contact/permanence.

Although many of the above difficulties (e.g. truancy, criminal activity, risk-taking behaviour, self-harm, developmental delay) may be more highly represented in the looked after children population, it is important to remember that they are not inevitable outcomes. Therefore, all psychological assessments must focus on the strengths and skills of any looked after child, identifying positive coping strategies, protective factors and potential resilience.

THE ROLE OF THE EXPERT

The contribution of expert witnesses is often a vital part of the decision making in many complex child cases before the Court. Courts have become increasingly reliant upon such evidence, but there is an inevitable tension between the use of experts and the drive to avoid delay in dealing with child cases. The duty of an expert witness is to inform the Court of matters that are relevant and within his or her area of expertise. Key summaries of the role of the expert, *inter alia*, can be found in Walsh (1998) and Wall (2000). The main points are:

- The evidence as presented to the Court should be, and should be seen to be, the independent product of the expert.
- An expert should not lose objectivity and take sides, and the evidence should provide independent assistance to the Court by way of objective, unbiased opinion in relation to matters within his or her expertise and should never assume the role of advocate.
- An expert should state the facts or assumptions upon which his or her opinion is based and should not omit to consider material facts that would detract from his or her concluded opinion.
- When an expert advances a hypothesis to explain a given set of facts, he or she owes a duty to:
  – explain to the Court that what he or she is advancing is a hypothesis;
  – inform the Court if the hypothesis is controversial.
- The expert also has a duty to place before the Court all available material that contradicts the hypothesis.
- An expert should make it clear when a particular issue or question falls outside his or her expertise. If an expert's opinion is not properly researched because it appears that insufficient data is available, he or she must say so, indicating that the opinion is no more than a provisional one and should also point out any qualifications about the truth of his or her assertions.
- If, after exchanging reports, an expert has a change of mind on a material matter, he or she should inform the other parties and the Court.

What to Expect from the Report

The report should be able to stand alone and provide any reader with information about the author of the report (full curriculum vitae), the nature of the instructions (listed in full) and the methodology employed (all enquiries, observations and assessments made). Individual psychologists are likely to

employ slightly different formats but the key issues that must be addressed
are:

1. The specific instructions should be answered.
2. The material considered (i.e. documents, statements, etc.).
3. Clear opinions and recommendations should be reached (but not conclusions, which are the remit of the Judge only).
4. The reasoning behind the opinions should be made explicit.

Examples of good practice would include a clear, well-written report in plain
English, avoiding excessive jargon. It should be expected that if the psychologist has access to any new, relevant information, that he or she will disclose
the information to the Court via their lead solicitor. Examples of bad practice would include psychologists who ignore instructions, fail to submit their
report in the time frame, who draw woolly, vague conclusions and/or who
include unrelated pages of research.

Recommendations in relation to looked after children are likely to focus on
three main areas:

(a) Future placements and permanency (e.g. rehabilitation to family, long-
    term fostering, adoption, separation or joint placement of siblings, spe-
    cialist residential provision for disabled children, secure accommodation
    for teenagers at risk of harm to themselves or others).
(b) Issues of contact, in relation not only to parents, but also to siblings, ex-
    tended family and possibly foster families (e.g. letterbox or face to face,
    frequency, setting, duration, long-term plans).
(c) Possible interventions and/or therapy (e.g. supportive educational pro-
    vision; play, family or individual therapy; physical or speech therapy;
    social skills training), which can be aimed at issues related to victimiza-
    tion, attachment difficulties, involvement with a delinquent peer group
    and educational difficulties.

For example, in relation to Emma, recommendations were:

(a) Place her long-term with her sister, given that there were clear protective
    factors in the sibling relationship and they had maintained frequent contact
    that was positive for both. Both also expressed a wish to be placed together.
    Given their ages and Emma's difficulties (e.g. behaviour, diabetes, query of
    autistic spectrum disorder), it was more realistic to presume that this was
    more likely to be stable, long-term fostering rather than adoption. Indeed,
    Emma's foster carers had expressed a wish to care for both girls and been
    assessed by social workers as suitable.

(b) Maintain supervised contact with mum due to concerns about her violent partner and concerns regarding her observed interactions with the girls, which were very over-intrusive resulting in high conflict. Given their ages, history and expressed wishes, contact frequency of six contacts per year was recommended. This upholds the relationship but should not be too disruptive to the long-term foster placement.

(c) Make behavioural management programmes available to the foster carers, if required, although their current setting of clear, consistent and loving boundaries had already impacted positively on her behaviour. In terms of educational provision, Emma had responded well to a classroom assistant and it was recommended that this was formalized at 10 hours per week. It was not perceived that individual therapy would be of benefit at that time, given that the placements were settled and the girls felt contained. However, it was recommended that this option be left open for the girls in the future, with the foster carers aware of how to access therapy, if required.

REFLECTIONS AND KEY ISSUES

Looked after children are not a homogeneous group. Indeed, this group of children have highly complex needs and professionals may well have a duty to provide additional time and consideration to them. They have experienced significant and often recurrent loss and separations and, as such, require more intensive and specialist support than many other children and adolescents.

Currently, there is some controversy about *when* an assessment or intervention is undertaken. Many services delay assessing or intervening with a child while he or she is in a state of uncertainty, stating that the child needs to be in a permanent placement prior to an assessment being undertaken. However, those working with the looked after child and, in particular, the Court, need vital information about the child while the child remains in a state of uncertainty in order to make those decisions. It behoves professionals to embrace such uncertainty and try to support the child through a difficult process. Indeed, the manner in which the child is informed and prepared for the meeting with the psychologist is absolutely key to the potential outcome. Children and adolescents cannot wait until the perfect moment.

APPENDIX 5.1: FULL REFERENCES FOR PSYCHOMETRIC ASSESSMENTS

Achenbach, T.M. (1991) *Manual for the Child Behavior Checklist/4-18, YSR, and TRF Profiles.* Burlington: University of Vermont Department of Psychiatry.

Battle, J. (1992) *Culture-Free Self-Esteem Inventory*, 2nd edition (CFSEI-2). Texas: Pro-Ed.

Beck, J.S., Beck, A.T. & Jolly, J.B. (2001) *Beck Youth Inventories of Emotional and Social Impairment*. London: Harcourt Assessment/The Psychological Corporation.

Bene, E. & Anthony, J. (revised 1985) *Bene–Anthony Family Relations Test*. UK: NFER–Nelson Publishing Company Ltd.

Birleson, P. et al. (1991) *Birleson Depression Scale*. UK: NFER–Nelson Publishing Company Ltd.

Briere, J. (1992) *Trauma Symptom Checklist for Children*. Odessa, FL: Psychological Assessment Resources Inc.

Butcher, J.N. & Williams, C.L. (1992) *Minnesota Multiphasic Personality Inventory – Adolescent* (MMPI – A). USA: University of Minnesota Press.

Butler, R.J. (2001) *Self Image Profiles* (SIP). London: Harcourt Assessment/The Psychological Corporation.

Conners, C.K. (1997) *Connors' Rating Scale – Revised*. New York: Multi-Health Systems.

Frydenberg, E. & Lewis, R. (1993) *Adolescent Coping Scale*. Victoria, Australia: Australian Council for Educational Research Ltd.

Goodman, R. (1997) The Strengths and Difficulties Questionnaire. A research note. *Journal of Child Psychology and Psychiatry*, **38**, 581–586.

Horowitz, M.J., Wilner, N.M. & Alvarez, W. (1979) Impact of Event Scale: A measure of subjective stress. *Psychosomatic Medicine*, **41**, 209–218.

Kovacs, M. (1992) *Children's Depression Inventory*. New York/Ontario, Canada: Multi-Health Systems Inc.

Millon, T. (1993) The Millon Adolescent Personality Inventory and the Millon Adolescent Clinical Inventory. *Journal of Counselling and Development*, **71**(5), 570.

Morgan, C.D. & Murray, H.A. (1930s) *Thematic Apperception Test*. Cambridge, MA: Harvard University Press.

Roid, G.H. & Miller, L.J. (1997) *Leiter International Performance Scale – Revised*. Illinois: Stoelting Co.

Rutter, M. (1993a) *Revised Rutter Parent Scale for School-Age Children*. UK: NFER–Nelson Publishing Company Ltd.

Rutter, M. (1993b) *Revised Rutter Teacher Scale for School-Age Children*. UK: NFER–Nelson Publishing Company Ltd.

Spivack, G., Haimes, P. & Spotts, J. (1967) *Adolescent Behavior Rating Scale* (DAB). USA: Devereux Foundation.

Spivack, G. & Spotts, J. (1966) *Devereux Child Behavior Rating Scale* (DCB). USA: Devereux Foundation.

Wechsler, D. (1992) *Wechsler Intelligence Scale for Children* – III[UK] (WISC–III[UK]). London: The Psychological Corporation.

REFERENCES

Ainsworth, M.D.S. (1989) Attachments beyond infancy. *American Psychologist*, **44**, 709–716.

Ainsworth, M.D.S. (1990) Epilogue: Some considerations regarding theory and assessment relevant to attachment beyond infancy. In M.T. Greenberg, D. Cicchetti & E.M. Cummings (Eds), *Attachment in the Pre-School Years: Theory, Research and Intervention*. Chicago: University of Chicago Press.

Ainsworth, M.D.S. & Bowlby, J. (1991) An ethological approach to personality development. *American Psychologist*, **46**, 333–341.

Akhtar, S. (1992) *Broken Structures: Severe Personality Disorders and their Treatment*. Northvale, NJ: Jason Aronson.

APA (American Psychological Association) (1994) Guidelines for child custody evaluations in divorce proceedings. *American Psychologist*, **49**(7), 677–680.

Arkowitz, H. (1991) Introductory statement: Psychotherapy in the light of learning theory. *American Journal of Psychiatry*, **120**, 440–448 (cited in Hollanders, 2003).

Bailey, D.B. Jr & Simeonsson, R.J. (1988) *Family Assessment in Early Intervention*. Columbus, OH: Merrill.

Bandura, A. (1977) *Social Learning Theory*. Englewood Cliffs, NJ: Prentice Hall.

Beck, A.T. (1976) *Cognitive Therapy and the Emotional Disorders*. New York: International Universities Press.

Beck, A. (1995) *Cognitive Therapy: Basics and Beyond*. New York: Guilford Press.

Beck, A., Freeman, A. & Associates (1990) *Cognitive Therapy of Personality Disorders*. New York: Guilford Press.

Bor, R. & Legg, C. (2003) The systems paradigm. In R. Woolfe, W. Dryden & S. Strawbridge (Eds), *Handbook of Counselling Psychology* (ch. 12). London: Sage.

Bowlby, J. (1951) Maternal care and maternal health. *World Health Organization, Monograph Series No. 2*. WHO.

Bowlby, J. (1953) *Child Care and the Growth of Maternal Love*. London: Penguin.

Bowlby, J. (1969) *Attachment and Loss. Vol. 1. Attachment*. London: Hogarth Press.

Bowlby, J. (1973) *Attachment and Loss. Vol. 2. Separation: Anxiety and Anger*. London: Hogarth Press.

Bowlby, J. (1980) *Attachment and Loss. Vol. 3. Loss: Sadness and Depression*. London: Hogarth Press.

Bowlby, J. (1988) *A Secure Base: Clinical Applications of Attachment Theory*. London: Routledge.

BPS (November 2000) *Code of Conduct*. Leicester: British Psychological Society.

BPS (2004) *Advice for Members Acting as an Expert*. British Psychological Society www.bps.org.uk.

Bretherton, I. (1999). Updating the 'internal working model' construct: some reflections. *Journal of Attachment and Human Development*, **1**(3), 343–357.

Bronfenbrenner, U. (1979) *The Ecology of Human Development*. Cambridge, MA: Harvard University Press.

Burton, M. & Davey, T. (2003) The psychodynamic paradigm. In R. Woolfe, W. Dryden & S. Strawbridge (Eds), *Handbook of Counselling Psychology* (ch. 5). London: Sage.

Burnham, J. (1986) *Family Therapy*. London: Routledge.

Cassidy, J. & Shaver, P.R. (1999) *Handbook of Attachment: Theory, Research and Clinical Applications*. New York: Guilford Press.

Clark, D.M. & Fairburn, C. (1997) *The Science and Practice of Cognitive Behaviour Therapy*. Oxford: Oxford University Press.

Covell, K. (1999) Promoting parenting plans: A new role for the psychologist as expert in custody disputes. *Expert Evidence*, **7**, 113–126.

Crittenden, P.M. & Claussen, A.H. (Eds) (2000) *The Organization of Attachment Relationships: Maturation, Culture and Context*. New York: Cambridge University Press.

DOH, DFEE & Home Office (2000) *Framework for the Assessment of Children in Need and their Families*. London: TSO.

DOH (1989) *Children Act 1989*. London: TSO.

Drabick, D.A. & Goldfried, M.R. (2000) Training the scientist-practitioner for the 21st century. *Journal of Clinical Psychology*, **56**, 327–340.

Elliott, M., Browne, K. & Kilcoyne, J. (1995) Child sexual abuse prevention: What offenders tell us. *Child Abuse and Neglect*, **19**(5), 579–594.

Freud, A. (1965) *Normality and Pathology in Childhood*. Harmondsworth: Penguin.

Freud, A. (1970) *Child Analysis as a Subspecialty of Psychoanalysis: The Writings of Anna Freud* (pp. 204–209). New York: International Universities Press.

Freud, S. (1923) The ego and the id. *Standard Edition*, **19**, 1–59.

Freud, S. (1938) An outline of psychoanalysis. *Standard Edition*, **23**, 139–208.

Fury, G., Carlson, E. & Stroufe, L.A. (1997) Children's representation of attachment relationship in family drawings. *Child Development*, **68**, 1154–1164.

Gilbert, P. (1984) *Depression: From Psychology to Brain State*. London: Lawrence Erlbaum Associates.

Gopaul-McNicol, S.-A. & Brice-Baker, J. (1997) *Cross-Cultural Practice: Assessment, Treatment and Training*. Chichester: John Wiley & Sons.

Gopfert, M., Webster, J. & Seeman, M.V. (1996) *Parental Psychiatric Disorder: Distressed Parents and their Families*. Cambridge: Cambridge University Press.

Graham, P. (1998) *Cognitive Behaviour Therapy for Children and Families*. Cambridge: Cambridge University Press.

Gumbiner, J. (2003) *Adolescent Assessment*. Chichester: John Wiley & Sons.

Hartman, A. (1978) *Finding Families: An Ecological Approach to Family Assessment in Adoption*. London: Sage.

Hollanders, H. (2000) Eclecticism/integration: Historical developments. In S. Palmer & R. Woolfe (Eds), *Integrative and Eclectic Counselling and Psychotherapy*. London: Sage.

Hollanders, H. (2003) The eclectic and integrative approach. In R. Woolfe, W. Dryden & S. Strawbridge (Eds), *Handbook of Counselling Psychology* (2nd edn; ch. 13). London: Sage.

Home Office (June 2003, implemented November 2003) *The Protocol for Judicial Case Management in Public Law Children Act Cases*.

Kelly, G. (1955) *The Psychology of Personal Constructs*. New York: Norton.

Klein, M. (1932) *The Psycho-Analysis of Children*. London: Hogarth.

Klein, M. (1959) *Our Adult World and its Roots in Infancy: The Writings of Melanie Klein* (vol. 3; pp. 247–263) London: Hogarth.

Lidz, C. (2003) *Early Childhood Assessment*. Chichester: John Wiley & Sons.

Luntz, B.K. & Widom, C.S. (1994) Antisocial personality disorder in abused and neglected children grown up. *American Journal of Psychiatry*, **151**, 670–674.

Lynam, D.R. (1996). The identification of chronic offenders: Who is the fledgling psychopath? *Psychological Bulletin*, **120**, 209–234.

Main, M. & Hesse, E. (1990) Parents' unresolved traumatic experiences are related to infant disorganized attachment status: Is frightened and/or frightening parental behavior the linking mechanism? In M. Greenberg, D. Cicchetti & E.M. Cummings

(Eds), *Attachment in the Pre-school Years: Theory, Research and Intervention*. Chicago: University of Chicago Press.

Main, M. & Solomon, J. (1990) Procedures for identifying infants as disorganized/disoriented during the Ainsworth Strange Situation. In M. Greenberg, D. Cicchetti & E.M. Cummings (Eds), *Attachment in the Pre-School Years: Theory, Research and Intervention*. Chicago: University of Chicago Press.

Maslow, A. (1973) *The Farther Reaches of Human Nature*. Middlesex: Penguin.

McGoldrick, M., Giordano, J. & Pearce, J.K. (1996) *Ethnicity and Family Therapy* (2nd edn). New York: Guilford Press.

McLeod, J. (2003) The humanistic paradigm. In R. Woolfe, W. Dryden & S. Strawbridge (Eds), *Handbook of Counselling Psychology* (ch. 6). London: Sage.

McNeish, D., Newman, T. & Roberts, H. (2002) *What Works for Children? Effective Services for Children and Families*. Buckingham: Open University Press.

Morton, N. & Browne, K.D. (1998) Theory and observation of attachment and its relation to child maltreatment: A review. *Child Abuse and Neglect*, **22**(11), 1093–1104.

Padesky, C.A. & Greenberger, D. (1995) *Clinician's Guide to Mind over Mood*. New York: Guilford Press.

Palmer, S. & Woolfe, R. (2000) *Integrative and Eclectic Counselling and Psychotherapy*. London: Sage.

Persons, J.B. (1989) *Cognitive Therapy in Practice: A Case Formulation Approach*. New York: Norton.

Pfeifer, J.E. (1999) Introduction: Psychologists, Courts and child custody disputes. *Expert Evidence*, **7**, 81–83.

Reder, P. & Lucey, C. (1995) *Assessment of Parenting: Psychiatric and Psychological Contributions*. London: Routledge.

Reder, P., McClure, M. & Jolley, A. (2000) *Family Matters: Interfaces between Child and Adult Mental Health*. London: Routledge.

Rogers, C.R. (1961) *On Becoming a Person*. London: Constable.

Rogers, C.R. (1969) *Freedom to Learn*. Columbus, OH: Merrill.

Rogers, C.R. (1978) *Carl Rogers on Personal Power: Inner Strength and its Revolutionary Impact*. London: Constable.

Samra-Grewal, J. (1999). Custody and access evaluations: Issues for mental health professionals. *Expert Evidence*, **7**, 85–111.

Saradjian, J. & Hanks, H.G.I. (1996) *Women who Sexually Abuse Children: From Research to Clinical Practice*. Chichester: John Wiley & Sons.

Spence, S.H., Donovan, C. & Brechman-Toussaint, M. (2000) The treatment of childhood social phobia: The effectiveness of a social skills training-based, cognitive-behavioural intervention, with and without parental involvement. *Journal of Child Psychology and Psychiatry*, **41**(6), 713–726.

Spinelli, E. (2003) The existential–phenomenological paradigm. In R. Woolfe, W. Dryden & S. Strawbridge (Eds), *Handbook of Counselling Psychology* (ch. 8). London: Sage.

Street, E. & Dryden, W. (1988) *Family Therapy in Britain*. Milton Keynes: Open University Press.

Thomas-Peter, B. & Warren, S. (1998) Legal responsibilities for forensic psychologists. *Expert Evidence*, **6**, 79–106.

United Nations (1989) *Convention on the Rights of the Child*. New York: United Nations.

Van Deurzen, E. (2002) Existential therapy. In W. Dryden (Ed.), *Handbook of Individual Therapy* (4th edn; ch. 8). London: Sage.

Van Ijzendoorn, M.H. & Bakermans-Kranenburg, M.J. (2003) Attachment disorders and disorganized attachment: Similar and different. *Attachment and Human Development*, **5**(3), 313–320.

Veltman, M.W.M & Browne, K.D. (2001) Identifying child abuse through favourite kind of day and kinetic family drawings. *The Arts in Psychotherapy*, **28**, 251–259.

Veltman, M.W.M & Browne, K.D. (2002) The assessment of drawings from children who have been maltreated: A systematic review. *Child Abuse Review*, **11**, 19–37.

Veltman, M.W.M. & Browne, K.D. (2003) Identifying abused children using assessments and observations in the classroom: A preliminary study. *Child Abuse Review*, **12**, 315–334.

Wall, Justice Nicholas (2000) *A Handbook for Expert Witnesses in Children Act Cases*. Bristol: Jordan Publishing.

Walsh, E. (1998) *Working in the Family Justice System: A Guide for Professionals*. Bristol: Jordan Publishing.

6

ENGAGING THE NETWORK: CONSULTATION FOR LOOKED AFTER AND ADOPTED CHILDREN

Helen R. Dent and Kim S. Golding

*We believe that we are there to help our colleagues with their tasks, but not to try to take over from them. Frequently we learn as much as they do.**

Consultation is an alternative to working directly with clients. It involves working with a part of the network surrounding the client, explicitly for that client's benefit, and in this way differs from direct work or therapy. Consultation can involve supervising or advising professionals who will be delivering direct therapy or it can involve helping other professionals to reflect on their work with the aim of delivering their services more effectively. When children are involved, the consultation remit also extends to working with parents and carers. In other words, a consultant works with consultees who have responsibility for a client or clients.

Consultation may just involve two or three people, but it can be a time-consuming procedure – a three-hour session with eight people adds up to 24 hours of professional/carer time. However, when working with children, particularly in complex situations, it is almost always necessary for contact to

---

*Reproduced from Nissim (1993, p. 12) by permission of The Fostering Network.

Thinking Psychologically About Children Who Are Looked After and Adopted
Edited by K.S. Golding, H.R. Dent, R. Nissim and L. Stott.
Copyright © 2006 John Wiley & Sons, Ltd.

be made between various people in their network, from parents and carers to health, educational and social service professionals. If the time involved in these contacts is added up, it is likely to be similar to the time involved in a consultation session. The two main differences are that in individual contacts, the time is hidden, so that it is not such an obviously large block of time. Secondly, in consultation, all of the professionals and carers who could be making individual contact can work directly and more effectively together. Interestingly, Caplan (1970) developed consultation to be a time-saving intervention when faced with a potential client population of 16,000 children and too few psychologists to see individual referrals (Labram, 1992).

The Laming Report (2003) has identified communication between agencies as a weakness that must be rectified if vulnerable children are to receive the protection they need. Consultation is a method of engaging the network, which is receiving increasing support from research into its effectiveness (e.g. Golding, 2004).

Saunders and Broad (1997; cited in Kelly et al., 2003) found that 77% of young people leaving care who had accessed CAMHS had found the service unhelpful. This clearly points to the need for finding a different way of helping children while they are in care. Street and colleagues (1991) consider that consultation is particularly suited to such situations as it is a flexible way of working, which 'allows for a collaborative reflection on the whole system, rather than seeking to put therapeutic energy into just one mode of working' (p. 319). Sprince (2005) suggests that consultation can be used to create a therapeutic network to support or take the place of direct interventions with children.

This chapter will explore different types of consultation for use in varied circumstances in work with looked after and adopted children.

DEFINITIONS AND MODELS

Consultation has been in documented use since at least 1548, when it was recorded as 'the act of consulting or taking counsel together; deliberation, conference' (*Oxford English Dictionary*, 1971, p. 885). It is an ancient form of providing help in religion, business, law and health, usually through giving expert advice, though the 1548 usage indicates a more egalitarian activity, akin to the types of consultation that will be discussed in this chapter. Within the discipline of psychology, occupational psychologists were the first to use this approach (Argyris, 1970). Consultation in the arena of mental health has now evolved into a range of practices involving different theoretical models and processes. These different models have certain characteristics in common.

For example, consultation is generally:

- initiated either by consultee or consultant;
- a direct service to consultees, assisting them to develop coping skills that ultimately makes them independent of the consultant;
- triadic in that it provides indirect services to third parties (clients);
- focused on work-related problems. The concept of work is broadly conceived. Work is considered to be the tasks undertaken by the group from which the consultee stems. For adoptive parents, foster carers and residential social workers this would be the work of caring for the children, and related responsibilities;
- varied to adapt to the consultee's needs.

While the consultant and consultee work together to identify problems and plan interventions, the consultee is seen as responsible for implementing these plans (e.g. see Ovretveit et al., 1992; Brunning & Huffington, 1991). This may be in the form of resolving problems or strengthening competencies (Wallace & Hall, 1996). Consultation therefore aims to help those who are working directly with a problem to be able to draw upon their own resources and develop their skill to the ultimate benefit of a client (Campbell, 1995). Additionally consultation can be used both to assess needs and to mobilize resources (Medway & Updyke, 1985).

Consultation is increasingly being adopted as the model of choice for psychologists working within a school setting (e.g. Labram, 1992; Dickinson, 2000). It has also been adapted for a range of consultee groups such as parents (Cobb & Medway, 1978), health professionals, clergy and police (Brown et al., 2001). Attention has also been given to providing consultation to networks of professionals (e.g. Potel & Moxham, 2000; Triseliotis et al., 1995; Dimmock & Dungworth, 1985).

Recent models of consultation can be seen as lying on a continuum ranging from a focus on process to a focus on content (e.g. see Cowburn, 2000; Wallace & Hall, 1996). Process consultation involves the consultant as a generalist facilitating the process of problem solving by working with the consultee. Consultation is seen as a collaborative process. Content consultation involves the consultant using specialist knowledge to solve problems while the consultee is passive. Brown et al. (2001) identified four major approaches to consultation. Two of these can be seen as falling at the content end of the continuum. Clinical consultation involves a health professional consulting with someone considered to have expertise in a clinical area. Typically the consultant will meet with the client and then advise the consultee on management of problems. Behavioural consultation similarly involves a consultant with expert knowledge guiding behavioural management of a problem. Mental health consultation, in contrast, encourages a collaborative relationship between consultant and consultee to promote the mental health of clients and to improve social support. Organizational consultation uses process or content consultation to help a consultee or consultees to manage an organization involving a client system with the same aim of promoting the well-being of clients.

Within consultation, the consultant can draw on a variety of other theoretical models: for example, humanistic, attachment and psychodynamic. Humanistic and attachment models can be particularly useful for understanding and meeting the carers' and the child's needs, and psychodynamic models for understanding and working with the network (see Chapter 2 and Sprince, 2000, 2002).

A large variety of psychological models have been used in consultation, which is reassuring, given the importance of flexible working tailored to each situation, for example:

- problem-solving model (Bergen, 1995)
- problem-focused model (Street et al., 1991)
- solution-focused model (Bremble & Hill, 2004)
- support model (Golding, 2004)
- systemic model (Campbell, 1995)
- psychoanalytic model (Sprince, 2002).

Whatever models are used, consultation offers an important space for consultees to step back and reflect on the myriad issues they are dealing with. These may include the client's problems; attempts to solve these; how effective these attempts are; whether their concerns are the same as the client's or as others in the network; what impact the situation is having on them personally; and how effectively the network is supporting its members and the child at the centre. Sprince (2005) considers that the intensity of projections of feelings within the network, and the urge to pass these on, prevent professionals from being able to engage in reflection. If reflection does not take place, then the depth of the child's needs and difficulties cannot be acknowledged.

Being a consultant is clearly a complex role. Research evidence has identified a formidable number of characteristics and practices associated with being an effective consultant in schools (see Knoff et al., 1995), of which many are relevant to consultations in the looked after children arena:

- openness
- ease with lack of immediate closure
- maintaining distance from consultee's problems
- combining problem solving with sensitivity to the consultee
- empathy, genuineness, active listening and paraphrasing
- using straightforward rather than technical language.

Other authors have identified the need to be comfortable with incomplete information (Caplan, 1970); the need to make all participants in the process feel equally valued (Golding, 2004); the ability to develop theoretically based hypotheses and to abandon them in the face of contradictory evidence (Caplan, 1970); coping with complexity (Harper & Spelman, 1994); taking a curious and reflective stance; and being clear about responsibilities and boundaries (Dickinson, 2000).

The current practice of consultation spans from one individual consulting another, to several agencies consulting a team. With such a range of practice on offer, it can be difficult to identify whether and what type of consultation might help a given problem effectively. Later in the chapter, a model will be presented which aims to aid decision making and clarify the usefulness of different models for different situations. However, some aspects of consultation, particularly the theoretical stance, will be in the control of the consultant, affected by his or her training, competence and preference, as well as his or her ability to match process to the needs of the consultees.

HOW CONSULTATION DIFFERS FROM DIRECT THERAPY, TRAINING AND OTHER MEETINGS

Consultation differs from direct therapy, in that it frequently does not involve the client face to face and it may not focus directly on the client's issues. When it does, it will be concerned with the consultees' understanding of and ability to work with these issues. Consultation is concerned with changing the context in which clients are experiencing their difficulties, whereas direct therapy usually helps the clients to change or adapt to their surroundings. Consultation may be used with the clients present, as Jones and colleagues (1997) have described in an account of a consultation service for adult mental health clients. This use of consultation has only recently been considered with looked after children but could be useful in some cases (Sprince, 2005). When the client is present, consultation differs from therapy in the following ways:

- the focus of the intervention is on the context in which the client experiences his or her difficulties;
- use of a reflecting team in the room during the meeting;
- encouraging the client to make use of resources in his or her community rather than relying on expert therapists.

Jones and his colleagues found that 'in many consultations ... an alternative construction of the person's problem effectively dissolved it' (p. 23) so that therapy was not needed. Some psychologists would define this way of working as 'therapy' in itself, and as good consultation is indeed therapeutic, the line between therapy and consultation can be hazy. A helpful distinction suggested by Wallace and Hall (1996) is that consultation facilitates problem solving whereas therapy facilitates personal growth.

Consultation differs from training in that it is tailored to a specific situation or client (e.g. a 7-year-old child who has many difficulties including displaying overtly sexualized behaviours) as opposed to training designed for the generic needs of a client group (e.g. a training programme about the needs of children who have been sexually abused). Similarly with counselling, the difference from consultation lies in the focus of the work. A consultant may make use of counselling techniques, which if carried out to improve the consultee's quality of life, would aptly be called counselling, but if used to enable a carer or professional to work more effectively with a child, would fall into the remit of consultation.

Various statutory meetings surround the lives of looked after children, such as reviews and case conferences. These generally have specific purposes, targets, attendees and timetables. The main difference between these meetings and consultation is that consultation can be set up to suit various needs of the child, the carers, the professionals or the network. Statutory meetings are clearly vital, but by their very nature are unable to be sufficiently flexible to meet every need in each case. Statutory meetings are agenda driven and therefore not able to provide a reflective space for attendees to think about the child and the placement in quite the same way. They are also constrained over who must be invited. This can prevent certain types of discussion – for example, it would be difficult for a carer to explore certain issues with the child or family of origin present. Reviews and case conferences are also decision-making forums and do not normally allow much time for an exploration of 'how it is' currently caring for or working with the child, for consideration of the child's history as context for this and for reflection on this information by members of the child's network. Consultation, in contrast to the review or case conference, is designed to be a supportive space in which these processes can happen.

THE RELEVANCE OF CONSULTATION FOR LOOKED AFTER AND ADOPTED CHILDREN

The relevance or usefulness of consultation for working with looked after children stems partly from the complex network of carers, professionals and birth family members that are involved with each child (see Chapter 2). This complexity also exists for adopted children, even though not all of the network members are as actively engaged. In addition to this complexity, the children bring powerful emotions with them, which are unconsciously transmitted within the network surrounding them (Sprince, 2002, 2005). Wilson (2005) has spoken of powerful feelings organizing social workers and other professionals. Consultation provides a reflective space within which to identify and contain these emotions, and to use them to deepen understanding of the child's experience. Deeper, shared understanding will underpin more consistent and effective action for the child by the consultees.

Consultation has also developed out of the therapeutic dilemma that it is unsafe to carry out therapy with a child who is not in a secure, long-term placement, yet some form of intervention is needed in order to help the child to reach this goal. Therapy with a child who has been so severely neglected or abused that he or she has had to be taken into care, will involve looking at painful issues. Therapists will only undertake such work if the child is in a settled, long-term placement, as it is important for the child to be able to draw upon close, reliable relationships as support during this process. Not having such support could render the therapy ineffective because the child is unable to engage in it sufficiently. At the other extreme, carers or teachers may feel unable to contain the heightened emotions that the child experiences during therapy, and this may threaten the viability of a foster or educational placement.

The most effective way to change a child's behaviour in the short term is in fact to change the context. This can be accomplished through various ways such as parent training programmes or family therapy, but for children who are looked after, consultation has emerged as a particularly effective way of making changes in the network. Bremble and Hill (2004, p. 30) have questioned, 'Is there an alternative to the current dichotomy of "change the children" or "change the environment"?' in an account of successful, multi-agency, solution-focused consultation. Their approach achieves both and they believe this is due to:

- the importance of the participants having their concerns heard and contained and as a consequence being able to contain the anxieties of others in the network;
- getting rid of the myth that 'expert' CAMHS staff hold the answer;
- changing the focus from the problem to the solution of a preferred future for the child and the network.

Golding (2004) also addresses the first two points with her focus on a 'collaborative approach which acknowledges the expertise of all those attending' (p. 75). In her work, the psychologist's role is to listen to the story and provide a psychological formulation to further the discussion. However, this expert role is used in a collaborative way. The psychologist respects the expertise of those in the room and offers a perspective which, when combined with the expert knowledge of all those attending, can move discussion and problem solving forward. The idea is that by combining expertise the consultant and consultees come to a new shared understanding of the child and his or her emotional and practical needs that can inform finding a way forward. It is therefore the combining of the expertise (facilitated by the psychologist) that leads to the outcome of the consultation. In the process, all of those attending have an opportunity to feel listened to and therefore this process is also supportive.

Adoptive parents share the frustration in accessing services for their children (Rushton, 2004), but are often coping with different issues from foster carers. Hartman and Laird (1990) have suggested that many adoptive families experience a lot of powerlessness in relation to their parenting:

- over their ability to become biological parents;
- in relation to the adoptive agency which decides whether or not they can adopt children;
- over the adopted children's behaviours which they perceive to be a result of heredity and past experience;
- over their ability to parent the children successfully.

They suggest that consultation empowers adoptive parents by involving them in the processes of deciding what interventions will help their children:

> An important practice principle, then, is to work in such a way that helps empower adoptive families, a way that increases their ability to shape their own situations. This principle implies an egalitarian, collaborative, consultative model in which all concerned contribute their own special resources and skills to the problem-solving situation.
>
> (Hartman & Laird, p. 228)

THE AIMS OF CONSULTATION FOR LOOKED AFTER AND ADOPTED CHILDREN

The two fundamental aims of consultation for looked after and adopted children will be to improve their immediate quality of life and their longer-term prospects. These aims may be achieved in many ways, which need to be more clearly specified for consultation to be effective. Some of the more common aims in relation to the network are to:

- promote a shared understanding of the child and the needs of the carer;
- facilitate more effective communication between professionals and throughout the network;
- hear and validate the different views in the network in order to promote shared understanding;
- improve the consistency of approach by all professionals;
- create a care plan that is adopted by all stakeholders.

Aims that focus on the carer are to:

- support the carers in their challenging role;
- help carers to become more 'therapeutic';
- support direct therapy for the child and carers.

As with all referrals it is important to be clear about the desired outcomes of the referral before either accepting the referral or planning the intervention. For consultation, this may also entail pre-consultation investigations with different parts of the system, or this may be an early aim of the consultation process.

A MODEL OF CONSULTATION FOR LOOKED AFTER AND ADOPTED CHILDREN

Given the wide range of consultation that has been reported for use with looked after and adopted children, we thought it might be helpful to create a simple model of types of consultation to aid decision making in practice. Consultation for looked after children can be grouped as shown in Figure 6.1.

Reasons for Choosing Spotlight or Wide Focus Consultation

The ultimate aim of consultation is always to provide some benefit or improvement to the child's life, though this may sometimes be achieved by focusing on the needs of one part of the network – for example, by providing support to the carers. Regardless of whether the primary aim of the consultation is to provide input focused on the needs of the child or on some other part of the network, the following method of deciding what type of consultation is needed can be used:

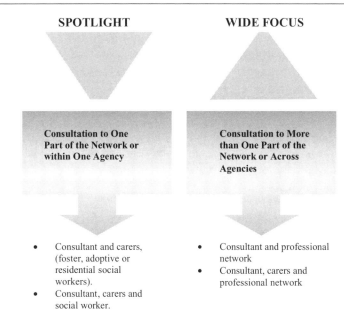

Figure 6.1   A model of consultation

- If the aim of the consultation is to achieve change in only one part of the network – for example, to provide support to foster carers who are doing a good job in stressful circumstances – then a spotlight consultation is likely to be an appropriate forum for providing support and for helping clients to consider other ways of understanding their difficulties and finding solutions (Jones et al., 1997).
- If the aim of the consultation is to achieve change in more than one part of the network – for example, if there are difficulties at the carer's home and at school, or concerns over health and contact with the birth family – a wide focus consultation will be more suitable. In a wide focus consultation it is important not to assume that all members of the network are seeking the same sort of help (Christie & Fredman, 2001).

SPOTLIGHT CONSULTATION

It is theoretically possible for spotlight consultation to be offered to any part of the network, but when working with looked after and adopted children it normally involves carers, with or without social service professionals.

Three case examples are included in this section to illustrate spotlight consultation with foster carers, adoptive parents and residential social workers.

The first case study is an example of a consultee-centred (Caplan, 1970) case consultation, in which a specialist professional helps a foster carer, with a focus on an individual child.

Case Example: Consultant and Foster Carers

A couple who had been providing foster care for a 5-year-old boy, Tom, for 10 months, were concerned about his behaviour. Initially he had been charming and easy to care for but over the past four months his behaviour had significantly deteriorated. He was behaving well at school and seemed to enjoy it a lot. The foster carers wished him to have therapy for the early abuse and neglect he had suffered as they felt this caused his difficult behaviour. They were particularly concerned that he had started calling his foster mum a filthy slut and refused to do what she asked. He generally behaved better with his foster dad.

Tom was referred to the CAMHS team for therapy. The clinical psychologist invited the foster carers to a meeting and gave them the option of bringing their family placement social worker and Tom's social worker if they wished.

The carers came on their own as they wished to have an early meeting and not wait for a convenient date for everyone. The psychologist spoke to Tom's social worker prior to the meeting in order to learn about his history. She then listened carefully to the carers' concerns and was able to explain some of his behaviours and suggest some changes to their management of him that might help immediately. In particular she engaged the couple in a discussion about how the husband could explicitly model appropriate ways of behaving towards his wife, as well as talking to Tom about this. The carers were able to come up with many ideas, such as thanking her in Tom's presence for cooking meals. They were reassured that Tom would be able to learn from their example, just as their own children had. The psychologist also suggested some modifications to the ways in which they were managing Tom's behaviour and recommended that they attend a group for foster carers on Facilitating Attachment. She explained that bringing in an outside expert to work directly with Tom at this stage might further undermine the foster mum's authority and interfere with the development of healthy respect and attachment.

The carers found the group helpful and with support from the psychologist were able to substantially improve Tom's relationship with his foster mum.

This next case study is an example of a systemic consultation concerning a 12-year-old girl whose adoptive parents have divorced and her adoptive mother has remarried. The consultants make use of a reflecting team in which one member conducts the interview and the other listens and takes notes. Towards the end of the session the interviewer's colleague is invited to reflect aloud on what he or she has just heard. These reflections are listened to by clients as well as the interviewer who afterwards resumes the discussion with the clients by asking for their feedback on the reflections. (If there is more than one person in the reflecting team they will have a reflective conversation with each other, also in the presence of the consultees.)

Case Example: Consultant and Adoptive Parents

An adoptive mother referred herself to a specialist adoption support service as she was concerned about her 12-year-old adopted daughter, Amy, who seemed to be very reluctant to make the transition from little girl to emerging adolescent and was presenting as very incompetent and immature. She had just started secondary school where the difference between her and her peers was becoming painfully obvious. She was also proving very difficult at home where she seemed to take no responsibility for her actions and seemed unable to learn from her mistakes. When she was booking an appointment it emerged that this adoptive mother was divorced from the partner with whom she had adopted Amy and had remarried and had a subsequent child by her second marriage. The adopting couple had two birth daughters who were young adults. They had adopted Amy from an extremely traumatic background, as her mother had committed suicide and her father was in prison for the murder of her little brother. The consultation team encouraged the adoptive mother to include both her ex-husband and her current husband in the session. In the event, the adopting couple (i.e. adoptive mother and ex-husband) attended.

During the course of the session (which lasted an hour and a half), it was possible through systemic questions to piece together the story of the early history, which was followed by a spell for Amy in a foster family to whom she had become very attached. Indeed the feeling had been mutual and there was still some contact face to face as well as by 'phone all those years later. The story of the adoption and later divorce of the adoptive couple was reviewed, as was the current situation, with Amy living with her mum, step-father and baby half brother but spending weekends with her adoptive dad and the younger of her two adoptive sisters who had chosen to live with her dad.

Feedback was offered to the 'couple' via the reflecting team discussion on the day and followed up in a letter, which they each received. (The adoptive mother was encouraged to share her copy of the letter with her husband.) Key issues were summarized as follows:

- Amy is in a three-way developmental intersection dealing with major issues of: (1) adoption, (2) living with divorce in a step-family situation and (3) being on the threshold of adolescence. She has a lot on her plate.
- She needs to start getting her head around her tragic history. The previous foster carers could be crucial and the focus of contact could shift from social

visits to the gathering of first hand memories from them of Amy's parents. This would not necessarily involve her so much as her adoptive parents who could first gather the information and then filter it back to Amy as and when appropriate. The former carers could also be encouraged to treat her as a young lady rather than as a lost little girl, which is how they remember her.

- A link was made between the need to block out early trauma and the impact this may have on learning, as reflection may be too painful, and living in the here and now may seem preferable. It was suggested that by beginning to open up the past through sessions with a post-adoption support worker Amy might be more able to reflect generally, and this could improve her general ability to remember and learn.
- The adoptive couple's evident commitment to Amy, in spite of the divorce, was held up as a model of resilience and coping. This also extended to her sisters who were seen as role models who were coping in the adult world and who had experience of surviving adolescence and divorce.
- In looking back, both parents were reminded of what they had achieved with and for Amy and how many obstacles they had surmounted. They were encouraged to have faith in what they had achieved and to start giving Amy space to expand even if this involved her making mistakes. These were described as learning opportunities rather than situations from which she needed protection. The couple were congratulated on their achievements which included continuing to co-parent post-divorce and to work collaboratively for all three of their shared children.

Consultation with Residential Unit Staff

Consultations with residential staff raise different issues from those with foster carers. There is a large group of staff who work in shifts and who care for a group of children in a place that is not a 'family home' with all that entails in terms of habits, rituals and traditions. Issues that may arise in providing consultation to residential units are:

- How do the units decide who should attend?
- Do the staff members see themselves as representatives for the staff group?
- If consultation concerns a particular child, which of their key workers should be in the meeting?
- It is not always possible to arrange the meeting to coincide with the key worker's shift.
- What role does the child's social worker have in this?

- It is important to ensure that the staff group are aware that the consultation is for them.
- The staff group are not always clear about what they want.
- It is vital to plan for achieving consistency following consultation.
- Plans being made very precipitously for the young people.

Consultations may focus on an individual young person in the unit, a generalized difficulty such as bedtimes or self-harm, or may address such issues as staff communication or morale. When focusing on a young person, there may be a need to involve professionals from other agencies and the consultation will take on a wider focus. On other occasions, it will be sufficient to work with the unit staff, for example, to reassure them that a young person's need for nurture and socialization (such as learning to eat at a table, using cutlery, in the company of others) is greater than their need for therapy. Maslow's (1970) Hierarchy of Needs is helpful on such occasions (see Figure 6.2).

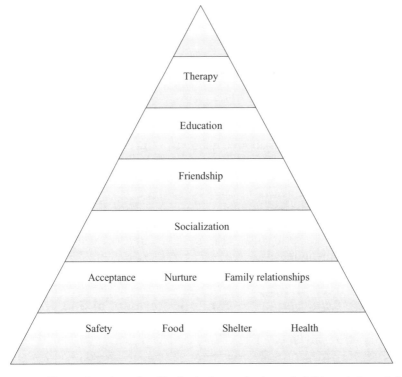

Figure 6.2 Hierarchy of needs of looked after and adopted children (adapted from Maslow, 1970)

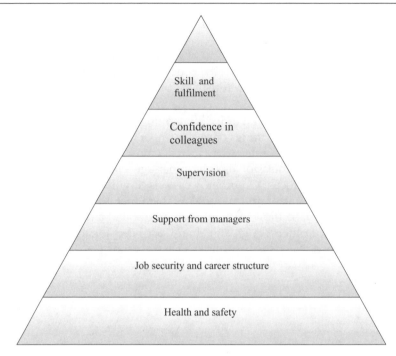

Figure 6.3   Hierarchy of needs of staff working with looked after children (adapted from Maslow, 1970)

Sprince (2005) also talks about a hierarchy of needs for professionals, who may have many fears, particularly of allegations by young people. She argues that professionals, too, need to feel safe in order to work effectively (see Figure 6.3).

The next case study, involving a consultant and some staff in a residential unit, illustrates how consultation may start with a focus on a young person's behaviour but develop to consider issues that have a bearing on this and on staff morale in the unit.

Case Example: Consultant and Residential Unit Staff

Andrew, a 15-year-old boy, had been accommodated in a residential unit for two years following several failed foster placements. He left home when he was 9 years of age because of sexual abuse by his mother, which was discovered when his friend and neighbour disclosed abuse by her also. The period in the residential unit was the most stable of his life, though his behaviour was a cause of much concern. He had formed a close relationship with Darren, one of his key workers. A referral was made to a clinical psychologist when Andrew's behaviour escalated. It had been known for some time that he shoplifted, drank alcohol and smoked cannabis, but he had recently started becoming aggressive and violent towards staff, including Darren. The staff wanted to find out what had caused the change and how to manage the behaviours.

The psychologist decided to hold a consultation meeting with as many people in the unit as possible, and a handover meeting of the shift in which Darren worked was chosen for this purpose. Ten people, including the deputy manager, came to the meeting.

Many concerns were expressed over Andrew's behaviour, but two recent changes seemed important. He had recently been allocated a new co-key worker, Mike, who was African. Andrew had insulted Mike with racist comments and Mike had retaliated by shouting at Andrew and refusing to let him have a bus pass. It also emerged that Darren was hoping to emigrate to Canada with his girlfriend, but was being careful not to let Andrew know until a date was set, as he was concerned about the effect that the news and the uncertainty would have on him.

In the consultation, the psychologist reflected on the meaning of secrets to Andrew and the possibility that he may be hypervigilant to adults concealing things from him. Darren still felt that his plans were not sufficiently certain to warrant telling Andrew. In discussion it emerged that there was a difference of opinion between the two shifts as to how much Andrew suspected about Darren's plans. There were also mixed views about Andrew's behaviour towards Mike, with some staff expressing support for Mike and others feeling that he shouldn't have reacted to Andrew in the way that he did.

The psychologist acknowledged the different opinions in the room. She facilitated a discussion around how people would manage the need for keeping some information private from their own children; and how they would react to racist remarks from their children and perceived over-reaction from their partner in this situation. Some themes that emerged in this discussion were:

- the need for discussion about why information should be withheld from the children and if agreed, both partners to adhere to this;
- agreement to be reached on how to manage behaviours of concern;
- one partner to support the other;
- if one partner was not happy about how the other treated the children, this should be raised without the children present.

The psychologist wondered whether any of these ideas could be used in the unit. This led to discussion over consistency between shifts and problems with handover meetings. The deputy manager asked if it would be possible to have some input specifically on these issues and it was agreed that the psychologist would facilitate an away day for the unit staff.

The consultation meeting had started with the aim of understanding and managing Andrew's aggressive and violent behaviour and had ended with a plan to work on aspects of staff organization and team working that affected the quality of care given to all young people in the unit.

WIDE FOCUS CONSULTATION

Wide focus consultation involves a larger group of consultees, usually from different teams or agencies. The aim may be to help the network to function more effectively and consistently in their interactions with the child who has been referred. Alternatively the aim may be to help the network to support the child's carers more effectively. Whatever the aim, the size of the meeting can make it challenging to manage.

One visual image used in consultation by Nissim (personal communication) is that of 'creating a clearing' from which to hack out paths into the undergrowth of information held by different parts of the network. The image can be extended to convey the uncertainty as to whether a concealed 'tiger' may be lurking or a 'beautiful plant' concealed in the undergrowth. Wide focus consultation has the task of enabling all parts of the network to join together in confronting the tiger or finding the beautiful plant. Another image used by Wilson (2005) is that of a dance. He talks of finding the pattern that is organizing the behaviour of the professionals, for example fear of complaints, and says that the task of the consultant is to introduce a difference. In this way, consultation is a context for repositioning practice.

In a wide focus consultation it can be helpful to have two consultants, one of whom may chair the meeting, to help to keep track of all the information, to offer different perspectives on the information shared and to help each other to reflect on the content of the meeting. Essentially it can be helpful to have two consultants given the increased complexity of wide focus consultation. There are different ways that these can be used, such as having clearly defined roles of chair and consultant or through use of a reflecting team with a rotating consultant who manages the consultation.

Being a facilitator or an expert may vary between consultation sessions or within a single consultation meeting, depending on the situation. Flexibility within the structure is likely to be associated with improved satisfaction and better outcomes from the process. Casey et al. (1994) have suggested that clinical psychologists often take on the role of assembling pieces of the puzzle to make the picture clearer. The same metaphor can apply to chairs of consultation meetings. In this post-modern era, we tend to be less comfortable with one dominant expert, but to prefer a consultant who also weaves in others' perspectives and knowledge. Ultimately the aim may be to help consultees to become observers in the process they are part of (Wilson, 2005).

Examples of Wide Focus Consultation

Two examples of wide focus consultation are offered in this section, each from multi-agency teams designated for working with looked after children. The first example comes from a team that works with the holistic health needs of children referred. The second example, the Worcestershire Model, comes from a team that was set up to provide support to carers.

In the first illustration, a specialist Looked After Children team has been asked to provide therapy for a 12-year-old girl whose foster carers are worried that she is staying out late in an unsafe area of town where drug dealing and prostitution are known to occur. The team has a policy of convening a consultation session as the starting point for working with each case referred. The sessions derive their structure from systems theory. The reason for this is that referrals to the team are usually made after other attempts to intervene have been tried. Many agencies, services and professionals may be involved with the child, their family and carers. The general aims of the team's consultations are to:

- gather together the carers and professionals involved with the child;
- share information about the child and how the different professionals are involved with him or her;
- encourage understanding among the professionals of each others' roles and perspectives;
- find a shared way of understanding the concerns;
- find ways of working consistently to support each other's interventions rather than set up contradictions which the child or carers will need to reconcile.

The team uses a chairperson who manages the meeting, another professional who listens and may offer an expert voice, and a scribe if there is anyone available to take on this role. Otherwise this task has to be managed as well as chairing or listening. Sometimes this 'home team' will ask for a break in which to reflect together on what they have heard, either in the room or outside. If this has not been decided in advance, the chairperson will normally take this decision.

Case Example: Consultants, Foster Carers, Social Services, Health and Education

Katy (12 years) had been in care for a year. Her mother was a heroin user and had been unable to provide good enough care since her husband left three years ago. Katy's younger brother Shaun (7 years) was taken into care at the same time, and was placed with the same foster carers. He remains there in a successful long-term placement. Katy was moved to another placement after six months because she kept on running away. It was thought at the time that she would be happier away from her brother. Katy was also experiencing increasing difficulties at school.

At the time of referral, Katy was in danger of being excluded from school and her foster carers had concerns over her behaviour and her safety. The referral to the Looked After Children team requested assessment and individual therapy for Katy.

The team decided that a consultation meeting involving the three agencies Education, Health and Social Services was needed to share information about Katy.

The team did not feel it would be in Katy's interests to carry out an assessment without knowing more about the whole system surrounding Katy. However, the suggestion of a consultation meeting was respectfully phrased as a time efficient way of gathering information from all relevant people, prior to making decisions about how best the team could help. The team made a commitment to help and not just conduct the consultation (unless the consultation was sufficient).

The team invited Katy's social worker, foster carers and the designated teacher for looked after children at her school to a consultation meeting and also asked them who else should be invited. The invitation list became as follows:

- Head teacher at Katy's school
- Designated teacher for looked after children
- School nurse
- Katy's social worker
- Family placement social worker
- Katy's current foster carers
- Shaun's social worker
- Social worker, Looked After Children team
- Clinical psychologist, Looked After Children team
- Assistant psychologist, Looked After Children team.

The first consultation meeting was well attended. The meeting was chaired by the social worker from the Looked After Children team. The assistant psychologist took notes. Notes from each consultation meeting are sent to everyone who has attended the meeting, in the first instance for corrections. It is decided in the meetings who else should ultimately receive the notes. Notes carry a record of the meeting and agreed action points.

Katy's social worker was first invited to give the history of and reason for the referral, followed by the concerns and experiences of the foster carers and then the other professionals present. The following story emerged, which contained new information for all present.

Katy's mother and father had just about coped with the two children despite the mother's heroin use, as their father did not work and was able to carry out some child care. Katy's father left when his wife had an affair and became pregnant. She miscarried and the affair ended, but in the meantime Katy's father had met someone else and moved to another town. He sent cards to the children, but developed suspicions that they weren't his children, and so did not wish to have contact. Katy and Shaun missed their father badly, but whereas Shaun blamed their mother for having the affair, Katy became angry with their father for leaving.

Katy's mother became short of money after her husband left and her heroin use increased. She became involved in prostitution in order to secure her supply. Social Services became involved when Shaun's school became concerned about neglect and made a child protection referral. This culminated in the children being taken into care.

Katy and Shaun were happy at first in their foster placement but started to have bitter arguments over their parents, which always ended with Katy running off. Initially she stayed away for a few hours, but when she was absent overnight the foster carers requested a different placement for her. They thought her relationship with her brother was the cause and they were concerned for her safety.

However, Katy continued to run off in three subsequent placements, usually when she was unhappy or when her carers tried to insist she did something she didn't want to do, such as homework.

Katy was also behaving inappropriately at school. She was considered to be capable of the work but not able to sustain concentration. She distracted other pupils by constantly chatting in class and was insolent to teachers. The school's solution of sending her to the Pupil Support Unit was no longer working as she had become just as disruptive there. Katy had also started leaving the school premises without permission.

The first task of the consultation session was to establish where responsibility for Katy lay if she ran off, as this was a cause of friction between all parties. School staff believed this lay with the foster carers and they believed it lay with Social Services. The social worker clarified that the police should be called.

Once this issue had been resolved, conversations focused on how to maintain both the foster and the school placement. The foster carers were able to begin to see how they could support the school staff and vice versa.

When asked about Katy's strengths, the school staff revealed that Katy had a talent for dance and sports. The games staff wanted her to be in the school netball team but concerns about what her behaviour might be like during 'away matches' prevented this from happening.

The foster carers were unaware of Katy's sporting ability, and became keen to encourage it. School staff were keen to include her in the netball team as a reward for good behaviour, but the foster carers were doubtful that this would work. They also felt it was unethical to deprive Katy of this opportunity. A compromise was reached with the foster carers offering to accompany the netball team to away matches if Katy were selected. The carers also planned to buy a basketball hoop for Katy's forthcoming birthday and to investigate local dance classes.

The major achievement of this consultation meeting was to allow school staff and foster carers to hear each other's concerns and to facilitate working together for Katy.

Katy became a member of the netball team, and behaved well during away matches. She told the foster carers that her Mum had been good at sports at school. She stopped running away from home and school, and concerns over drugs and prostitution decreased.

Her behaviour during school and in the foster home is improving slowly and she has made friends with another girl in the netball team. There are many issues that still need to be worked on, but the discovery of Katy's talent, and the willingness of the network to foster this has become a major resilience factor for Katy.

The Worcestershire Model of Consultation

The Integrated Service for Looked After Children (ISL) aims to improve the life chances of children and young people living within Worcestershire by enhancing the support provided for the carers, schools, and direct to the children. A core service within ISL is the Worcestershire Model of Consultation (Golding, 2004). This provides consultation for carers supported by their professional network and includes relevant professionals from the statutory agencies and, when appropriate, from the voluntary sector. The consultation provides a reflective space in which carers and the related network can explore the child in placement in a way that both supports the carers and provides ideas for a way forward. The consultation allows those involved with the child to reflect on their own role and plans and to focus on how this fits with the roles and plans of others involved. The whole network can gain shared understanding of the child, insight about current issues involving the child and a common belief in how to best aid that child while supporting the carer and their family. The therapist and chairperson aim for a collaborative model for the consultation in which they work in partnership with the consultees in exploring problems and finding potential solutions. The chairperson attends to the process of the consultation, ensuring that the story is told and that everyone has an opportunity to feed into the telling of the story. Within this the chairperson ensures that the carer has time and space to tell their story with a unique opportunity to 'tell it as it is'. The chairperson has to keep in mind the aims of the consultation and to ensure that the process meets these aims, dealing with any distractions as they arise. The therapist listens to the unfolding story, seeking clarification when relevant. His or her role is to provide a psychological formulation that will move the discussion forward. In other words, psychological theory and understanding are used to provide a possible explanation of the child's current functioning and behaviour in the context of past experience. The consultants then facilitate discussion leading to increased understanding and joint problem solving. The psychological expertise brought to this process is the unique responsibility of the therapist, but the use of this expertise becomes a collaborative process.

Case Example: The Worcestershire Model

Jon is a 5-year-old boy who experienced severe neglect and physical abuse within his family of origin. His mother suffers from depression and occasional psychotic episodes. His father is prone to violence. Both parents are drug users. Jon was removed from their care when he was $3^1/_2$ years old. He lived in three short-term foster placements before moving to his current pre-adoptive placement. Within this placement he is difficult to manage because of extreme overactivity, temper outbursts, and difficulty separating from his carers. A CAMHS therapist and a paediatrician already support Jon and his family, while education workers support Jon at school. A referral is made to The Integrated Service for Looked After Children (ISL) for further therapeutic help for the family. A consultation is recommended so that the pre-adoptive carers with their professional network can meet and reflect on the best way forward. The consultants are a social worker who acts as chairperson and a clinical psychologist. Consultees are the pre-adoptive mother and father supported by their fostering social worker, the child's social worker, the class teacher, the therapist and the paediatrician.

The aims of the consultation are to:

- explore Jon's current behaviour within the context of his early history;
- reach a shared understanding of Jon's behaviour, emotional and educational difficulties;
- explore with the carers and the school staff ways to manage Jon's behaviour and support his emotional and educational needs;
- plan how the network can support the carers and the school in these tasks.

The early part of the consultation provides an opportunity for the parents to share with the meeting the progress they are making in helping Jon to settle with them and also the considerable difficulty that they are experiencing in managing Jon on a day-to-day basis. They use this opportunity to talk of their concerns about Jon's behaviour not improving and their worry that they are not helping him. They also conveyed their emotional exhaustion in looking after Jon alongside their elder adopted daughter who has severe learning difficulties. They wonder whether the therapy is helping Jon and whether some form of medication might be a useful route to pursue. Jon's class teacher adds to this story, describing the disruptive influence Jon has had on the school, but that with full-time support and a very structured routine he is beginning to settle. She is very concerned about what will happen when the funding for the support ends. The social worker provides the background information and shares her concerns that Jon might not settle and that the placement might disrupt. She is also concerned about the lack of life story work that has taken place with Jon. The therapist describes the non-directive play therapy she is using with Jon and her feeling that Jon is currently stuck in exploring the early chaos in his life. The paediatrician is wondering whether to diagnose Jon with ADHD or attachment disorder. He is reluctant to begin medication because of Jon's age but is giving this some serious thought.

The consultants empathize with the consultees on how emotionally draining it is to care for and support Jon and reflect how uncertain everyone is about the way forward. They congratulate the carers on doing such a good job in helping Jon to settle with them but acknowledge the degree of difficulty this presents and the concerns about the impact on their elder daughter. The psychologist then facilitates a shared understanding of Jon as a child with emotional regulation difficulties and a compulsive need to control within relationships, describing how these might have arisen out of his early experience of being parented. Both the symptoms of ADHD and of attachment disorder are seen as being an effect of these core difficulties. This leads to a discussion of the relative merits of medication and alternative parenting strategies to help Jon. The consultant also draws attention to the resilience that Jon displays through his intelligence and ability to learn and his developing capacity to trust his parents and to use them to help him to feel secure. There is a general acknowledgement that Jon requires a lot of support and structure. Ways of achieving this in school and at home are considered.

Following discussion of these ideas the network decides:

- The paediatrician will continue to monitor Jon but will not prescribe medication currently. She will also support the school in obtaining a Statement of Educational Needs so that continuing support can be secured.
- A teacher within ISL will offer some extra short-term support to the school. The aims of this are to help the school to make the best use of the mainstream support available to them, and to help the staff to further develop their strategies for helping Jon.
- The carers, and the fostering social worker are invited to attend the fostering attachments group run within ISL. Here they can explore alternative parenting strategies.
- The fostering social worker decides to look at some opportunities for respite care for Jon to allow his parents some exclusive time with their daughter.
- The therapist decides to change his approach to involve the carers in the therapeutic work so that Jon's fragile attachment to them can be encouraged. He also agrees to include a life story element to this work supported by the social worker, cautioning however that the pace of this will need to be slow.
- The consultees agree that regular network meetings will be useful to ensure that they continue to work together to help Jon.

CONSULTATION FOR THE NETWORK

An important function of consultation that is not always openly expressed, is to encourage all members of the network to remain fully engaged in the enterprise of improving the quality of life of the focus child, and not to 'hand over' responsibility for providing a cure to 'experts'. As Sprince (2000, p. 431) has written, 'Few of us would consider taking an individual child into therapy without working with the family. For looked after children, parental responsibility is often in the hands of a complex organization of carers.... We have an obligation to learn to work more effectively with that larger family.' In consultation for the network this may helpfully extend to involving biological families, if they are able or willing to cooperate. Sprince (2005) has suggested that including the family of origin can both lead to increased empathy from the foster carers and to birth parents being better able to support the foster placements. Her accounts of psychoanalytically oriented consultation to organizations that work with looked after children (Sprince, 2000, 2002) illustrate how consultation can help the network to contain and work with the anxieties generated around children who have been traumatized by their early experiences.

Once the network around the child is functioning consistently and effectively, further interventions may be indicated. For example, extra support may be decided upon for the carer/family through further consultation, training or counselling. This aims to increase the ability of the carer to parent therapeutically or to help the family to function more healthily. The advantage of starting with consultation for the carer and the network is that the planned interventions will be consistent with other approaches and that the network will support these interventions.

However, if multiple simultaneous interventions are already occurring, consultation can help to facilitate consistency so that everyone working with and caring for a child agrees with, understands and supports each other's work, as in the following case example:

> Marcia spends half a day a week with a family support worker, attends an NSPCC run therapeutic group for sexual abuse survivors for an hour and a half each week and has recently been referred to the Pupil Support Unit at school. Each of the professionals working with Marcia had a different idea about the reason for her difficulties and a different strategy for helping her. This was not surprising, since until Marcia was referred to the Looked After Children team and a consultation meeting was called, not all of the professionals were aware of each other's involvement with her. Consultation facilitated a shared understanding and enabled a more streamlined approach by everyone in the network. The support worker became more engaged in supporting the school's initiatives during her afternoon with Marcia and both the support worker and school learned strategies from the NSPCC counsellor for responding to Marcia's sexualized behaviours.

Consultation for the network can also be a forum for discovering why 'tried and tested' interventions are not working; for example, why a child who has been responding well to boundaries in a successful foster care placement, has suddenly started to challenge the rules and to reject previously desirable rewards. The cause may lie in any part of the network from school to contact with the family of origin. A consultation meeting can be an efficient way of uncovering this and reflecting upon solutions.

EVALUATION OF THE EFFECTIVENESS
OF CONSULTATION

Medway and Updyke (1985) undertook a meta-analysis of 24 studies that explored mental health and school consultation. They concluded that consultation had a positive impact on consultees and clients with more pronounced effects on consultees. There was no difference in effectiveness between mental health, behavioural or organizational-based consultation for consultants, consultees or clients. In comparison to counselling, consultation has been shown to be more effective across a range of studies. These studies, however, refer to school situations and cannot be generalized to other settings. Little comparative research has been conducted outside of the school setting (Brown et al., 2001).

Evaluations of consultation services for looked after and adoptive children are rare. However, Nissim and Blow (2000) have reported mostly positive (e.g. we felt the professionals listened perceptively and helped us to talk through our difficulties; excellent opportunity to get different professional perspectives) and some negative (e.g. your discussion with each other we thought could have been done behind closed doors although we understood your strategy) experiences by adoptive and foster carers and social work users of a Family Placement Consultation Service.

Golding (2004) has demonstrated that the carer's understanding of the child changed following consultation. This finding was statistically significant but the issues underpinning the changed level of understanding were complex. Overall carers perceived the children as having more severe problems following consultation. The carers are living with little change in the children on a daily basis. Often they feel that lack of improvement in the child is a consequence of their fostering and they question whether their fostering practice is appropriate. Consultation appears to help carers to understand the severity of the problems the child brings into the placement. This leads to a different view of their relationship with the child. For example one foster carer commented:

> 'Having had no real direction or diagnosis of C. it was difficult to understand why no progress or anything seemed to make any difference to C.'s behaviour, which seemed to be deteriorating. Having talked to K. things fell into place, and we had less personal views of the reasons why C. was so abusive and violent.'

This increased understanding can in turn help foster carers to hold realistic expectations about what they can achieve, and this can have a positive impact on the placement. A social worker commented that:

> 'The consultation provided the carers with a greater understanding of the child's needs. The carers had high expectations of what they could receive from this child and by having a better understanding of his needs their expectations have lessened, which has helped the placement to be a little more stable.'

Foster carers reported feeling more supported and that their confidence had increased following the consultation. This suggests that gaining a new perspective on the child is helpful, but frustration at the lack of direct services for the children is also apparent.

The issues are complex, but it appears that consultation currently offers more to the consultees in the network than to the child or young person who has been referred, though this may be affected by the timing of the evaluation. Since the network needs to be functioning effectively, if the child's needs are to be met, it is clear that the child will benefit from the consultation later than the network, and possibly after evaluation measures have been taken. Consultation does at the very least appear to offer a robust and adaptable method of engaging the network. Sprince (2005) has stated that network meetings and meetings with workers are more effective than giving direct therapy for the children. This makes great sense and can be illustrated with an extreme example – when a child is in an abusive environment, it is recognized that changing this context is more important than offering therapy to the child.

ISSUES AND TENSIONS

Consultation is not a panacea for the problems of effective professional liaison. There are many issues that cannot always be resolved, and tensions that must be attended to if consultation is to be effective. Some of the more common issues and tensions are discussed in this section, but the wise consultant should expect and be prepared to help the meeting to work through unexpected problems that surface.

The consultation meeting may not be sufficient to contain the anxieties of all consultees. When one person feels greater anxiety there is a risk that he or she may precipitate action concerning the child that is out of step with the overall plan, thus reducing its effectiveness. Such idiosyncratic action can arise in any part of the network, from foster carers, teachers, health professionals or social workers. For example, the pressure of work in social work teams can create high levels of anxiety, which may lead to a search for 'cures' for children. This, combined with frustration at the slow pace at which other professionals can work, may result in a 'scatter-gun' approach to making referrals, rather than relying on the consultation plan. It is part of the consultant's role to ensure that all such concerns are heard and taken account of in consultation, to protect the coherence of the child's network.

Consultation for looked after children rarely involves the child or young person in the meeting, though consultations in other settings such as Adult Mental Health Services and CAMHS often do include the client. This raises issues of confidentiality and consent such as if, how or when the child is to be informed about the consultation; who can or should give consent; and how the family of origin should be involved particularly when the child is voluntarily accommodated. Who should be informed of the content of the meeting can also be an area of uncertainty. These issues need to be discussed and resolved either before or during the first consultation session.

Consultation is time intensive, as discussed at the beginning of the chapter. This unfortunately reduces time for other interventions. Golding (2004) found that while carers were satisfied with the consultation service, those who were most satisfied had consultation plus other support interventions. There is a need to balance time for consultation with time for other activities. The amount of time involved in consultation needs to be justified by its effectiveness; however, the long-term benefits are not known.

Within the consultation, time for 'Telling the Story' needs to be balanced with time for discussion of the story. It is not always easy to get this right. It is also important to get the right balance between consultant as expert and consultant as facilitator. Expertise can both facilitate discussion and end it. The consultant needs to make careful judgements about what level of expert formulation the network can make use of at each stage.

There are differing views about whether the consultant should meet the child. On the one hand, meeting the child gives the consultant extra information. On the other hand, not meeting the child enables the consultant to be more objective and more receptive to others' views about the child. It also means that the members of the network can feel that they are the experts about the child.

In consultation it is important to make sure that aims are clear and to identify and decide how to accommodate alternative agendas that may exist in the network. It is also important to ensure that the roles and responsibilities of all members of the network, particularly consultants and social workers are clear, since, by default, responsibility for making decisions about the child will fall to the social worker.

> In one case, when consultation sessions had led to a substantial improvement in a young person's challenging behaviour, the social worker's manager decided that the girl no longer needed her support worker and stopped the provision. This sadly coincided with difficult home contacts, and the girl's behaviour deteriorated severely, resulting in exclusion from a previously successful educational placement.

In this case the problem had been lack of communication over the decision. But similar issues can arise when senior managers are not present at consultation meetings. The social worker can leave the meeting, having formed a very different view of what should happen for the child but have difficulty convincing a manager who has not had the benefit of sharing the understanding arrived at in consultation. Senior managers are understandably most concerned when there are financial implications to the decision. Part of the task of the consultant is to make decisions about the level of seniority of staff invited to consultation sessions. Nevertheless, the consultant does not have the power to require attendance, and so it is the members of the network who will in the end decide who attends. Another strategy for addressing this issue can be to send feedback letters to senior managers, with the consent of participants, when issues crop up that need to be dealt with at their level.

CONCLUSIONS, CHALLENGES AND THE WAY FORWARD

To return to the beginning of the chapter: Is consultation worth the time investment? In the process of writing this chapter we have become even more convinced of the value of consultation for helping to facilitate positive outcomes for looked after and adopted children. However, since consultation is such a flexible tool, ultimately each consultation session will need to be judged on whether or not it has achieved the aims set for it.

It is proving a challenge to design well-controlled, ethical outcome studies to measure the overall effectiveness of consultation (Wolpert, personal communication) so there may not be a robust evidence base for some time. Direct therapy for children that is supported by evidence may seem to be a better choice, but clinical experience suggests that these approaches have not worked so well for looked after children (e.g. Minnis & Del Priore, 2001).

Consultation appears to be a workable solution to the dilemma of 'change the child or change the system', but it needs to be carefully managed as levels of anxiety in the network can run high. Many clinical and word-of-mouth reports suggest that it is so far the best way of integrating and engaging the network in the enterprise of improving outcomes for looked after children.

Some direct quotes from consultees are an encouraging conclusion to this consideration of consultation:

'I felt totally refreshed and positive after the meeting – the report gave me another boost. Coincidental or not, things have much improved – I feel relaxed and in control.'

(Foster carer)

'I still lacked confidence in what I was doing despite the progress that I knew J. had made. The positive feedback from the meeting was a big confidence booster which in turn helps me to help and understand J. even more.'

(Foster carer)

REFERENCES

Argyris, C. (1970) *Intervention, Theory and Method.* Massachusetts: Addison-Wesley.

Bergen, J.R. (1995) Evolution of a problem-solving model of consultation. *Journal of Educational and Psychological Consultation*, **6**(2), 111–123.

Bremble, A. & Hill, J. (2004) A model of multi-agency psychology consultation. *Clinical Psychology*, **34**, 29–33.

Brown, D., Pryzwansky, W.B. & Schulte, A.C. (2001) *Psychological Consultation. Introduction to Theory and Practice* (5th edn). Boston: Allyn & Bacon.

Brunning, H. & Huffington, C. (1991) The 'consultancy model': Empowering ourselves and our clients. *Clinical Psychology Forum*, **73** (November), 28–29.

Campbell, D. (1995) *Learning Consultation. A Systemic Framework.* London: Karnac Books.

Caplan, F. (1970) *The Theory and Practice of Mental Health Consultation.* London: Tavistock.

Casey, M., Harris, R., McDonald, K. & Todd, G. (1994) Opportunities for consultation. *Clinical Psychology Forum*, **65** (March), 36–38.

Christie, D. & Fredman, G. (2001) Working systemically in an adolescent medical unit: Collaborating with the network. *Clinical Psychology Forum*, **3** (July), 8–11.

Cobb, D.E. & Medway, F.J. (1978) Determinants of effectiveness in parent consultation. *Journal of Community Psychology*, **6**, 229–240.

Cowburn, M. (2000) Consultancy to groupwork programmes for adult male sex offenders: Some reflections on knowledge and processes. *British Journal of Social Work*, **30**, 635–648.

Dickinson, D. (2000) Consultation: Assuring the quality and outcomes. *Educational Psychology in Practice*, **16**(1), 19–23.

Dimmock, B. & Dungworth, D. (1985) Beyond the family, using network meetings with statutory child care cases. *Journal of Family Therapy*, **7**, 45–68.

Golding, K.S. (2004) Providing specialist psychological support to foster carers: a consultation model. *Child and Adolescent Mental Health*, **9**(2), 71–76.

Harper, D. & Spelman, D. (1994) Consultation to a professional network: Reflections of a would-be consultant. *Journal of Family Therapy*, **16**, 383–399.

Hartman, A. & Laird, J. (1990) Family treatment after adoption: Common themes. In D.M. Brodzinsky & M.D. Schechter (Eds), *The Psychology of Adoption* (pp. 221–239) New York: Oxford University Press.

Jones, S., Moss, D. & Haltom, R. (1997) A consultation service to adults referred as having mental health problems. *Clinical Psychology Forum*, **105** (July), 21–26.

Knoff, H.M., Hines, C.V. & Kromrey, J.D. (1995) Finalising the consultant effectiveness scale: An analysis and validation of the characteristics of effective consultants. *School Psychology Review*, **24**(3), 480–496.

Labram, A. (1992) The educational psychologist as consultant. In S. Wolfendale, T. Bryans, M. Fox, A. Labram & A. Sigston (Eds), *The Profession and Practice of Education Psychology. Future directions.* Cassell.

Laming, H. (2003) *The Victoria Climbié Inquiry: Report by Lord Laming.* Cm. 5730. London: TSO.

Maslow, A. (1970) *Motivation and Personality* (2nd edn). Harper & Row.

Medway, F.J. & Updyke, J.F. (1985) Meta analysis of consultation outcome studies. *American Journal of Community Psychology*, **13**, 489–505.

Minnis, H. & Del Priore, C. (2001) Implications from two studies. *Adoption and Fostering,* **25**(4), 27–38.

Nissim, R. (1993) Who Cares for Carers? Practical support. *Foster Care,* **73**, 12–13.

Nissim, R. & Blow, K. (2000) The family placement consultation service: Mutual feedback and change. *Context,* **52** (December), 3–4 and 6.

Ovretveit, J., Brunning, H. & Huffington, C. (1992) Adapt or decay: Why clinical psychologists must develop the consulting role. *Clinical Psychology Forum* (August), 27–29.

Oxford English Dictionary (1971) Compact Edition.

Potel, D. & Moxham, N. (2000) 'Working together' from principles to practice. *Clinical Psychology Forum,* **140**, 28–32.

Rushton, A. (2004) A scoping and scanning review of research on the adoption of children placed from public care. *Clinical Child Psychology and Psychiatry,* **9**(1), 89–106.

Saunders, L. & Broad, B. (1997) The health needs of young people leaving care. Leicester: DeMontfort University. In C. Kelly, S. Allan, P. Roscoe & E. Herrick (2003). The mental health needs of looked after children: An integrated multi-agency model of care. *Clinical Child Psychology and Psychiatry,* **8**(3), 323–335.

Sprince, J. (2000) Towards an integrated network. *Journal of Child Psychotherapy,* **26**(3), 413–431.

Sprince, J. (2002) Developing containment. Psychoanalytic consultancy to a therapeutic community for traumatised children. *Journal of Child Psychotherapy,* **28**(2), 147–161.

Sprince, J. (2005) *Towards an integrated network. A psychoanalytic perspective on consultation.* Paper presented at the 7th Annual Fostering and Adoption Conference, Bristol: UBHT, 1 March.

Street, E., Downey, J. & Brazier, A. (1991) The development of therapeutic consultations in child-focused family work. *Journal of Family Therapy,* **13**(3), 311–333.

Triseliotis, J., Sellick, C. & Short, R. (1995) *Foster Care Theory and Practice.* Batsford: BAAF.

Wallace, W.A. & Hall, D.L. (1996) *Psychological Consultation. Perspectives and Applications.* Pacific Grove: Brooks/Cole.

Wilson, J. (2005) *Muddles and multiple perspectives – A systemic, collaborative approach to consultation.* Paper presented at the 7th Annual Fostering and Adoption Conference, Bristol: UBHT, 1 March.

7

FINDING THE LIGHT AT THE END OF THE TUNNEL: PARENTING INTERVENTIONS FOR ADOPTIVE AND FOSTER CARERS

Kim S. Golding

This Thing That We Do

Frustration, elation, anger and fear,
An abundance of feelings,
I've felt through the years.
Repairing emotions,
Say nothing, just hear,
Holding a child,
And sharing a tear.
Rebuilding of families,
Is what we hold dear.
Supporting a parent,
When all is not clear,
Then preparing a child,
When moving draws near.

The purpose or reason,
Is not always plain,
So prepare yourself,

Thinking Psychologically About Children Who Are Looked After and Adopted
Edited by K.S. Golding, H.R. Dent, R. Nissim and L. Stott.
Copyright © 2006 John Wiley & Sons, Ltd.

For feeling the pain.
The feeling of anger,
We have to restrain,
When the damage we're healing,
Is causing a strain.
From shedding a tear,
I will never refrain,
However painful,
I'll do it again,
Just remember the reason,
Is giving, not gain.

But we would not do it,
If we got no pleasure,
Each child touches me,
My memories I treasure.
The sharing of lives,
Fun, sorrow and leisure,
The gift of a child,
Joy no man can measure.
The rebuilding of families,
Or creating of new,
Makes it worthwhile,
This thing that we do,
This thing is called Fostering,
And you can help too.

(Reproduced by permission of Kerry Hill)

Kerry's poem conveys something of the complexity of parenting a foster child and illustrates some of the tasks not present when raising a birth child. In writing this poem Kerry was thinking of her role as a short-term foster carer. In this role she has the dual task of helping the child to belong and be part of the family while also helping the child to move on. Kerry is also an adoptive parent. For long-term foster carers and adopters the task is no less complex as the child suffers the loss of previous families, the difficulties of trusting this new family, and the feeling of difference in not having been born within the family. Foster and adoptive carers therefore need a high level of parenting skills to provide the special care these hurt children need. This chapter acknowledges the complexity of this parenting task and explores the way professionals can support these carers and parents.

Freud (1959) records one of the earliest descriptions of an indirect intervention with a parent; the aim of this was to improve the behaviour and emotional well-being of a child. He instructed a father in strategies for resolving the underlying phobic impulses and symptoms of his son. This early intervention is an example of parent training, but in this case the parent is trained in psychodynamic interventions. More typically indirect interventions have focused on training parents in behavioural techniques. Behavioural parent training began in the 1960s. This aimed to modify negative child behaviours, to strengthen the family unit and to provide parents with new resources to enhance skills and efficacy in parenting. Typically these interventions involve health professionals in guiding parents to accurately identify problems, carry out an assessment, and implement a treatment plan. Therefore parents, acting as co-therapists, are the primary agents of change for their children. More recently, parent training has drawn on a wider theoretical base than behavioural and social learning theory, with a focus not just on managing behaviour but also on sensitively responding to and empathizing with the child's needs and emotional difficulties.

This chapter and Chapter 8 will explore the use of parenting interventions within foster and adoptive care. In this chapter psychological models that can be usefully applied to interventions will be explored, together with a discussion of a range of group and individual interventions developed for foster and adoptive families. Chapter 8 will build on this with discussion of a comprehensive service for parents of adopted children.

THE TASK OF PARENTING A FOSTERED OR ADOPTED CHILD

Whether a new child is born into or enters a family via adoption or fostering, a major readjustment is needed. The presence of another individual within the family impacts on all family members and on the pattern of interactions previously developed. The whole family has to work hard to adjust to the new reality and, to varying extents, to manage the loss of the family that was before the child arrived. This is a process of family reconstruction involving changes to family practice and family narratives (Hart & Luckock, 2004).

However, there are a range of tasks with which foster carers, and many adoptive parents, may need help and guidance that go beyond the normal adjustment to a new child. These tasks make the process of family reconstruction more complex and difficult. Parenting interventions need to take into account the complexity that carers face in parenting a child, which also involves:

- Relating to the family of origin. Foster carers relate to the families directly, facilitating the children's continuing relationship with them through direct and indirect contact. Adoptive parents help children to understand and adjust to the fact of their adoption. This is an ongoing process that is never complete but is revisited at different developmental and life stages. Additionally, adoptive families are increasingly involved in accepting and facilitating different levels of contact with families of origin either through indirect letterbox contact, visits to siblings adopted by different families, or, in the case of open adoptions, contact with birth parents and other family members.

- Parenting siblings can include birth siblings, non-related siblings and/or a combination of biological and adopted or fostered children (and sometimes all three!). The parents have to help these siblings to develop healthy relationships. Rivalry can be intense between siblings with a shared or similar history of not getting their needs consistently and predictably met. Additionally, it is not uncommon to see siblings re-enact past abusive experience within the sibling relationship, therefore needing a higher level of supervision than is usual. The carers' biological children can struggle to accept and build a relationship with the new member of the family. They may resent the loss of attention from their parents, have unrealistic expectations of what their new brother or sister brings to the family or be concerned about the impact of abusive behaviour on their parents.

- Fostering or adopting a child has an impact on the whole family and their support network. This affects siblings, marital partners and the wider family and friendship network. It also impacts on the community that the carers live within. Getting on with the neighbours and socialization at the school gate can take on very different meanings when the fostered or adopted child's challenging behaviour has impacted upon these adults and their families. Parenting interventions tend to focus on the dyadic relationship between carer and child. This can fail to acknowledge and support the difficulties the whole family network are having in adjusting to the reality of adoption or fostering, and can miss opportunities to provide more systemic help.

Despite this complexity, foster and adoptive parents, like all parents, need to develop a healthy relationship with the children they are parenting. They need to provide stability for the children and the experience of a continuous relationship within which the children feel valued and accepted. Typically, however, adopted and fostered children will resist such environments because they do not meet their expectations of the world. They will resist trusting and responding to the carer, leading to anxiety, distrust, criticism, anger and contempt. Alternatively they may relish the attention and sympathy that they are now receiving, leading to a yearning for all the care and affection that they have needed but not received in the past (Bowlby, 1988). Either way the children's behaviour can overwhelm the parenting skills of their new parents, sometimes leading to the breakdown of the placement.

There are likely to be many factors that impact on the quality of the relationships that develop within fostering and adoptive families. Interventions need to acknowledge these multiple factors. Thus the age of the child and experience of previous placements will combine with characteristics such as temperament and degree of sociability. The experience and expectations of the carers, the needs of the whole family and the degree of support available will all impact on the development of relationships with the foster or adopted child. While interventions will not be able to address all these factors it is important to maintain an awareness of them when tailoring interventions for individual families.

In a study of late-placed children in adoptive and foster placements, Quinton et al. (1998) found that stability of placement depended upon parenting skills, perceptions and experience. There was a close relationship between the child's behaviour, the parenting style and placement stability. Around 60% of new parents were experiencing at least some difficulty with their parenting role. Commonly difficulties were experienced in responding sensitively, expressing warmth and in day-to-day management. When faced with unusually challenging behaviours, experienced parents felt deskilled but found it hard to ask for help. Poorer parenting was strongly associated with problems in the development of mutually satisfying relationships and with the child's behaviour. The authors conclude that the quality of the relationship was critical. Parents with a satisfactory relationship were better able to tolerate behavioural difficulties and to handle the children better. The child who was slow to attach and develop a relationship, however, frequently taxed the capacity of new parents to maintain their positive feelings. These parents needed help to maintain their warmth and sensitivity and not to withdraw and reject the child.

In a study of 83 children adopted between 10 and 43 months, Lieberman (2003) throws light on why development of a satisfactory relationship can be problematic. She found that parents tended to overlook or minimize the children's signals that they were anxious or needed care. They misinterpreted difficult behaviour as a sign that the child did not care for them rather than understanding this as a communication of anxiety and fear of loss. They often responded to the behaviour with discipline rather than with firm but comforting behaviour. Thus they failed to reassure the child of their continued availability. The author concludes that:

> Good enough parenting is often not good enough for an emotionally disturbed child. In this sense, adoption is a radical intervention only if the adoptive parents become adept interveners, able to decode and respond appropriately to the child's psychological needs.
>
> (Lieberman, 2003, p. 282)

The remainder of this chapter focuses on the provision of parenting interventions. These interventions aim to improve the quality of the relationship between the carers and children, and to help the carers to develop skills in managing the children. It is important that these interventions do not ignore the functioning of the family as a whole or the complexity of a parenting task that involves forming healthy relationships with a child who is unaccustomed to participating in such relationships. Consideration also needs to be given to helping the child to adjust to multiple relationships both in current and past families.

THEORETICAL MODELS AND THEIR INFLUENCE ON INTERVENTIONS

When devising interventions for adoptive and foster carers there is a range of theoretical models that can be useful. These models provide both a framework for understanding the difficulties the children present and guidance that can help the parents or carers to enhance their parenting skills matched to the needs of the children in their care. In this section a number of models will be described and their relevance to fostered and adopted children explored.

The Developmental and Transactional Models

Developmental models provide a context for understanding the child and the stage of development he or she has reached. This will have an important influence on the parenting intervention. Childhood is a period of ongoing stages leading to major changes in physical, cognitive, social and emotional development. In this section particular attention will be given to transactional models of development. These models provide an explanation for how maturational change within the child and the influence of the environment combine and interact, leading to growth and development.

Child development is the outcome of complex transactions between the child, biology and the environment (Richardson, 1994). The child is actively relating to the environment and being acted upon by the environment in a transactional process (see Figure 7.1). This has led to an ecological model of development (Bronfenbrenner, 1977). For example, the parent–child relationship is seen as reciprocal and bidirectional. Variations in families are explained by an interaction of characteristics of the person and the context in which the person is involved. Intra-familial (within family) and extra-familial (wider environment) contexts are important in the development of families, and it is these that provide the ecological context in which the family develops (e.g. see Crnic, 1990).

Transactional Interactions

Development is influenced by:

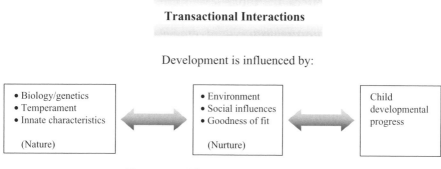

Figure 7.1 The transactional process

The importance of the environment and, in particular, the social world into which the infant is born is emphasized by research that reveals the sophisticated abilities of infants to direct their attention to other people. Babies come into the world already tuned in to faces, voices and biological motion, with a particular interest in the face and voice of their mothers. Babies are born ready to enter into a relationship (Hobson, 1993, in Oates, 1994). Thus development is primarily a social process and the formation of relationships is a basic starting point for development (Oates, 1994). The initial social context is the family context. This remains pivotal but is supplemented with a growing range of social contexts as the child grows, including school and various community settings. Child development therefore occurs within the context of a family and community, which is also developing and changing. The stages and changes that are ongoing through a child's growing up comprise the backdrop for a child's developing abilities and social adjustment.

The interaction between the child's developing abilities and the experiences he or she meets within the world will lead to a range of risk and protective factors that will influence the child's adjustment. Risk factors predispose the child to developing psychological problems while protective factors reduce this risk or predispose the child to recover from risks more easily. Protective factors increase the resilience of the child to cope with stress and difficulties, while risk factors reduce this resilience. For example, intelligence, temperament and self-esteem can constitute a risk or protective factor. Some children are born genetically vulnerable or are at increased risk because of birth or pre-natal injuries. Parenting practice, family health or family problems can also influence the balance of risk and protective factors.

Children who are fostered or adopted have an increased likelihood of encountering a range of risk factors including early experience of abuse and neglect, family difficulties and biological factors stemming from pre-natal experience of drugs and maternal stress.

These children often struggle to take advantage of good-quality responsive and available carers who can protect and nurture them. Children cannot elicit or respond to the sensitive care on offer. Living with children who persist in not trusting parents, whose self-perception continues to be that they are undeserving of love and whose behaviour displays these beliefs on a day-to-day basis, can shape the parents' perception of them. The children's needs and behaviours in response to this in turn affect the social environment such that the carers become less able to provide responsive, available parenting (Howe & Fearnley, 2003). Interventions need to address these transactional difficulties.

Lieberman (2003) suggests that such persistent failure to achieve an emotionally satisfying and reciprocal relationship with their child can lead to the parents feeling hopeless. Adoptions can fail when parents are convinced that either they do not have the skills to successfully raise the child or there is something wrong with the child that is intractable and prevents the development of healthy relationships. Parents are left feeling guilty, angry and regretting the adoption.

Jason joined his new family easily at the age of $3\frac{1}{2}$. He settled in quickly and they felt confident that he was becoming one of the family. However, after a few months they began to struggle. Jason became very rejecting of his adoptive mother, refusing to let her do anything for him. The mother in turn became overwhelmed by feelings of failure and guilt and the family began to question their wisdom in adopting this little boy. Psychological intervention helped this family to change their view of Jason's behaviour. They began to understand that his resistance to them was an expression of the fear he felt about becoming emotionally close to a parent again. With this new understanding the family felt able to take on the parenting task again.

Developmental models therefore highlight the importance of a good understanding of how children develop, the stage of development they have reached, and the risk and protective factors influencing them. These will guide the tailoring of interventions with carers to the developmental needs of the child. An emphasis on the importance of transactional relationships additionally focuses the intervener on helping the carer to parent the individual child, taking into account the complex relationship between the two of them and within the family more widely.

The concept of goodness of fit can usefully guide the advice and support being offered. Thus the child's characteristics and the expectations of family members are explored, often highlighting why difficulties in the relationships have developed.

To return to the example of Jason, he was a bright boy who fitted in well at the local playgroup and was beginning to develop the cognitive skills expected of his age. However his early experience of neglect and abuse had influenced his emotional development. In many ways he was functioning emotionally as an infant. Within the home he struggled to occupy himself, wanted to remain in sight of the carer at all times, and became very distressed when he didn't get his needs met immediately. This led to a lot of frustration for his parents whose expectations were for a typical $3\frac{1}{2}$ year old. It also created tension with their biological son, Andrew who had not expected that adopting a brother would take so much of his parents' time.

As Jason demonstrated clingy, demanding behaviour his parents became tense and irritated. They felt guilty about the time spent with Jason and were torn between meeting his needs and giving time to Andrew. This in turn led to Jason becoming distressed and even more demanding. The fact that Jason behaved well at playgroup, occupying himself for lengthy periods there, led the parents to become concerned that they were failing with Jason at home. They redoubled their efforts to help Jason to manage without their constant attention. Overall this resulted in a poor 'goodness of fit' between Jason and his parents. Their expectations and his needs were not in accord. As they were helped to view Jason as an emotionally younger child who needed a large degree of attention and nurturing from his parents, their expectations reduced. They began to think about their parenting role as one in which they provided Jason with nurturing that he had not received earlier in his life. They found activities to do with him that focused on the developing relationship between themselves and Jason, and found ways to involve Andrew in these activities. They also adjusted their daily routine so that they had more time to spend with Jason while Andrew was at school, taking time over nurturing activities such as mealtimes and bath times. After school, activities for Andrew were divided between them or became a focus when Jason was in bed.

While Jason could still be demanding at times his clinginess reduced and he even began to spend short periods of time occupied with his toys, providing a parent was nearby. The 'goodness of fit' between Jason and his parents had improved as their expectations adjusted in line with his needs. In turn the relationship between Jason and Andrew, while still fraught at times, improved. Jason now had more confident and less frustrated parents who found they had a happier boy to look after.

This example illustrates the need to take into account the complexity of caring for children who have experience of previous dysfunctional parenting. The children frequently behave in ways that fail to elicit caregiving. In particular, as they sense a threat to the availability of the carer they will behave in ways that serve to push the carer away further. If children can receive nurturing care at these times they will be able to organize their behaviour around this availability rather than around the feared unavailability of their carer (Dozier et al., 2002). Thus it can be seen that a parent–child relationship is akin to an intricate, reciprocal dance (Stern, 1985). The child and parent both signal and respond to each other's signals. Children who are fostered and adopted, however, tend to provide signals that are complex, self-contradictory and difficult to interpret (Marvin & Whelan, 2003). Interventions can provide support and guidance for carers in interpreting the signals and meeting the emotional needs of the children.

Fahlberg (1996) suggests that the foster carer use the arousal–relaxation cycle. This is an example of a healthy transactional relationship. The cycle is apparent in the first year of life and is seen as pivotal in allowing the child to develop trust and feelings of security. Thus an infant will naturally experience times of higher arousal when he or she experiences discomfort or distress. The carer will help the infant by soothing and then relieving the distress. The infant experiences emotions being regulated and discomfort easing, leading to relief and a period of relaxation.

This cycle can also be used in older children who are experiencing relationship difficulties (see Figure 7.2). Carers respond to the needs expressed by often distressed and difficult behaviour, and use the period of relief and relaxation following an outburst to get closer to the child. The child feels understood and supported, and at the same time is being helped to develop improved abilities to regulate emotion.

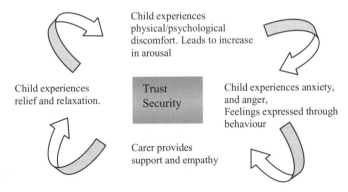

Figure 7.2   Arousal–relaxation cycle (adapted from Fahlberg, 1991)

Older children, who are unused to receiving responsive nurturing, will often resist the carers' efforts to support and empathize and the carers then need to find creative ways to offer support and empathy.

For example, a carer found her 9-year-old foster child in a rage 'trashing' the front room. She did not know what had triggered this but she could see how upset and angry he was. She knew from experience that he wouldn't cope with a direct approach from her. She therefore sat down at the side of a room and began to relate a story. She told a story of a lion in a zoo:

Once upon a time there was a lion who lived in the zoo. Now this lion had lived in the zoo for a number of years. He was a bad-tempered lion and for this reason he had to live in an enclosure all on his own. This made the lion very angry. He roared at anyone who came near. Animals came by but they all ran away when he roared at them. A monkey came by. He tried to be friendly but the lion roared and he ran away. The elephant came by and offered the lion a bun, but the lion roared and the elephant ran away. Then one day a bear came along. Now the bear was a wise bear. He knew that the lion needed a friend. He wanted to help the lion. When the lion roared he didn't run away. He offered to be the lion's friend. . . .

The carer got no further with the story; at this stage the boy ran to her and cried in her arms. The carer spent some time soothing and comforting him after which they together restored her room.

Interventions with carers can therefore be used to explore the complex interactions that have developed between the child and family members. Carers are helped to adjust their parenting style to suit the needs of the child. The therapist and carers work together to plan how the ideas might be implemented within their home and fitted to their own existing parenting styles. The carer is helped to recognize and respond to the emotional and developmental needs of the child.

However, the difficulty of caring for children with emotional difficulties should not be underestimated. The extent to which carers are able to maintain a reflective stance is important. This allows them to collaborate with the therapist to understand and develop successful interventions. At times the carers' own emotions overwhelm them to the extent that they are no longer reflective and can no longer support the child.

Thus a foster couple were struggling with their 14-year-old foster daughter, Claire, who had become verbally abusive and rejecting of them. As this went on day after day the carers found it increasingly difficult to cope. The foster mother began to believe that Claire didn't want to live with them any more and that she was enjoying being so rude and difficult. She tried to remain calm and to support Claire but she was increasingly finding it difficult to maintain her empathy and not to feel angry. This in turn was leading to further abusive behaviour from Claire. The couple began to argue about the reasons for Claire's behaviour while their older foster daughter began spending more and more time at her friend's house.

This was emotionally exhausting for the carers and there was considerable concern that the placement would break down. The carers had regular support from a psychologist who encouraged them to keep going and to believe that there was a reason for this change in behaviour. The carers had one more go at finding out what was upsetting Claire. Finally she admitted that she had been receiving unsolicited text messages from her mother. Claire and her carers had a tearful evening together during which Claire was finally able to express her anxiety and confusion.

An understanding of a child's developmental needs and exploration of transactional relationships that have developed between the child and family members can therefore usefully inform interventions aimed at improving relationships and family adjustment.

Social Learning Model

The social learning model, which has stemmed out of behaviourism, assumes that behaviour is initiated and reinforced by the environment (Hollin et al., 1995). We learn ways of behaving because of the consequences that follow it. Social learning theory adds emphasis to this learning occurring within a social context, and pays more attention to cognitive processes, especially observation and modelling. Thus rewards, punishments and other contingencies and events are mediated by people within relationships (Herbert, 1991). Behaviour is learned by watching and imitating others in addition to shaping and reinforcement. As children watch others they form concepts about possible behaviours, and these concepts will then guide their own actions. Observation of their own actions, and their consequences, will lead to modification or strengthening of the concepts (see Bandura, 1977, 1986). This model explains how children learn appropriate behaviour for the society or culture in which they live (socialization). The theory, therefore, has a particular relevance for applying psychological thinking to children whose family culture has changed because of fostering or adoption.

A useful example of a social learning explanation of behaviour is that provided by Patterson (1982). He considered the family socialization process that underlies the development and maintenance of conduct-disordered

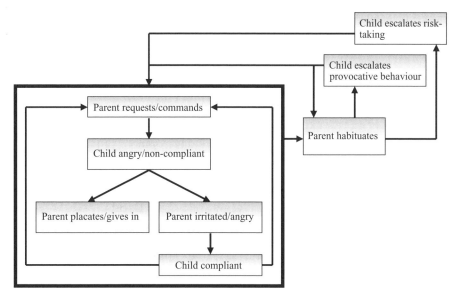

Figure 7.3 Coercive pattern of interactions

behaviour in children. It is not uncommon for this pattern of behaviour to be brought into the adoptive or foster home by the children. Negative reinforcement is seen as central to maintaining the coercive interactions between family members (coercive hypothesis). Behaviour is maintained or escalates in order to avoid a negative consequence. For example, non-compliance in a child leads to the parent withdrawing the command (negatively reinforcing non-compliance). Alternatively, the parent might respond with coercive behaviours such as yelling at the child. If the child then complies, this coercive behaviour of the parent is negatively reinforced and such coercive patterns of interacting tend to persist and escalate over time. Threats and nagging escalate but are only inconsistently acted upon. Thus the child learns to regulate the attention of his or her parent by alternating angry and compliant behaviours. As the parent habituates to the behaviour of the child, getting used to this level of non-compliance and therefore not responding to it, the child will escalate his or her behaviour to the point that the parent responds again, and an escalating coercive pattern of interactions is set up (see Figure 7.3).

Social learning theory therefore predicts that children will learn patterns of behaviour that are influenced by their relationship with their parents. Thus the children develop expectations about family life and they bring these expectations with them into their new foster or adoptive homes. Children tend to cling to these expectations, pushing the carers into particular transactions.

Carers feel caught in a trap of interactions that are not their own. Interventions can help carers to understand these interactions better. This enables them to take charge and guide the children into more healthy ways of relating with them.

Many evidence-based parent training programmes are informed by social learning theory. Research has demonstrated the links between parenting practice and child behaviours (e.g. Patterson, 1986) and between the alteration of parenting practice and changes in child behaviours (O'Dell, 1974; Kazdin, 1997). Such research has led to the development of parent training programmes often delivered in a group work context for parents of children displaying problematic behaviours. A number of these programmes have been extensively evaluated, demonstrating lasting effects for two-thirds of families treated and up to four years following (Dadds, 1995; Webster-Stratton, 1997).

Parent training programmes are a popular way of delivering indirect interventions to groups of foster and adoptive carers. They are cost-effective and have an added advantage of building in peer support for the carers. For example, *The Incredible Years* parent training programme (Webster-Stratton & Hancock, 1998; Webster-Stratton, 2005) was originally developed for use with biological parents, but has also been successfully used with adoptive parents (Gilkes & Klimes, 2003) and foster parents (Pallett et al., 2002; Golding & Picken, 2004). This adopts a collaborative approach in which the therapists and carers work as partners to consider parenting techniques and how they might be adapted and used in different situations. A combination of teaching, discussion and role-play is used to allow foster carers to reflect on and practise different ways of managing children. The programme introduces social learning theory and techniques organized around a parenting pyramid. The first part of the programme focuses on building positive relationships. Effective parenting is viewed as one that has a positive base at its foundation. A positive foundation promotes feelings of confidence and self-worth in the child; it helps the child to feel loved, fostering a secure base for ongoing emotional development, and promoting feelings of attachment and warmth between the child and the carer. The programme therefore begins with building this positive foundation. Non-aggressive disciplinary techniques such as time-out, ignoring behaviour and logical and natural consequences can then be used, built upon this foundation of positive parenting skills. The collaborative model of training, used within this programme, is one that particularly lends itself to well-motivated foster and adoptive carers who already have an adequate level of parenting skills but can be helped to adapt this to the particular needs of the children for whom they are caring.

Golding & Picken (2004) describe the adaptation of this parenting programme for groups of foster carers. The parenting pyramid provided a framework for the group but was extended and adapted to explore issues of relevance to caring for looked after children. The collaborative approach allowed issues around caring for looked after children to emerge naturally. Discussion and role-play helped the group to consider these in relation to the behaviour management techniques being discussed. For example, when the technique of ignoring was explored, the carers were concerned about using this technique with children who were oversensitive to feeling rejected and unloved. Role-play was used to explore ways that difficult behaviour could be ignored while the carers still managed to convey their acceptance and affection for the children themselves. Discussion of children who struggle when praised and who habitually sabotage rewards highlighted the usefulness of low key descriptive commenting (e.g. 'I liked the way that you played with your brother while I cooked tea. You shared the lego out and didn't get cross when he wanted the train'), and finding small rewards that children can enjoy. Similarly, the perennial problem of caring for children who need to be in control led to useful discussion and exploration of 'when–then' commands and the helpfulness of offering two choices.

The behaviour of foster children can be perplexing at times. As the behavioural management techniques were explored, issues were raised that lent themselves to a psycho-educational component within the training. In this way carers were helped both to develop their parenting skills to the needs of children with complex difficulties and to increase their understanding of the children. Thus during the course of the group a number of diverse themes were discussed alongside the exploration of techniques. For example:

- Why foster children find it difficult to form secure attachment relationships.
- The impact of traumatic experience on the development of foster children.
- The development of play and social skills when early experience is lacking.
- The link between behaviour and how children feel about themselves and others.
- Special problems such as eating difficulties, sexualized behaviours.
- The influence of own childhood experience on being a carer.

Carers report high levels of satisfaction following attendance at such groups. They feel that it has led to improvements for the children and for their relationship (Golding & Picken, 2004; Pallett et al., 2002). Generally the limited experimental research that has been done also suggests that carers are highly satisfied with the training. However the training does not significantly reduce the children's problems (Minnis & Devine, 2001; Hill-Tout et al., 2003). This should not lead us to underestimate the usefulness of such groups. The support they provide, and the increase in confidence and feelings of self-efficacy for the carers, can be a significant factor in helping them to maintain placements, and provide stability and security for children despite their on-going difficulties.

The social learning model is therefore an important model that can guide our understanding of the behaviour being displayed by adoptive and foster children and can inform interventions aimed at developing the parenting skills of the carers. Existing parenting programmes based on social learning principles can usefully be used with foster or adoptive carers. In this way carers can be helped to understand social learning theory and to explore the role of their behaviour in managing the children. Specific behavioural techniques can be used to provide the carer with tools for managing the child in their care. However, these programmes do not address the specific issues for children who have an experience of abusive or neglectful early care and who bring this experience with them into foster or adoptive homes. It is likely that parenting programmes will need to be adapted to take into account the special needs of this group of children. An understanding of the transactional process occurring and the attachment needs of the children will complement the social learning perspective that underlies many parent training programmes.

ATTACHMENT THEORY-BASED MODELS

While many children in foster and adoptive care will, over time, form satis-factory attachment relationships with their carers, a substantial minority can find living with parents difficult (Rushton et al., 2003). These are the children who are hardest to help; they find it difficult to trust and they appear to invite carers to reject them. These children are anxious and afraid but this is often hidden under a veneer of angry, aggressive and controlling behaviours.

Psychological support to help the parents and carers of these children is essential if the children are to have a chance of living long-term within one family. Without this experience they will move from placement to placement, never forming satisfactory attachment relationships, and will grow into adult life unequipped for the experiences ahead of them. The parents or carers need help to understand the day-to-day experience of caring for the children, to maintain empathy for the children despite the nearly intolerable behaviour they are subject to, and to provide a caring experience within which the chil-dren can emotionally develop.

Quinton et al. (1998) suggest that the provision of stable and loving homes is a necessary but not sufficient starting point for helping children to re-cover developmentally from early, traumatic experience. Similarly, Hayden et al. (1999) highlight the importance of good understanding and appropri-ate skilled management of traumatized children's behaviour. Without this understanding and skill, carers frequently use inappropriate and sometimes abusive forms of control. A starting point therefore for psychological support is an understanding of how children's current behaviour and feelings are linked to their past experience. If carers can gain this understanding they will be in a better position to manage the behaviour while helping the children to manage the intense feelings they are experiencing.

Attachment theory can provide a model that can be used by practitioners to help carers to gain understanding and to increase their parenting skills. Within an attachment framework practitioners can guide carers in the development of parenting skills matched to the individual needs of the child based on an understanding of the influence of their past experience. In this way carers can gain additional skills in facilitating the development of a secure attachment between the child and themselves. While it is unrealistic to expect this to solve all the problems these children present, it will contribute to the development of resilience and emotional growth. This will increase the chances that the children will grow up and go out into a world where they can both manage themselves and engage in relationships with others.

Attachment theory and its application to therapeutic work with children living in foster and adoptive homes are explored in Chapter 12. In this current section the use of parenting programmes based on attachment theory and how this can inform group or individual work with foster or adoptive carers for children of a range of ages will be discussed.

Traditional parenting models that inform parent training programmes focus their main attention on the management of the behaviour of the child. Thus the Incredible Years Programme referred to earlier is focused around a series of behavioural strategies with the aim of improving the relationship between parent and child and increasing parental skill at managing the child's behaviour. Programmes such as these pay less attention to the emotional needs of the family and the child. Parenting a foster or adoptive child with complex emotional difficulties places a strain on the normal parenting skills of these parents. Programmes that might prove useful have been developed with biological families in mind. For example, Bavolek and Comstock (1983) developed a programme that uses cognitive and affective techniques with the aim of building empathy among all family members. Originally developed to help parents at risk of abusing their children, this might also be suitable for parents and carers who are finding it difficult to empathize with their foster or adoptive child's situation in the face of confusing and challenging behaviour.

Foster and adoptive parents caring for children with extreme difficulties can experience high levels of anxiety, failure and fear that they will not be able to continue to parent the child. Psychological support to these families must be able to provide a high degree of containment for this anxiety. The Solihull approach (Douglas & Ginty, 2001; Douglas & Brennan, 2004) was developed as a psychotherapeutic and behavioural approach for health visitors working with children with sleeping, feeding, toileting and behavioural difficulties. In a small-scale study, this approach has been found to decrease parental anxiety and reduce severity of child's difficulties after a three-session intervention. In contrast to health visiting practice that provides advice and guidance to parents, this approach more directly facilitates the relationship between parent and child. In this way the parent is empowered and resilience is created for the child (Whitehead & Douglas, 2005). The core principles of this approach of containment, reciprocity and behaviour management are ones that could usefully be applied in supporting the carers of foster or adoptive children. The parents are helped by an approach that:

- contains the anxiety and overwhelming feelings of the parents and therefore restores their ability to think and solve problems;
- focuses on the reciprocity between the parent and child providing advice to help them to be more in tune with each other;
- provides behavioural management advice.

Attachment theory has guided the development of 'The Circle of Security Project' (Marvin et al., 2002). This provides parent education and psychotherapy with the aim of altering attachment patterns in high-risk parent–child dyads. Parents are helped to be more sensitive and responsive to the child's signals. They learn to reflect on their own and their child's behaviour, thoughts and feelings. They are additionally helped to consider their own history of attachment relationships and how this might affect current caregiving patterns. The success of projects such as this in providing biological parents with improved understanding and greater skill, leading to the development of more secure attachments for the child, is important in demonstrating the usefulness of models of parenting based on attachment theory.

The provision of interventions aimed at enhancing carer sensitivity to the emotional needs of their children has been found to be helpful for biological parents and their young children (Van Ijzendoorn et al., 1995). It is clear that sensitivity can be improved, but it is less clear how far this has a longer-term impact on the attachment security of the child. Attention to the parents' attachment state of mind is also needed. These interventions hold promise for foster and adoptive parents where the children struggle to experience security of attachment. Research in this area is currently quite limited, but initial results from one or two studies suggest that such interventions can impact on the child at the physiological as well as the behavioural level (Fisher et al., 2000; Dozier et al., 2002). Attachment-based interventions for parents and infants are explored more fully in Chapter 12.

Foster care frequently requires children to form new attachments in middle childhood and adolescence despite their distrust of 'parents'. Parenting interventions need to overcome this distrust while attending to the dual needs of meeting the previously unmet emotional needs of the child, akin to the development of secure attachment with infants, while promoting age-appropriate competence at school and in the community (Schofield & Meek, 2005). The authors propose an attachment-based multidimensional model of parenting the older child in foster care. Interventions attend to the carers' thinking and feeling about the child. This influences their behaviour, which in turn impacts on the child's thinking, feeling, and behaviour. They describe five dimensions of parenting that interact to provide a secure base for the child:

- Promoting trust and availability.
- Promoting family membership.
- Promoting self-esteem.
- Promoting reflective function.
- Promoting autonomy.

There are therefore a range of programmes that can usefully influence the development of parent training for foster and adoptive carers. In Worcestershire a programme for foster carers has been developed that draws elements from all these different programmes, combined with knowledge gained from practitioners who have written about attachment theory and its application in practice (Hughes, 2004; Delaney, 1998; Fahlberg, 1996; Howe et al., 1999).

This programme has been used with individual foster carers and through a 'Fostering Attachments Group' (Golding, 2003). The programme begins with a psycho-educational component explaining attachment theory and the development of different attachment patterns. The aim of this component is to increase the understanding of the carers for the children in their care and to help them to link the child's current behaviour with his or her past experience. This in turn helps the carers to feel less victimized by the often direct behaviour they are experiencing and to develop empathy for the child despite the challenge that he or she is presenting. The development of understanding and the focus on how this understanding can lead to different ways of parenting the child in turn helps to contain the high levels of anxiety and failure the carers are often experiencing.

The practitioner, and the carers, then explore different ways of working with children that have been suggested by attachment theory. This has been developed into a house model of parenting (see Figure 7.4). This model helps carers to focus on how to provide a positive family atmosphere and how to avoid being drawn into a re-enactment of the child's early experience.

Carers are encouraged to control the emotional rhythm of the house. In this way they foster a secure base within which the child can learn emotional regulation skills and the ability to be reflective. Within this family atmosphere children can be helped to feel that they belong to the family and to experience mutual enjoyment with family members.

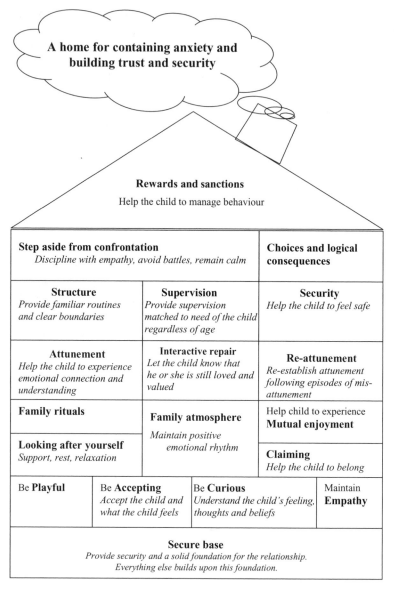

Figure 7.4   The house model of parenting

Carers learn to build attachments through attunement and interactive re-pair. They remain emotionally engaged and available by maintaining a stance of curiosity, acceptance, playfulness and / or empathy (see Hughes, 2004). Cu-riosity leads to understanding of the child, and aids understanding for the child. With this understanding comes acceptance, without which the carer will find it difficult to be either playful or empathic. Discipline will become angry and confrontational. Acceptance means demonstrating to children that their inner life of thoughts and feelings is noticed and valued. Discipline will then start with empathy and warmth for the child. Acceptance is not the same as tolerance; it does *not* mean that the carer should just 'put up' with difficult behaviour. Acceptance does mean starting where the child is, understanding the child's inner life and how this is being communicated. The carer expresses empathy for the inner thoughts and feelings of the child. The carer can then provide the guidance, feedback and limit setting that will eventually help the child to express thoughts and feelings in a less challenging way. Finally, the carer spends time with the child, helping him or her to become re-attuned. The relationship is repaired because the carer reminds the child that he or she is still special to them. Following inevitable breaks in attunement because of the need to discipline, or because the carer becomes angry and non-empathic, the carer and child again become emotionally engaged with each other.

Security and trust are increased by an appropriate degree of structure and supervision tailored to the individual needs of the child. This all provides a containing structure for the child, symbolized by the house.

The top of the house and the roof builds on this containment by exploration of ways to manage difficult behaviours. In particular carers are helped to find ways to step aside from confrontation, to provide discipline with empathy, and to help the child to enjoy praise and rewards.

While much of the discussion focuses on looking after the child, some important attention is also given to carers looking after themselves, and consideration of their own experience of being parented and how this impacts on their fostering.

Evaluation of the fostering attachments group suggests that carers find it supportive, leading to increased confidence and improvements in the child's behaviour, although controlled experimental studies have not been carried out (Golding & Picken, 2004).

At times the group discussion can have significant emotional impact on the carers. The painful exploration of the damage that is created by early adverse environments, the difficulty in enabling children to recover from this, and sometimes the impact of their own early histories on their fostering can all lead to feelings of sadness. For example, one carer reported: 'I felt reassured that other people feel so frustrated at times. It was a session that provoked sadness in me and I feel quite low at the end.' Another carer was profoundly moved by a discussion of the avoidant attachment pattern and talked afterwards of his own early experience and the impact this has on his fostering. The fact that these carers continue to feel positive about attending the group despite this painful exploration provides an indication of the supportive nature of such group work.

Attachment theory provides a framework for understanding why children can feel insecure within their new families. This has led to a range of interventions that can inform the parenting of these children. Parenting interventions move beyond the management of behaviour towards helping carers to foster feelings of security, safety, and trust within the children. This is an important starting point towards helping them to recover from early traumatic experience and separation. The children can then experience more secure attachment relationships, enabling them to thrive within foster or adoptive homes.

THE EVALUATION OF PARENTING INTERVENTIONS FOR FOSTER AND ADOPTIVE PARENTS

A number of authors recognize the importance of specialist interventions for foster and adoptive carers, but little research has systematically considered the impact of such interventions. One qualitative study of short-term carers found that foster carers felt the need for and benefit of specialist support. This was most frequently available at times of crisis, rather than being planned as part of the support package at the beginning of the placement (Sellick, 1992). Hayden et al. (1999) suggests that the independent agencies are furthest ahead in recognizing the importance of accessible interventions from psychiatric and psychology services. Quinton et al. (1998) caution that if interventions are not sufficiently intensive, the impact may not be great enough to alter outcomes for the child.

It is difficult to evaluate whether interventions improve parenting skill or family functioning, although numbers of placement breakdowns can be used as a guide. For example, Quinton et al. (1998) found that social work support was helpful in maintaining placements even where the placements were rated as unstable by the carer. Using placement breakdown or stability as an indicator of the success or failure of an intervention overlooks the multiple reasons why placements break down, not all of which are related to parenting skills or family functioning.

Consideration of the child's behaviour as an index of success of the intervention is similarly fraught with difficulty. For example, an increase in behaviour problems does not necessarily indicate that the placement is failing. Barth et al. (1988), in a study of adoptive parents, found that attachments could develop between child and parent even when behaviour is worsening. It is also possible that behaviour is worsening or improving because of factors outside the placement – in school, with contact with birth families or within the peer group, for instance.

Carers report high levels of satisfaction when they receive parenting support (Golding & Picken, 2004; Minnis & Devine, 2001; Hill-Tout et al., 2003;

Pallett et al., 2002). Parenting interventions can keep carers going and enable them to develop their practice leading to less breakdown and reductions in difficult behaviour (Sellick & Thoburn, 1996), but little is known about the mechanism by which the intervention can enhance skills or how this in turn impacts on the functioning of the child. More research is needed to explore the tailored use of parenting interventions to increase the skill and confidence of the carer and to enhance the emotional and behavioural functioning of the child. There is even less research exploring the impact of parenting interventions on complex family functioning.

It is also important to consider how well psychological interventions complement existing services being provided for carers from core social service, education and health teams. Difficulties can arise when conflicting views are held, leading to different sets of advice being given to carers. It may be that the different services hold different ideas about appropriate aims and goals. For example, education-focused services aimed at engaging children within school and a focus on achievement and qualification might be at odds with advice that the priority for an adopted child is to develop a good-quality relationship with the carer, perhaps recommending a period out of school. Similarly, interventions that recommend a high degree of physical contact between the carer and the child may feel uncomfortable to a fostering social worker who is concerned about protecting the carer from the potential for false allegations from the child. The guidance provided within the context of 'safe care' can leave a carer uncomfortable with nurturing parenting tasks such as cleaning a child's teeth or offering a distressed child a cuddle. Such discomfort may increase with advice recommending high levels of nurturing involving appropriate touch and contact.

These difficulties highlight the need for the provision of intervention services within the context of cohesive, inter-agency working. This should involve good communication between all agencies involved with a carer or family, and joint decision making about priorities for intervention. Additionally, carers need support to deal with the many agencies with whom they have to interact.

CONCLUSION AND THE WAY FORWARD

The systematic use of psychological interventions with carers is only recently being explored. The parent training interventions are furthest ahead in researching efficacy. Studies of group interventions suggest that carers find such interventions to be supportive and helpful, but it is unclear whether such interventions have any lasting impact on the child. It is likely that such interventions will need to be provided over a longer rather than a shorter term and that some attention to the unique needs of the children being cared for will be important.

> The foster carers in front of me look tired and ill. They describe what it is like day-to-day caring for Annie, a small child who is displaying severe tantrums, eating and sleeping difficulties. They express concern at Annie's head-banging behaviour, and worry that they no longer have the capacity to continue caring for her. We explore together Annie's past history of neglect and abandonment. We think about her behaviour within this context, as a reflection of severe separation anxiety and fear of abandonment. I offer to help them to find a different approach to parenting Annie, one that can take into account her fears and can provide her with enough security and predictability that she can begin to benefit from the stability she is being offered. The carers describe their relief. They already look less ill and tired as they describe feeling as if they have found light at the end of the tunnel. I continue to support them for the following year. At times we struggled to keep the light in view, but we continued to work together to find a way of parenting Annie, one that helped her to feel more secure and comfortable with being parented. She remained in the placement until she successfully moved to an adoptive family.

Carers fostering or adopting children with complex emotional difficulties have a stressful parenting task ahead of them. The continuing difficulties that these children can present lead to lack of confidence, feelings of failure and ultimately the breakdown of placements to the detriment of everyone. Support and appropriate parenting advice is an essential part of the services that these carers need. Finding and following the light at the end of the tunnel is a task that can be made easier with the right level of support and training.

This Child – Not of Birth

In time it has grown
Like a flower in the earth
The love that I feel
For this child not of birth.

Or was it instant this feeling?
I'm not really sure
From when did I love him?
I just know this love's pure.

Sometimes we feel angry
And helpless and scared
At the pain he has suffered
His emotions impaired.

No sense of belonging
His hurt is too deep
So we talk of beginnings
Good memories we keep.

I look down in wonder
At this child in his bed
Too scared of knowing
What dreams fill his head.

So I hide my own pain
Show him feelings of pride
But my emotions are shattered
I just cry inside.

But the joy he has brought me
With each step that he takes
This warm feeling inside me
Love stronger it makes.

But there's one thing I can tell him
That I know gives him worth
And that's that I chose him
My child – not of birth.

(Reproduced by permission of Kerry Hill)

REFERENCES

Bandura, A. (1977) *Social Learning Theory*. Englewood Cliffs, NJ: Prentice-Hall.

Bandura, A. (1986) *Social Foundations of Thought and Action: A Social Cognitive Theory*. Englewood Cliffs, NJ: Prentice-Hall.

Barth, R.P., Berry, M., Yoshikami, R. & Goodfield, R.K. (1988) Predicting adoption disruption. *Social Work*, **33**, 227–233.

Bavolek, S.J. & Comstock, C.M. (1983) *The Nurturing Programme for Parents and Children*. Schaumberg, IL: Family Development Associates.

Bronfenbrenner, U. (1977) Toward an experimental ecology of human development. *American Psychologist*, **32**, 513–531.

Bowlby, J. (1988) *A Secure Base. Clinical Applications of Attachment Theory*. (2nd edn) London: Routledge.

Crnic, K.A. (1990) Families of children with Down Syndrome: Ecological contexts and characteristics. In D. Cicchetti & M. Beeghly (Eds), *Children with Down Syndrome: A Developmental Perspective* (pp. 399–423). Cambridge University Press.

Dadds, M.R. (1995) Families, children and the development of dysfunction. *Developmental Clinical Psychology and Psychiatry*, **32**. London: Sage.

Delaney, R.J. (1998) *Fostering Changes. Treating Attachment-disordered Foster Children*. Oklahoma City: Wood & Barnes Publishing.

Douglas, H. & Ginty, M. (2001) The Solihull approach: Changes in health visiting practice. *Community Practitioner*, **74**(6), 222–224.

Douglas, H. & Brennan, A. (2004) Containment, reciprocity and behaviour management. Preliminary evaluation of a brief early intervention (the Solihull Approach) for families with infants and young children. *International Journal of Infant Observation*, **7**(1), 89–107.

Dozier, M., Higley, E., Albus, K. & Nutter, A. (2002) Intervening with foster infants' caregivers: Targeting three critical needs. *Infant Mental Health Journal*, **23**(5), 541–554.

Fahlberg, V.I. (1996) *A Child's Journey Through Placement*. London: BAAF.

Fisher, T., Gibbs, I., Sinclair, I. & Wilson, K. (2000) Sharing the care: The qualities sought of social workers by foster carers. *Child and Family Social Work*, **5**, 225–233.

Freud, S. (1959) *Analysis of a phobia in a five-year-old boy*. Collected papers: Case histories. New York: Basic Books. [See Bratton, S.C. (1998) Training parents to facilitate their child's adjustment to divorce using the filial/family play therapy approach. In J. Briesmeister & C.E. Schaefer (Eds), *Handbook of Parent Training, Parents as Co-therapists for Children's Behaviours* (2nd edn; pp. 549–572). New York: John Wiley & Sons.]

Gilkes, L. & Klimes, I. (2003) Parenting skills for adoptive parents. *Adoption and Fostering*, **27**(1), 1–7.

Golding, K. (2003) Helping foster carers helping children. Using attachment theory to guide practice. *Adoption and Fostering*, **27**(2), 64–73.

Golding, K. & Picken, W. (2004) Group work for foster carers caring for children with complex problems. *Adoption and Fostering*, **28**(1), 25–37.

Hart, A. & Luckock, B. (2004) *Developing Adoption Support and Therapy*. London/Philadelphia: Jessica Kingsley Publishers.

Hayden, C., Goddard, J., Gorin, S. & Van der Spek, N. (1999) *State Child Care, Looking After Children?* London/Philadelphia: Jessica Kingsley Publishers.

Herbert, M. (1991) *Clinical Child Psychology. Social Learning, Development and Behaviour*. Chichester: John Wiley & Sons.

Hill-Tout, J., Pithouse, A. & Lowe, K. (2003) Training foster carers in a preventative approach to children who challenge. Mixed messages from research. *Adoption and Fostering*, **27**(1), 47–56.

Hobson, R.P. (1993) *Autism and the Development of Mind*. Hove: Lawrence Erlbaum. [See J. Oates (1994) First relationships. In J. Oates (Ed.), *The Foundations of Child Development* (pp. 259–298). Oxford: Blackwell Publishers/Milton Keynes: The Open University.]

Hollin, C.R., Epps, K.J. & Kendrick, D.J. (1995) *Managing Behavioural Treatment. Policy and Practice with Delinquent Adolescents*. London/New York: Routledge.

Howe, D. & Fearnley, S. (2003) Disorders of attachment in adopted and fostered children: Recognition and treatment. *Clinical Child Psychology and Psychiatry*, **8**(3), 369–387.

Howe, D., Brandon, M., Hinings, D. & Schofield, G. (1999) *Attachment Theory, Child Maltreatment and Family Support. A Practice and Assessment Model*. Mahwah, NJ: Lawrence Erlbaum Associates.

Hughes, D.A. (2004) An attachment-based treatment of maltreated children and young people. *Attachment and Human Development*, **6**(3), 263–278.

Kazdin, A.E. (1997) Parent management training: evidence, outcomes, and issues. *Journal of American Academy of Child and Adolescent Psychiatry*, **36**(10), 1349–1356.

Lieberman, A.F. (2003) The treatment of attachment disorder in infancy and early childhood: Reflections from clinical intervention with later-adopted foster care children. *Attachment and Human Development*, **5**(3), 279–282.

Marvin, R.S. & Whelan, W.F. (2003) Disordered attachments: Toward evidence-based clinical practice. *Attachment and Human Development*, **5**(3), 283–288.

Marvin, R., Cooper, G., Kent, H. & Powell, B. (2002) The Circle of Security Project: Attachment-based intervention with caregiver–pre-school child dyads. *Attachment and Human Development*, **4**(1), 107–124.

Minnis, H. & Devine, C. (2001) The effect of foster carer training on the emotional and behavioural functioning of looked after children. *Adoption and Fostering*, **25**(1), 44–54.

Oates, J. (1994) *The Foundations of Child Development*. Oxford: Blackwell Publishers/ Milton Keynes: The Open University.

O'Dell, S. (1974) Training parents in behaviour modification: A review. *Psychological Bulletin*, **81**(7), 418–433.

Pallett, C., Scott, S., Blackeby, K., Yule, W. & Weissman, R. (2002) Fostering changes: A cognitive-behavioural approach to help foster carers manage children. *Adoption and Fostering*, **26**(1), 39–48.

Patterson, G.R. (1982) *Coercive Family Process*. Eugene, Or: Castalia.

Patterson, G.R. (1986) Performance models for antisocial boys. *American Psychologist*, **41**, 432–444.

Quinton, D., Rushton, A., Dance, C. & Mayes, D. (1998) *Joining New Families: A Study of Adoption and Fostering in Middle Childhood*. Chichester: John Wiley & Sons.

Richardson, K. (1994) Interactions in development. In Oates J. (Ed.) *The Foundations of Child Development* (pp. 211–257). Oxford: Blackwell Publishers/Milton Keynes: The Open University.

Rushton, A., Mayes, D., Dance, C. & Quinton, D. (2003) Parenting late-placed children. The development of new relationships and the challenge of behavioural problems. *Clinical Child Psychology and Psychiatry*, **8**(3), 389–400.

Schofield, G. & Meek, M. (2005) Providing a secure base: Parenting children in long-term foster care. *Attachment and Human Development*, **7**(1), 3–25.

Sellick, C. (1992) *Supporting Short Term Foster Carers*. Aldershot, Avebury.

Sellick, C. & Thoburn, J. (1996) *What Works in Family Placement?* Barnardos.

Stern, D.N. (1985) *The Interpersonal World of the Infant*. New York: Basic Books.

Van Ijzendoorn, M.H., Juffer, F. & Duyvesteyn, M.G.C. (1995) Breaking the intergenerational cycle of insecure attachment. A review of the effects of attachment-based interventions on maternal sensitivity and infant security. *Journal of Child Psychology and Psychiatry*, **36**, 225–248.

Webster-Stratton, C. (1997) From parent training to community building. Families in society. *Journal of Contemporary Human Services*, March/April, 156–171.

Webster-Stratton, C. (2005) The Incredible Years: A training series for the prevention and treatment of conduct problems in young children. In E.D. Hibbs & P.S. Jensen (Eds), *Psychosocial Treatments for Child and Adolescent Disorders. Empirically Based Strategies for Clinical Practice* (2nd edn). Washington, DC: American Psychological Association.

Webster-Stratton, C. & Hancock, L. (1998) Parent training for parents of young children with conduct problems: Context, networks and therapeutic processes. In J. Briesmeister & C.E. Schaefer (Eds), *Handbook of Parent Training. Parents as Co-therapists for Children's Behaviour* (2nd edn; pp. 98–152). Chichester: John Wiley & Sons.

Whitehead, R.E. & Douglas, H. (2005) Health visitor's experiences of using the Solihull Approach. *Community Practitioner*, **78**(1), 20–23.

8

BEING ADOPTED: PSYCHOLOGICAL SERVICES FOR ADOPTING FAMILIES

Julie Hudson

Bringing up a child whether of birth or not, is a remarkable journey. The adoptive parent will share many experiences common to all parents. There are, however, important differences. Falling in love and understanding the internal world of the child can be especially difficult when the child's past experiences consist of abuse, neglect and trauma. Help and advice need to be offered in a context that acknowledges the adoption process. Within this the prospective parents may perceive a strong need to demonstrate that they can be good parents. Providing services for adoptive parents can prove ineffective if this process is not fully understood.

Nick's heart sank when Karen proudly showed him a set of beautifully made behavioural charts for Liam, ten minutes after he had sat down. Liam, aged 8, and his sister, Janie, aged 4, had been placed with Karen and Jim, for adoption, almost 16 months ago. The adoption had been postponed once and disruption seemed likely.

Nick, a clinical psychologist from the new local service for looked after and adopted children, had been asked to visit the family by their adoption support social worker. Liam was increasingly seen as either totally demanding of his adoptive parents' undivided attention, or having violent rages whenever things

Thinking Psychologically About Children Who Are Looked After and Adopted
Edited by K.S. Golding, H.R. Dent, R. Nissim and L. Stott.
Copyright © 2006 John Wiley & Sons, Ltd.

did not go his way. Behaviour programmes rewarding Liam for any periods of calm, acceptable behaviour had been effective but didn't seem to work any more. Jim had video-taped Liam's most recent rage in the hope that showing Liam just how horrible he was would shock him into changing.

Karen and Jim had received regular support from their adoption worker, who visited frequently. She referred the family to the local Child and Adolescent Mental Health Service (CAMHS) nine months ago. She managed to decrease the waiting time from seven months to four months through her persistence as to the risks associated with the escalation of Liam's challenging behaviour. CAMHS had been impressed with the high standard of parenting Karen and Jim were offering, and with their patience and commitment to both children. Liam's progress in sleeping and eating, in the context of his early neglect and abuse, was seen as evidence that he would gradually learn to trust them and his aggressive behaviour would reduce. They were discharged after two sessions.

Nick declined to watch the video of Liam and instead showed a video clip he had brought with him about the impact of early neglect. He talked about how hard it was to make sense of the pervasive need to control, seen in abused and neglected children. He empathized with the exhaustion, both emotionally and physically, of both parents and told them how he could work with them, and their support worker, about different ways of responding to both Liam's and Janie's behaviour. They agreed but didn't feel hopeful, as they had tried everything.

Two months later Liam was sent home from school for punching his teacher in the face. This was the final straw. Karen and Jim insisted that the children had to be moved that same day. They refused to change their minds. They did not allow the children to say goodbye to people, as they were terrified about the destruction Liam would do to their home, and to them. Both Liam and Janie returned to live with foster carers in the placing authority.

As the above case example illustrates appropriate support and help can arrive too late when mental health services are not set up to meet the particular needs of adopted children, and when parents are offered help that doesn't seem to meet their needs.

A wide range of factors can contribute to the desire for adoptive parents to prove that they have been able to form a family perceived as 'normal' by their extended family and neighbourhood networks. This is particularly so if close relatives and friends are not supportive of the choice to adopt. Adoptive parents have often been through infertility treatments. They therefore have a strong need to construct a positive identity as parents although this differs from what is often thought of as the 'natural' way of becoming a parent. Adoptive parents have often experienced a different route to looking after a child compared with foster carers. Their histories can be similar but the chosen path of adoption to form a family has different consequences. Cultural stories surrounding adoption can also interact with individual motivational factors, and this all creates an atmosphere where adoptive parents develop beliefs that they should feel grateful and 'get on with it' on their own.

Within this chapter it is argued that new adopters need a psychologically based service, as a matter of routine. Interventions are needed which suggest that adoption can be a difficult and testing process. This warrants parental access to specialist services, regardless of the circumstances of the child and the experiences of the adults, and presents a context of adoption support where 'having some difficulties' is anticipated and perceived as normal. Help is offered to overcome these difficulties, but this is a different context of support from one that suggests that things are likely to be fine and to 'wait to see' if problems arise before asking for help. The latter context implicitly raises, once again for many adopters, some element of failure around requesting professional help.

A framework is needed to routinely follow-up adopted children throughout their childhoods. In this way mental health services can be targeted to those most in need in a non-stigmatizing way. This process highlights the need to overcome the potential difficulties for newly placed adopted children in gaining access to Tier 3 specialist child mental health services, which include:

- Awareness that behaviours indicating concern in new adoptive placements (e.g. emotional withdrawal and generalized oppositional behaviour) may differ from those symptoms that are usually used as indicators for a prioritized service (e.g. self-harm or weight loss).
- The importance of accessible services for children who move from one geographical area to another.
- The need for services for children in transition from foster to adoptive care.

The Adoption Support Services Regulations (DOH, 2003), under the Adoption and Children Act (DFES, 2002) place a duty on local authorities to provide a range of specific support services. These enable adoptive parents and adopted children to receive good services wherever they live.

In the context of these regulations, and associated funding, a multi-agency group has developed a model of adoption support. This has social, psychological and physical health components. The psychological component of this package includes consultation, training and direct therapeutic intervention to children and their adoptive parents. This incorporates principles from attachment theory, cognitive-behavioural approaches and systemic approaches influenced by the work of Howe et al. (1999), Archer (1997, 1999), Archer and Burnell (2003), Delaney (1998a, 1998b), Delaney and Kunstall (1997) and Levy and Orlans (1998). The prime influence is the work of Dan Hughes (1997, 1998,

2004). This chapter focuses on one aspect of the model: indirect intervention through consultation to parents and social workers.

One key aim of this model is to minimize the likelihood that adoptive parents will 'take it personally' when difficulties arise. Perceiving problems as 'your fault' is a normal response for many parents when things go wrong with a child, regardless of the extent to which they were involved in the child's conception. The consequence of this perception, should it become entrenched, can create an atmosphere within the home of adult shame, non-communication about feelings and helplessness. This occurs alongside defensiveness when others raise concerns. These factors can immobilize a new adoptive parent's capacity to develop the type of family atmosphere and parenting attitude required to care effectively for children with severe attachment difficulties.

The model starts with the premise that adopting any child who has experienced neglect, trauma and loss combined with lack of continuity of care and permanent loss of birth parents could present difficulties (e.g. Smith & Brodzinsky, 2002). This includes the risk of attachment difficulties (Gauthier et al., 2004) and mental health difficulties (Rushton, 2004; Hodges et al., 2003; Steele et al., 2003, and see Howe, 1998, for a detailed review). The provision of good-quality psychological and therapeutic services as early as possible is seen as an effective use of scarce resources.

PATHWAYS TO LASTING RELATIONSHIPS: INTERVENTION STEPS AND EXAMPLES OF PRACTICE

A great deal is required from both foster carers and adoptive parents to help the recovery of a child who has experienced trauma and loss. Hughes (1997) suggests that it is helpful if they can:

- provide affective attunement and experience mutual enjoyment with their child;
- demonstrate differences from abusing adults and carers;
- demonstrate empathy and support around their child's trauma and shame;
- share their thoughts and emotions with their child;
- address any lies, distortions and minimizations;
- become involved in developing any joint plans and strategies for life at home, at school and with friends.

This model places the adoptive parent in a central role. It is therefore crucial that adoptive parents receive support and validation from their professional network regarding their authority as parents and their importance to their child.

Extracts from the story of one composite family of two parents (Jane and Tim) adopting two siblings (Ben and Lisa) are used to illustrate key psychological processes. The story covers the period before matching to 12 months after the children move in.

PAVING THE WAY

The Provision of a Psychological Teaching Component in Adoption Preparation Courses for Prospective Adoptive Parents

This input should highlight the impact of loss, trauma, neglect and severe attachment difficulties on the formation of new family relationships. If potential pitfalls are highlighted, it is crucial to be clear as to the extent and nature of the local support that will be available to work through any difficulties. It is equally important to evince a strong sense of hopefulness that any difficulties can be overcome, in time. An invaluable future link can be developed if the professional offering the prospective intervention can also provide an input into the initial training. This provides a sense of continuity and a basis for the beginning of trust.

An outline of the training content is summarized in Appendix 8.1.

Jane and Tim attend the adoption preparation course run by their local social services. They meet six other potential adopters. They also meet the social workers, paediatrician and clinical psychologist who offer both early and long-term support. They hear personal stories from new and long-term adopters. They hear about the impact of neglect and trauma, watch videos, and reflect on what it may be like for them to live with a child who has serious difficulties in forming trusting and loving relationships. They talk about how worried they feel about the length of time it can take a child to trust new carers, particularly after hearing some adopters say they managed the first year more like a job. They recognize how hard it will be for them if they live with a child who persistently lies to them and plan to think more about why this is so. They were relieved at hearing, first hand, how positive over time the experience of forming a new and loving family can be. This put any negative aspects into an overall context.

Detailed Analysis of Psychologically Relevant Historical and Current Information

As a substantial amount of paperwork accompanies the adoptive process, it is important to become familiar with statutory reports, although formal permission will need to be requested to gain access to these reports. A 'Form E', usually compiled by the child's social worker, can provide comprehensive information about the whole situation for the child, including behavioural and emotional factors. A 'Form F' provides comprehensive information about the circumstances, motivational factors, and family background of the adoptive parent or parents matched with a child.

Court reports can be requested, which requires formal permission being sought from the relevant Court. Similarly, relevant social work or expert reports can provide useful information. Observations describing parent–child interactions, and a range of professional opinions, can be obtained from Child Protection Case Conference minutes. The latter has proved to be a rich source of detailed information of specific interactions over time between adult carers and children.

An analysis of this information, from a developmental and psychological perspective, enables the formation of hypotheses that guide initial and future interventions.

The relevance of this task is highlighted in the report of associations between the Adult Attachment Interviews (AAIs) of adoptive mothers and the emotional themes arising in doll play narratives obtained from their recently adopted children. Steele et al. (2003) found to their surprise that, as early as three months after the adoptive placement started, it was possible to: 'discern significant influences upon the child as subtle as the adopter's state of mind with regard to attachment' (p. 200). Thus one possible cost of a child's early loss, abuse and neglect, is hyper-vigilance to the state of mind of a caregiver.

An early paper-based analysis has proved invaluable over time. This is frequently referred to in subsequent consultations, even years later, when trying to make sense of perplexing child behaviour or complex child–parent interactions. Initial opinions as to key developmental factors, attachment style, core beliefs, or persistent adaptive behaviours are revisited and revised repeatedly in the light of new information. During this process of clinical formulation as progressive hypothesizing, constant attention is given to ensure that 'self-fulfilling prophesies' are not being developed. It is essential that hypotheses at this stage are never put across as expert opinions, but as 'guesses' in the context of how often workers are surprised by what actually happens.

Intervention from an Attachment-based Psychological Perspective around Matching

Matching is the process by which an appointed local panel formally agrees to a particular child being placed with particular adoptive parents. This is a difficult and emotive process. Psychological intervention at this point can provide an assessment of the potential level of the child's developmental, emotional and educational needs during their first years in the adoptive home. This is linked to potential needs in relation to the adoptive parental circumstances, such as their styles of coping, stress management and attachment.

The initial findings of Steele et al. (2003) may aid the assessment of adopters, the matching process and the case for identifying individualized plans for early adoption support. This suggests that unresolved losses or mourning in a parent may exacerbate the emotional worries of a recently adopted child. Risks are increased if the child is late adopted, and has had a number of foster placements prior to being placed for adoption. Their work highlights the importance of normal carer–child interactions, including a mix of matching and rupturing of attention and affective states. With adoptive adult caregivers whose states of mind are dominated by their own unresolved loss or trauma: 'the availability of the adult to engage with a child, especially one that may be experiencing challenging and negatively tinged behaviour, may leave too many of the ruptures untended' (p. 201).

These findings highlight the importance of considering psychological need from the perspectives of both children and the adopting adults. Potential difficulties are hypothesized pre-matching. The process is to recognize need and plan for short- and long-term resources rather than to select prospective adopters in or out. This includes considering financial implications, and suggesting who will provide the interventions, should the placement go ahead. It may also be necessary to clearly state, from a psychological perspective, that unless there is clear evidence of the appropriate resources then the match should be reconsidered. This shifts the emphasis away from the suitability, or not, of the adopters, to accepting the findings and implications of a psychological assessment of both need, and risk, should the placement go ahead without the anticipated support.

The example below demonstrates how such an analysis can provide different perspectives about a child's needs at adoption panel, and to adopters. This can affect the adoption process, an understanding of placement needs and subsequent intervention.

It is six months since Jane and Tim attended the Prospective Adopters Training. They are about to be considered as a match for two half-siblings, Ben, aged 8 and Lisa, aged 3. The children live 200 miles away in a different Local Authority area. Three weeks before matching panel, Lisa communicates to her foster father that her grandad has been sexually abusing her for as long as she can remember. This became known through Lisa asking her foster father if her new family will have a grandad who will play her special game. Grandad has only recently had his final contact with Lisa.

Jane and Tim checked the box on their Form F, indicating that they would rather not take a sexually abused child. The Local Authority in the placing area feels that it is still appropriate to present the match to the panel this month.

In Jane and Tim's area, the support social worker urgently requests a two-hour pre-match joint consultation. This is agreed and a consultation is held including the local paediatrician and clinical psychologist, Jane and Tim, their support social worker, and Lisa's and Ben's social worker. The outcome recommends further intervention including:

- Finding out all known information about the sexual abuse.
- Assessment of the impact on Lisa, and her understanding, given her young age.
- An assessment as to whether Ben may have been sexually abused.
- Further assessment of Jane and Tim's understanding of the possible short- and long-term impact of sexual abuse.
- Further assessment of their capacity to care for Lisa and Ben in the light of this new information.

It is recommended that the panel decision be delayed until after these interventions have been completed. This is a tough recommendation and is carried out in the context of acknowledging the reservations of the placing agency.

Consideration of Child, Adult and Interactive Factors at the Point of Matching

Child and adult factors need to be understood and potential interactions between these explored. These include characteristics and attachment styles of the children, and the impact of sibling dynamics when more than one child is adopted; motivational factors for the adopters; and the potential impact of unresolved loss (see Steele et al., 2003). Additionally, parents may have experienced, and sometimes not acknowledged, previous child or adulthood abuse (e.g. from parents, peers or partners). All such factors can influence how the child settles in and how the parents adjust to the new parenting task. At this stage it is necessary to begin to build a relationship with the adults, with their support workers present, in which permission is given for examination of emotionally painful issues and events.

> The interventions recommended pre-matching have been completed and the match has recently been agreed at panel. Jane and Tim are both planning to return to full time work within three months of Lisa and Ben being placed with them. The needs of Lisa and Ben are considered during consultation. This takes into account their potential difficulties as a sibling pair with histories of early neglect, physical abuse, known sexual abuse to Lisa and witness to spouse abuse. It is recommended that they would benefit from one carer being physically and emotionally available whenever they are at home. The impact of this is discussed with Jane, Tim and the professional system. The potential extra resources required to provide consistent high-quality childcare when Jane and Tim are at work are also considered.
>
> After prolonged discussion as a couple, Jane approached her employer, who agreed that she could take 12 months off work, returning on a part-time basis. Jane feels great about this and acknowledges how pulled she has felt between long-term career aspirations and obligations, and her previously unspoken wishes to be a full-time mother. This enables Tim to talk about his worries of feeling marginalized as a parent if he is the only one in full-time paid work. They talk about this in depth during consultation and plan together how they can share tasks to reduce the likelihood of this happening.

Integrating Child and Adult Factors

Within the context of a two-hour psychological consultation hypothetical emotional responses can be considered, and normalized, without being minimized. It can be important to note that past trauma-induced feelings, beliefs and adaptive strategies may be evoked again through the adoptive process, independent of the amount and outcome of previous therapy or counselling.

> Seven years before marrying Tim, Jane experienced a two-year adult relationship in which she was emotionally humiliated and physically assaulted. This occurred gradually after a wonderful beginning, and was an extremely difficult time for her. Jane chose not to tell her family or her friends until she managed

to finally end the relationship. She thereafter received excellent support and validation for her choices.

The foster mother describes Ben, aged 8, as needing to be in control in a big way. He has occasionally hit and punched her when she insists he does as she asks.

Jane is asked how she might respond if similar feelings of victimization arise but this time from a small 8-year-old male child. She is asked to consider whom she would talk to about this?

Jane is taken aback to be asked about this as it had not occurred to her. She recognizes that she may not wish to go over all this again with her current partner. This may evoke feelings of past adult shame, which she felt had long ago been put to rest. Jane cries and shares this with Tim and they discuss together how they will manage this, if it arises. They both give permission for this to remain a potential theme for future consultations, if Ben does become physically aggressive, or emotionally intimidating.

This type of intervention can evoke negative responses, as such possibilities may not have been considered previously. It may be viewed as intrusive and unnecessary at the time. These potential responses highlight the importance of providing a context (during a consultative rather than a therapeutic intervention) of a consistent, long-term and trusting relationship with clear boundaries and confidentiality limits from the start. Feedback from adopters, over time, indicates that this early process of hypothesizing emotionally painful events, combined with rehearsal of responses, as a parental dyad was extremely helpful. If hypothetical situations then occur in reality, these early discussions give a meaning to the evoked adult response, a context in which to understand and explore emotions and a rehearsed solution. This decreases the chances that the parent involved 'takes it personally', feels overwhelmingly shamed, helpless or a failure as a parent, and thereby chooses to 'keep silent' about his or her perception of what is happening.

OPENING THE GATE: INTERVENTION SOON AFTER CHILDREN AND PROSPECTIVE ADOPTIVE PARENTS MEET

Initial Consultation

If the matching process has been straightforward, the first routine psychological consultation will be arranged during or soon after introductions have taken place. Consultations are planned for up to two and a half hours.

Adoptive parents, their support worker, the child's social worker and, sometimes, previous foster carers, are invited. If there are developmental, neurological or physical health issues, it can be helpful if joint working arrangements enable a community paediatrician to join the consultation at this early stage. This enables the relevant professionals and the adoptive parents to take a holistic approach to a child's physical and psychological health from the start.

Two key aims of consultation at this point are to provide psychological input into the 'first impressions' and to introduce the theory behind, and ideas for, the effective parenting of children who have experienced loss, abuse, neglect and have serious attachment difficulties.

Adoptive parents are taught parenting concepts arising from the application of attachment theory. This is returned to frequently during subsequent consultations, which include the importance to babies and children of the cycles of affective attunement, misattunement plus shame, followed by re-attunement and repair. These cycles happen thousands of times for the securely attached child. They promote attachment, socialization and conscience development and disruption of such cycles leads, to long-term consequences. The impact of pervasive shame is highlighted. This can be a barrier to developing a conscience. A child who feels overwhelmed with shame (how you feel about yourself) has difficulty feeling guilt or remorse (how you feel about others).

Adoptive parents are encouraged to make sure that these sequences of attachment occur as often as possible. Emphasis is placed on the importance of non-verbal attunement through sharing emotion and focused attention where enjoyable experiences are increased and stressful experiences are contained.

Emotional communication with the child, non-verbally as well as verbally, is seen as a key factor. The aim being to help the child to become more aware of his or her inner life, thoughts, feelings, wishes and intentions, as well as traumatic memories. These experiences enable a child to feel an affective (emotional) bond with caregiving adults, with whom emerging emotional awareness can be shared and communicated.

Adults are encouraged to plan how to behave as parents. They may want to be lax with discipline at first to make up for past hurts done to the child, or to plan 'Special Times', like parties or holidays abroad, to show how much the child is wanted. Both are examples of common early adoptive parenting responses that would be discouraged under this model. It is recommended that clear and comprehensive rules about family life are set from the start. The theory behind this thinking is discussed in detail alongside adopters' anticipated views that the approaches suggested are too negative, severe and restrictive.

Hughes (1997), whose work highly influences this model, explains the reasons for such clear and comprehensive family rules. These include helping the child to avoid 'failure' by presenting what is expected. Adoptive parents are encouraged to put these rules and expectations across in a matter-of fact tone with empathy for their child's response. Such rules are simply seen as a helpful way for the child to be able to learn how adults and children live together in this family. During the first days of the placement it is possible that:

- the child is going to be more receptive to adoptive parents' rules than later;
- choices and consequences are more easily perceived as parental teaching rather than punishment;
- both parents and child are less likely to be angry at each other and that parents may therefore have more empathy for the child's behavioural choices and he or she may be less likely to be oppositional, indicating that power struggles are therefore less likely to occur now than they might later;
- the child is less likely to see the choices and consequences as being a rejection of self.

Hughes (1997, p. 217) states:

> Later, the child is more likely to personalize the consequence. It becomes a statement about him, rather than a result of the family's rules and his current behavioral choice. The child is more likely to feel secure when he knows quite clearly what is expected of his behavior. Given such security, he will be somewhat more receptive to forming an attachment than if he needs to put a great deal of energy into keeping himself safe.

In summary, psychological intervention during the initial days and weeks after a child moves in explicitly aims to assess a range of child factors, adult factors, adult–child interactions and the role of support networks. Child factors include:

- A detailed analysis of children's behavioural and emotional responses to the events of the transitional period.
- The way children are appearing to feel comfortable with the adults.
- Whether children are showing any outward signs of grief regarding past or recent losses.
- The extent to which children have returned to previous adaptive strategies.

Adult factors include:

- The extent of 'click' felt by the adults at first and subsequent meetings.
- The impact of exhaustion combined with anxiety and excitement.
- How the adults are managing the combined stress of the above.
- The adult's ability to use reflective thinking when under stress, such as about parent–child interactions.

Jane and Tim took seriously the importance of setting clear family rules, with empathy, about: 'This is how we do things in our family.' Bedroom rules and bedtime patterns were firmly established from the time of Lisa and Ben's first overnight stay. These were tested in many ways, including Ben appearing to choose bedtimes as the time when he wanted to talk about his past traumas. Jane and Tim had been prepared for this and managed it beautifully by setting aside four 'Talk Time' sessions each week. Ben was helped to shift his wish to talk to these times. This meant that Ben did not take over whole evenings, Lisa had her share of bedtime and Jane and Tim successfully managed their guilt about appearing unkind and heartless when stopping Ben talk about his past abuse.

After six weeks of living there, Jane spoke of a worrying incident. A 4-year-old friend from playgroup had come downstairs happily talking of playing sexy games under the duvet with Lisa in the adult's bedroom. Jane and Tim were horrified and the other parents were told. After discussion they realized how much their bedroom and bedtime rules had slipped without their notice, as the early start went so well. The ease at which this can happen was put in the context of both children trying to re-enact the familiarity of the bedtime chaos of their family home in a one-bedroomed flat. Boundaries and rules were reinstated, as was increased supervision. Clear explanations were given to Lisa and Ben as to why they were not ready yet for less supervision and more flexible bedroom rules. They both accepted this with no complaint or oppositional behaviour.

Consultation as a Long-term Psychological Intervention

Subsequent consultations are offered routinely throughout the period prior to the final adoption hearing, and into the first year after the adoption has been formalized. Evaluation has shown that this process works successfully as a screening tool. It provides a flexible, responsive and non-stigmatizing assessment as to which families require and will benefit from other interventions, alongside the indirect consultation model.

These interventions include:

- Relationship-based attachment therapy to carer and child (see Chapter 12).
- Group work, facilitated by professionals, focusing on parenting children with severe attachment difficulties (see Chapter 7).

A number of key psychological processes emerge over the initial one to two years following an adoptive placement. A small number of these are identified in the following sections, alongside associated intervention strategies.

This proactive model of regular indirect intervention through consultation enables these themes to be identified, and addressed positively as they arise, before potentially negative and unhelpful parent–child interactions become established.

FIRST STEPS ON TO NEW PATHWAYS

Development of a 'Coherent Narrative'

It is crucial to be able to tell a clear story about your life, your memories, experiences and emotions, including the good and the tough times. This includes being able to reflect on your story when necessary, sharing it with someone else and not being afraid or ashamed of it. This process helps considerably to define who you are and to make sense of your feelings and your responses. Helping children who have experienced abusive parenting in the past to see that their behaviour was understandable given their situation (normalization of the behaviour) can reduce their shame because then their behaviour has a place in a coherent narrative (clear life story).

The early intervention steps identified as part of 'Paving the Way' lay the foundations for the adoptive parents to make sense of past significant information. They can help the child to incorporate past narratives into a current narrative. This includes becoming a member of their new and permanent family. The model uses this process, often termed 'Life Story' work by social workers, as a crucial process that gradually unfolds over time for the adopted child. For further discussion see Price (2003).

For some children, social work practice will have included videos of their adoptive parents, made by them, and given before introductions. This may be combined with a scrapbook welcoming them into their new family. Children will differ in the extent of responsive narrative work that has been completed prior to the adoptive placement. The child is a key player, with personal memories and questions guiding the process. An opportunity will be missed if 'Life Story' work becomes a single event when social workers, who may work many miles away from where a child is placed, hand over the child's life storybook to the adoptive parents six months into the placement.

It is likely that in the weeks leading up to the adoptive placement, children will have had their 'final visits' to many key attachment figures from their past. For practical reasons it can sometimes happen that children have formal goodbye visits with their mother or father just weeks before they move. At this point, if the child has become as securely attached as possible to foster parents, the layering of actual loss, potential loss and feelings of abandonment are immense. Early consultations integrate this information alongside discussions as to how to ensure that children's responses at this time are not lost in the face of just how many things are happening concurrently.

Consultations also provide a forum to discuss the psychological significance of the process of transferring information from the social worker and past foster carer (representing the past) to the adoptive parents (representing the future). The rationale is explained in the context of research evidence as to the importance of children having, or developing, a coherent narrative in their recovery from trauma, abuse and loss (Hughes 1997, 1998; Howe et al., 1999; Cairns, 2002).

This process can set the scene for how children integrate their construction of past events and their established core beliefs about themselves, others and the world, into their future view of life (Feast & Howe, 2003).

An example of a common theme that develops in the early months is the integration of core beliefs and constructs of birth mother and father, and foster mother and father into a psychological construct of an adoptive mother and father. The model presented here encourages the child's social worker to have an active key role at this point, always in conjunction with the adoptive parents.

This can be a worrying process for adoptive parents, as they may be concerned:

- that they will do or say the 'wrong thing';
- whether they should just listen, and acknowledge the story of how the children's parents weren't able to care for them, or be the carriers of the positive characteristics of their birth parents;
- that repeated queries about a birth mother and father indicate that the child is not ready to be adopted;
- that the child is rejecting them personally, and this can become even more distressing if the child screams in oppositional anger that he or she hates them and wants to go home to his or her foster parents or 'real' mother or father.

Sixteen weeks after moving to live with Tim and Jane, Lisa asked Jane if she could put their new Life Story book alongside the one she always kept under her pillow of her time living with her mum. The next night, Lisa asked if her mum could come and live with them. Lisa wanted Tim and Jane to look after them both. On hearing kindly, but clearly, that this wasn't possible, and the reasons why, Lisa became distressed, screaming at Jane that she hated her and wanted to leave the next day to go back to her foster carer.

Ben heard this and the next night asked Jane, 'How will I know if my mum is dead?' He also talked of his devil dreams, where a smiling kind devil came to visit him, cuddled him, and then changed into an evil devil who tried to eat him.

Tim and Jane are becoming emotionally exhausted by the children's distress around the loss of their birth mother. They begin to feel that this is the children's way of telling them they are not happy and do not want to live with them.

During consultation the importance of understanding and absorbing the children's grief and rage was discussed. A place in the house was made, with memory boxes, tapes of songs and videos, where they could go at agreed times to 'remember mum' together. It was recalled, by their social worker, that one of mum's partners frequently called their mum 'devil', as a term of affection. This was retold to Ben who recalled other memories of that time. After four weeks the family visits to the 'Remember Mum' place in the house lessened, at the children's pace. Ben's dreams went and Lisa moved her Life Story book about her mum to this place, keeping the one from her adoptive parents under her pillow.

Integrating Past Information

Sharing the Past that is Known to Adults in the Professional Network

Many children would prefer to keep their past experiences hidden and avoid all attempts by the adults to talk about their past. Difficulties can arise when an adoptive parent does not feel able to be part of the process of helping a child to integrate his or her past into their future as an adoptive family. Consultations can aim to tease out the meaning, for the adoptive adult, behind choosing not to make links between current challenging behaviour in the form of physical aggression to a parent, and the child's past experiences of physical abuse.

The Wish to Cause no Pain

Adoptive parents' core beliefs can include the belief that by helping children to recall a past they appear reluctant to remember, they will be responsible for causing the children emotional pain. It is believed that the children will thereafter blame the adoptive parents and lose any trust that has been established that they will keep them safe. The children will end up hating the adoptive parents and resenting them for doing this. Based on these beliefs, the adoptive parents do not feel prepared to take the risk, even in the face of psychological explanations as to why this is important. The risk of directly causing pain to children is simply too great to take.

Looking further behind the meaning of this for a parent during consultation may uncover deeper anxieties relating to the parent's own past experiences of hurt or abuse. The hidden meaning may be the belief that 'I will be overwhelmed by my own feelings if I allow myself to really empathize with what it felt like for my child (someone I love) to be abused and neglected.'

These are complex and emotional issues to explore with adults with whom the psychologist has a consultative rather than a therapeutic contract. At such times it is helpful to revisit matters of contract and confidentiality. Sometimes, it may be helpful for the adult to receive direct therapeutic intervention. Interventions are not readily available within the NHS for such work and decisions may need to be made as to how this is followed up, and who can offer adult-focused work.

Sharing the Past that is not Known to the Professional Network

Adopted children are likely to have traumatic experiences and memories that they have not shared with anyone else. At some point it is possible that children will find ways to communicate these experiences to the adoptive parents. This could be through behaviour, dream telling, pictures or using words. The meaning behind this process for a child can vary and it is important to help adoptive parents to reflect on the possibilities for their particular child. These can include, 'I am letting you know that I trust you enough to tell you this . . .' or 'This will really check out if you can love me and accept all my bad bits' or 'I will go mad if I keep this stuff to myself any longer'.

Children will have known about their own experiences for years. They will have found adaptive strategies to cope and carry on without telling anyone. The carer will be developing a relationship with the child based on the known information. Discovering new and distressing information, such as previous sexual abuse, may place the adoptive parent in shock. The adult will need to process the impact of the information and integrate a different kind of acceptance for his or her child. This can come when that child is most likely to be hyper-vigilant about all parental responses, particularly those that may indicate anticipated rejection. This is a time when they therefore need the most reflective care. 'How can he seem so together when I am falling apart' was a crucial question posed by one adoptive parent faced with this situation.

When this happens, work may need to be undertaken in consultations about the constructive integration of adult–child narratives.

SIGNPOSTS IN FOREIGN LANDS: LEARNING A NEW LANGUAGE

Adoptive parents, and their families, are unlikely to have extensive experience of children who have severe attachment difficulties. There is little time to grasp relevant concepts before it is necessary to understand the children enough to respond to their challenging behaviour effectively. Steele et al. (2003) highlight the likelihood that children's attachment behaviour will be elicited at a high intensity during the early days of a new placement, when 'almost any experience would either be sensed or expected as a threat, without necessarily being based in the reality of the new situation' (p. 202).

A psychological perspective can help to unravel the pertinent aspects of complex ideas, such as the impact for their particular child of:

- disrupted attachment processes
- persistent fear response
- hyper-arousal
- dysregulation
- dissociation.

The National Clearinghouse on Child Abuse and Neglect Information (US Department of Health and Human Sciences, 2001) summarizes the different roles of professionals and caregivers in the context of the developing understanding, from research, of the impact of early abuse and neglect on early brain development. 'Even caregivers with the best of intentions can misunderstand a child's behaviour, fashion their response based on that misunderstanding, and then wonder why their response was not effective' (p. 9).

It is important that knowledgeable professionals work with caregivers to help them to understand. They can consider together what can be done to help children to recover from their lost potential.

> Interventions cannot be constrained to weekly therapy appointments. Interventions must address the totality of the child's life, providing frequent, consistent 'replacement' experiences so that the child's brain can begin to incorporate a new environment–one that is safe, predictable and nurturing. (p. 10).

When core concepts are grasped, two further difficult steps remain. One is forming the belief about the length of time it can take children to begin to trust. The other is recognizing the persistent nature of the core beliefs that children bring with them. A child's core beliefs about self, others, the world and relationships can include:

- I am unlovable.
- I am special.

- I am bad.
- I don't deserve good times.
- I deserve special treatment to make up for all the bad things that have happened to me.
- People are only after what they can get.
- Bad times always follow good times so I'd rather not have any good times.
- The adults will always let you down in the end.
- If you let yourself love someone you will always end up hurt.
- The only way to stop getting hurt again is to be in control of everything and everybody.

Adoptive parents can become perplexed and confused when, 6 to 12 months into their newly formed family, they witness a return of concerning behaviours from their adopted son or daughter.

> Six months after moving in, things were going well. Ben was due to go on a special trip to an adventure park with his paternal grandfather and Tim's niece, Harriet. Ben was excited all week. Two days before the trip, while in the garden playing with Harriet and Lisa, Lisa came rushing in crying, 'Ben's killing Harriet'. Ben had, in fact, tripped Harriet up, and had kicked her when she fell to the floor. This was the first time he had been known to be aggressive in any way to Harriet. Harriet didn't seem bothered. Jane, Tim, and Grandpa were mortified. They managed to hold off giving a severe consequence until the adults had thought together. Harriet and his grandpa were becoming special to Ben, and Jane and Tim were perplexed. No apparent trigger could be found for Ben's aggressive outburst.
>
> During consultation the hypothesis was raised that Ben was terrified of the special trip as he was sure he would 'mess up' in some big way. He took control of his fear by acting in a way that would ensure that he wouldn't be allowed to go. Ben's difficulties in managing social situations were acknowledged. This suddenly made sense to Jane and Tim.
>
> Using 'Curiosity' statements and reflective dialogue, such as 'We wondered how it could be that you could hurt...', this was discussed with Ben later. Jane and Tim took responsibility for organizing something that Ben was not yet ready for. They told him he needed more practice at 'getting along', but with them physically present to help him. They would all go to the Park, with Harriet, during the next weekend.
>
> The consequence for kicking Harriet was to apologize in person and to teach her how to play his favourite trading card game.

One key aim of consultations is to help adoptive parents to understand and make sense of the meaning for children behind their behaviours. Psychological intervention with the adoptive parents at this point, as the adult and child narratives collide, can meet the need for some form of translation as to what is going on. It can also provide vital hope for the future at a time when adopters are most exhausted and their own psychological reserves are depleted.

> Eight months since moving in, driving past Ben's new school late one night after a good day out, Jane joked, 'We could drop you off now, Ben, so you would be here ready for the morning.' Lisa immediately said, 'It's O.K, Ben, I'll look after you. We'll be O.K.' It suddenly struck Jane that Lisa had taken her seriously.
>
> In the next consultation, Jane spoke of her shame at having made such a callous remark without thinking. She couldn't get it out of her mind – she felt so sad that Lisa's own internal world meant that (despite all the love and thoughtful care that she was receiving) she had actually believed that Jane could do such a thing. The enormity of loving children who find it so hard to trust hit home. As her understanding of the internal worlds of her two children increased, Jane wept for them and for herself.

UNCHARTED TERRITORY: PATHWAYS TO SAFE OR TREACHEROUS GROUND

'More than Ordinary' Parenting

This model addresses ways of trying to provide effective care for neglected, traumatized and abused children who also have attachment difficulties. This group of children can find it hard to control their emotions, may try to control everything in their life and often find it hard to ask for, or let their carers, help (Hughes, 1997, 1998; Howe et al., 1999). One aim of consultation is to help adoptive parents to understand and develop the different styles of parenting that are likely to be required. Reasons why some parenting interventions, such as those focusing on behavioural regimes and incentive schemes, may not produce much lasting change are explored.

The parental attitude referred to earlier is fundamental to the effectiveness of this approach. See Chapter 7 for a detailed description and discussion of this parenting model. This attitude includes:

- *Acceptance* – This includes the behavioural choices the child makes now, avoiding the use of 'trial periods' and 'last chances'.

- *Curiosity* – This includes wondering about the meaning behind the behaviour for the child. It is different from asking a child why he or she did something. Having an attitude of curiosity includes an attitude of being sad rather than angry when your child messes up and can get through to a child in a way that anger cannot.
- *Reflective and non-judgemental talk* – This can be part of being curious. It involves making 'best guesses' about what a child may be thinking and feeling, saying this aloud, and keeping it connected to the present. It can be about having a conversation with yourself without anticipating a response.
- *Empathy* – It is important to stress that empathizing with the underlying reasons for a child's behaviour does not mean that you condone the behaviour. A consequence (related if possible) should follow. If consequences seem to be occurring too frequently, it may be necessary to get back into more extensive 'adult supervision'.
- *Playfulness* – A playful attitude is crucial and can be a key factor in helping children to recover, particularly if they may have given up on the idea of having good times.

An Example of Responding to Challenging Behaviour

An example is described of the impact of a combination of sibling adaptive behavioural and emotional responses. It is one that clinical experience indicates arises frequently when adopting a sibling pair and effective responses can prove particularly challenging as a parent.

The Persistent Need to Control Combined with Persistent Demands for the Presence of the Main Carer by One Child and Extreme Self-reliance in the Other Sibling

Children with serious relationship and attachment difficulties can try to feel safe by attempting to control all aspects of their environment through their anger, rage, depression or compliance.

If children are habitually oppositional and defiant, they may come from a background where they had no control and things happened to them that were unpredictable. For example, when they cried, they were hit or when they were hungry they weren't fed. The children may not have been able to do anything to lead to more predictable responses, having no control at all over their environment.

One way for a child to subsequently feel safe is to try desperately to control everything that happens in the environment. So when the adoptive parent says 'No' (which means that the adult rather than the child is in control), the child becomes anxious, adults in control threaten feelings of safety. The child is then likely to fight the carer over even the smallest of things, with any request developing into a battle.

By planning to, and succeeding in, making carers angry for much of the time, children may feel safe because they believe they are in control. They may continue to feel that if they are in charge of the family atmosphere, they are less likely to be abused or hurt, even though they are no longer living with people who hurt them. Behaving like this may also reduce the risk of getting close enough to someone for the perceived inevitable consequence to follow of feeling hurt, rejected and abandoned.

Key issues often raised are how to manage a child's behaviour and how do adults get back in control. If the focus is on trying to control the child, much energy can go into 'putting out fires' every day.

If children's early experiences of parenting consisted of warm, loving care alternating with unpredictable parental neglect, they may have developed the adaptive strategy of persistently demanding the physical or emotional presence of their carer. These children may have the following core beliefs about their carer: 'You must never leave me alone'; 'You must always be there for me'; 'If you leave me alone for a minute, I will become scared that you will never come back or that someone might hurt me or that you will forget about me'; 'I will never forgive you for making me feel like that again'.

Lisa was overheard telling an adult friend of Jane, 'You know, I really like living here. The only trouble is they think they are in charge of me.' Jane's friend perceived this as a humorous and sweet comment. However, Jane and Tim were feeling, nine months after Lisa moved in, that this aspect of Lisa's behaviour was not responding to anything they did.

Half way through a consultation Tim expressed his fears that they would never get it right for Lisa. Battles over tiny matters were escalating. He was coming home from work to a tearful and exhausted Jane. Lisa was making so many positive changes in many other areas of her life, but their frustration was increasing at her need to feel in control at all costs. This seemed to be increasing and was impeding emotional progress in key areas. After calling Jane 'mum' for many months she reverted to calling her 'Jane' after oppositional outbursts. Jane admitted to finding it hard to like Lisa at times and she was finding reasons for delaying the process around the formal final adoption hearing.

A hypothetical intervention is described using the above example.

It was acknowledged during consultation that both Jane and Tim were rapidly losing the capacity to respond to Lisa's hostility with empathy. Lisa was increasingly in control of Jane's emotional life and behavioural responses. Jane was beginning to feel a complete failure.

The events of the preceding few weeks were tracked in detail, including an incident following a family party in London. Lisa woke up ecstatic in the hotel in which they had decided to stay, rather than travel back. She danced around singing 'We're yours now'. She had mistakenly seen the family party for a cousin's twenty-first birthday as their formal adoption party. Jane and Tim were perplexed at how this had happened given how they had described in detail the actual process of going to Court.

The impact of both children's understanding of the adoptive process, and what this incident may have meant to them psychologically, was discussed in the consultation.

The impact of Lisa's understandable misreading of cues not having been adequately addressed by her parents was reflected upon. There had previously been many examples of Lisa beginning to love and trust them. It was hypothesized that this seemingly small incident had a huge impact on Lisa and Ben. The children's core beliefs about adults always letting you down in the end were returned to. This incident may have been enough for Lisa to become highly anxious that Jane and Tim would never adopt them, increasing her fear that they would reject them at some point, as everyone else in her life had. It was hypothesized that Lisa may have returned to her pervasive controlling behaviours to protect herself from potential hurt.

Jane and Tim talked about how awful they had really felt about this. So awful that they hadn't been able to bear talking about it. They acknowledged their guilt about having avoided managing Lisa's confusion and disappointment as well as not anticipating her subsequent rejecting behaviour. Jane and Tim talked of how hard it had all been lately. Jane felt so resentful of Tim's easy playful relationship with Lisa. Themes of 're-enactment of past' were returned to.

Ben's more detached and avoidant style, including core beliefs associated with 'I can manage on my own', was discussed in terms of how this can seem easier to manage emotionally for some parents. This way of interacting with others may fit more easily with cultural expectations of a neglected and traumatized child. It was wondered how much Ben may be benefiting from Lisa doing all the visible emotional work while he carefully watched the adults' responses. It was hypothesized that Ben was also likely to be feeling anxious about whether the adoption would continue.

During the consultation, Jane and Tim practised saying some actual words to Ben and Lisa (Reflective Dialogue), rehearsing the attitude of acceptance, curiosity and empathy.

Things have been tough for us lately. We have had so many battles and so many hurtful things have been said. It will be hard but we will work through this together. No matter what happens we are a family now and we will find a way. (Acceptance)

We were also wondering if Ben was worried about the adoption. We were trying to make sense of all this. You know, we were remembering the other day and wondering what on earth it might have been like to find out that you had not been adopted that day in London. (Curiosity)

You must have thought it had all been sorted. Maybe that reminded you of all the times you had been let down by adults. That must have been so hard for you both. (Empathy)

We were so busy we never took the time to think about this with you. Sometimes we make mistakes and miss important stuff and that may make you anxious. We do love you and want you to be our family. (Acceptance)

It was predicted that Lisa might bury her head or shout 'No. Shut up. I hate you ...'.

Responses to Lisa doing this were practised, giving acceptance and empathy about Lisa maybe not wanting to think about all this again. It was anticipated that both children would respond to being physically held and hearing about specific examples of just how special they are.

It was suggested that Jane and Tim return to previous ways of 're-parenting' Lisa.

Jane and Tim were phoned that night and two weeks later by the consultant. Immediately afterwards, as anticipated, Lisa had become extremely distressed. She tore up special pictures, broke a plate, and thumped her brother. She did, however, totally accept all the consequences given. She engaged fully in being re-parented, even asking to be rocked and sung to by Jane. Within one week, Jane was beginning to have loving feelings again for Lisa.

This example is an illustration of the importance of adoptive parents receiving the same attitude during consultation from professional supports as they are being asked to offer to their child. If the adoptive parents are not offered acceptance and empathy for all their responses, it may be harder for them to move on to take the action necessary to repair difficult times with their children. That is, to accept their child, from which follows curiosity as to what the meaning might be behind what they do. This is followed by empathy for how hard they are trying and just how tough the task is for them of learning to live in a family again, to trust the adults who are parenting them.

ESTABLISHING A LASTING RELATIONSHIP: PATHWAYS TO INCREASED SECURITY

Consultation as Children and Adults get to Know Each Other Well

Ongoing consultation aims to address how adult–child relationships are developing over time. Hodges et al. (2003) report preliminary findings comparing themes from story stem assessments of children adopted in the first year of life with older previously maltreated children, placed for adoption. Changes were tracked in their attachment representations over the first year of placement in their new families. This suggests that ongoing work is likely to be required with the families of some later-adopted children. At the one-year assessment, in this study, positive attachment representations increased – for example, of adults helping and limit setting. However, negative attachment representations did not decrease – for example, seeing adults as aggressive or rejecting.

Building Bridges between Past and Present

Falling in Love: Adult Perspectives and the Significance of Public Acknowledgement

Falling in love is a subjective experience. It is hard to do justice to the associated emotions by analysing this process following the making of a new family through an adoptive placement. During regular consultation over the first year, it is often possible to mark an incident of startling significance for adults when they recognize what it means for them to fall in love with a child. This is particularly so with adults who have not given birth to their own children.

Adoptive parents can describe this as an almost physical sensation. It feels emotionally painful to acknowledge the affect that goes alongside knowing you have no choice but to put another person before yourself, regardless of the personal consequences.

> Jane talked about Lisa's first day at school. She felt emotionally exhausted having had little time for herself for many months. She had anticipated relief, and associated guilt, on returning to an empty house. However, once home she felt a huge gap and longed to see Lisa again. She was amazed at how much she missed Lisa. Jane reflected that this was the point when she began to realize what it means to love your own child.

> Discussion ensued about loving a child to whom you did not give birth and the loss of all those first experiences that Jane and Tim had missed out on – giving birth, the first smile, first steps. The first day at school was equated with the first day at playgroup – a publicly recognized time for a parent to pace at home, crying, resisting the temptation to phone, waiting for the allotted time to pick up the 2 year old. The impact of having little opportunity to publicly acknowledge the time of falling in love with the adopted child was highlighted as the formal hearing usually post-dates this by a long time.

The significance for the adopters of consultation enabling an independent outside person (the consultant) to celebrate this process with them is hard to objectively gauge. Clinical experience indicates that once this process has been talked about in consultation, the child thereafter seems to be accepted unconditionally by his or her adoptive parents, regardless of whatever challenging behaviour is subsequently presented. The issue becomes one of how to get through the hard times, rather than whether the hard times mean that the adoption may never work out. This observation may make clearer the meaning behind the personal impact of witnessing this process and sharing the affect, as a professional supporting the adoption process.

Securing the Gate

It is important to check out and assess the hope that within 9–18 months after moving in, a child may begin to experience and attempt to make some sense of differences between his or her early parenting, the potentially effective but transient parenting of foster care and the promised permanency of adoptive care. Regular indirect psychological intervention throughout the first two years after moving in enables thoroughness in the task of attempting to track changes in a child's overall development. It facilitates the process of understanding the meaning of particular behaviours in the context of the child's developing attachments.

This task depends, in part, upon the extent to which the adoptive parents have developed the capacity for reflective thinking about their child, themselves and the interactions between the two. A key aim at this point, often into the second year after moving in, is to have developed a shared understanding of the tasks of the adopters and the psychologist, through consultation. This has a bearing on how the adoptive parents subsequently use the offer of psychological intervention, at their request, during the next few years.

Testing Changes: The Audition

Tim was looking after both Lisa and Ben, while Jane was visiting a friend. A pattern was becoming established. Ben had refused to come in for lunch earlier in the day with the consequence that the time he delayed would be taken away from his bedtime reading with Tim. At bedtime, Tim, as always, calmly restated the consequence and carried it out.

Ben tried every possible verbal barter known to persuade Tim to read to him for the usual time, even down to giving up the playstation for a month. Tim, as before, calmly restated the consequence, without engaging in debate, and carried it out. For the next hour Ben went through, in turn, every challenging behaviour strategy he knew to try to control Tim and get him to either change his mind or become angry. These strategies included attempting to strangle himself with his dressing gown cord over the banisters and threatening to smash a very precious vase that once belonged to Jane's dead grandparent. Lisa watched all this with fascination but little observable fear or anxiety.

During the consultation, the adults were all amazed at Tim's ability to continue to parent with acceptance, curiosity and empathy. At no time did he respond to Ben's hostility with irritation or anger. It was also noted that after an hour Ben offered his own solution, acceptable to both, which was: 'Well, Dad, will you teach me to read better, starting tomorrow?'

Tim and Jane had thought about this potentially perplexing and concerning incident at length prior to the consultation. Tim was not amazed by his own parenting. During reflection after the event he had recognized a subtle difference in Ben's affect. He didn't feel Ben's emotions to be escalating out of his own control, as had always been the case on previous, usually less dramatic, incidents. Tim's confidence, with hindsight, came from recognizing that this was a different kind of test from before. Tim felt Ben was beginning to 'Get It' that these parents really were different from his birth parents. Tim felt the meaning of the process for Ben was to doubly check out if his adoptive parents could really look after him and Lisa properly, and safely. Whether they could contain all Ben's negative affect, without making Ben feel bad.

It was hypothesized that Ben's core beliefs about relationships were beginning to change to: 'Some adults really can accept me no matter what I do; Jane and Tim really can look after me.'

This has been described in some detail as an example of how to measure the effectiveness of this type of indirect intervention, focusing on new adoptive parents Jane and Tim. They are equally as remarkable as all the new adoptive parents who have been offered this model of intervention.

When the parents are in charge in this way and have the concept of an open, long-term, responsive service with a support network they know, they can judge when things are getting stuck and when to ask for assistance. This process may be aided by parents using the checklist in Appendix 8.2.

REFLECTIONS AND THE WAY FORWARD

Observations so far from implementing the consultation component of the model are outlined in the following three sections.

I. Highlighting Areas of 'Best Practice' to Maximize Positive Outcomes for Adopted Children

This involves the recognition, normalization and evaluation of key processes involved in adult cognitive and behavioural change over time. These include:

- Integration of loss and grief for what will never be, anticipation (pre-adoption), excitement and fear (at matching and during introductions).
- Using known coping strategies, or developing new ones, to manage reality, such as exhaustion (first 3–9 months), and feelings of 'it's a job, not a family'.
- Acknowledgement of the process of falling in love. Making sense of and normalizing feelings if this does not happen.
- Being and feeling a parent and a family as well as an adopter.

2. Patterns for Adult High Concern which Trigger Requests for More Professional Input

These include:

- Recognition of the impact of the persistent nature of the need to control on parents, and on the child's emotional development.
- An increase of direct verbal and physical expression of aggression to the carer, usually one more than the other, often the main carer, often the mother.
- New information from the child about the child's past, such as previous sexual abuse.

- Troubles at school for children who are academically able but who have emotional difficulties. They are not yet ready to manage the complexities of a school environment without a safe adult figure nearby to help them to translate the world.
- Splitting parents into one good and one bad.
- Worries about not feeling able to like a child.

The latter two factors are often linked to:

- Successful re-enactment of the past abusive and neglectful family environment in the adoptive family, where the adults have joined the child's emotional world, rather than the other way round.

3. Adoptive Parent Perceptions of which Aspects of Intervention made a Positive Difference

These include:

- Being informed about the importance of high structure and routine from the start, being given a clear idea about how to do this, and planning for this before their child moved in.
- What it really means to 'accept what was' and linking difficulties in accepting their child with their own personal issues, as an adult.
- Having the opportunity, and being encouraged, to consider their own personal issues, such as re-experiencing, as an adult, feelings of victimization as a child.
- Learning together about the type of parenting strategies that help their child and them to move on. Learning ways of keeping calm rather than feeling irritated for long periods.
- Input at a local and strategic level to the education service about the specific needs, including additional resources required, of children with primarily emotional difficulties.

Plans for Long-term Intervention

One long-term aim of this model is a reduction in adoption breakdown; middle adolescence appearing to be a time of particular risk. To assist this outcome, plans include routine call-back appointments, jointly offered by a paediatrician and a clinical psychologist, at key developmental stages, such as when children are aged 9–10 years and 13–14 years.

So far, it is encouraging that over the two years the model has been operating, no adoption breakdowns have occurred with the 20 children referred at the time of matching. These children will receive long-term consideration, enabling follow-up data to be collected throughout their childhoods.

APPENDIX 8.1

Training Programme for Prospective Adopters: An Outline of the Psychological Component

Building Relationships: Basic Principles

Feelings and Thoughts are as Important as Behaviour

It is helpful to keep on trying to look behind behaviour to make sense of the thoughts, feelings and beliefs underneath.

Knowing about the Past can Help with Understanding what is Happening Now

Attachment styles and influences on core beliefs.
Coping and adaptive behavioural strategies.
Development: physical and psychological.

Relationships are a Good Place to Start

Looking after yourself.
Family atmosphere.
Family structure, routine and rituals.
Spending time together:

● Supervision and 'adult physical presence'.

Behaviours and emotions.

● Understanding them, living with them and helping children cope in different ways.
● Managing behaviour: 'Choices and Consequences' as a method of discipline.

Steps Along the Way: Developing an Attitude for Effective Parenting

(Influenced by Hughes, 1997, 1998)

A	Acceptance	*Of whomever the child is now, emotionally and behaviourally.*
C	Curiosity	*'How come . . . I wonder how it has happened that . . . ?'*
C	Containment	*Remaining in control of your emotions in times of stress.*
E	Empathy	*'This must be so hard for you . . .'*
P	Playfulness	*Whatever the adult's or the child's age.*
T	Thinking and reflecting	*Taking time for a calm step back to try to make sense of what is going on.*

APPENDIX 8.2

Making Sense of and Managing Behaviour: A Checklist

If you feel stuck on a large number of these queries it may be time to phone to discuss whether a consultation might be helpful.

About your Family and You

- How is the atmosphere in your family? How well are you looking after yourself? To what extent can you remain emotionally contained when your child is trying to make you angry?
- Are you getting enough breaks or respite – in meaningful ways for you?
- Is there a reasonable and clear structure and routine in your family routines?
- Are there any special times built in for you and your child?

About your Child

- To what extent does your child need to control aspects of his or her life?
- How well can your child manage (regulate) his or her feelings?
- To what extent is your child stuck in feeling shame?
- To what extent can your child tell a clear story about his or her life so far?

Making Sense of Specific Behaviour

What is the Meaning Behind your Child's Behaviour?

- Try to make sense of behaviour, as something you and your child work out together.
- It is helpful to keep on trying to look behind behaviour to make sense of the connections between the thoughts, feelings and beliefs underneath.

Coping Strategies

- Attempt to accept and understand the coping or adaptive strategies your child has developed to deal with his or her trauma. Respect your child's defences; they were developed for a good reason and have been helpful in the past. Gently challenge their continuing usefulness in the present. To what extent can your child self-soothe?

What is the Feeling Behind your Child's Behaviour?

- Notice if, when, and how your child becomes overwhelmed by his or her feelings. Do feelings build inside your child to the extent that he or she doesn't know what to do? When this happens does he or she dissociate (freezing, seeming not to be there, trance like) or dysregulate (become very active with a high arousal level)?
- Aim to talk about both positive and negative emotions. Have no taboos about conversation.

How is your Child making Sense of your Behaviour and What are the Implications for your Child's Beliefs about How you Think and Behave?

Children often misread others' motives and make false assumptions. If children don't have a secure sense of self (in terms of how they can effectively get others to positively respond to them), it is hard for them to make sense of other people's motives. Develop an understanding of your child's assumptions about the reasons why you and others behave as they do towards him or her.

REFERENCES

Archer, C. (1997) *First Steps in Parenting the Child who Hurts: Tiddlers and Toddlers.* Adoption UK. London: Jessica Kingsley.

Archer, C. (1999) *Next Steps in Parenting the Child who Hurts: Tykes and Teens*. Adoption UK. London: Jessica Kingsley.

Archer, C. & Burnell, A. (Eds) (2003) *Trauma, Attachmeent and Family Permanence. Fear Can Stop You Loving.* London: Jessica Kingsley.

Cairns, K. (2002) *Attachment, Trauma and Resilience. Therapeutic Caring for Children.* London: BAAF.

Delaney, R. (1998a) *Raising Cain. Caring for Troubled Youngsters/Repairing our Troubled System.* Oklahoma City, Oklahoma: Wood 'N' Barnes.

Delaney, R. (1998b) *Fostering Changes. Treating Attachment-disordered Foster Children.* Oklahoma City, Oklahoma: Wood 'N' Barnes.

Delaney, R. & Kunstal, F. (1997) *Troubled Transplants. Unconventional Strategies for Helping Disturbed Foster and Adopted Children*. Oklahoma City, Oklahoma: Wood 'N' Barnes.

DFES (2002) *Adoption and Children Act 2002*. London: TSO.

DOH (2003) *Adoption Support Services Guidance*. To accompany the Adoption Support Services (Local Authorities) (England) Regulations 2003, TSO.

Feast, J. & Howe, D. (2003) Talking and Telling. In A. Douglas & T. Philpot (Eds), *Adoption. Changing Families, Changing Times* (pp. 139–145). London: Routledge.

Gauthier, Y., Fortin, G. & Jeliu, G. (2004) Clinical application of attachment theory in permanency planning for children in foster care: The importance of continuity of care. *Infant Mental Health Journal*, **25**(4), 379–396.

Hodges, J., Steele, M., Hillman, S., Henderson, K. & Kanuik, J. (2003) Changes in attachment representations over the first year of adoptive placement: Narratives of maltreated children. *Clinical Child Psychology and Psychiatry*, **8**(3), 347–363.

Howe, D., Brandon, M., Hinings, D. & Schofield, G. (1999) *Attachment Theory, Child Maltreatment and Family Support: A Practice and Assessment Model*. Basingstoke: Macmillan.

Howe, D. (1998) *Patterns of Adoption*. Oxford: Blackwell Science.

Hughes, D. (1997) *Facilitating Developmental Attachment: The Road to Emotional Recovery and Behavioural Change in Foster and Adopted children*. Northvale, NJ: Aronson.

Hughes, D. (1998) *Building the Bonds of Attachment: Awakening Love in Deeply Troubled Children*. Northvale, NJ: Aronson.

Hughes, D.A. (2004) An attachment-based treatment of maltreated children and young people. *Attachment and Human Development*, **6**(3), 263–278.

Levy, T. & Orlans, M. (1998) *Attachment, Trauma and Healing. Understanding and Treating Attachment Disorder in Children and Families*. Washington, DC: Child Welfare League of America Press.

Price, P. (2003) The 'Coherent Narrative'. Realism, resources and responsibility in family permanence. In C. Archer & A. Burnell (Eds), *Trauma, Attachment and Family Permanence. Fear can Stop You Loving* (pp. 46–61). London: Jessica Kingsley.

Rushton, A. (2004) A scoping and scanning review of research on the adoption of children placed from public care. *Clinical Child Psychology and Psychiatry*, **9**(1), 89–106.

Smith, D.B. & Brodzinsky, D. (2002) Coping with birthparent loss in adopted children. *Journal of Child Psychology and Psychiatry*, **43**(2), 313–223.

Steele, M., Hodges, J., Kanuik, J., Hillman, S. & Henderson, K. (2003) Attachment representations and adoption: Associations between maternal states of mind and emotion narratives in previously maltreated children. *Journal of Child Psychotherapy*, **29**(2), 187–205.

US Department of Health & Human Sciences (2001) *In Focus. Understanding the Effects of Maltreatment on Early Brain Development*. National Clearinghouse on Child Abuse and Neglect Information.

9

MORE THAN WALLS: THE CONTEXT OF RESIDENTIAL CARE

Ruth Nissim

The topic of residential care is a vast and complex one, and the scope for psychological interventions is potentially broad. At the same time, residential care in Local Authority settings is now offered to only a minority of looked after children (albeit those with the most severe and complex needs) and as such is a small part of the complete endeavour. Equally, it can often be a small part of the activity of psychologists – even those with a dedicated role for looked after children. This is just one of the many contradictions that beset this topic.

For this reason, this chapter aims to explore and clarify the significance of residential care itself before looking, in Chapter 10, at psychological interventions. An opening section on historical perspectives is followed by a look at the contemporary context of residential care, and from these some key themes and issues are extracted. This provides a useful context to reflect, in Chapter 10, on how thinking psychologically might be helpful for other professionals and might guide interventions from psychologists.

HISTORICAL PERSPECTIVES ON RESIDENTIAL CARE

The history of children being looked after is itself part of a larger history of childhood (Ariès, 1962). It contains a complex tangle of traditions of which

Thinking Psychologically About Children Who Are Looked After and Adopted
Edited by K.S. Golding, H.R. Dent, R. Nissim and L. Stott.
Copyright © 2006 John Wiley & Sons, Ltd.

two are extracted here: the parents who choose to place their children away from home, and those who have little or no choice.

Early examples of children being placed away from home voluntarily date back to pre-Christian times, but invariably they went to other families. Throughout the Middle Ages in Europe it became common practice for more affluent families to seek places for their children in families of higher social status (Boswell, 1991). For poorer families, placing children away was an employment opportunity, as well as achieving housing, food and clothing at someone else's expense. They might even bring a meagre income back to the family of origin (Ariès, 1962). Again, children were going to wealthier families.

The prospects for unwanted children were rather different; they were much more likely to be reared in an institution. In England, prior to the Poor Law of 1536, it was the Church that played a key role in England in caring for unwanted children. Following the dissolution of the monasteries this 'safety net for the very poor' was removed (Triseliotis et al., 1995, p. 4) and a new set of institutions created, providing education for children of the nobility, and accommodation for the poor and destitute. Some contemporary British public schools can trace their origins back to this period. If by chance you were abandoned at the Ospedale della Pietà in Venice in the early eighteenth century, your prospects were likely to be transformed by the presence of Antonio Vivaldi, who offered a first-class musical education to selected female foundlings. However, this was a remarkable exception, which ended with his death in 1741 (Latham, 2002). Institutions for the poor took a downward turn during the nineteenth century, with the development of foundling hospitals across Europe:

> ... which neatly gathered all of the troubling and messy aspects of child aban-
> donment away from view, off the streets, under institutional supervision. Behind
> their walls, paid officials dealt with Society's loose ends, and neither the parents
> who abandoned them, or their fellow citizens had to devote any further thought
> or care to these children.
>
> (Boswell, 1991, pp. 431–432)

A reading of the literature of this period amply illustrates the nature of these establishments. *Nicholas Nickleby* by Charles Dickens (1978) is a well-known example, with its infamous Dotheboys Hall!

Institutionalization became common and was provided not only by the state (in the form of the workhouse) but also by voluntary societies (usually of a religious nature), who took unwanted children off the streets (Morgan, 1998). From there, thousands were shipped to the colonies from the latter part of the nineteenth century to as late as 1956 (Triseliotis et al., 1995). Extraordinarily, the Poor Law Boards were still providing for the care of unwanted children

400 years after their inception, and it was only after the Second World War that the Children Act 1948 replaced this legislation. The Curtis Report (1946) had drawn attention to the adverse effects of institutionalization of children on their development, and this is one of the first examples of psychology influencing residential issues. The research of Goldfarb (1943) and Spitz (1945) had demonstrated the need for a more individualized approach to child rearing and this research was referred to and affected the subsequent legislation that firmly advocated family-based care as preferable to institutional care.

The Children Act 1948 replaced Poor Law provision with state care and statutory services, and through the 1950s substitute family care took precedence. However, research evidence began to emerge during the 1960s, which suggested that many of the foster-placements were breaking down (Trasler, 1960; Parker, 1966; George, 1970), and this led to a decline in the use of fostering and a return to the use of residential care. The state decided to increase its power to intervene in family life, as enshrined in the Children and Young Persons Acts of 1963 and 1969. Now children being compulsorily removed from their families were likely to be placed in residential care, and a number of new facilities were built during the 1960s to accommodate them.

In this decade the reasons for reception into care began to shift towards the entanglement of the criminal justice system with the care system. Minor misdemeanours often led to unintended consequences for a young person, who might have stolen a bar of chocolate and ended up in residential care. This was popularly known by social workers at the time as the 'Mars Syndrome' (J. Randall, personal communication, 2004). Equally, problems with education, especially non-school attendance, could have the same result. However, although youngsters with this profile were often removed from home, it became evident that being away did not act as a cure either for their 'delinquency' or for their difficulties with the education system. Research began to show that removal from home was not an effective solution to these problems (Thorpe et al., 1980).

By the end of the decade the inadequacies of the public care system were again being challenged by research evidence, which showed that many children who were remaining in residential settings for prolonged periods could have benefited from family-based care (Rowe & Lambert, 1973). The next new Children Act of 1975 marked a return to family-based care. At the same time it reduced the rights of parents and often excluded them entirely. Family-based care did not include the family of origin under the 1975 Act.

As the impact of this legislation began to emerge, there was mounting evidence of unsuccessful outcomes for children in the care system (Thorpe, 1980; Holman, 1980; Triseliotis, 1980; Rowe et al., 1984; Milham et al., 1986; Berridge & Cleaver, 1987), and this provided the foundation for the Children Act 1989 (DOH, 1989). The Climbié inquiry report (Laming, 2003) opened another chapter in providing legislation to protect vulnerable children culminating in the Children Act 2004 (DFES, 2004b) and the programme for change described in *Every Child Matters, Change for Children* (DFES, 2004a). The emphasis has shifted from a concern with whether children should live within or outside of their families to a need for multi-agency planning and active partnership of local, statutory, voluntary and community organizations to improve the well-being of children. This encompasses safeguarding and promoting the welfare of vulnerable children and promoting the educational achievement of looked after children. The impact of the current Children Acts (DOH, 1989 and DFES, 2004b) on the provision of residential care will be discussed in more detail later in this chapter.

CONTEMPORARY CONTEXT

Scandals

Residential care carries a burden of history that colours the perceptions not only of the public but also of professionals. It also colours the views of those who live and work there. Moreover, in recent decades a spate of scandals has surrounded British children's homes, doing nothing to enhance their reputation as a valid provision for looked after children. Scandals are meat and drink to the media, and the coverage of these events often serves to diminish rather than advance public perceptions. The fact that disclosures of abuse and other malpractice often pertain to episodes, which took place over 20 years before they are made public, is seldom a consideration in the consciousness of those who are hearing about it for the first time.

Reviewing the main scandals to come to light in the last 20 years: Kincora Boy's Hostel, Belfast (DHSS, 1986), Frank Beck in Leicestershire (Kirkwood, 1993), Pindown in Staffordshire (Levy & Kahan, 1991) and North Wales (Crimmens & Pitts, 2000), certain themes are striking. The victims are boys and the perpetrators male. This, of course, reflects the patterns of care in that period, where boys were both more likely to be in care, and also more likely to be in residential care, than girls. All-boy establishments were the norm in the 1960s and 1970s, and by and large staff, especially senior staff, were male.

A worrying theme for this book is the use and abuse made of psychology, perhaps most notably in the Pindown regime, where residents were controlled through a mixture of material and psychological deprivation. It is likely that some use was made of the research on the effects of sensory deprivation on behaviour and adjustment. It is also possible that describing the regime as 'psychological treatment' may have given it an ill-deserved cloak of respectability. In both Leicestershire and Staffordshire there were charismatic individuals masterminding such malpractice. However, the more recent disclosures in North Wales reveal the cynical collaboration of groups of paedophiles who gained access to vulnerable young people while employed as residential social workers. Using information available on the Internet, they were able to apply for jobs in the same establishments so that they could collaborate on creating the context in which abuse could occur and work together to maintain secrecy.

Common to all these scandals was the abuse of power, which is a feature of all forms of abuse. This combined with the opportunities conferred by intimate care giving to disastrous effect. This was partly because the victims could neither speak nor be heard; partly, too, because of the closed nature of the establishments, which were barely known, still less understood by many senior managers and staff in other parts of the same system. Silence and secrecy could only end with the adulthood of the victims concerned and it is the case that the majority of such investigations have been instigated by them.

Research Evidence: A Brief Review

Reference has already been made to the impact of the research of Goldfarb (1943) and Spitz (1945) on policy regarding the use of residential care. Among other things, they identified the following key issues; isolation of children (from the community); carer:child ratios of one to eight; very little personal/individualized attention; minimal opportunities for peer interaction; low levels of stimulation. These combined to affect child development adversely.

Skeels (1966) followed a group of 25 institutionalized children in the 1930s, and found that, 21 years later, those who had experienced an 'enriched environment' had become self-supporting adults. The enriched environment consisted of reducing staff:child ratios and personalizing the care of the children in a way that allowed meaningful relationships to develop. The children became attached to a particular adult and this was thought to be the foundation for their future success as adults.

Research on children's homes benefited from two excellent British studies, which were published through the 1980s. Berridge (1985) made a detailed examination of 20 children's homes in three Local Authorities covering different regions of England. Three types of home were identified: small 'family group' homes, medium 'adolescent hostels', and large 'multi-purpose' homes. He found that around half of all the residents were waiting for long-term placements, usually with foster families. This echoes the celebrated study referred to earlier (*Children Who Wait*, Rowe & Lambert 1973), who estimated that around 7,000 were in residential care who could/should have been given

Table 9.1 Patterns of use of Local Authority care (adapted from Rowe et al., 1989)

Age	Living at home	Fostered	Adopted	Residential
Under 5	6%	77%	8%	6%
5–10	7%	65%	1%	25%
11+	11%	15%	—	62%
Average (based on totals)	10%	37%	2%	37%

family placements. It appears that over a decade later, many were still waiting. Moreover, Berridge (1985) found that a third of all the residents in his study had already experienced one or more breakdowns of long-term foster placements. Rowe et al.'s (1989) huge study involving over 9,000 children in six Local Authorities usefully juxtaposed family-based and residential care, both in terms of patterns of use, and of outcomes. Drawing on her data, Table 9.1 has been created to show the position she reported in relation to the use of residential care.

Rowe et al. (1989) not only found very high patterns of use of residential care for adolescents. They also report better outcomes, as measured by the disruption rates. They found that short-term fostering for adolescents was more likely to fail than to succeed (53% disruption rate) and that long-term fostering, while a lot better (at 27% breakdown rate), was still less stable than residential care, where disruptions were put at 16–21%.

Cliffe's (1991) study in Warwickshire, which followed outcomes after all its residential establishments were closed, acknowledged that some adolescents experienced an unacceptably large number of unsuccessful foster placements. They concluded that a suitable residential facility might have met their needs more appropriately.

In 1991, Parker et al. had looked at the issue of disabled children living in residential care. As Berridge and Brodie (1998) point out, there are serious problems of definition here, because if Emotional Behavioural Difficulties is included as a category of disability or impairment then 'well over a third (37%) of all school age children "in care" in England in the late 1980s in residential units were disabled' (Berridge & Brodie, 1998, p. 20). For a summary of residential care research up to the beginning of the 1990s, see Bullock et al. (1993).

The difficult area of making satisfactory provision for adolescents living away from home finally came into focus in its own right only in the 1990s with research from the DOH (1996) and a National Children's Bureau Study (Sinclair et al., 1995) which looked at, among other things, the respective roles of family-based and residential care. Triseliotis et al. (1995b) in their Scottish study were on the whole favourably impressed with the work children's homes were doing with adolescents, but rather less so with residential special schools catering for children with emotional behavioural difficulties.

The large-scale study undertaken by Sinclair and Gibbs (1996) looked at 48 children's homes in England providing over 200 places. By following up residents for six months they were able to look at the impact of being in residential care on outcomes. Sadly, children who had had good experiences did not show better outcomes at six-month follow-up. The study did identify factors that led to good-quality care, as did Whitaker et al. (1998) in their study of 39 homes, three from each of 13 Local Authorities. Their data were derived from 39 unit managers' accounts of their experiences of managing children's homes. In addition, six of the homes were followed up in detail through a series of monthly visits over about a year, which involved whole staff groups.

They concluded (pp. 235–236) that:

- Front-line staff need regularly scheduled, ongoing opportunities to learn from their own experience.
- Maximum use needs to be made, by those who formulate plans and make decisions, of the information and understandings, which staff members hold.
- Front-line staff need to be protected from unnecessary distractions, preoccupations and stress.
- People and organizations in the wider network involved in the care, education, or control of young people need to work together in an integrated way.

In 1998 (a good year for residential research) Berridge and Brodie revisited the study they had reported on in 1985 (referred to earlier). In reviewing changes, they noted that 'much uncertainty and dissatisfaction had developed nationally over the role and functioning of children's homes' (p. 23). They felt this had been exacerbated by a series of widely publicized cases. They noted that between 1985 and 1995 a pattern of decline in the role of residential care had emerged both nationally and internationally, such that the numbers of children had more than halved. They welcomed the positive measures taken by Government in an attempt to raise standards of residential care and also welcomed the greater volume of child care research that was providing a better understanding of the experiences of children looked after by Local Authorities. The research showed that residential care is still used extensively, especially for adolescents. It also showed that, for comparable groups of young people, 'children's homes are equally effective in meeting their objectives as their main alternatives, especially foster care' (Berridge & Brodie, 1998, p. 24).

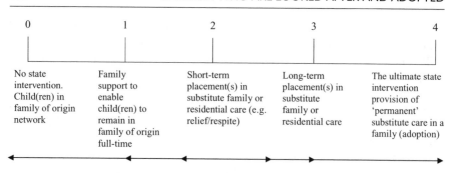

Figure 9.1   Continuum of care interventions

Residential Care as a Valid Option

In making a case for the validity of residential care as an appropriate option for some, usually older young people, its position on the 'continuum of care' is illustrated in Figure 9.1.

The continuum illustrates where residential care can start to have a role, i.e. in short-term episodes (2) essentially designed to promote the return of the child to their family of origin network. In practice, it is most often used in this way to support families where the children have significant learning or physical disabilities. Children with emotional and behavioural difficulties are more likely to enter residential care as the result of the breakdown of family-based care (either their own family or a substitute family). Berridge (1985) identified four broad categories of resident:

1. Younger sibling groups for whom it was a first and temporary placement who were admitted as emergencies (10% or so).
2. Approximately 50% of residents were waiting for longer-term placements (with foster families usually).
3. Young people separated from their families of origin for most of their lives who have already experienced a succession of unsuccessful substitute family placements (about 20%).
4. Around 25% were adolescents (mostly girls) who had come into the system recently from their families of origin and were still in contact with them.

When Berridge and Brodie (1998) followed up their study, they found that the first category no longer existed, which they thought was probably due to the wider availability of foster families for emergencies who could take sibling groups. The second group contained more young children (one-third were under 12) and fewer adolescents than a decade earlier, but they found very few long-stay cases in all age groups. The fourth group were now the major group with girls remaining predominant. Berridge and Brodie noted that they typically arrived after a short-term fostering had either failed or expired its allotted time. They were shocked by the rapidity and frequency of moves between different children's homes. In their sample, 75% of residents had previously lived in other children's homes and 'no fewer than three-fifths had been at the current home less than 3 months' (Berridge & Brodie, 1998, p. 82). They also found 'an important new group of consumers of residential care: children with severe learning disabilities and their families' (Berridge & Brodie, 1998, p. 82).

The new configuration of residents serves to highlight the ambiguous position of short-term residential care (2), as illustrated on the continuum of care (Figure 9.1). The arrows placed in both directions show that, for some, it is supporting/enabling the family of origin to maintain their duty of care, where, for others, young people are on their way to other arrangements that will take them further away from their families of origin. The range of residents' needs and the inherent ambiguity in the role of many such establishments in no way detract from their importance. Rather the reverse; it shows that they are much needed by a variety of young people and their families. How they are used is a separate question, which should not distract from the necessity for such places to exist.

Rehearsing the continuing extensive use of residential care is not, in itself, proof of its validity. Consideration of the residents themselves is useful. Typically, they are known to have experienced serious abuse of various forms as well as neglect. Berridge and Brodie (1998) noted that levels of known abuse had risen in the follow-up study. They found that the proportion of residents presenting behavioural problems had more than doubled. Although lengths of stay were much shorter, many children had experienced both fostering and residential care prior to their current placement. Levels of contact with the families of origin were higher. Education remained a serious problem, especially around attendance and exclusion from schools.

Research over the last 20 years or so on children living in substitute families has consistently shown that there is a group of children for whom this is not a realistic long-term option. While episodes of short-term family-based care can be beneficial, where the aim is relief/respite (Fisher et al., 1986), medium-term and longer-term stays in families can be associated with poor outcomes (Berridge & Cleaver, 1987; Rushton et al., 1986; Farmer & Parker, 1991; Wedge & Mantle, 1991).

Rowe et al. (1984) found that approximately 25% of placements in families intended to be long term did not last as long as they were needed, and 33% did not last as long as expected. Garnett (1992) found that 40% of the children in their study had experienced five or more changes of placement through their adolescent years. For a more detailed consideration of outcomes, see DOH (1991).

The author's study (Nissim, 1999) was able to identify a constellation of characteristics of children and young people that were not only associated with unsuccessful outcomes but which enabled predictions to be made about outcomes prior to placements being made in long-term substitute families. Moreover, certain characteristics when present together, combined to heighten the risk of unsuccessful outcomes. In particular, two kinds of outcomes were highly predictable: placement endings and multiple placements. Essentially it was possible to identify in advance those youngsters whose placements would end prematurely, and who would go on to have three or more subsequent placements within two years.

These findings echo those of Berridge and Brodie (1998) almost to the letter. It seems we can characterize contemporary residents in children's homes as being those who have experienced abuse and/or neglect in their family of origin where they may have remained for a significant length of time. They will retain strong if highly dysfunctional attachments to their family of origin and often to the community in which they originated. Their development will have been disrupted by this early adversity and this will typically have led to emotional behavioural disorders. One major consequence of this will have been their inability to manage the demands of the education system. These characteristics will have led to repeated disruptions in their care arrangements, involving moves in and out of the family of origin network as well as moves around the care system itself. For such young people residential care may be the most suitable way to meet their needs.

The valid roles of residential care are listed below, not in order of importance, nor implying that roles are mutually exclusive. It may be the case that one individual will have need of several of these roles at different stages of his or her development:

- Periodic relief/respite for individuals and parents enabling individuals to remain in the family of origin.
- A neutral place for individuals to retreat to for sanctuary following trauma.
- An opportunity to reflect on and rebuild relationships with family of origin network from a safe distance.
- Partial (shared-care) or full rehabilitation to family of origin network where appropriate.
- Partial or full relinquishment of ties to family of origin network promoting the likelihood of more successful outcomes in alternative placements.
- A care base where material and emotional needs are met, and individual development is promoted within and beyond the establishment.
- A safe base from which to address the challenges of independence and adult life.

THEMES AND ISSUES

There are so many themes and issues arising from the preceding sections of this chapter that there is a danger of feeling overwhelmed by the material. In order to lend clarity to the analysis let us consider the themes from the various perspectives of those involved in the process, utilizing the Onion Model described in Chapter 2.

Residents

In the previous section of this chapter the main categories of contemporary residents were described drawing on Berridge and Brodie's (1998) research. These were linked to the profiles of children who are unable to manage being cared for in a substitute family (Nissim, 1999).

The predicament of such a youngster is given eloquent expression in this poem:

Like a Book

Sometimes I'm treated like a book
With me torn, tattered covers someone takes me out to read
without any please, I'm handed over to the next person to read
They never seem to turn the page over,
So they never see
All the heartache that's built up in the real me
So if you get to pick me up
Make sure you don't give me to another
Make sure you read what's inside of me
Don't judge me by the cover
Or you will never see . . .

(Leeroy, D. (no date) reproduced by permission of
Northants County Council)

In addition there is an important new group of residents – children with severe learning disabilities – who are cared for in separate establishments. Typically these children will have levels of impairment that require intensive adult input in order for basic daily routines to be managed. They all require special education. The severity and chronicity of their predicament can be further compounded when frustration builds, but the capacity for communication is unable to give it expression. Extremes of challenging behaviour can occur when youngsters are unable to make themselves understood, and are difficult to reason with.

Irrespective of the particular predicament of each resident, some themes are common to all. They are separated from their family of origin, and whatever the characteristics of that family, this must, at some level, be counted as a loss. They will have been removed by the actions of adults, whether these were their own parents, or professionals. The extent to which their voices were heard at the point this decision was made on their behalf is a crucial issue, and leads directly to the question of children's rights. Incidentally, these themes are equally pertinent to children of the privileged placed by their parents into boarding school, often for the greater part of their childhood. Whether the placement was a state intervention, or a matter of parental choice, the extent to which placed children gave informed consent is a key issue in residential care. Of equal importance is the experience of each resident once in the home. Very vulnerable young people may find themselves in the company of others whose problems are equally severe. Survivors of abuse may be living with perpetrators, who may, themselves, also be abuse survivors. In such situations, there is a case to be made for single-sex facilities, an option much favoured by the public school system. While not altogether precluding further abuse, this can reduce the likelihood of some forms of previous abuse recurring. The demands placed on each resident in terms of making and maintaining relationships with fellow residents is a huge issue, in all residential settings.

Family of Origin and Kinship Networks

The potency of the family in residents' hearts and minds can scarcely be exaggerated. Yet they remain the least studied group, in the context of residential care research and seem, as a group, to receive the least attention, in terms of positive practice patterns of social work, once their children live in residential care. If we reflect, briefly, on a profile of the families, we know that their context is one of disadvantage. Bebbington & Miles's (1989) very large study highlighted the following common features: high proportion of single-parent families, typically on low incomes/income support, not owning their own homes, living in 'poor' neighbourhoods, overcrowded accommodation, large family size (four or more children), lack of social/community support networks.

In addition, parents themselves may have experienced childhood abuse and/or neglect and have experienced periods in care, especially in residential care. The impact of these factors on their capacity to parent their children satisfactorily holds the key to understanding their relationships with their children. It can also shed much light on their relationships with social workers and Social Service departments in general. Failing to work successfully with these families is often a major cause for their children failing within the care system; yet patterns of constructive collaboration seem hard to achieve.

It is important to emphasize that the families of children with severe learn-ing disabilities may not fall within this description, and it is perhaps for this reason that patterns of positive practice in relation to families are more often a feature of homes for these children. Indeed, there is much for 'mainstream' homes to learn here, in terms of the levels of involvement and inclusion in the care of their children accorded to parents.

Residential Workers

The most recent detailed study of the characteristics of contemporary resi-dential workers (Whitaker et al., 1998) looked at 34 homes across the UK, reflecting a range of locations. They found that there were almost twice as many women as men, both genders being predominantly British white. Of 467 staff looked at, only 14 had full social work qualifications (the managers are not included here); seven had nursing qualifications and a further nine had (unspecified) degrees. A total of 38 had some credentials (City and Guilds, Certificate in the Residential Care of Children and Young People) and some in-service training. This works out at around 15% holding some qualification.

Of 34 homes considered, nine had no vacancies, 25 did – approximately two per home, where the average number of staff (including all of them) was 13.7. In all there were 51 childcare staff vacancies. Many homes were using agency staff or borrowing staff from other homes to cover these gaps. This study broke down the tasks of residential workers into five broad categories:

- Working with the group of residents.
- Working with individual residents.
- Surviving as a staff team which meets the needs of children.
- Working with, and being managed by the Social Service department.
- Networking with families of origin, health, education, youth justice and the community/neighbourhood.

Of the large number of themes for residential workers the following are se-lected as being particularly pertinent:

- *Gender* – While twice as many women as men work in residential units the residents are still more likely to be male, although the balance is shifting with an increase in female residents (now 44.5%). This raises the question of choice for young people, in relation to key workers, not to mention reflecting patterns from the family of origin, often headed by a single female parent. It also raises wider issues of gender and power in our society.

- *Race* – The majority of staff of both genders are British white, but 12% of residents are from other racial groups. This again raises issues of choice for residents, as well as reflecting patterns of race and power in our culture.
- *Staffing* – Reference has been made to understaffing as a chronic feature of residential care. The consequences include difficulties in making up balanced shifts and organizing predictable rotas. The use of staff from other homes or agencies can be disruptive and destabilizing, creating extra pressure on regular staff. This may in turn lead to absenteeism and sickness among them, thus perpetuating this unfortunate cycle.
- *Qualifications* – The lack of qualifications is a significant theme, which has a number of consequences. While increasing efforts are made to train staff *in situ*, with the expansion of NVQs, in-service training initiatives and release of staff to attend external courses, these are all fraught with practical difficulties. In a context of serious understaffing, releasing staff can become difficult or impossible, especially when they are regular team members who know the home and its residents. Moreover, their absences will have an impact on the experience of residents.
- *Residents* – The tasks of managing and working with young people, both as individuals and as a group become even more challenging and pressurizing, as numbers of homes reduce, and the clientele are ever more vulnerable and demanding.

The Homes, the Social Workers and their Managers

Today, children's homes are small, mixed, with an average age of resident of 14 years. Approximately 88% of residents are described as British white (*source:* Whitaker et al. 1998). Most homes are situated in residential areas, and are adaptations of existing buildings, rather than purpose built.

There has been a major reduction in residential provision in recent decades. This has led to a concentration of the most vulnerable and disturbed being placed in residential care, as well as the increasing pattern of placing seriously disturbed youngsters into substitute families. In addition, the expense of placing young people with severe problems out of county/borough has reduced the number of such placements at a time of shrinking budgets for Local Authorities. All these factors have served to intensify the nature and the mix of residents in a way that does not serve the cause of residential care well.

Problems are compounded when referrals and admissions are made reluctantly, at the last minute and on an emergency basis as the result of other placements ending. The impact on both residents and staff can be very traumatic, and reactions of distress may serve to confirm prejudices about the undesirability of making residential placements. As discussed in Part III, it is important not to conclude from the problems associated with delivering good-quality residential care that it is therefore not necessary, and cannot be successful.

The social workers who refer children to residential placements may have grave misgivings about the wisdom of this course of action. Fisher et al., (1986) found that many social workers were opposed to residential care, and this could lead to poor outcomes, such as placement instability and traumatic unplanned admissions when placements were made as a last resort (Packman et al., 1986). More recently qualified social workers will often have little knowledge or experience of the residential sector and their first experience of it may be when they are 'forced' to use it as a placement for one of their young people who has prematurely come to the end of an existing placement in a family. The implications of this will be discussed in the next section.

Patterns of management of children's homes do not reflect the profiles of the staff teams. Whitaker et al. (1998) found that while the majority of the staff were women, male managers predominated. They were an experienced group (average 15 years in residential care) but many were only partly qualified.

By contrast, all the managers of teams of social workers would have to hold a full qualification, as would the social workers themselves, but this group typically have far less experience than their opposite numbers in residential care. When residential managers encounter professionals from other agencies who have more qualifications, this can create tensions and potential power struggles which may be counter-productive.

Children's Services: The Agency

At the time of writing this book a process of change is occurring leading to the development of Children's Services, combining education and Social Services. A strategy for residential care will be a component within these services. This will create the context for the policy and practice of each home, including explicit statements about its purpose and function, admissions criteria, etc. There should be policies that will be particularly relevant to residential settings (about managing challenging behaviour, smoking, etc.), although policies on these topics will also exist for departments as a whole. Where, at any of these levels, policies are imprecise, ambiguous and poorly disseminated, worse outcomes can be expected (Packman et al., 1986). It goes without saying that the absence of policy is also dangerous, either because homes will be run without a framework to guide them, or because they invent their own to fill the policy vacuum. There will also be a knock-on effect of policies in other areas of Children's Services on the position of the residential sector. Dale (1987) linked the 'institutionalization' of black children to doctrinaire opposition to trans-racial fostering, which was based on political ideology rather than the research evidence. Certainly Berridge and Cleaver (1987) and Fratter et al. (1991) reported that trans-racial fosterings were no less successful than same race ones, and Tizard and Phoenix (1989, 1993) reported successful outcomes for trans-racial placements. Yet black children can be kept waiting in residential care for a same race family placement because of fostering policy. As recently as 2001, the author had the same debate with social workers about a black boy who was, himself, willing to be placed trans-racially, his priority being to go into a family, but who was kept waiting in a children's home (where his behaviour and adjustment deteriorated), for a black family.

Other Agencies

Reference has already been made to the likely problems young people in residential care will experience in the education system. Only a moment's reflection is needed to see that patterns of abuse, neglect and repeated change and loss do not form a good preparation for fitting into mainstream schools. Hostility to adults, a necessary defence in their private lives, will not serve them well in their relationships with teachers. Equally, feelings of inadequacy and vulnerability in relation to others of their own age, will make it difficult for them to feel that they are on equal terms with peers. This may lead either to withdrawal – at its most extreme school refusal – or to patterns of aggression, both verbal and physical. This may be further complicated by the difficulties experienced by the school in communicating with the children's home. Shift patterns, sickness and absenteeism may all make it hard to build relationships with a child's key worker, for example. Equally, the home may find it as difficult to make contact with a year tutor. Where communication is most needed, it is often most absent. Meetings can, for many of the same reasons, be hard to organize. Inevitably they may occur in the absence of key people from either setting. Patterns of mutual misunderstanding can easily develop which are not in the best interests of residents. Residential workers, who may themselves feel overawed by their better-qualified opposite numbers in education, may not be best placed to advocate convincingly in education settings.

Where young people attend special schools issues may be different, as both staff will be working with a similar client group. Here the dangers may lie more in the area of competition than of misunderstanding. Comparisons may be made between the resources (human and material) that the two agencies have available to meet the same children's needs.

The author observed a striking example of this in a small country town where the Social Services care facility for children with severe learning difficulties was an old Victorian house on three floors, which was entirely unmodernized. Their equivalent Victorian educational facility had been progressively modernized and extended to become a state of the art provision, attracting a dynamic young male head teacher and first-class teaching team. A female, who was unqualified but had 30 years' experience, with a staff team, who were all female and all unqualified, ran the children's home. While the school had a sophisticated and effective behavioural regime, the home was struggling to manage the same children. Strategies used by the school could not be translated across, as they were predicated on levels of staffing and skills simply unavailable in the home. They were both working with exactly the same children.

This can also be an issue in health settings – especially in residential settings where typically the best staffing resources are made available to those with significant mental and physical health needs. This may be in stark contrast to what can be offered by the equivalent children's homes, trying to meet the needs of the most vulnerable youngsters with a fraction of the resources.

Case Example

In a large city the author worked in an NHS regional adolescent unit at the same time as offering services to a Social Services run residential facility for adolescents. Although the buildings were similar – both purpose built in the 1960s – in every other respect the differences were legion. Some of the key differences are summarized below.

- **Staffing** – In the NHS facility there were more staff, all better qualified and offering a wider range of skills as they were from many different professional backgrounds. This allowed multidisciplinary teams to be created for each individual resident, tailored to the particular needs of each.
- **Admissions** – They were planned, purposive and time-limited in the NHS facility, and were kept under weekly review. This contrasted with typically unplanned Social Services emergency admissions that tended to drift without purpose.
- **Treatments** – A range of individual, group and family therapies was available in addition to the personalized regime set up for each resident's daily care in the NHS setting. In the Social Services establishment there was no treatment

and the regime was entirely group oriented with very little personalized care planning.

- **Education** – While both facilities offered education on site, the NHS was fully staffed, resourced and supported, while the reverse was the case in the other setting.
- **Investment** – The investment in the NHS facility was much greater, this being chiefly spent on numbers and quality of staff. It was this that made all the differences referred to above possible.

In the area of Youth Justice the issues are different. Until recently, the systems of service delivery were the responsibility of Social Services departments, and the relationships between them and children's homes closer, both at an organizational level and in terms of the staff teams. Indeed, a significant role for residential care traditionally was to provide temporary placements for young people 'remanded to care' by the Courts. These days, while delinquency may be part of a resident's profile, it will not be the main or only reason for the placement. Nevertheless, relationships need to be made and maintained between children's homes and Youth Justice staff. Equally, such relationships are needed between the police and the wider Criminal Justice system. Children's homes may well find themselves labouring under the burden of history and of misapprehensions about contemporary residential care, in their relationships with these systems.

In addition to all the issues raised in this section, we need to be mindful of the different agencies' relationships with each other. These relationships occur irrespective of any particular individual but may be brought into focus over particular cases, or indeed around a particular establishment. Consequently this is an extremely important level of context for children's homes, but one where they may feel particularly disadvantaged and powerless.

Society and Community

In the second section of this chapter, the issue of scandals in residential care was highlighted. This creates part of the context within which the public views residential care. Prevailing politics also plays its part; a central government, which promotes adoption, is likely to legislate accordingly, for example, by pushing for early removals of children from their damaging families to permit them to be placed for adoption, rather than encouraging extensive support so that such families can be helped to keep the care of their children. Nor can such things be divorced from economic policy. A welfarist government may legislate for, and assign more funding to, the support of disadvantaged families, who are the major source of looked after children. The balance of power in Local Authorities will also partly determine how funds are allocated to particular departments. Within each department, Children's Services will have its own set of priorities. It may be the case that residential care remains a tiny part of all this activity, but its role and status are further reduced when it is not a priority at any level. The issue comes full circle for each home, as it tries to take its place in a community and a neighbourhood representing other values, perhaps most frequently 'family values'.

The Law

Over the years, changes in legislation have had an impact on the provision of residential care. The single most important shift from the Children Act 1975 to the Children Act 1989 was the introduction of the paramountcy principle – the welfare of the child is paramount. Whereas in 1975, the long-term welfare of the child was often thought to entail severing ties with the family of origin, in the 1989 Act, the importance of the family of origin was strongly emphasized. With its emphasis on prevention through partnership, and failing that, extensive attempts at rehabilitation, the Act greatly enhanced the status of the family of origin.

In relation to looked after children, the 1989 Act seemed to favour family-based care, which included maintaining links with the family of origin and in some ways sits uneasily with Adoption Law, which seeks to provide a permanent alternative family: the position of residential care, as so often, is far down the list of priorities.

The Children Act 2004 provides a legal framework for a programme of reform set out in *Every Child Matters, Change for Children* (DFES, 2004a) that will additionally impact on the delivery of residential care for children and young people. This legislation moves to focus on the structures and supports that need to be in place to improve outcomes and protection for all children. The vision created is of increased support, earlier intervention, effective protection and greater accountability and integration of services ensuring that children and young people will have improved life chances and improved living environments wherever they are living. At the time of writing it is too early to tell what impact this latest legislation will have on placement choice and the use of residential care.

Both the 1989 and the 2004 acts emphasize the importance of taking into account the views and wishes of children. This sits uneasily with legislation that encourages family-based care. Where there are differences of opinion between young people and social workers, the *Convention on the Rights of the Child* (United Nations, 1989) allows another legal avenue to be pursued. However, it too is emphatic in its preference for children to be reared by their parents, and makes no mention of other forms of care. While in no way implying that the law as it stands is wrong, this brief review shows how current legislation does little to help the cause of residential care.

CONCLUSION

The context of residential care is complex and often contradictory. It is, on the one hand, the first choice for privileged parents wanting the best for their children. They will pay handsomely for the advantages they believe are conferred by an education that is delivered away from home, of necessity involving residential care. On the other hand, residential care is typically viewed by Local Authorities as of marginal relevance to a minority of children, many of whom are placed reluctantly, and not from choice.

The youngsters concerned are among the most disadvantaged, damaged and vulnerable members of our society and their needs are extreme and complex. Other agencies, such as health and education, will offer residential provision for such young people that has enhanced staffing, additional funding and adapted facilities designed to meet their special needs. Local Authorities in their own residential care facilities do not make the same investment although they will often commit very substantial sums in order to place some of their most needy young people in independent specialist residential care settings around the country. One could be forgiven for thinking that the aggregated out-of-county budget might go a long way towards enhancing in-county provision. This would not only make better economic sense but also be much closer to the spirit of keeping children in or near their own families and communities.

The weight of history and the social structure of our society go some way towards explaining these paradoxes. The tradition of residential education for the privileged is very different from the workhouse tradition of the underprivileged. It could be argued that little has changed. Yet the institutions themselves have the potential to be more equivalent. They are addressing the same fundamental tasks but as long as the differences in class, income and status remain, so will the differences between the institutions.

Residential care for looked after children is a valid option, and in spite of the scandals and stigma attached to it, persists in surviving. There is no doubt that residential care not only fulfils a need but is potentially an intervention of choice, not just for the privileged, but also for those most in need. If one day this Cinderella service's fairy godmother turns up and says she can go to the ball, as beautifully dressed as her sisters, who knows what might be achieved! In the meantime this chapter has set the current context of residential care and

Chapter 10 will consider a range of psychological interventions against this background.

REFERENCES

Ariès, P. (1962) *Centuries of Childhood – A Social History of Family Life*. New York: Vintage Books.

Bebbington, A. & Miles, J. (1989) The background of children who enter Local Authority Care. *British Journal of Social Work*, **19**(5), 349–368.

Berridge, D. (1985) *Children's Homes*. Oxford: Blackwell.

Berridge, D. & Brodie, I. (1998) *Children's Homes Revisited*. London: Jessica Kingsley Publishers.

Berridge, D. & Cleaver, H. (1987) *Foster Home Breakdown*. Oxford: Blackwell.

Boswell, J. (1991) *The Kindness of Strangers*. London: Penguin. [See J. Triseliotis (1995) Adoption – evolution or revolution? *Adoption and Fostering* **19**(2), 431–432. In M. Hill & M. Shaw (1998) *Signposts to Adoption*. London: BAAF.]

Bullock, R., Little, M. & Milham, S. (1993) *Going Home: The Return of Children Separated from their Families*. Aldershot: Dartmouth.

Children Act (1948) London: HMSO.

Children and Young Persons Act (1963) London HMSO.

Children and Young Persons Act (1969) London HMSO.

Cliffe, D. with Berridge, D. (1991) *Closing Children's Homes: An End to Residential Childcare*? London: National Children's Bureau.

Crimmens, D. & Pitts, J. (Eds) (2000) *Positive Residential Practice*. Lyme Regis: Russell House Publishing.

Curtis Report (1946) *Care of Children Committee*. London: HMSO.

Dale, D. (1987) *Denying Homes to Black Children*. London: Social Affairs Unit.

DFES (2004a) *Every Child Matters, Change for Children*. London: TSO.

DFES (2004b) *Children Act 2004*. London: TSO.

DHSS (1986) *Committee of Inquiry into Children's Homes and Hostels*. DHSS Northern Ireland.

Dickens, C. (1978) *Nicholas Nickleby*. Middlesex: Penguin Books. First published 1839.

DOH (1975) *Children Act 1975*. London: HMSO.

DOH (1989) *Children Act 1989*. London: TSO.

DOH (1991) *Patterns and Outcomes in Child Placement. Messages from Current Research and their Implications*. London: TSO.

DOH (1996) *Focus on Teenagers*. London: TSO.

Farmer, E. & Parker, R. (1991) *Trials and Tribulations – Returning Children from Care to their Families*. London: TSO.

Fisher, M., Marsh, P., Phillips, D. & Sainsbury, E. (1986) *In and Out of Care: The Experiences of Children, Parents and Social Workers*. London: Batsford.

Fratter, J., Rowe, J., Sapsford, D. & Thorburn, J. (1991) *Permanent Family Placement – A Decade of Experience*. London: BAAF Research Series 8.

Garnett, I. (1992) Leaving care and after. In M. Shaw (1994) *A Bibliography of Family Placement Literature*. London: NCB.

George, V. (1970) *Foster Care: Theory and Practice*. London: Routledge & Kegan Paul.

Goldfarb, W. (1943) Effects of early institutional care on adolescent personality. *Child Development*, **14**, 213–223.

Holman, R. (1980) Exclusive and inclusive concepts of fostering. In J. Triseliotis (Ed.), *New Developments in Foster Care and Adoption*. London: Routledge & Kegan Paul.

Kirkwood, A. (1993) *The Leicestershire Inquiry 1992*. Leicester: Leicestershire County Council.

Laming, Lord (2003) *The Victoria Climbié Enquiry*. London: TSO.

Latham, A. (Ed.) (2002) *The Oxford Companion to Music*. Oxford University Press.

Levy, A. & Kahan, B. (1991) *The Pindown Experience and the Protection of Children*. Stafford: Staffordshire County Council.

Milham, S., Bullock, R., Hosie, K. & Haak, M. (1986) Lost in care: The problems of maintaining links between children in care and their families. In M. Shaw (1988) *Family Placement for Children in Care. A Guide to the Literature*. London: BAAF.

Morgan, P. (1998) *Adoption and the Care of Children*. London: IEA Health and Welfare Unit.

Nissim, R. (1999) *Substitute family placement: A systemic perspective on pre-placement factors, placement outcomes and the relationship between them*. Dissertation submitted for PhD, Reading University.

Northamptonshire County Council (no date) *A Dozen Thoughts Plus One. Poems by Young People in Care in Northamptonshire*. Northamptonshire County Council.

Packman, J., Randall, J. & Jacques, N. (1986) *Who Needs Care? Social Work Decisions about Children*. Oxford: Blackwell.

Parker, R.A. (1966) *Decisions in Child Care: A Study of Prediction in Fostering*. London: Allen & Unwin.

Parker, R., Ward, H., Jackson, S., Aldgate, J. & Wedge, P. (Eds) (1991) *Assessing Outcomes in Child Care*. London: TSO.

Rowe, J. & Lambert, L. (1973) *Children Who Wait*. London: BAAF.

Rowe, J., Cain, H. & Garnett, L. (1989) *Child Care Now: A Survey of Placement Patterns*. London: BAAF Research Series 6.

Rowe, J., Cain, H., Hundleby, M. & Keane, A. (1984) *Long Term Foster Care*. London: Batsford/BAAF.

Rushton, A., Teseder, J. & Quinton, D. (1986) *New Parents for Older Children*. London: BAAF Discussion Series 10.

Sinclair, R. & Gibbs, I. (1996) *Quality of Care in Children's Homes. Report to the Department of Health*. York: University of York.

Sinclair, R., Garnett, L. & Berridge, D. (1995) *Social Work and Assessment with Adolescents*. London: National Children's Bureau.

Skeels, H. (1966) *Adult Status of Children with Contrasting Early Life Experiences*. Monograph of the Society for Research in Child Development, Vol. 37, pp. 595–602.

Spitz, R.A. (1945) Hospitalisation: An enquiry into the genesis of psychiatric conditions in early childhood. *Psychoanalytic Study of the Child*, 1, 53–74.

Thorpe, R. (1980) The experience of children and parents living apart: Implications and guidelines for practice. In J. Triseliotis (Ed.), *New Developments in Foster-care and Adoption*. London: Routledge & Kegan Paul.

Thorpe, D.H., Smith, D., Green, C.J. & Paley, J. (1980) *Out of Care: The Community Support of Juvenile Offenders*. London: George Allen & Unwin.

Tizard, B. & Phoenix, A. (1989) Black identity and trans-racial adoption. In I. Gaber & J. Aldridge (Eds) (1994) *Culture, Identity and Trans-racial Adoption*. London: Free Association Books.

Tizard, B. & Phoenix, A. (1993) *Black, White or Mixed Race?* London: Routledge.

Trasler, G. (1960) *In Place of Parents*. London: Routledge & Kegan Paul.

Triseliotis, J. (Ed.) (1980) *New Developments in Foster Care and Adoption*. London: Routledge & Kegan Paul.

Triseliotis, J., Sellick, C. & Short, R. (1995a) *Foster Care Theory and Practice*. London: Batsford/BAAF.

Triseliotis, J., Borland, M., Hill, M. & Lambert, L. (1995b) Teenagers and the social work services. In D. Berridge (1997) *Foster Care – A Research Review*. London: TSO.

United Nations (1989) *Convention on the Rights of the Child*. New York: United Nations.

Wedge, P. & Mantle, G. (1991) *Sibling Groups and Social Work*. Aldershot: Avebury, Gower.

Whitaker, D., Archer, L. & Hicks, L. (1998) *Working in Children's Homes. Challenges and Complexities*. Chichester: John Wiley & Sons.

PART III
THERAPEUTIC SPACES FOR DIRECT WORKING

10

HOME FROM HOME: INTERVENTIONS WITHIN RESIDENTIAL SETTINGS

Ruth Nissim

In Chapter 9 the field of residential care was reviewed, both historically and in terms of its current context. The decision to provide this review before starting the discussion on psychological thinking and interventions is deliberate. Any attempt at intervention should follow from an understanding of the predicament not only of the individual resident but also of the setting and its context. While popular opinion may view psychologists as working with individuals, and psychology as the study of the human mind, both the subject and its practice can be considerably broader in scope. This becomes particularly pertinent when reflecting on individuals who are living in a group situation, and carers who are part of a staff group. This chapter begins with reflections on how thinking psychologically might be useful for other professionals before focusing specifically on the range of possible interventions from psychologists. The chapter ends with a discussion on the role of psychology within residential settings.

PSYCHOLOGICAL THINKING FOR OTHER PROFESSIONALS

An attempt to summarize the range of psychological theories that other professionals might choose to draw upon to inform their thinking is, in this chapter, inappropriate. However, a brief summary of what is available may serve to illustrate the breadth of theories potentially under consideration. Where theories have been described elsewhere in this volume they are not repeated here, but it is important to point out that attachment and systemic theory, for example, have much to contribute to this topic.

Theories of individual functioning can inform an understanding of individual young people and show how they relate to the other young people and to the adults with whom they are living. Thus psychodynamic theory considers that the psyche is divided into three domains – the unconscious (id), the partly conscious (superego) and the conscious (ego). The way that these three interact together and with external reality determines behaviour and development. Childhood experiences are thought to determine personality as the individual moves through different developmental stages. The first and most famous exponent of this theory was Freud over 100 years ago (Freud, 1923) but the ideas have undergone many revisions and transformations since then and are still very much in current usage. Chapter 2 explored how psychodynamic thinking can further our understanding of the way networks of people around the child work together. This thinking can equally be helpful in exploring groups of people living and working together, as in a residential home. An understanding of how past experience can have an unconscious impact on the current interactions between people can help to make sometimes inexplicable behaviour understandable.

Moving away from a consideration of unconscious determinants upon behaviour and development, other theories focus more on what is observable and environmentally determined. Learning theory suggests that learning occurs as a result of classical, instrumental or operant conditioning. Pavlov, in the now famous experiment, demonstrated the process of classical conditioning whereby when two stimuli are presented simultaneously, the response to one is also evoked by the other. Thus when dogs were presented with food at the same time as a bell was rung the dogs 'learned' to salivate to the sound of the bell (Pavlov, 1927). This set the scene for exploration of a variety of conditions within which stimuli could be demonstrated to elicit responses. To fully explain the complexity of human behaviour however, this S–R psychology needed to be complemented with the more complex and elaborate theories of operant conditioning proposed by Skinner (1974). This demonstrates that patterns of behaviour that meet with favourable consequences (positive reinforcement), or reduce the occurrence of negative consequences (negative reinforcement), are more likely to become more frequent while behaviours resulting in unfavourable consequences (punishment) are likely to become less frequent. Adverse learning experiences in childhood, as well as the way the individual is responded to in the present, provide the explanation for dysfunctional patterns of behaviour.

While learning theory restricted its explanations to what was observable and environmentally determined, cognitive theories additionally placed emphasis on thinking and reasoning processes. These theories highlight the importance of attributions. The individual's belief as to the cause of any particular event or circumstance will determine his or her response to it. Typical patterns of thinking (cognitive styles) are identified which explain the stance taken by a particular individual (see Beck, 1976).

An understanding of psychodynamic, behavioural and cognitive theories can provide help to those trying to understand the behaviour presented by young people living in residential care. As these theories focus on individuals they tend to lead to interventions which are directed at individual residents. Key workers, for example, might try to help a young person to make sense of his or her past experience and link this to the individual's current behaviour, perhaps making unconscious processes conscious for that person (e.g. 'You had to compete with your sister for your mum's attention; maybe that is why you are getting angry with me when I am spending time with the other young people'). Alternatively, the key workers might work with the staff group to set up conditions within which desirable behaviour is rewarded or they might help a young person to develop different beliefs about why something is happening (e.g. 'when I discuss with you your difficulty in returning to the home by the time agreed, I think you believe that I don't like you; actually I care about you and want to keep you safe').

Group living is clearly a more complex process than these individual approaches suggest, and socio-cultural theories can help to address some of this complexity. This approach attributes many aspects of individual and group development to the social and cultural context within which the individuals find themselves. Intervention focuses on the management of this social and cultural context. Theories of group behaviour can additionally contribute to an understanding and management of this context. Adolescence is a developmental stage when youngsters are particularly susceptible to peer influence and show a predilection for socializing in groups. This is more apparent in some cultures than in others. In America, for example, an individualistic focus encourages autonomy, and peer influences are very dominant at this life stage. In China, however, where being part of a group has a more important focus, the influence of the family remains stronger.

Organizational psychologists can also offer theoretical perspectives that might be useful in residential settings. At the individual level, there is a solid body of research on vocational guidance, the process of attempting to match aspirations of young people with their abilities and opportunities. There is also a good deal of research on the development of people, the so-called 'science of training'. The most developed aspect is that of the application of Social Learning Theory to the use of role playing and strengthening of self-efficacy. Comprehensive reviews of the field are offered by Ford (1997) and Kraiger (2002).

At the group level, there is much research on what supports effective group performance. Often this starts with group observation using a model like that proposed by Schein (1987), and interventions are then planned to assist with improving the effectiveness of the processes or the sense of well-being within the group. A useful general text is that by West (1994); a more detailed approach is given in chapter eight of Kraiger (2002), entitled, 'What we know about designing and delivering team training'.

At the organizational level, the main focus is on facilitating change. The initial phase is to examine the pressures for change (both internal and external). It is then necessary to carry out some analysis of the aims, structure (who talks to whom), and climate (in what spirit) to discover if the present shape and method of organizing processes is likely to support the aims. An intervention is then made to try to ensure that the style of management, the processes being used and the relationships between people are likely to lead to the achievement of the outcomes thought most desirable (i.e. the shared aims). A follow-up evaluation will identify 'where we think we are now' and, therefore, what needs to be done next. Change is a continuous process and, after the initial intervention, should be driven by an internal champion.

The field covered by organizational psychology is very wide and other research has been conducted that might be relevant to residential care settings, for instance on 'motivation at work', 'stress' and 'communication within organizations'. A good introductory text, which gives some idea of the scope of the discipline, is Arnold (2005).

This brief review of a range of theories of individual, group and organizational aspects of human behaviour indicates the vast amount of information that is available. They are all potentially relevant to working in residential care and it is increasingly common for theoretical perspectives to be accompanied by practice applications in the literature.

It is important to point out that here the different theories have been artificially separated, although the modern trend is towards combining elements from different areas. Indeed, there is a recognized school of psychology that describes itself as integrative or holistic, and favours exactly what the name implies. More typically, different theories can be selected as lending themselves better to different levels of working.

In this chapter, five levels of working in residential settings are described. It will be apparent that different theories will be better suited to each of the levels referred to. Psychological theories and their application to residential settings are by no means the exclusive preserve of psychologists. For those working with individuals who live in children's homes it might be a useful exercise to reflect on the models of individual functioning described here. To what extent are you drawing on any single one or perhaps a combination of theories? Are there any with which you may be less familiar, or which you feel are unsuited to this particular client group? Perhaps there may be scope for expanding the range of theories you typically use in your work. For example, although learning theory is described by some as being mechanistic and superficial, it can be a very effective tool in the context of the chaos and complexity that can typify residential care. It is not that learning theory has all the answers, but its very clarity and simplicity can be helpful in the face of what may seem to be overwhelming and intractable problems. Sometimes focusing on some very specific behaviours and making explicit their likely consequences can demonstrate the potential for change in a way that gives hope and a sense of achievement that can then be built upon.

The same exercise may be considered around interpersonal theories, for colleagues whose main level of working is with parent–child and family relationships, as they relate to residential care. This is often a neglected aspect of the work endeavour, as professionals struggle to move children back to family-based care, but whether children return to their family of origin network, move into a substitute family or remain in a residential setting, they carry their history and current understanding of interpersonal relationships in their hearts and minds. This is an area of work that is greatly assisted by the theoretical frameworks described in this book and elsewhere. It is as crucial for children no longer living in families as it is for those who struggle to remain in them.

Where colleagues are working with groups of young people in residential settings the relevance of theories about group behaviour will be self-evident. It is tempting to dismiss residents in children's homes as being a deviant group where patterns of deviant behaviour are likely to be learned and maintained. This view helps to confirm the view that being in a children's home is a bad thing. However the group effects, which are so powerful for all adolescents, can be constructively harnessed both within and beyond the home itself. Within the home, structured or semi-structured groups can be used to promote group cooperation and self-expression. Beyond the home, individual residents can be encouraged to participate in more typical groups, e.g. sports clubs, etc., which open up their access to the outside world.

Finally the body of theory available about people in work contexts is likely to be relevant to each of us as individuals, enabling us to reflect on our own setting and our position within it. It also allows us to observe other organizations, drawing on different theories to clarify what can seem to be overwhelming and unintelligible systems. Whether one's role is inside or outside the residential setting, this level of theorizing about people and organizations can be of assistance in moving individuals away from what can become very biased and subjective viewpoints.

For now, a case scenario is presented, which, while being a composite, draws all its features from real life practice. The aim is to show how psychological thinking can have a positive impact when used by other professionals in a residential setting.

Before Psychological Thinking

An adolescent boy was described as angry and violent, especially towards staff, and this was causing them to experience great problems in managing him. The staff team's theory was that he was anti-adult and hostile to authority in general. Their aim was to show him that adults could be effective authority figures, and they made strenuous efforts to challenge his behaviour and bring it under control. This only resulted in worse outbursts from the boy, so they all found themselves in an impasse. There were consequences too, for the other residents. Some were scared of him and tried to avoid contact; others saw how readily he flared up and enjoyed goading him into action, on their behalf. The advantage for them was that he was blamed for violent incidents, which they had partly engineered and, as such, should have held some responsibility for. This made them feel powerful, but at the same time they were playing a dangerous game, and it was always possible that staff might believe him when he said they had started it. He might also turn on them, in his temper. The atmosphere in the peer group was anxious and unsettled.

The situation was hardly better for staff who were starting to split into two distinct factions. Some, mostly female staff, felt that challenging the boy was counter-productive, only increasing the number of outbursts and creating a terrible atmosphere. Others were intensifying their attempts to try to gain control, but repeated failure was doing nothing for their status or morale. Some staff were undecided, and generally coped by avoiding that particular young person. The credibility of this divided staff team was very low with the residents, and was beginning to be noticed outside the home. The social worker for the boy was critical of the way her client was being managed, and her remarks back at the office did nothing to enhance the reputation of the home with the fieldwork team.

After Psychological Thinking

Following more detailed and systematic observation of the boy by a worker who was freed up to do this task and record it properly, it became clear that the angry outbursts were worst at particular times of day. This was eventually linked specifically to those times when residents were taking showers. A range of behaviour other than the outbursts themselves was noted, including repeated questions from the boy about who was where, repeated checking of the shower-room, with requests that the worker check it on his behalf.

On the basis of the additional information, the team developed a new theory about the boy whom they now saw as fearful, anxious and vulnerable. They understood his outbursts to be a way of dealing with his fears, especially the one associated with the showering process.

A new theory led to a new intervention; it was agreed that, as an experiment, he should take his shower, alone, at a separate time, but only following thorough checking of the area by a member of staff. The worker would, having done the prior checks, stand sentry in front of the shower protecting the boy from unwanted intrusions, and ensuring his safety. Such was the success of this approach that it was applied to a number of other situations. The theory around the boy's fear and vulnerability generated interventions to increase his sense of safety and security in a number of situations in the home. Soon the number of outbursts greatly reduced.

With such good results, a better atmosphere was created within the peer group. Those residents who had been fearful were less so, and those setting up the boy were exposed as the boy's trust in staff increased and he was able to tell them about being set up and was believed by them.

In the same way, the staff gained confidence from seeing their intervention working and this improved cohesion and morale within the team. It also had a knock-on effect, in that the policy on showering was changed to increase privacy and reduce adverse group effects. This was discussed and negotiated with residents, who welcomed it as a positive improvement. Naturally, the social worker was pleased to see her client's improvement and the general improvement in the atmosphere in the home when she visited.

This did not go unnoticed at head office, where the discussion turned on aspects of abuse that the boy had almost certainly experienced in the family of origin. The likelihood that he had experienced homosexual assaults in the context of bathing was a theory that they were beginning to consider much more seriously in light of the developments in the children's home. This was to be the focus of future social work with this client and his family.

This scenario illustrates how thinking more psychologically can have positive consequences not only for individuals but for groups of both residents and staff. If followed through, such thinking may also have a long-term impact on patterns of social work practice, both within and beyond residential settings.

INTERVENTIONS FROM PSYCHOLOGISTS

The special contributions that psychologists might make are grouped below into six key areas:

- Child psychologists are familiar with normal and abnormal child development 0–19 years, and through the range of disabilities, and have knowledge of different theories of human development and behaviour.
- Psychologists have a wide range of assessment techniques and tools at their disposal, which are not available to other professionals. They are also able to devise special assessment procedures tailored to particular demands. Assessment can be done at individual, group and family levels, and can be administered either by the psychologists, or by others, as is most appropriate. This area was dealt with more fully in Chapter 5.
- Psychologists do not expect to undertake assessments in isolation but expect them to lead to a planned strategy of care or treatment. Such treatment could encompass individuals, groups or families, and could be delivered directly by the psychologists or by others, as appropriate.
- Many psychologists are qualified teachers with teaching experience. All will have had experience of teaching psychology to other professionals and will have contributed to the training and supervision of their own profession.
- All psychologists receive training in research methodology, experimental design, data collection and statistical analysis. All will have conducted a research project during their training and many continue to pursue research once in post. Psychologists can therefore offer an understanding of research methods and statistical analysis and the part these things can play in understanding and explaining problems.
- In the early 1990s the Manpower Advisory Group (which at that time acted as a focus for manpower issues in the National Health Service) made an analysis of psychology practice. What they found to be unique in this group (as opposed to other professional groups) was 'a thorough understanding of varied and complex psychological theories, and the ability to apply these to new problems to generate interventions'. Let us use this as our definition of consultancy, which is applicable to all levels of work from individuals to large organizations. (Consultation was covered more fully in Chapter 6.)

A model of working is advocated that encompasses five different levels of activity. The numbering of the levels of working implies neither a hierarchy nor a sequence, as it is necessary to consider working on more than one level simultaneously.

The pattern of practice for the psychologist is summarized in Table 10.1.

Table 10.1 Pattern of practice for the psychologist

Levels of working	Psychologist's activity
1. Direct work	Development of treatment/interventions for: • individuals • groups of residents • families of residents
2. Indirect work through consultation	Regular consultation services to staff teams in relation to: • individuals • the group of residents • the ethos and regime used to care for them
3. Training and support	Contributing to existing training strategy. Developing new initiatives, especially in respect of psychological skills and knowledge.
4. Policy and practice	Contributing to policy and practice in relation to: • each home (e.g. purpose and function, admissions policy, etc.) • Residential Strategy for the Local Authority (which encompasses all their homes) • Children's Services strategy
5. Research and evaluation	Collection of data: • to act as baseline • to inform practice • to enable outcomes to be measured over time • production of reports as feedback

Practice Examples

Practice examples are taken from the author's experience of working in residential settings over 20 years, and include practice from the 1980s in an Observation and Assessment Centre for Boys, in the 1990s in a number of Local Authority Children's Homes, and, at the turn of the millennium, an in-depth period of working exclusively in one Local Authority Community Home with Education. While these illustrations are drawn from a psychologist's practice, such interventions could equally be utilized by psychologically minded and appropriately supervised practitioners from other disciplines.

Level 1: Direct Work

The extent to which it is possible or appropriate to work at this level will depend upon a number of considerations. One of the most important is the total amount of psychology time available to the establishment(s). Where this is limited, the psychologist must try to maximize the impact on all residents, and will probably decide to work mostly at Level 2 (see p. 289) in order to achieve this. Other considerations will include the likely length of stay of residents, the purpose and function of the home, the attitude of staff and, most importantly, the views of the individual concerned.

It is notoriously difficult to develop individual work with young people whose experiences have been of abuse and neglect by adults. This has invariably resulted in a deep mistrust of adults, which is often compounded by many changes of adult carers over the years. The young people have good reason to be wary of letting down their defences, as in their past, this has led to disastrous consequences of abuse and abandonment.

It may be feasible to engage in direct work when delivering a psychology service to only one establishment which allows time to work at all five levels. It becomes possible to focus on individuals who are likely to stay for longer periods and to spend time building up a relationship with not only that young person, but also his or her key worker, social worker and, where possible, family of origin network. Preferably, the psychologist should find a location within the home and be seen in that office/consulting room frequently so that over time he or she is regarded as 'part of the place'. Certain 'rules' become known about seeing this person, of which perhaps the three most important might be:

1. You only come if you want to.
2. You only stay as long as you want.
3. You do not have to come on your own.

Creating a 'safe' environment where young people have some control over what happens is crucial in the context of their typical life experiences.

Individual work can range from one-off sessions, through to more extended pieces of work. The techniques used can include play therapy (using a range of toys, doll's house, etc.), geneograms (family trees), word games, drawings, standardized psychological materials and counselling through conversation. A young person may work mainly through keeping a diary, which allows significant exploration of family relationship and abuse issues, without the information needing to be spoken in response to questions.

An adolescent girl took to hovering in the corridor outside the psychologist's office perhaps hoping to bump into the psychologist. Sometimes, she would call on the nurse who had an office next door, and it was agreed that the nurse would bring her to meet the psychologist. After they were introduced, she took to tapping on the door but would not come in. She was always with a group of other residents – never alone. Eventually, they were all enticed in with offers of drinks and biscuits, and this enabled her to look around. There was much talk among the young people about the psychologist, why she was there and how it was decided that a young person could see her. It was made clear that all that was needed was for the young person to tell the key worker, who would fix up a time. A protracted process ensued which consisted of extremely brief visits by the girl, at first with a key worker, then with her friends and eventually alone. They extended over time, but always at the pace of the girl, until about half an hour was tolerated, around two months after the initial introduction was made. It was moving to see this hostile, well-defended abuse survivor sitting on the floor playing with the doll's house as if she was 5 years old. She had certainly worked hard to achieve this, her choice of activity.

This composite case, based entirely on fact, serves to highlight the difficulty of engaging young people in direct work, and perhaps illustrates why traditional methods of service delivery are unsuited to the task. This type of young person is almost impossible to get to a strange clinic, to meet a complete stranger with whom he or she may be expected to communicate for up to an hour. It is equally difficult, for different reasons, for the psychologist, or any other helping professional to make meaningful contact under such conditions, and raises important issues about service delivery, which are picked up later in the chapter.

There is some evidence of the difference between the effectiveness of traditional methods of service delivery (via CAMHS clinics) and the on-site approach described here. Before the author started, there was only one resident (in a total population of 24) receiving direct individual work; two years later there were 14 residents receiving a service, on average attending three sessions each with the resident psychologist within the course of one year.

The development of group work with such young people is challenging for the same reasons. Without great care, youngsters may feel very exposed and vulnerable in the presence of other young people and all their defences will be mobilized. It can be a long hard struggle to make a safe environment in which very painful issues of abuse and neglect can be explored constructively.

Together with residential worker colleagues, the author developed a Girls Group in an establishment where boys predominated. The same rules applied as for individual work, except that boys were not included and therefore could not be brought along. The girls themselves set the agenda and made the rules. They also made decisions about how to deal with incidents within the group. For example, if someone walked out in a mood, it would be decided if she should be followed, either by a worker or another girl. Equally, if a burning issue was discussed – for example, privacy – it might be agreed that a delegation from the group would report back to the head of home. The group created a context in which issues specific to being a female could be aired and taken forward, and created the impetus for the boys to have a group of their own.

Before the arrival of the psychologist, no group work had been attempted within the establishment, and it had not proved possible to include residents in any of the groups being run in the CAMHS context. After two years, there were seven residents participating regularly in a group, which ran for 10 sessions.

Working with the families of origin poses additional problems, because of the considerable hostility that families often feel towards the Social Services as an organization, and to staff and institutions within it. Many of the families of residents have had their parental rights removed in acrimonious circumstances, and it is difficult for them to trust professionals. Moreover, many of the parents themselves have histories of abuse and neglect, which resulted in their being taken into care as children. Some have particular experience of residential care; indeed, some parents may have lived in the same home in which their child is now placed!

It is common for social workers to find themselves in an impasse when it comes to direct work with the families of residents. This can have disastrous consequences for the residents, as it may result in them becoming stranded in the home, because their families refuse to work with Social Services. Equally, social workers who may not want the young person to remain in residence, are unable to move the young person on because they cannot find a substitute family, even if the young person was willing to try one. Neither can they return the young person to the family of origin network, in the absence of proper discussion and negotiations.

It is sometimes possible for the psychologist to assist in these circumstances, where they have the knowledge and skills to work with hostile and angry families. This is invariably best achieved through working closely with the case-responsible social worker. It can be unhelpful to exclude the social worker and thereby fall into the trap of being set against them by the family. A brief example illustrates what can be achieved through working collaboratively.

A severely maltreated girl was removed from her mother's care, and placed in the home, while Care Proceedings were pursued. The mother was actively opposed to the proceedings, and the social worker was unable to plan the girl's future care without a Care Order, which she had so far been unable to obtain. They were in an impasse. The work of the psychologist, which was commissioned by the social worker, initially took place with the mother and daughter, and it became clear that this powerful relationship was extremely dysfunctional, in that both were trapped by feelings of mutual loyalty. The girl was longing to be cared for safely away from home but could not say so for fear of hurting her mother. Equally, the mother knew that her addictions rendered her incapable of maintaining satisfactory parenting but she did not want to further harm her daughter by rejecting her. The work consisted of building up visits home for the girl, under social work supervision, with the aim of assessing the viability of a reunion. Discussions about these visits formed the basis of the therapeutic work. The visits were so violently unsuccessful that the mother was eventually able to acknowledge that she could not care for her daughter, and withdrew her opposition to the Care Proceedings. Following the Care Order, the girl was placed in foster care, and the foster mother attended a couple of sessions with the psychologist, the girl and her mother, prior to that placement starting.

In this case, the residential worker for the girl was actively involved in the whole process, was looked upon more favourably by parents, and was better able to work with them collaboratively than the case-responsible fieldwork social worker. Before the psychologist started, family work occurred with only one resident. Two years later, eight families were seen over the course of a year, typically for only one or two sessions with the psychologist, although work often continued without her.

With direct work at individual, group and family levels there is a distinct advantage in being a non-Social Services professional with no power to place or remove children. But this is not in itself sufficient. A considerable level of understanding of abuse, neglect and disadvantage needs to be combined with a wide range of therapeutic skills, which can be adapted to a range of settings and circumstances. This direct work is not for the inexperienced or faint hearted. Often young people and their families need to test the clinician's resolve through behaviour that can involve verbal and physical aggression. If the worker is unequal to the test, the work cannot be done. If the work can be done, it can have a significant positive impact for residents and their families.

Level 2: Indirect Work through Consultation

This is probably the level of working most often adopted by psychologists with limited time and more than one home to cover, but it is also an important level to work at where more time is available for one home. The first task is to become familiar with the establishment, and the best way to achieve that is by working on shift, especially in the evening and at weekends, if time and circumstances permit. All too frequently outsiders come in and advise homes without appreciating the nature of the setting concerned. Being prepared to join the residential workers has several advantages, including improving the psychologist's understanding, visibility and credibility as an interested party, both to staff and residents. Following this, more typical patterns of practice include:

- Regular (e.g. monthly) reviews of all residents with staff team.
- In-depth discussion of specific individuals, emerging from regular reviews.
- The development of special strategies for individuals as well as more general ones for the group as a whole.
- Discussions about the nature of the regime, aspects of the rules, ethos, etc.
- All sessions written up and any advice given carefully recorded for reference in the absence of the psychologist.
- Inclusion of case responsible social workers when in-depth discussions of an individual resident are planned.
- Inclusion of senior managers when wider issues, e.g. rules, regime, are under discussion.

Level 3: Training

The psychologist can contribute to existing training strategies, either within the home, or as organized by a central training department. Examples of practice include contributing to staff induction – for example, by introducing the role of the psychologist, presenting work on understanding young people's behaviour, working with families, etc. The psychologist is well placed to assist with existing training on the health of looked after children, focusing particularly on mental health issues.

The psychologist can also set up new training initiatives based on their growing understanding of the needs of a particular home, or group of homes. Examples of topics covered include: assessment, observing and recording behaviour, promoting positive behaviour, attachment, family therapy, etc.

In addition, the psychologist can develop evaluation sheets so that any training event developed in-house is properly evaluated, and any useful feedback is incorporated into future practice.

Level 4: Policy and Practice

The extent to which the psychologist is either able or willing to contribute to policy and practice will depend on his or her level of experience, seniority and interest in this level of working. However, none should be practising in a children's home without some level of awareness of the key features of the Local Authority's Residential Strategy. This will itself be part of a wider children's strategy, the essence of which also needs to be grasped, as residents in the home inevitably arrive from and depart to other parts of the care system. Very often the psychologist will also be working in these other settings.

At the level of policy and practice for a particular home, psychologists can make a significant contribution, often drawing on their experience of working at Levels 1, 2 and 3 as just described. Examples of practice include the development of an Assessment of Level of Needs matrix for all referrals to an establishment; the development of statements of purpose for homes; contributions to the overall Residential Strategy, especially to policy on admissions to residential care.

Level 5: Research and Evaluation

As with the preceding section, the extent to which the psychologists are able/willing to work at this level will depend on a number of factors – for example, the amount of time they have available, and the importance of this type of activity for their personal practice. However, it will be routine to keep good records and produce reports of activity at all the preceding levels of working. This not only acts as a baseline, at the outset, but enables practice to be tracked over time, and the feedback used to inform future practice. It may also shed some light on the impact of practice on outcomes.

Internal and External Outcomes

External outcomes can be clearly linked to describable events. In the context of residential care, these might include such things as whether the placement of an individual lasted as long as was planned, or whether it ended prematurely. At the level of the establishment itself, outcome indicators might include things like turnover of residents, numbers involved in running away, etc. Internal outcomes refer to the inner world of experiences, opinions and relationships which combine to form the subjective meaning of the placement for anyone involved, from whatever perspective they hold.

The purpose is not the search for one outcome, whether external or internal. Nor is it an attempt to reconcile contradictory views, as just described. Rather it is to illustrate the nature and extent of the outcome endeavour in all its complexity.

Table 10.2 illustrates how information collected by a psychologist can be used to show the impact of changes in practice on outcome. It is drawn from the author's practice.

An example of an internal outcome finds expression in the following quote by Gina who was in care between 14 and 16 years of age.

The staff were brilliant. They'd sit down and listen to you. They wouldn't, like, just act like you weren't there. They'd sit down and, like, come and stand outside and have a cigarette with you, you know, like they'd get really close. Like a couple of the staff, they'd come and sit in my bedroom and talk to me if I was feeling down, they'd come and talk to me.

(Skuse & Ward, 2003, p. 178)

At the opposite end of the spectrum, an excerpt from a director of Social Services' letter to a psychologist – following receipt of a report – reads:

Thank you . . . I found it to be an excellent report with strong valuable messages for myself and senior management . . . regarding the services we should endeavour to achieve at (the Children's Home). I would endorse that in looking at the changes that need to be made in Children's Services that you are consulted in terms of how we move this forward . . . .

Psychologists may use information to expose gaps in the services to looked after children. An example of this occurred when an audit of health records of residents revealed that only 20% had any record of their health available within the home. This led to major changes in practice, which are reported on in Chapter 3.

Psychologists may be able to undertake their own research in residential settings, or to encourage trainee psychologists to conduct research (this is a necessary part of their training) in partnership with them. The latter is more common, given major constraints on time, and the huge logistical problems which research in such settings entails. It also has the advantage of introducing

Table 10.2   The impact of change in practice on outcome

Information collected	Time one (N = 24 res.)	Two years later (N = 27 res.)	Outcomes include
Admissions in one month:	18	3	Young people experience less change; peer relationships can develop; staff can develop relationships with residents
Discharges in one month:	19	1	
Average length of stay:	1 month	7 months	Individual group and family work becomes feasible
Episodes of running away:	62	33	Increased stability of residents group; more acceptance by individuals of placement
Length of absence:			Absences are brief, staff able to successfully follow-up and return residents
<24 hours	31	29	
>24 hours	31	4	

trainees to an important specialist area of practice, which might not otherwise be available to them.

Other Activity

A brief summary of some other activities undertaken by psychologists while working in residential settings acts as a conclusion to this section:

* Chairing a multidisciplinary, inter-agency project group on the health of looked after children.
* Participating in recruiting, selecting and evaluating residential workers, mainly through the design of forms for the purpose.
* Promoting user involvement for the families of residents.
* Health promotion, especially mental health, for residential staff.
* Contributing to a special project set up to meet the needs of the most complex cases shared by Health and Social Care, through methods of selection of young people, training and support of staff and ongoing evaluation of outcomes.
* Involving other psychologists from the region in the topic through mounting conferences/workshops.
* Involving the British Psychological Society in the area of residential care, via the Special Group for psychologists and Social Services.
* Representing the BPS at the Warner Enquiry into Residential Care (DOH, 1992).

DISCUSSION

The topic of residential care is vast and contains a body of literature, both research and practice based, of which a selection is provided in the references. Almost none of this literature derives from the activity of psychologists, and it is fair to say that social work thinking and practice have dominated the discourse. The question was posed earlier in the chapter, 'What can psychologists offer?' Patterns of practice have been described which cover a range of levels of activity from working with the individual resident through to wider organizational issues that impact on residential care.

Getting the Best out of Psychologists

If Social Services departments are to use psychologists in residential settings, they will want to ensure that they maximize their impact and get the best out of them. Equally, psychologists themselves need to practise in a way that demonstrates their value, as they are an expensive commodity, particularly in the context of how staff in residential settings are paid. There are certain conditions, which are conducive to positive practice:

- *Dedicated time* – If psychologists can offer their services on a planned, regular and predictable basis, not contingent upon referrals of individuals or in reaction to the latest emergency (there will always be one!), this enables relationships to build up over time, which later form the basis for constructive collaborative work.
- *Experienced practitioners* – The innumerable challenges of working in residential settings make it particularly demanding and it is preferable if practitioners are more mature and experienced. Additional experience of working in Social Services settings is a distinct advantage, and specialist knowledge of residential work is also desirable.
- *Management support* – The importance of this can scarcely be exaggerated. Experience suggests that the successes of psychologists are inextricably linked to how they are viewed and supported by management. In one case example, the ending of a service occurred after three key people left Social Services. These were the Director, the Head of Children's Services and the manager of the Psychology Service. In spite of excellent support elsewhere in the system, the position of the Psychology Service was lost as none of the three replacements championed the service. Eventually that Psychology Service was disbanded and the psychologists made redundant. Ironically, within a short time, it was felt necessary to recruit and employ two new psychologists. While this could be taken as positive feedback, in that the need for a Psychology Service was recognized, it also shows how short-sighted (and costly) had been the management decision to terminate the service.

  The definition of 'management support' includes the provision of good working conditions and appropriate remuneration; endorsing the model of service delivery; actively tackling problems and obstacles and doing so effectively; treating the psychologists respectfully and allowing them appropriate levels of autonomy; accepting and acting on the feedback from the psychologists about patterns of practice within social services; seeing the service as an asset rather than a threat. Where this style of management support is present, psychologists can be very effective.
- *Model of service delivery* – The model of working at a number of different levels was described earlier. This has proved particularly suitable for psychologists entering a system for the first time as opposed to offering services from an outsider position. It allows for an extended understanding of the context in which the service is being delivered, and this enables a range of

interventions to be developed, all of which are designed to achieve change, but which focus on different parts of the system. At different times during the life of a psychology service some levels of working will be more important than others. Indeed, at times it will be necessary to work at one level first, before another level of work can start. Where the psychologist had a strong position within the system, and high levels of communication with the managers, it allows a flexible and timely response to the issues uppermost at any particular time in the evolution of each residential setting.

- *Inter-agency collaboration* – When psychologists are employed by and/or are based within Social Services it is crucial to retain strong active links with Child Health in general, and especially with CAMHS and Child Psychology from the local Trust. This maintains an inter-agency perspective that widens understanding in a number of ways. There may be obstacles to successful inter-agency partnership in both the NHS and Social Services and being jointly managed has the potential of being problematic. However, where managers show a mutual respect of each other's work and agency, through good communication they can collaborate well in relation to the psychology service. This can lead towards strengthening of the relationship between the two agencies. Current guidance as outlined in *Every Child Matters, Change for Children* (DFES, 2004) encourages working together and to some extent the integration of agencies involved in delivering services to children.

- *The attitude of the homes* – Where psychologists experience children's homes as wanting a service, and collaborating to achieve a shared agenda for action, they are able to have a significant impact. This has occurred not only when a lot of time was dedicated, but also when a much smaller amount was used to good effect. Given a favourable stance from the home, it is possible not only to achieve set goals, but to offer added value in the range of methods described earlier in the chapter. The essence of any success resides in the partnership between the home and the psychologist – the more positive and robust it is, the more the psychologist can achieve. It should be emphasized, in this spirit, that any such achievements owe at least as much to the homes themselves.

The corollary of identifying factors that are conducive to success is to say that, without them, the prospects of success for psychologists in Local Authority residential settings are very limited. However, beyond simply reversing the positive factors rehearsed above, there are other obstacles to success, some of which hark back to the nature of residential care itself. These include:

- *Staffing problems* – Staffing shortages, combined with sickness and absenteeism, can make it difficult for psychologists to develop a relationship with staff groups who keep changing and may comprise many temporary agency staff. At worst, it becomes impossible for teams to be released from the 'shop floor', and as and when they are, they are in a serious state of exhaustion. The attention of the psychologist may not be welcome!

- *Attitude of social workers with case responsibility for young people and their families* – Sadly (as has been referred to earlier in the chapter) it has been a common experience for psychologists to hear social workers speaking in highly negative terms about residential care in general as well as about particular homes. At worst, communication can be non-existent, and decisions and plans may be made in a high-handed, unilateral fashion. Naturally, where social workers show some interest in and understanding of residential care, and of the predicament of particular homes, a more fruitful partnership is possible.

- *Policy and practice* – As discussed earlier, policy in relation to residential care can be ambiguous and at times non-existent. Where policies do exist, they seem to be susceptible to being overruled when necessity dictates – for example, a policy decision to have planned admissions to all except designated emergency beds, can be overruled at times. The fact that this leads to unmanageable mixes of residents and creates instability and disrupts staffing arrangements, seems to be of less importance than the imperative to solve an emergency at short notice. Later the home might be criticized for failing to manage successfully. The position of residential care within the overall 'vision' for children's services is at times unclear. One could be forgiven for forming the impression that, although many would like to dispense with residential care altogether and use agency/out-of-county provision, this is recognized as uneconomic. However, rather than enhancing existing services, they often remain underfunded and undervalued, as a 'necessary evil'.

- *Underfunded and undervalued* – Throughout 20 years working with, in or for Social Services departments the author has seen this agency as underfunded and undervalued. Children's services have seen the diminution of resources (both human and material) while the small numbers of children and families entitled to a service have become ever more severe, complex and needy. Against this background, the pressure on professionals has risen and the adverse impact on services has been demonstrable. Indeed, a number of psychological services have perished, in spite of strong evidence of their effectiveness, when Local Authorities were no longer able to afford them.

Consequently, psychologists must accept that in choosing to work in Social Services settings, and particularly in the residential sector, they themselves run the risk of experiencing the patterns of instability, change and loss, which are a feature of this work.

Children – lost and found

I

In a bleak landscape
harsh winds bite bitter
chilling to the bone
Splintery shards of ice pierce to the heart
A deafening silence stills the air
The words hang frozen on cracked lips
unspeakable, unheard

Leaving the fire banked up
she sets off to work
wrapped up against the cold
her rucksack packed with extra clothes
hot drinks and hope
She knows the place
has found them there before
half dead from cold

The picking up is not so bad
so frozen stiff they don't resist
don't speak, won't eat or drink at first
(but later try and stop them)

It gets bad once defrosting starts
Their pain becomes immense
Intolerable
The terror worse that what is left is
shattered fragments
beyond all repair
Or, worst of all, there's nothing left
There's no one there

She soldiers on, her broad back braced
against the weight, the cold, the pain
The hell that they are facing
on their long journey

II

The fire is low but still alight
in the fading gloom of the unlit room
when at last they stagger in together
each exhausted

She's tired of being strong
of keeping hope alive
of getting nothing back for all this time
of working on her own, week in, year out
watching her colleagues watching her
uncomprehending, uncompassionate

She flops down, flat out, eyes closed
still fully dressed in wet shoes, dirty clothes
He's shocked from his own stupor
by this body, deathly still
and going to her side
he touches her icy hand, he feels she's cold
So he banks the fire up
She's tired, he thinks
as her breathing deepens into sleep

(Ruth Nissim, March 2005. Reproduced with permission)

Psychological Ways of Working with Residential Care

If Social Care Services cannot afford to buy in or retain their own psychologists, is there any other way in which they can contribute? As has already been suggested earlier in the chapter, you don't have to be a psychologist to think psychologically or to gain access to the vast psychological literature that is now freely available via the Internet. The number of taught courses has multiplied and modular systems of learning allow for only those relevant aspects to be studied. It is hoped that the material in this chapter has illustrated how psychological thinking and practice can be relevant and accessible to other professionals working in residential settings.

THE WAY FORWARD

It is difficult to divorce the way ahead for psychologists working in residential settings from the future of the settings themselves. There are so many factors affecting these establishments over which the psychologist can have little or no influence. However, in making a personal and professional commitment to any home, psychologists can start to build meaningful relationships with staff, residents and their families. As mutual trust and confidence is built up a positive force for change can be created and many things become possible, some of which have been illustrated in this chapter.

It is important that such endeavours do not occur in isolation. Partnerships with social workers need to be improved, perhaps through joint training initiatives pre-qualification, which would allow the foundations to be laid for later working practices. This needs to be a reciprocal process where each profession aims to understand more about the ideas, values and professional practices of the other. Improvements in mutual respect and understanding might enhance the levels of constructive partnership achieved, which can only be to the advantage of the homes, their staff and residents.

Residential care has for too long been a Cinderella service, in comparison to residential provision for young people delivered by Health and Education. For them, the greater your problems and needs, the more specialist and better qualified the staff and facilities become. They are funded and managed with the aim of delivering top quality 'Rolls Royce' services. It seems, in our culture, that if your problems are social in origin then you are less deserving and not entitled to the best. This is as true for the agency and its staff as it is for the children and their families. It is to be hoped that the creation of Children's Trusts and the rapprochement of Health and Education with Social Services in respect of meeting children's needs, will result in the excellence that is currently available in some parts of the system spreading to the other parts.

Psychological thinking has much to offer the residential sector, and so do psychologists. Although it is a difficult area for all who work in it, individual professionals must ask themselves how they can help children and families to get the best possible service in these settings. Surely there can be no doubt as to their need or their entitlement.

REFERENCES

Arnold, J. (2005) *Work Psychology: Understanding Human Behaviour in the Workplace* (4th edn). Harlow: Prentice-Hall.

Beck, A.T. (1976) *Cognitive Therapy and the Emotional Disorders.* New York: International Universities Press.

DFES (2004) *Every Child Matters, Change for Children.* London: TSO.

DOH (1992) *Choosing with Care: The Report of the Committee of Inquiry into the Selection, Development and Management of Staff in Children's Homes.* London: TSO.

Ford, J.K. (Ed.) (1997) *Improving Training in Work Organizations.* New Jersey: Lawrence Erlbaum.

Freud, S. (1923) The ego and the id. *Standard Edition*, **19**, 1–59.

Kraiger, K. (Ed.) (2002) *Creating, Implementing, and Managing Effective Training and Development.* San Francisco: Jossey-Bass.

Pavlov, I. (1927) Conditional reflexes. In M. Herbert (1991) *Clinical Child Psychology. Social Learning, Development and Behaviour.* Chichester: John Wiley & Sons.

Schein, E.H. (1987) *Process Consultation.* Reading, Mass.: Addison Wesley.

Skinner, B.F. (1974) *About Behaviourism.* London: Cape.

Skuse, T. & Ward, H. (2003) *Outcomes for Looked After Children: Children's Views of Care and Accommodation.* An Interim Report to the Department of Health. Loughborough University: Centre for Child and Family Research .

West, M.A. (1994) *Effective Teamwork.* London: BPS.

11

OPENING THE DOOR: HOW CAN THERAPY HELP THE CHILD AND YOUNG PERSON LIVING IN FOSTER OR ADOPTIVE HOMES?

Kim S. Golding with Ann Courtney and Jane Foulkes

> Sarah, a pale, thin 14-year-old girl sits in front of me. She has to leave her five-year foster placement. The carers cannot cope with the constant lying, stealing and fighting. Sarah cannot cope with the false promises from her mum that she will be able to return. She sits in front of me now and pours out her anger at a friend who has recently let her down. I hear the anger Sarah feels at a placement breaking down, at a mother who cannot be there for her, but most of all at herself for not being good enough. I sit there and listen and wonder how can I help. What intervention can help Sarah through a childhood that has let her down? What psychological theory can help me to understand the fear and dread of matching yourself to the world and finding yourself lacking. I struggle to find a way to help. I fear for Sarah's future.

There is a range of psychological interventions that might be applied to helping the child and young person living in adoptive or foster care. These interventions need to take into account the special needs of children who have

Thinking Psychologically About Children Who Are Looked After and Adopted
Edited by K.S. Golding, H.R. Dent, R. Nissim and L. Stott.

experienced abuse, neglect, loss and separation earlier in their life, children who feel shame in themselves and lack of trust in others. Within this chapter a number of traditional intervention approaches are described with discussion of how these might be adapted to the needs of looked after and adopted children. This is supplemented in Chapter 12 with a focus on a range of specialist interventions that have been developed specifically with the needs of these children in mind.

Since the 1920s therapists have sought to help children displaying signs of emotional disturbance. The initial impetus came from psychoanalysis. Pioneers such as Melanie Klein and Anna Freud found ways to apply methods developed with adults for children. The opening of the first child guidance clinic by Dr Emmanuel Miller in 1927 and The Children's Centre by Dr Margaret Lowenfield in 1928 broadened the provision of psychotherapy. In 1949 Dr John Bowlby founded the first training course for child analysts (Lush et al., 1999). Alongside these developments Virginia Axline was further developing play therapy, later immortalized in her book *Dibs: In Search of Self* (Axline, 1964) and interventions were developed to provide briefer treatment with more attention to the environment and the family (Rutter, 1975). Epic books such as 'Helping Troubled Children' (Rutter, 1975) ensured that child interventions were here to stay.

The impetus to provide therapy for children in substitute care can be traced back to the Second World War and the needs of child evacuees (Lush et al., 1999). The development of interventions for neglected and rejected children began in the 1960s. Wolff (1969, p. 236) provides advice with a remarkably modern ring to it:

> What such children need more than anything else is an adult who will assume parental responsibility. They do not need a doctor, they need a parent. But, because of their past deprivations and experiences of stress, such children need a very special kind of parent. They need a person or group of people who will guarantee unconditional affect and support, who are prepared to forgo, often for many years, the satisfactions that parents normally get from their children and who will bring to their task professional understanding not only of childhood behaviour but of their own responses both to the children in their care and to the parents whose inadequacies have brought the children to this plight.

This was also the decade in which the fact of child abuse was being faced and treatment of abused children, often placed in foster care, was being considered. The pioneering work of the Kempes ensured that this was a topic of therapeutic interest that would not go away (Kempe & Kempe, 1978).

Psychological interventions are not just the province of the therapist. Therapy begins within a stable substitute home, and is provided by the team around the child. This can include carers or parents, social workers, teachers and mentors. Sometimes the provision of such an environment is sufficient to allow the child to explore and resolve issues and experiences. Hunter (2001) cautions that providing children with the message that their grief and distress can only be received by a psychotherapist can be unhelpful, suggesting that the carers cannot bear their hurt. Practitioners are developing ways of working with these children alongside this therapeutic network. This involves both adapting traditional interventions and developing new interventions. Opening the door to new ways of working with children and young people, which supports the fragile progress they are making within their new homes.

TRADITIONAL INTERVENTIONS: ISSUES AND ADAPTATIONS

A Structure for Therapy: Adopting a Holistic Approach

There is a bewildering range of interventions that might help the child. These interventions can be tailored for the individual child or young person, the family or the wider community, e.g. the school, local neighbourhood and support network (see Figure 11.1).

Children who are adopted or fostered often live within a more complicated range of contexts than children living with their birth families. An essential issue to address is how to use all these contexts to provide a supportive environment within which the child is accepted and can grow and thrive. Only from this starting point can the child be helped towards improved social adjustment and better mental health.

Too narrow a focus on individual therapy can lead to an expectation that children will adjust to a world for which they are not equipped. The therapy becomes a way of 'making children fit'. When therapy becomes part of a wider ecologically based and holistic approach, we all have a responsibility to help children to feel more comfortable and secure. Therapy then becomes one component of a comprehensive treatment plan within which a range of interventions is directed at the multiple levels of child, family and wider environment (Pearce & Pezzot-Pearce, 2001). Therefore simplistic debates about the usefulness of traditional or innovative interventions, or the need to work individually with the child or to work with the family and community are not helpful. What are needed are flexible intervention packages that can use any from the whole range of interventions combined in a way that meets the needs of the individual child or young person, and his or her family and community (see Figure 11.2).

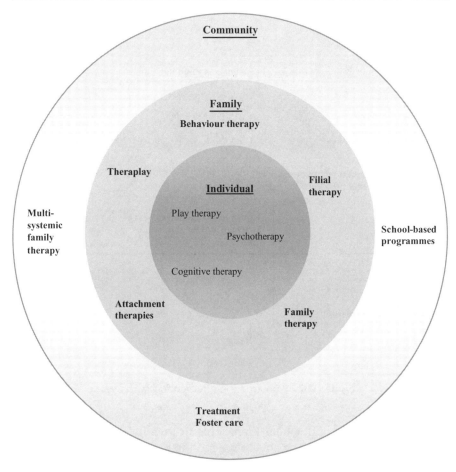

Figure 11.1   Types and levels of interventions

The range of therapeutic possibilities that might contribute to such intervention packages are considered below. Discussion will focus on how these might be adapted to meet the needs of looked after and adopted children.

Psychoanalytic Psychotherapy

Psychoanalytic psychotherapy assumes that fears and anxieties relate to primitive states of mind developed in the face of past experience. This in turn leads to the development of self-defences. These are obstacles to trust and communication. Therapy therefore attends to these self-defences so that

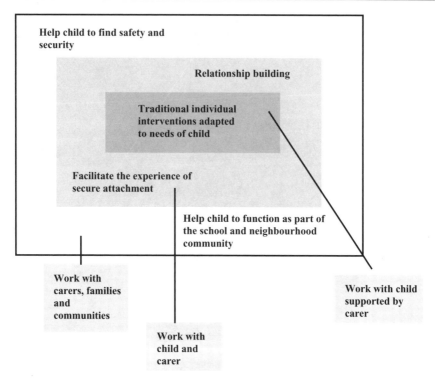

Figure 11.2   Constructing intervention packages

therapist and child understand them. This in turn helps the individual to own this past and thus to be able to function in healthier ways in the future (Hunter, 2001).

The therapist helps to free the child from compulsions to repeat the past and thus enables him or her to benefit from current relationships. Toys and artwork are used to provide the child with means of communication. The therapist provides containment of feelings as well as interpretation to encourage insight development.

Hunter (2001) suggests that applying this therapy to children who are deeply mistrustful and traumatized requires adaptation, and without such adaptation these children will remain unreachable. In particular, these children might need a therapist who is more communicative and receptive than is traditional. This accords with Hughes (1997) who suggests that traditional models of psychotherapy, which aim to foster self-reliance, do not provide enough containment of anxiety or feelings of safety. Thus the quiet of the therapy room might be experienced as overwhelming.

The therapist needs to be aware of the near unbearable experiences the child brings to the therapy. It is important that the therapist acknowledges the experience of abuse encountered by the child (Hunter, 2001). Alvarez (1983) advises on the use of interpretations with a positive ending, as the child tends to pick up on and magnify the negative in what he or she is told. For example, Hunter (2001, p. 173) suggests changing 'you believe that I will abandon you because you are angry and jealous' with 'because you experience all those angry and jealous feelings, it makes it hard for you to believe I can want to come back.' A number of authors point to the importance of liaison with the caring network around the child so that they can support the therapy (e.g. Hunter, 2001; Boston & Szur, 1983/1990).

Play Therapy

Play is used in a variety of interventions with children, as a method of engaging them, of developing a therapeutic relationship and of maintaining their involvement in the work that is to be undertaken. In addition, a number of the approaches outlined in this chapter, such as psychoanalytic psychotherapy and cognitive-behavioural therapies, use play to engender insight or learning.

However in play therapy, it is the play itself that is therapeutic and used as the child's natural medium of self-expression. Thus a child uses play to express his or her feelings and problems, as an individual might use speech in adult therapy. Play gives concrete form and expression to children's inner worlds. Unmanageable reality is transformed by symbolic representation into manageable situations, over which the child can gain a sense of mastery, by engaging in self-directed exploration.

Play therapists use a variety of differing approaches but most emphasize the need to create conditions of security within the playroom (by consistency and reliability), and through the core conditions of acceptance, empathy and congruence (Rogers, 1951) respond to the child's communications at an *affective* rather than a cognitive level.

Children use a variety of ways to express themselves, often using toys from an earlier stage of development, to re-experience and reintegrate past experiences into current functioning.

> A 9 year old I worked with for a year, who had a long history of neglect and abusive relationships and had been 'tricked' by adults on many occasions, began each session with a series of games of 'hide and seek' where we were 'separated' and came back together again. (This was despite the obvious limitations of a small room, which meant that any real hiding was impossible, especially

for an adult!). I repeatedly had to do 'all the work' to bring us together as he tricked and tried to mislead me. Eventually he was able to integrate his own experience of me as an adult who was 'transparent' and responded in a genuine fashion, and my feelings of helplessness and frustration when I, as 'the child' was 'tricked'. My reliability and availability resulted in an increase in his trust of me, and of other adults in his life.

Other children choose to use role play, often by reversing roles. In these situations children can recreate and re-experience, in a non-threatening way, unresolved issues from their past. By taking the more 'powerful role' of abusive parent, or angry teacher for example, they are distancing themselves from their own experience in a way that feels safer. The therapist in the child's role recreates a healthy and 'normal' reaction. Children are able to simultaneously explore the feelings and actions of the adult, hear the 'child's' responses from the therapist, and gain some mastery over a painful situation, perhaps by changing the outcome, or expressing their own strong, and previously hidden feelings.

An 11-year-old boy, who had experienced several very distressing moves from home, sometimes with his mother and sometimes with a social worker, repeatedly recreated 'moving day'. He used the boxes that contained my toys, rather than any of the toys, to represent a 'car', which he drove, as I was removed from situation after situation and 'abandoned' to strangers. He gradually accepted that my protests and distress (and his) were not 'stupid' and babyish as he initially claimed, and became able to acknowledge some of his own neediness and wish for comfort.

Sometimes the child will identify a problem in the playroom and work on it directly. On other occasions, after the child has had the opportunity to clarify his or her difficulties symbolically, he or she will work on them in the period between sessions. For this reason, it is important that the child is in a stable situation, with carers who can support the therapy. With the support of therapist and carer, the child is enabled to come to a resolution that is appropriate to his or her level of development, and current functioning.

However the child chooses to use the sessions, the therapist does not interpret or explain the symbolism or metaphors to the child. The child's feelings are acknowledged, or mirrored and understood, and are communicated by the therapist within the metaphor used by the child, as in 'that lion cub is so sad and scared, because the daddy lion is fighting and roaring at everybody'.

Many children within the care system present with developmental delays, cognitively, emotionally or physically and play therapy is particularly appropriate for these children. It is able to address multiple problems simultaneously, it does not rely on verbal skills, and is flexible in adjusting to children's changing developmental needs (see Ryan & Wilson, 1995).

Relatively few treatment outcome studies for abused or neglected children exist in the psychological literature to date, and little empirical research has been conducted on the relative values of individual, family and group therapy approaches (Pearce & Pezzot-Pearce, 1997; Russ, 1995; Ryan, 1999). Therefore, most discussions of play therapy interventions are still based on clinical, rather than empirical, evidence. However, the limited research available (see Ray et al., 2001) suggests that play therapy is an effective intervention for a broad range of children's difficulties.

Adaptations to traditional play therapy hold particular promise for fostered and adopted children.

Filial Therapy

This is a modification of non-directive play therapy, and has been advanced over several decades within play therapy research and practice (Guerney, 1983; Van Fleet, 1994; Van Fleet & Guerney, 2003). Filial therapy is an intervention in which parents or carers are trained as therapeutic agents. Carers are taught the basic skills of child-centred play therapy by lectures, demonstrations and role plays. They then move on to practice these skills, with the observation and supervision of the therapist. Parents then transfer these sessions to their own homes, with ongoing support and supervision. Finally, generalization of the skills acquired is transferred to a wide variety of parenting situations and difficulties.

The skills taught to carers include: *structuring* the special play sessions, to help the children to feel able to use the time in their own individual way; *empathic listening*, so that the carers pay close attention to the feelings the children are expressing, particularly in their play; *imaginary play*, responding to the children's role plays; and *limit setting*, a three-step approach for setting limits and enforcing consequences.

Both foster carers and adoptive parents (as well as birth parents) have found that these play sessions enhance their relationship with their child, as well as enable the child to work through particular worries or concerns.

Filial therapists emphasize relationship-building goals generally, although some are developing a more specific attachment framework, when training carers (see Hunter, 2003).

Research on longer and short-term filial therapy training programmes for issues ranging from bereavement, chronic illness, learning disabilities, imprisoned parents, to single parents have been reported. Its effectiveness in advancing parental acceptance and reducing children's problems has been verified, although random control trials have not yet been conducted (Van Fleet, 1994; Kale & Landreth, 1999).

There are no filial therapy outcome studies on working specifically with children in the care system and their carers. However, case experience suggests that it is particularly effective. For example, filial therapy powerfully avoids the message identified earlier in this chapter (Hunter, 2001) that suggests 'I cannot bear to listen to you so I'll send you to a professional'. It ensures that children who have already experienced loss and separation are not encouraged to develop a close, but necessarily brief, relationship with another adult. It prevents the child 'splitting' the therapist and carer(s) to avoid dealing with important issues. It can effectively work on old patterns of relating and behaving, based on earlier, and now outdated internal working models, and create changes in the new system, in both adult and child.

Theraplay

Like filial therapy, theraplay is based on a belief in the importance of helping parents and carers to understand their children's needs more fully and develop strategies for meeting those needs.

It is a short-term dynamic therapeutic approach using *structured* play, as opposed to filial therapy, which follows a non-directive play therapy model. Theraplay was originally developed by Anne Jernberg and others at the Theraplay Institute in Chicago, and has its roots in object relations theory, self-psychology, psychodynamic therapy and developmental psychology (Jernberg & Booth, 2001).

It is a treatment for enhancing attachment, self-esteem, trust in others and 'joyful engagement'. Therapists work *with* carers and children. Interactions in the sessions focus on four essential qualities found in healthy parent–child relationships: *Structure, challenge, engage and nurture.* Structuring activities are those that help to clearly delineate time and space and teach mastery through the internalization of rules (for example, wait until I count to 3, *then* you can burst the balloon/kick the football). Challenges are activities that encourage the child to go beyond their current abilities – particularly in ways of relating intimately with others, or expressing strong pent up emotions, in safe playful ways (for example, arm wrestling). Engaging activities are arousing, exciting and stimulating, and help children to experience where they end and the rest of the world begins. They enhance children's experience of themselves as separate individuals (for example, pee-bo). Nurturing activities involve care taking, to help children to understand that they can get what they need, and will not be rejected for that need (for example, singing, cuddling, applying lotion to the child). Recreating and replicating early attachment behaviour is a major feature of theraplay, with an emphasis on finding ways to increase eye contact, enjoyable physical contact, and nurturing.

Theraplay is tailored to give corrective experiences in physical co-regulation through its extensive use of touch, eye contact and 'parentese', the calming and stimulating way of speaking throughout the activities. In theraplay changes can be seen as taking place in the 'moments of meeting' or 'attunement of high intensity states' between a child and therapist or parent, in which intense resonance expands experience for both (Mäkelä, 2003). It is the element of intense surprise and 'challenge' which allows for the 'possibility of a novel state being first experienced and then incorporated by both' (Tronick et al., 1998).

Theraplay has been used for children with autism or pervasive developmental delay, with ADHD, with attachment difficulties and for depressed as well as angry and aggressive children. Like filial therapy, it is an effective intervention for children who have experienced loss in their past, and enables those involved in caring for the child to work together.

Currently the Theraplay Institute is seeking to generate research, and develop evidence for the effectiveness of this method that extends beyond individual case material.

Cognitive and Behavioural Therapy

Behaviour Therapy

Behaviourism based on the operant model of learning (Skinner, 1974) emphasizes the role of the environment in explaining behaviour. This theory has led to techniques of behaviour modification to help people to change. For example, parents might be taught to reward the behaviour they want their child to display and ignore the less desirable behaviours.

This approach places importance on the initial assessment and highlights the need for careful recording and observing. The children can demonstrate perplexing, even paradoxical behaviour. The child who eagerly looks forward to an outing but as the day arrives behaves in the very way that he or she knows will spoil the chances of going; or the child who, following a day when he or she appears especially close and loving with the parent, will then seek out and destroy a favourite article belonging to the parent.

Without a good understanding of the behaviours the child displays it will be difficult to plan interventions that will be helpful. Importantly this careful individualized assessment can avoid interventions based on assumptions concerning, for example, what the child finds rewarding in a situation. Positive reinforcers for children who have experienced a history of abuse, neglect and loss can be unexpected. Children may find a range of behaviours rewarding that we might feel would be uncomfortable for them. Causing emotional and physical pain to others, saying 'no', engaging in and winning power struggles, and avoiding emotional engagement are examples of surprising but common motivators for children whose early life has taught them that you shouldn't get close because others can't be trusted.

Similarly the rewards we may expect to offer might lead the child to feel anxious and unworthy. Commonly children will sabotage planned rewards and treats as they convey to us that they are not worthy of such attention. Alternatively they might behave well to get a particularly attractive reward, but as soon as the treat is attained they revert to their former behaviour. Parents are left feeling manipulated and ineffectual.

Behavioural programmes work because ultimately children want and value a relationship with the parents. They will try hard to earn rewards and treats, but most importantly they want to please their carer. For children who have learned not to trust carers this can be very different. They may fear such relationships. They may want to be self-reliant and therefore work hard not to have a relationship, or they may want and cling to a relationship while fearing its loss. This fear can be so intense that they sabotage the relationship to bring the feared loss forward.

> A foster carer described to me her own history of abuse and neglect as a scapegoated child. Anticipating the next beating was much worse than eliciting it. She became the difficult, challenging child that her parents had always believed her to be.

For the foster or adoptive child the ending of the relationship may be much more comfortable than waiting and anticipating its ending.

Thus interventions must attend to the positive development of relationships. It is additionally important to have a good understanding of the child and the behaviour displayed. Advice must take into account the particular context for the child. For example the popular technique of 'time-out' in which the child is removed from the source of reward following misbehaviour is commonly recommended. This distancing technique typically also removes the child from the parent for a period of time. This can trigger or perpetuate feelings of abandonment for children who have experienced earlier loss and abandonment (see, e.g., Archer & Burnell, 2003).

Cognitive-Behavioural Therapy

Cognitive psychology attributes importance to inner processes of thinking, beliefs, and attributions in understanding behaviour. Cognitive therapies are aimed at helping people to alter these processes in a way that improves their overall functioning. A combination of these two approaches, as found in social learning theory, guides cognitive-behavioural therapy (CBT). Not surprisingly, this therapy combines a focus on environmental influence with that of attention to inner processes. In CBT thinking is central. Feelings and behaviours are determined not by the situation per se but by the appraisal the person makes of the situation. This in turn is influenced by early childhood experiences leading to the development of core beliefs and associated assumptions. Thus children who experience early abuse and subsequent placement with foster carers may develop core beliefs that they are unlovable with the related assumption that if they get close to a carer they will be rejected. Their subsequent behaviour can be understood as a strategy to ensure that they do not get close. The therapy involves challenging thoughts, through cognitive restructuring and behavioural experiments.

Cognitive-behavioural techniques have been used directly with children and young people. Here too some adaptation to traditional ways of working may be needed for the adopted or fostered child. For example, cognitive therapy relies on a degree of abstract thinking ability. Children can find reflecting on their own interpersonal experiences difficult. Thinking ability is commonly quite concrete with limited ability to engage in verbal interventions, and difficulties with consequential thinking. Language difficulties and developmental delay will compound this (Pearce & Pezzot-Pearce, 2001; Hart & Luckock, 2004). Adaptation to cognitive techniques is needed. For example, Knell (1998) introduced puppets and animals to model cognitive strategies. Russell and Van den Brock (1988) developed structured narrative activities within which alternative endings to stories are explored. The authors also suggest encouraging children to focus on relationships or aspects of relationships that have not been abusive to alter or challenge assumptions and attributions. Hart and Luckock (2004) advise involving the parent or carer in the child's cognitive-behavioural therapy.

Treatment Foster Care

The design of this intervention has been based on the principles of social learning theory (Moore & Chamberlain, 1994; Chamberlain & Smith, 2005). This is a wrap-around, multi-level programme for young people aged 10–16, aimed at helping them to successfully live in foster care. Typically these children will have complex needs including a high level of conduct problems, psychological, emotional and relational difficulties. Foster carers are the central part of the treatment team. They care for one child at a time and have increased levels of support and payment. Children are provided with a high degree of structure based on a point and level system. In addition they are closely supervised, provided with support for school, development of recreational skills and weekly sessions with an individual therapist using social learning and cognitive approaches. In addition, attention is given to facilitating positive contact with the birth or adoptive family as appropriate. The programme aims to provide young people with a secure base, systematic responses to their behaviour, opportunities to develop normative and prosocial behaviour, opportunities for improved relationships with their families and increased problem-solving, academic and relationship development skills.

When applying cognitive-behavioural interventions to children whose life experiences have had a major impact on their emotional development, the likelihood of core deficits in emotional regulation and reflective function need to be considered. The children may experience difficulty modulating and integrating emotional states. Rage emerges suddenly and intensely, and impulses often determine behaviour. Capacity for reflective function, the ability to interpret the behaviour of others through an understanding of mental states is poorly developed. Children need help to recognize feelings they may not be aware of, to regulate and manage emotional arousal and to interpret their own behaviour and that of others. Only when they are not overwhelmed by emotion, and have some capacity for reflective function will children be able to benefit from cognitive and behavioural approaches. A holistic approach that considers thinking, behaviour and emotion may be optimal for children and young people whose emotional, behavioural and cognitive development has been compromised by their early experience (see Figure 11.3).

Systemic Approaches

Interventions that adopt a systemic approach focus not just upon the individual with the presenting problem but place the individual within context. For example, the intervention may focus on the individual within a family, within a school, or within a community.

Multi-systemic Family Therapy

This therapy focuses on the young person, the family and the wider systems within which they are living (Henggeler et al., 1998). Such an approach holds out promise for working with children whose family and community networks are complex.

In systemic therapies the therapist aims to maintain multiple perspectives on all problems. Ruth Nissim suggests that the systemic psychotherapist

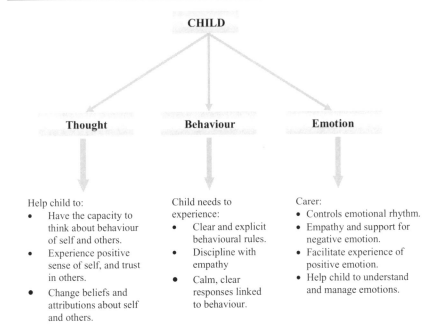

Figure 11.3   Cognitive–emotional–behavioural interventions with children

should keep the following list of relationships in mind when working with children who are looked after or adopted (Nissim, 2004, personal communication):

1. Relationship with self, both past self and present self.
2. Relationship with the family of origin (including parents, siblings and extended family).
3. Relationship with peers (in a variety of settings, e.g. school, neighbourhood, leisure activities).
4. Relationship with past and current carers, including residential carers.
5. Relationship with past and present social workers and the Social Services agency.
6. Relationship with health and education agencies, plus other agencies that may have been involved with the child.
7. Relationship with past and present communities.
8. Relationship with the law.

It can be helpful to explore these different relationships with the young person. Gaps in knowledge or understanding can become the focus of future work.

This type of work can involve the young person alone or the young person with the family or support network.

> An adolescent girl with an extensive history of abuse became very involved within the session in arranging information about her relationships on the board. She rubbed this out at the end of the session, thus feeling in control of the material she had shared. The next week she brought her diary to show the therapist. Within this she had drawn what she termed 'an abuse family tree' using different colours to highlight the names of those who were abusers. She found it difficult to talk about this aspect of her life but in this way managed to effectively engage in some important communication with the therapist.
>
> (Nissim, 2004, personal communication)

Family Therapy

This is a systemic approach that has its theoretical roots in the range of psychological theory, including behavioural and analytical theory. The problems within the family are viewed through a particular lens depending upon theoretical notions of family.

In family therapy families are helped to move from entrenched behaviours and patterns of interaction, which are preventing them from finding their own solutions to problems. The family is helped to view itself from a different perspective thus helping it to identify alternative solutions (Herbert, 1991). Patterns of verbal and non-verbal communication between family members, especially how different members give and receive feedback with each other, can provide clues as to the cause of the difficulties and the interventions that might be of help.

Family therapy has an underlying assumption that the problems for which the families are seeking help have arisen within this same family. Adoptive parents report that therapists often do not take into account that they have adopted a child. This can leave parents feeling misunderstood and blamed (Archer & Burnell, 2003) while the child's past experience of traumatic family relationships and the impact these can have on potentially healthy relationships within the adoptive family are ignored (Archer, 2000). Interventions need to take into account the problems that adoptive or foster children bring with them that influence their capacity for entering into healthy family relationships. The therapist can look for patterns and themes within the child's past history that may shed light on current patterns of behaviour and interaction.

There are also themes – commonly found in the stories of children who are looked after and adopted – that can impact on the children's functioning and ability to settle within the family. For example, the theme of not being good enough is frequently found in children who are trying to make sense of having to leave their family of origin. Hartman and Laird (1990) have suggested a number of themes that commonly arise within adoptive families. They suggest that if these are ignored they can hinder the family's healthy functioning. For example, they identify powerlessness, 'bad seeds' in which families dread the power of the past, the need to be perfect parents, cutting off and connecting, and leaving home as powerful themes relating to the dynamics of the adoption situation. Systemic therapy can allow these themes to be raised and explored by the whole family thus reducing their power to impact on the family dynamics.

Systemic psychotherapists can draw upon a range of questioning techniques to help them to engage their clients in thinking about painful issues. For example, hypothetical questions ('what if … ?') can allow a more indirect focus upon the issue. Future questions can help people to think beyond the here and now while relationship questions can help them to think about things from the perspective of another ('What do you think your mum would do/think/say?'). Comparative questions can help people to think about themselves in relation to others. This might include, for example, thinking about self in relation to a past or future self, in relation to someone more or less powerful, in relation to being more or less loved and valued. Ranking of importance questions can allow individuals to step back and think about their own values and needs.

> The use of future questions allowed the network around one young man to gain a better idea about his needs and desires. He had been severely deprived and was living within a residential unit on a long-term basis. When asked how he saw his future he appeared not to comprehend the question. He was used to living in the here and now and was unaccustomed to thinking in any other way. His past was too painful to think about and his future did not feel like his own. This question, however, facilitated some important exploration for him. He started to think of himself as someone who was entitled to a future, and a future that he could make happen. Following on from this he wrote about 'My Future' for his case conference. He had not attended these meetings, and continued not to want to attend them, but his writing allowed his voice to be heard. In particular his desire to be fostered was expressed. Having lived for so long within a residential unit this was not an option that had previously been explored.
>   (Nissim, 2004, personal communication)

Clearly young people together with their adoptive, foster or residential families can be helped by a systemic approach. This will allow a focus on the range of complex interactions within and outside the family and needs to take into account the presence of multiple families in the child's life. At its simplest this will include family of origin and current substitute family, but can also include a number of interim foster families. Minuchin (1995) has argued for the use of an ecological approach that takes into account this complex system of family environments and the wider context of the range of professionals supporting these families.

APPLYING INTERVENTIONS. ISSUES AND DILEMMAS

The Need for Stability Prior to the Commencement of Psychotherapy

One of the commonest reasons given for not providing psychotherapy for children or young people is that they are not in a sufficiently stable environment. This can be very frustrating for those who are trying to ensure that the child is getting all the help he or she needs. Frustration grows when the child's difficulties are viewed as a source of the instability, and yet the help to resolve the difficulties is not available because of this very instability. Social workers and others supporting the family can feel in a no-win situation while adoptions break down or children move from placement to placement.

It is important that both the referrer and the person assessing the referral are clear about the reasons why it is felt that therapy is needed and that good communication exists between them. Sometimes a decision not to offer therapy is communicated in a simplistic way that leaves the referrer feeling that what is needed is unattainable. Instead the referrer needs support to draw up an optimal intervention plan. For example, a child might have moved from a foster home to an adoptive home. Perhaps the move has come suddenly and in an unplanned way. I have known, for example, children having to move precipitately because of bereavement within the foster family. A child may feel bewildered having to get used to a new home, school and friends, and the distress this causes can lead to the display of very troubling behaviour. The social worker witnessing the distress refers to a therapist. However, the child may neither welcome nor be able to use yet another stranger at this time (Hunter, 2001). The therapist may feel that the child needs a period of stability with supported parents before assessment for a therapeutic intervention takes place. In this situation it makes more sense for the new parent to become the emotional anchor for the child than for the therapist to take this role (Hunter, 2001). It is not a case where no intervention is needed, but the intervention could most usefully be directed towards the parents, helping them to support and manage the child. This becomes even more problematic for the child who is moving from placement to placement. When behaviour is so difficult that it is not contained within a single placement it may well be that therapeutic interventions are considered to improve the capacity in the child for stability. Here again careful consideration and discussion are needed. It is likely that the child will be as resistant to forming a relationship with the therapist as he or she has been with a carer. Further, without containment and support between sessions the child is very unlikely to be able to engage in painful, therapeutic work. An intervention plan is needed that promotes a network approach to supporting a placement in containing the child. Only when this is achieved might it be considered appropriate to engage the child in more individual work.

There should be no hard and fast rules about the provision of psychological help and decisions need to be made on a case-by-case basis. In addition to the use of a professional network supporting and containing a placement for the child, there may be other forms of psychological help that can be provided for the child or the family. These will have, as their aims, improvement in the stability of children. For example, some cognitive-behavioural work might help children to develop skills that improve their capacity to live within the family. Systemic and family therapy approaches can also be used to help the whole family to work together towards stability. The need for psychotherapy with the child might be delayed or even made less necessary by the provision of this psychological help.

Some thoughts are, however, being given to the use of psychotherapy with children at points of transition. Hunter (2001) suggests that short-term or crisis interventions using psychoanalytic psychotherapy can be appropriate and has found that even children living in short-term or temporary placements have been able to use such therapy effectively. Lanyado (2003) describes working therapeutically with a child during transition from fostering to adoption. She recommends staying with the 'here and now' experience of the change, allowing the child to form a coherent narrative of the event. This can foster an experience of transition that is integrated into the child's internal world. Similarly, Kendrick (2000) advocates the use of therapy to provide support to children through transitions. She suggests that this can serve to reduce the impact of the trauma of moving, providing the child with an increased capacity to form secure attachments when he or she finally moves in to a long-term placement.

The Myth of 'Fixing the Child'

Children develop ways of coping, based on their early experience of abusive, neglectful or lost relationships. They bring these ways of coping into their foster and adoptive homes, using their experience of early parenting to guide how they should behave with their new carers. Moving children into foster and adoptive homes provides an improved environment and the opportunity for better relationships. It is anticipated that the children will then change their behaviour. The behaviour that has been successful in their early lives is unsuccessful in their new life and causes them problems. It is hoped that they will adapt, developing loving relationships within their family, a positive approach to learning in school and successful friendships within the community. Often however this doesn't happen. A common response to this is to suggest that the child has a problem. Therapy is seen as a way of fixing this problem. The child is not benefiting from the love and protection now being provided, and therefore needs some 'expert' help. This is the myth of 'fixing the child' – the desire to have the child fit in to a new world.

The task faced at this time, however, is not to provide therapy for the child. There needs to be adaptation on both sides. The child needs time and patience, tolerance for 'disturbed' behaviour and an opportunity to gradually learn to live a different way. The carer goes on a journey with the child, adapting the world to suit the child while the child learns to adapt to the demands of the new family. The therapist can go with them on this journey, but should not take the journey from them. The time for therapy might arrive but first an ecological and systemic view is needed, one that pays attention to the needs of the child and the family so that their journey can take them along the right path. The therapist at this stage can provide containment: containing parental anxieties as the child struggles and wobbles; containing the child's anxieties as he or she tentatively tries out different ways of relating to the world; and containing the anxiety of the network as they work towards stability and permanence for the child.

Engaging the Child

When providing psychological interventions to children who are adopted or fostered it is important to think about how to engage them in the psychological work. Traditionally therapeutic services have been offered centrally from mental health locations, and failure to attend has been viewed as the intervention no longer being required. Young people with a history of difficult relationships, however, will not fit readily to this model. They may have grown up with parents with mental health difficulties and be fearful that attendance at the 'clinic' means that they are doomed to go the same way. They have no reason to trust the professionals they encounter, and may resist attending the sessions or dip in and out of therapy. They will feel especially uncomfortable if they think they have no control within the therapy sessions.

They will anticipate the worst of the therapist, often voting with their feet. We therefore need creative and imaginative ways to engage children, with more effort directed at helping them to attend and greater provision for accepting them back when they are avoiding more sessions than they are attending. Therapy needs to be paced appropriately, and this often means going more slowly than is usual, with careful attention to how the child is coping. Being too direct may not just set the intervention back but may bring it to a premature end.

> Karen was referred for therapy following a traumatic accident. Karen had experienced physical and sexual abuse earlier in her life. She now lived within the looked after system and appeared deeply traumatized by her experiences. Therapy proceeded very slowly. Karen attended with her carer for extra support and was given control of the time and pace of each session. The first 10 sessions were used by Karen to explore whether she could trust the therapist. Thereafter she began to talk about the accident and allow some exploration of her past experience. This work was very slow as Karen could only tolerate around 10 minutes of such therapeutic work in each session. During this time there were increasing concerns about the behaviour that Karen continued to display within the placement. The therapist was under pressure to address this within the sessions. Unwisely submitting to the pressure she broached the subject. Therapy came to an abrupt end as Karen left the room. Although she attended a few more sessions she no longer engaged with the therapist in any way. Her placement ended and Karen subsequently moved out of county.

Supporting the Child and their Family through Periods of Resistance

When direct therapeutic work is provided for the child attention still needs to be given to the support that is provided. Commonly the child's behaviour will worsen during the initial stages of therapy, and parents will need to be adequately supported at this time. It is also likely that the child will feel threatened as the therapist begins to connect with his or her needs. Children who have experienced hurt within caregiving relationships are likely to experience a core conflict that needs to be overcome. They desire to reach out to the therapist who offers care and support and also dread being hurt by this person. This is why, even when children enter therapy readily, they are likely to demonstrate resistance at an early stage. They will need to be supported through this resistance.

Therapy should proceed at the child's pace, while not allowing complete avoidance or distraction from the work that needs to be done. The support network around the child must also be maintained with close collaboration and communication between those who are supporting the child. At times of increased resistance and apparent deterioration within the child, the network can have concerns about whether this approach is the right one. Discussion and negotiation are important within a shared understanding that therapy is hard work and will involve ups and downs. When this doesn't happen, therapy can be ended prematurely.

A 9-year-old girl, Rebecca, entered therapy enthusiastically and quickly engaged with the therapist. However, after the first few sessions her enthusiasm waned. As the therapist touched on emotion her main defences of self-reliance and avoiding feelings were threatened. She no longer wanted to come and told her social worker that she wanted the therapy to end. Keen to listen to her the social worker agreed that she should stop attending the sessions. This was the second time that Rebecca had requested an end to a piece of therapeutic work. What she learned both times was that she would be supported to avoid integrating and processing her painful experience of abuse and loss. The therapist continued to work with Rebecca's parents but Rebecca's behaviour deteriorated. She became more self-reliant, distant and passively aggressive. This culminated in her request to replace long-term fostering with a series of short-term placements. Rebecca did not want to emotionally commit to anyone. After considerable work with the network supporting Rebecca, therapy was recommenced. Rebecca's communication that this was too hard was however listened to. The pace of therapy was slowed down, and Rebecca was given more control over this. Additionally more indirect ways of exploring her feelings were used through the joint creation of poems and artwork.

Working with Children with Special Difficulties

Within the group of foster and adopted children there are those who have greater difficulties and who find it even harder to access and respond to therapy. These children may be sexualized. They may harm others sexually, physically or emotionally. They may engage in offending behaviour. These are the children who tend to be seen as tainted or corrupted in some way. They are often seen as troublemakers and, therefore, undeserving and can be viewed as a threat. In addition, they can make carers, therapists and other professionals feel uncomfortable, doubting their own ability to intervene successfully.

The extreme behaviour of these children can often mask their pervasive feelings of worthlessness. As adults focus on the behaviours and the level of concern this raises, the feelings of the children and young people are overlooked. The young people are overwhelmed by shame, but with no adult to help them to tolerate and contain this emotion they have to rely on rigid, defensive strategies (Hughes, 2004). As a result of early experiences of abuse and neglect and of attachment needs not being met, the children are left with a negative view of themselves and their capabilities. They find it difficult to trust others and are reluctant to explore the world, which appears to be a very frightening place. They are driven to find self-reliant ways of protecting themselves from further harm, and to experience safety. They do this by trying to regain some sense of power and control over themselves, others and their environment. (For a discussion of children's use of controlling strategies, see Crittenden et al., 2001, and Solomon & George, 1999).

Some children take their feelings of anger, shame and humiliation out on others, abusing, lashing out, fighting or causing damage. Identifying with the aggressor and turning the other person into a victim allows them to release some of their feelings and gain a sense of the world as controllable. Other children take their pent-up emotion out on themselves, punishing and controlling their bodies by self-harm sometimes culminating in parasuicide attempts. Still others try to dull the pain of intolerable thoughts and feelings about their experience with drugs and alcohol. Many combine all three strategies. Sadly, while these strategies help to some extent in the short term, in the long term they result in the young people feeling worse about themselves and being further isolated from others who shun them because of these challenging behaviours. Unable to find better means of coping behaviour becomes more entrenched until they have lost the control of themselves and their environment that they were so desperately seeking (see Figure 11.4).

The complex combination of trauma and attachment difficulties, that the young people have experienced, leads to extreme difficulties in trusting others or themselves. They believe that they are beyond help. They become very fragile and secretive, afraid that if they reveal something of themselves they will not be able to control how much they say and it will all come tumbling out. They feel that they are to blame for the original trauma and their current behaviour. Their dilemma is the conflict between wanting to be believed and understood, helped and comforted on the one hand and the risk of exposing themselves to possible disbelief, judgement, further rejection and abandonment on the other. The older the children and the more entrenched their coping strategies, the more they and the network involved with them can lose sight of the fact that these children and young people were or continue to be victims themselves. Instead they become labelled as perpetrators and are seen as less deserving of help.

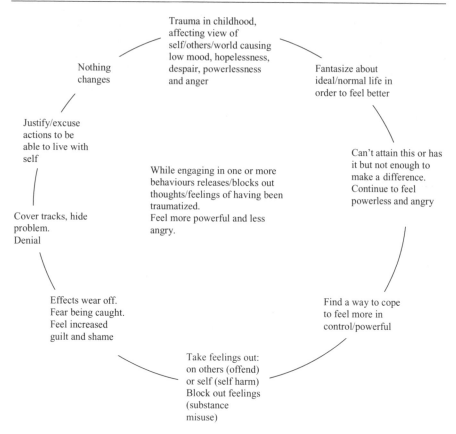

Figure 11.4   Cycle of abuse (adapted from Ryan & Lane, 1997)

If these young people are not helped or if the help provided is inappropriate or unsuccessful it is not only regrettable for them but also for any of their potential future victims. This will include their partners and children as the cycle of abuse continues. Working with this group of young people is, therefore, vital in order to break this cycle if at all possible. However, the lack of such work is evident within the case histories of many of these children. For example, in a study of 96 children who had experienced or perpetrated sexual abuse, less than half had received therapeutic help and less than one-third had received help addressing their own experience of abuse. This study found that those children who had access to therapeutic help and were given the opportunity to discuss their past experience of abuse within their current placement, displayed the most behavioural improvement (Farmer & Pollock, 1998).

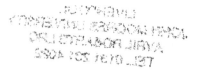

Traditionally psychotherapy has been very prescribed. It has taken place in an office, with the client and therapist alone, over 50-minute sessions. The children and young people frequently report that they have been unable to talk or have felt unheard within settings that they describe as formal, cold and uncaring (Farmer & Pollock, 1998). In order to engage these individuals, a much more flexible approach is required (e.g. Ryan & Lane, 1997).

For children and young people who have in one way or another felt powerless for most, if not all, of their lives the issue of control is a central one in therapy. These young people have generally had to acquire strategies to try to regain some measure of control by exercising power over others in terms of inappropriate sexual, physical or verbal behaviour. While boundaries are crucial to enable them to begin to feel safe, it is also important to help them to feel that they have some power or control in the therapy situation. In this way they can gradually build trust in the therapist. For example, they can have the choice in how far they participate. The venue; the time and the length of each session; who else is there and what is discussed can all be negotiated to some extent.

The venue is a crucial issue for an anxious young person who does not feel safe anywhere or trust anyone. Younger children most often choose to be seen at home where they feel safer and more relaxed. They also have someone on hand if they become upset. Sometimes children want and need someone with them. This might only be for part of an initial session or for the first few sessions but can make the difference between a child agreeing to try therapy or not. Older children tend to want to be seen away from the home environment but may still want someone with them initially until they have become more accustomed to working with the therapist. Having a third party present clearly has implications for confidentiality. However, with this group of children it is important to ensure that carers do not feel undermined by an 'expert', being left with no idea of what has happened within the sessions. Good practice suggests that at the very least a carer/parent is seen or contacted prior to sessions so that an information update can be given and, following the session, the therapist can give an indication of whether there are likely to be any issues or concerns. If the work involves the carer/parent throughout, confidentiality becomes three-way rather than two.

Whatever the situation, a confidentiality warning to the child, regardless of age, is important so that the boundaries are understood. Given that trust is such a crucial issue, believing that something was confidential and finding out that it was not will further damage the child's ability to trust and will probably result in his or her withdrawal from therapy and an unwillingness to re-engage in future. Similarly, if having told the therapist something, assuming that it will be passed on, and nothing is done, the child will lose faith in the therapist's ability to protect or keep anyone safe.

This attitude of flexibility and negotiation can take children and young people by surprise, accustomed as they are to being told how things will be. Once the boundaries are given, including confidentiality, no hurting self or others, etc., the remainder can be mutually agreed within certain parameters. As a result the child feels listened to, consulted and has an investment from the start. If nothing else, this approach intrigues children and they are keen to know how it develops and whether the therapist can maintain it!

Children who have been hurt, particularly sexually, are often anxious about having to retell their histories in detail. Some want and need to do this while others prefer to rely on the therapist having obtained the relevant information beforehand. Good communication with other professionals involved in order to obtain as full a picture as possible is important. Embarrassment and shame are common barriers to be overcome and the more confident and relaxed the therapist is the easier it is for the child to be able to discuss issues he or she may have been unable to disclose to anyone previously. In telling past events and how they have dealt with them, children are afraid of not being believed, being judged, blamed, getting into further trouble or getting someone else into trouble. They require a great deal of reassurance and empathy.

Work with adult perpetrators stresses the importance of beginning with the offending behaviour and working on that so that strategies can be put into place to prevent further offending (Laws, 1989; Finkelhor & Browne, 1986; Morrison et al., 1994). If young persons have entrenched abusive behaviour it is clearly important to have appropriate boundaries and strategies in place to help them to manage that behaviour, prevent re-offending and protect the public. However, as they are so much nearer their own victim experiences it may be more appropriate to start with their victimization and move forward. In this way they can begin to make the link between what has happened to them and how they are attempting to deal with that via their current behaviour (e.g. see Ryan, 1999). This is especially the case with those who deny their behaviour as a result of intense shame and fear of the consequences.

A 16-year-old boy who had been referred for sexually inappropriate behaviour did not want to come and only did so under duress. He was adamant that he had not done what was alleged and he refused to discuss the incidents concerned. He presented as extremely angry and aggressive. To have pursued the allegations at this stage would have been counter-productive and could have resulted in his withdrawal from therapy. Instead, the therapy focused on his history and his feelings about what had happened to him within his birth and adoptive homes. He described how he had felt rejected, abandoned and utterly powerless. He decided that he would meet his own needs and improve his situation by ensuring that no one ever beat him or got 'one over' on him. He made demands and used aggression to ensure that these were met. As a result he did feel more powerful, but, he confided, he was also lonely and viewed himself and his behaviour in a very negative light. We discussed how he might better meet his needs in more constructive, non-aggressive ways. To his surprise he discovered that he got much better results using these non-coercive means. Over time he became less angry, more relaxed and more able to see that he had a choice about the way he behaved, which did not mean giving up his own needs. While he never acknowledged the sexually inappropriate behaviour, he was able to discuss other inappropriate behaviour that he used to maintain a sense of control. This helped him to make progress towards changing his behaviour.

Within therapy it is most useful to work from the general to the specific. The therapist shares understanding of abuse/offending cycles. This helps the young person to feel confident that the therapist will be able to help him or her to make sense of past and present and the thoughts and feelings that he or she has been trying so hard to escape. The aim is to help the child or young person to examine the motivation for his or her behaviour, to be able to make sense of it and to confront and deal with issues in a different, more constructive manner.

CONCLUSION AND THE WAY FORWARD

Later adjustment for children is not just dependent upon their early experiences. As Clarke and Clarke (2000, p. 99) eloquently put it, 'early experience represents no more than a first (and important) step on a long and complex path through life'. Later experiences can open up or close down opportunities for recovery from detrimental early experience (McAuley, 1996). At intervals children will encounter 'turning points' in their development when the environment in which they find themselves has the potential for psychological change. This chapter has explored the way that therapeutic interventions can contribute to such turning points. Such interventions need to take into account the special needs of children and young people living in adoptive and foster homes and must attend to the environmental and holistic needs of the child. Research is needed to guide the development of such interventions, not only by considering the way that traditional interventions can be adapted but also by guiding the development of new interventions, as considered in the next chapter.

Sarah again sits in front of me. Two years have passed since I last saw her. During this time she has 'tested out' a range of family members and peer groups to live with. She has flirted with drugs and alcohol, and has experienced increasing levels of social anxiety. She asks to see me again. She uses the time to touch base. She talks fast and intensely, leaving me little time to comment or reflect. She makes me laugh and she makes me cry, but within this I see some signs of insight, of a growing ability to reflect on her situation. I still fear for her immediate future but I have some optimism now. She still has a hard road ahead of her but I have a hunch that she will come through this and survive. The door is open for Sarah and I believe she will be able to help herself and seek help from others when she most needs it.

REFERENCES

Alverez, A. (1983) Problems in the use of counter-transference: Getting it across. *Journal of Child Psychotherapy*, **9**, 1.

Archer, C. (2000) *Making Sense of Attachment in Adoptive and Foster Families*. Northamptonshire: Adoption UK.

Archer, C. & Burnell, A. (2003) *Trauma, Attachment and Family Permanence. Fear can Stop you Loving*. London: Jessica Kingsley Publishers.

Axline, V. (1964) *Dibs: In Search of Self*. New York: Penguin Books.

Boston, M. & Szur, R. (1983/1990) *Psychotherapy with Severely Deprived Children*. London: Maresfield Library/Karnac Books.

Chamberlain, P. & Smith, D.K. (2005) Multidimensional treatment foster care: A community solution for boys and girls referred from juvenile justice. In E.D. Hibbs & P.S. Jensen (Eds), *Psychosocial Treatments for Child and Adolescent Disorders. Empirically Based Strategies for Clinical Practice* (2nd edn). Washington, DC: American Psychological Association.

Clarke, A. & Clarke, A. (2000) *Early Experience and the Life Path*. London: Jessica Kingsley Publishers.

Crittenden, P.M., Landini, A. & Claussen, A.H. (2001) A dynamic-maturational approach to treatment of maltreated children. In J.N. Hughes, A.M. La Greca & J.C. Conoley (Eds), *Handbook of Psychological Services for Children and Adolescents* (pp. 373–398). Oxford: Oxford University Press.

Farmer, E. & Pollock, S. (1998) *Sexually Abused and Abusing Children in Substitute Care*. Chichester: John Wiley & Sons.

Finkelhor, D. & Browne, A. (1986) *A Sourcebook on Child Sexual Abuse*. London: Sage.

Guerney, L. (1983) Introduction to filial therapy. In P. Keller & L. Ritt (Eds), *Innovations in Clinical Practice: A Source Book* (vol. 2, pp. 26–39). Sarasota, FL: Professional Resource Exchange.

Hart, A. & Luckock, B. (2004) *Developing Adoption Support and Therapy*. London/Philadelphia: Jessica Kingsley Publishers.

Hartman, A. & Laird, J. (1990) Family treatment after adoption: Common themes. In D.M. Brodzinsky & M. D. Schechter (Eds), *The Psychology of Adoption*. Oxford/New York: Oxford University Press.

Henggeler, S.W., Schoenwald, S.K., Borduin, C.M., Rowland, M.B. & Cunningham, P.B. (1998) *Multi-systemic Treatment of Antisocial Behaviour in Children and Adolescents.* New York: Guilford Press.

Herbert, M. (1991) *Clinical Child Psychology. Social Learning, Development and Behaviour.* Chichester: John Wiley & Sons.

Hughes, D.A. (1997) *Facilitating Developmental Attachment. The Road to Emotional Recovery and Behavioural Change in Foster and Adopted Children.* Northvale, NJ: Aronson.

Hughes, D.A. (2004) An attachment-based treatment of maltreated children and young people. *Attachment and Human Development,* **6**(3), 263–278.

Hunter, J. (2003) *An attachment perspective of the relationships within filial therapy.* Unpublished MA Thesis, University of York.

Hunter, M. (2001) *Psychotherapy with Young People in Care.* Hove, East Sussex: Brunner–Routledge.

Jernberg, A. & Booth, P.B. (2001) *Theraplay: Helping Parents and Children Build Better Relationships through Attachment Based Play* (2nd edn). San Francisco: Jossey-Bass.

Kale, A. & Landreth, G. (1999) Filial therapy with parents of children experiencing learning difficulties. *International Journal of Play Therapy,* **8**(2), 35–56.

Kempe, R.S. & Kempe, C.H. (1978) *Child Abuse.* London: Fontana/Open Books and Open Books Publishing Ltd.

Kendrick, J. (2000) 'Be a kid': The traumatic impact of repeated separations on children who are fostered and adopted. *Journal of Child Psychotherapy,* **26**(3), 393–412.

Knell, S. (1998) Cognitive-behavioural play therapy. *Journal of Clinical Child Psychology,* **27**, 28–33.

Laws, R. (1989) *Relapse Prevention with Sex Offenders.* New York: Guilford Press.

Lanyado, M. (2003) The emotional tasks of moving from fostering to adoption: Transitions, attachment, separation and loss. *Clinical Child Psychology and Psychiatry,* **8**(3), 337–349.

Lush, D., Hunt, M. & Radford, P. (1999) The association of child psychotherapists: An organization evolving over fifty years. *Journal of Child Psychotherapy,* **24**(1), 5–27.

Mäkelä, J. (2003) What makes Theraplay® effective: Insights from developmental sciences. *The Newsletter of The Theraplay® Institute,* Fall/Winter.

McAuley, C. (1996) *Children in Long-term Foster Care. Emotional and Social Development.* Aldershot, Hants: Avebury.

Minuchin, P. (1995) Foster and natural families: Forming a co-operative network. In L. Combrinck-Graham (Ed.), *Children in Families at Risk: Making the Connections* (pp. 251–274). New York: Guilford Press.

Moore, K.J. & Chamberlain, P. (1994) Treatment foster care: Toward development of community-based models for adolescents with severe emotional and behavioral disorders. *Journal of Emotional and Behavioral Disorders,* **2**, 22–30.

Morrison, T., Erooga, M. & Beckett, R.C. (1994) *Sexual Offending against Children. Assessment and Treatment of Male Abusers.* London: Routledge.

Pearce, J.W. & Pezzot-Pearce, T.D. (1997) *Psychotherapy of Abused and Neglected Children.* New York: Guilford Press.

Pearce, J.W. & Pezzot-Pearce, T.D. (2001) Psychotherapeutic approaches to children in foster care: Guidance from attachment theory. *Child Psychiatry and Human Development,* **32**(1), 19–44.

Ray, D., Bratton, S., Rhine, T. & Jones, L. (2001) The effectiveness of play therapy: Responding to the critics. *International Journal of Play Therapy,* **10**(1), 85–108.

Rogers, A.G. (1995) *A Shining Affliction.* New York: Penguin Books.

Rogers, C.R. (1951) *Client-centred Therapy.* New York: Houghton Mifflin.

Russ, S. (1995) Play psychotherapy research: State of the science. In T. Ollendick & R. Prinz (Eds), *Advances in Clinical Child Psychology* (pp. 365–391), New York: Plenum Press.

Russell, R.L. & Van den Brock, P. (1988) A cognitive-developmental account of story-telling in child psychotherapy. In S.R. Shirk (Ed.), *Cognitive Development and Child Psychotherapy* (pp. 19–52). New York: Plenum Press.

Rutter, M. (1975) *Helping Troubled Children*. London: Penguin Books Ltd.

Ryan, G. & Lane, S. (1997) *Juvenile Sexual Offending. Causes, Consequences and Correction*. San Francisco: Jossey-Bass Publishers.

Ryan, V. (1999) Developmental delay, symbolic play and non-directive play therapy. *Clinical Child Psychology and Psychiatry*, **4**(2), 167–185.

Ryan, V. & Wilson, K. (1995) Non-directive play therapy as a means of recreating optimal infant socialization patterns. *Early Development and Parenting*, **4**(1), 9–38.

Solomon, J. & George, C. (1999) *Attachment Disorganization*. New York: Guilford Press.

Skinner, B.F. (1974) *About Behaviourism*. London: Cape.

Tronick, E.Z., Bruschweiler-Stern, N., Harrison, A.M., Lyons-Ruth, K., Morgan, A.C., Nahum, J.P., Sander, L. & Stern, D.N. (1998) Dyadically expanded states of consciousness and the process of therapeutic change. *Infant Mental Health Journal*, **19**(3), 290–299. [In J. Mäkelä (2003) What makes Theraplay® effective: Insights from developmental sciences. *The Newsletter of The Theraplay® Institute*, Fall/Winter.]

Van Fleet, R. (1994) *Filial Therapy: Strengthening Parent–Child Relationships through Play*. Sarasota, FL: Professional Resource Press.

Van Fleet, R. & Guerney, L. (2003) *Casebook of Filial Therapy*. Boiling Springs, PA: Play Therapy Press.

Wolff, S. (1969) *Children under Stress*. Middlesex, England: Allen Lane, The Penguin Press.

12

'FORGOTTEN MISERIES': CAN ATTACHMENT THEORY HELP TO GUIDE INTERVENTIONS?

Kim S. Golding

A therapist sits with a child and a carer. They all look at each other, and consider the space between them. The child looks anxious, apprehensive, not sure what is coming next. The carer looks hopeful, will today give her some answers she needs? The therapist considers how to begin, how to create an opening that will take them within the space. The hour passes. The therapist ponders. What did she learn today? The child is scared, reluctant to trust, reluctant to give up defences that appear to work so well. She was glad to leave. This was hard for her, allowing the carer to witness a little of what she is feeling, but might it be bearable? The carer leaves puzzled. Is this going to help? No instant answer but there was something, a look, a slight leaning in, the suggestion of a relationship that could be different. The therapist smiles, it is a beginning.

Attachment theory has important implications for children growing up in substitute care. Children who live in foster, adoptive or residential homes all share a loss of or separation from their biological families. Additionally most of these children and young people will have experienced inadequate parenting early in their lives, and many will have had to cope with multiple placements following their removal from their family. These experiences will

Thinking Psychologically About Children Who Are Looked After and Adopted
Edited by K.S. Golding, H.R. Dent, R. Nissim and L. Stott.
Copyright © 2006 John Wiley & Sons, Ltd.

have had an impact on their early development of attachment relationships as well as on their later capacity to form an attachment to a new carer.

Abuse and neglect of children are associated with the development of insecure attachment relationships. Crittenden (1988) found that among children who have experienced abuse or neglect, only 5–13% form secure attachments to their carer. Gross neglect is associated with attachment problems, inattention, over-activity and social difficulties (quasi-autistic). The pathways to these outcomes are, however, complex with environmental and genetic factors both contributing (Taylor & Rogers, 2005).

Insecure attachment is a risk factor for, and secure attachment a protective factor against, later difficulties. Children from abusive or neglectful environments are therefore at increased risk of later problems although the mechanisms by which this occurs and the comparative importance of attachment over other hostile elements of the early environment are not fully understood (Rutter, 1995).

Attachment theory can guide our understanding of the effects of early abuse, neglect, separation and loss on the child's ability to form healthy attachments with new parents. It can help us to make sense of the child's subsequent behaviour. Increasingly, practitioners working with these children and young people are also looking towards attachment theory to guide their interventions (e.g. Cairns, 2002; Hughes, 2004).

Attachment-based therapies are growing in popularity, complementing the more traditional therapies discussed in the previous chapter. These interventions are diverse with a range of treatment goals, including facilitating sensory integration for the child; increasing sensitive and emotionally attuned caregiving; and helping children to feel safe enough to relinquish their controlling behaviour (see Howe, in press). This chapter will explore these therapies, considering the context of attachment difficulty that the children present and discussing the way these methods are linked to the theory that has bred them.

ATTACHMENT THEORY

Attachment theory suggests that infants are biologically predisposed to form attachment relationships from which they can experience security and comfort (e.g. Bowlby, 1969, 1988). The child develops a range of attachment behaviours that are designed to keep the carer close, to act as a secure base. Such behaviours are triggered by threats of separation, physical rejection or alarming conditions in the environment. These attachment behaviours are complemented by explorative behaviours when the child is feeling safe. Bowlby further suggested that the early experience of attachment relationships leads to the development of a cognitive model (internal working model) of these relationships which influences and is modified by later relationships.

The very earliest years of a child's life are critical for his or her later development and ability to develop and form close relationships. Secure attachments allow children to develop trust in others and self-reliance in themselves. Bowlby suggests that securely attached children with positive expectations of self and others will approach the world with confidence. Thus when faced with potentially alarming situations the child will tackle them effectively or will seek help to do so. Where an attachment figure is insensitive, neglecting or rejecting, an insecure attachment will develop. This is reflected in the organization of the behaviour that the child demonstrates (Ainsworth et al., 1978). In order to elicit care from inconsistent carers, the child may maximize attachment behaviour. This is expressed through demanding and clingy behaviour.

Emotional distress is extreme with a resistance to being soothed and comforted (ambivalent–resistant attachment). Alternatively, the child may minimize attachment behaviour to maintain closeness to carers who are already rejecting. This is expressed through passive and withdrawn behaviour with little display of emotional distress (avoidant attachment). In both cases these behaviours are organized to increase the chance that parents will be responsive when children need them, and thus can be seen as adaptive for the particular environment in which the children find themselves. Long-term development can, however, be compromised for children who have a history of insecure attachment (Weinfield et al., 1999).

More seriously, a disorganized attachment relationship can develop when carers are frightened or frightening to the child. The child is unable to organize his or her behaviour at times of stress in order to receive emotional support because the carer is both the source of fear and potential safety (Main & Solomon, 1986). As they become older these children solve this dilemma through self-reliance. They become controlling in their behaviour. They do not trust the carer so they take control of the relationship. Rather than the attachment being disorganized, the child develops highly organized but controlling ways of interacting with the parent that build upon early patterns of avoidant or ambivalent relating (Crittenden et al., 2001).

A small proportion of children who have had no experience of early attachment relationships, either because of severe neglect or impoverished institutionalized care, will demonstrate a failure to develop selective attachments (O'Connor et al., 2001). These children can be disinhibited, i.e. indiscriminately friendly, but unable to engage in mutually satisfying relationships; or they can be inhibited, displaying a failure to or fearful pattern of approaching the carer when distressed.

Interactions between parent and child often tend to reinforce the early attachment patterns. Additionally these early attachment relationships act as a guide for children in later relationships. They bring to these relationships 'memories of past interactions and expectations of future ones' (Rutter, 1995, p. 554). From early attachment experience children develop expectations about themselves and about future relationships (Weinfield et al., 1999).

ATTACHMENT THEORY INTO PRACTICE: BEGINNING WITH BOWLBY

A useful starting point to consider how attachment theory can guide intervention is with Bowlby's own writings about therapy. Bowlby was predominantly concerned to develop a theory of attachment, and in doing this to address – as he saw it – the unscientific aspects of psychoanalysis (Bowlby, 1969, 1973, 1980). While he had an interest in promoting change in child-rearing practices he actually wrote little about the implications of attachment theory for clinical practice (Lieberman & Zeanah, 1999). However, relatively late in his career he did redress this somewhat in a book that explicitly explored the clinical applications of attachment theory (Bowlby, 1988). While predominantly concerned with adult therapy, his ideas have relevance for working with children and their carers.

Bowlby states that the first task for the therapist is to provide security. The therapist provides a secure base from which the 'patient' can explore and express his thoughts and feelings. Bowlby stresses the importance of the therapist being 'reliable, attentive and sympathetically responsive ... to see and feel the world through his patient's eyes, namely to be empathic' (Bowlby, 1988, p. 140). With continuing debate about what is or is not an intervention based on attachment theory, these guidelines can provide a useful yardstick against which interventions can be compared. Thus interventions that are coercive and encourage anger can be seen as counter to these guidelines and as less likely to provide for the child corrective attachment experiences (Lieberman & Zeanah, 1999).

Bowlby (1988, p. 137) writes that the aim of therapy is to enable the 'patient' to construct or reconstruct working models of self and attachment figures. To consider ideas and feelings about others that have been unimaginable and unthinkable. In this way Bowlby suggests '... he becomes less under the spell of forgotten miseries and better able to recognize companions in the present for what they are'. For children living within the looked after system, these 'forgotten miseries' have most frequently arisen within their early relationships with parents. An important task for carers and therapists, therefore, is to provide a therapeutic environment within which children can learn a different view of themselves and enjoy different, healthier relationships. Children can then develop positive expectations of attachment figures, and from this base can begin the journey towards understanding their past.

The parenting task is a difficult one. Children entering foster care are ill equipped for eliciting or responding to sensitive and responsive care. They will find it difficult to let go of their past experience and trust in the parenting being offered. Carers will need support as they find themselves coerced into particular transactions that meet the child's own expectations about the world. The carer of a child with an insecure and avoidant style of relating will quickly feel not needed as the child does not ask for, and resists, attempts at being helped or nurtured. Caring for a child with an insecure and ambivalent/resistant attachment style, on the other hand, can elicit feelings of incompetence and failure, as the carer feels unable to soothe the child. Such understanding can inform parenting interventions that help the child to benefit from substitute care. In turn this allows the child to move along a different, healthier developmental pathway with expanded possibilities (Bowlby, 1988). Crittenden et al. (2001) suggest that by providing children with a greater range of adaptive solutions to problems, they are able to move beyond the narrow range of environments that their early experience has equipped them for.

APPLYING ATTACHMENT THEORY: A MODEL FOR INTERVENTION

Substitute care provides an opportunity for children to form attachments with carers who are able to meet their emotional needs. Interventions aim to develop this ongoing relationship between the carer and child providing the foundation for growth that lies beyond the development of attachment security. Thus children will develop resilience and a positive sense of identity. They will more successfully learn to interact with peers, and to develop friendships (Hart & Luckock, 2004).

Attachment theory can therefore provide a useful model, guiding the provision of services for children living in substitute care that focus on the child or young person and the social environment within which he or she lives. Such a framework can guide the development of interventions for carers, the child and carer together, and the child alone (see Figure 12.1).

As the first column indicates, the intervention may need to begin with working with the carers, exploring their own attachment history, and improving their ability to act as a secure base for the child. Unresolved loss or trauma may need to be worked through if they are to have a secure state of mind that is able to address the attachment needs of the child in their care.

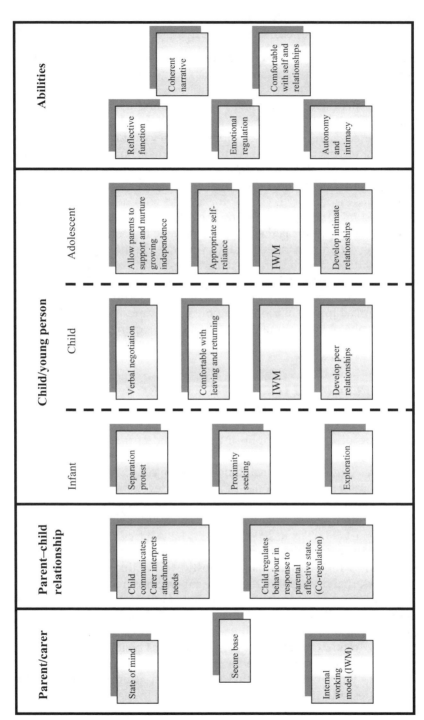

Figure 12.1 Attachment theory: A model for intervention

The focus then moves to the second column and the carer–child relationship. The carer needs to be able to understand the child's communications about nurturing, however distorted these may be, and help the child to regulate emotion in the face of these often disturbing needs.

Attention needs to be given to the developmental stage of the child (column three), although it should be noted that these developmental stages are not always met within the same chronological age range as those children who have grown up in less adverse circumstances. It is not unusual for children living in substitute care to be emotionally and socially much less mature than their peer group. This can be hidden behind pseudomaturity as the children try to manage by themselves, but it needs to be taken into account when planning interventions. Interventions may need to address the multiple needs of children from across the developmental range. For example, a child might need the typically infant experience of a carer who is constantly preoccupied with and available to him or her, while at the same time being supported to develop age-appropriate behaviour to cope with school and peer groups (Schofield & Meek, 2005).

At infancy, or when this stage of development has not been successfully completed, children need help to express their attachment needs successfully so that they can use the carer as a secure base from which they will be comfortable to explore and develop within their world. This builds upon the experience of primary intersubjectivity shared between infant and caregiver since birth. This is an affectionate and alert engagement between the infant and carer with each attending to the subjective experience of the other (Trevarthen, 2001). This intersubjective sharing of affect (Stern, 1985) is an essential first step towards secure attachment and an integrated sense of self (Hughes, 2004).

As children leave early infancy, interactions with carers extend to include joint attention to events and objects outside of the relationship itself. Trevarthern calls this the stage of secondary intersubjectivity, and it sets the stage for continuing development during childhood. With language development there is an increase in verbal negotiation between children and carers as children are increasingly comfortable with leaving and returning. Children develop an internal working model, a cognitive/affective model of how relationships work. This means that they have a memory of relationships, which influences how they will respond in later relationships.

By adolescence the young people are developing self-reliance balanced with the need for close and intimate relationships. The internal working model, guiding expectations for caregiving relationships, is increasingly stable and will have broadened to include expectations of others within a wide range of relationships. Parents continue to be important to support and nurture this growing independence. Supported by a nurturing attachment relationship during childhood, the young people will develop a capacity for autonomy

and intimacy while developing abilities for emotional regulation and reflective function. In short, they will feel comfortable with themselves and
with relationships and will have created coherent meaning around their life
experiences.

ATTACHMENT THEORY AND INFANT–PARENT INTERVENTIONS

Interventions with biological parents and infants can provide ideas for working with foster and adoptive carers. The earliest such intervention had its roots
in psychoanalysis, but was also influenced by the developing ideas found
within attachment theory (Lieberman & Zeanah, 1999). This was parent–
infant psychotherapy, an intervention aimed at tackling the old 'ghosts' that
have invaded the nursery (Fraiberg, 1980). A combination of emotional support, developmental guidance, crisis intervention and insight-oriented therapy was provided for the parent with a particular focus on the parent's feelings and behaviour towards the baby. This intervention was based on the
premise that disturbance in the parent–child relationship was a manifestation of unresolved conflicts of the parents with important adults from their
own childhood.

A synthesis of infant–parent psychotherapy with ideas suggested directly
by attachment theory has led to the development of interventions designed
to enhance parenting ability by increasing parents' sensitivity to the cues
provided by their infants and increasing the consistency of their responding
to these cues. An additional intervention goal has been to alter the parents'
own mental representations of attachment. The therapist helps the parents
to understand their own state of mind based on an exploration of their past
experience, especially in childhood. These interventions have been provided
within the context of enhancing social support and improving parental mental
health and well-being (e.g. Bakermans-Kranenburg et al., 1998; Svanberg &
Jennings, 2001; Marvin et al., 2002).

A meta-analysis of 70 studies suggests that such interventions are successful
for enhancing maternal sensitivity and, to a lesser extent, infant attachment
security in biological mothers (Bakermans-Kranenburg & Van Ijzendoorn,
2003).

The Sunderland Infant Programme has demonstrated the use of such interventions to provide early intervention for high-risk parent–infant dyads.
A combination of video feedback, interaction and developmental guidance and individualized psychotherapeutic interventions led to increases
in both parental sensitivity and infant security of attachment (Svanberg, in
preparation).

There are indications that interventions need to be continuing and multi-modal, extending beyond the goal of increased maternal sensitivity, when supporting foster and adoptive parents. For example, Stams et al. (2001) provided an intervention aimed at enhancing maternal sensitivity in adoptive parents. The intervention changed mothers' ability to respond sensitively, increased security of attachment and improved infant exploratory competence in early childhood, but there were no enduring intervention effects at follow-up when the children were 7 years old. The authors speculate that the intervention may have improved sensitivity without altering the underlying attachment representation that the mothers held. The mothers could not adjust their responses to the changing demands of the children as they moved through different developmental stages.

While adoptive care can provide infants with opportunities for care and nurturing that would otherwise not be available to them, this option also represents traumatic separation from birth mothers (Verrier, 1993). Enabling children to remain with birth parents is an important focus for intervention. The use of foster homes to provide a secure base for mother and child while the mother receives intensive therapeutic and parenting help is therefore an exciting option for attachment interventions (Kretchmer et al., 2005).

Mary Dozier and colleagues have developed an attachment and bio-behavioural catch-up intervention for foster carers and children placed as infants (see Dozier et al., 2002; Dozier, 2003; Lewis et al., in press). This intervention is based upon research demonstrating the effects of disrupting the child–parent relationship at a time when there is a biological need to maintain this relationship. Children are left with anomalous patterns of cortisol production associated with difficulties in regulation of physiology, emotion and behaviour and with a reduced capacity to develop trusting relationships with their foster carers. Additionally their early experience leaves children quickly overwhelmed and with reduced coping skills when the carer is perceived as threatening. That this threat can be unintentional is apparent in the authors' example of the threat that is experienced when the carer states or implies that the continuance of the placement is dependent upon the child's behaviour (Lewis et al., in press).

Diary studies of foster carers demonstrate how insecure attachments develop between foster carer and child. The carer fails to respond to the underlying neediness masked by displays of avoidant or resistant attachment behaviour. This results from the child leading the interaction to elicit caregiving that is expected based on previous experience of inadequate care (Dozier, 2005). The carer responds to the child in a complementary fashion. Thus the carer will turn away from the child displaying avoidant patterns of relating (the child acts as if he or she does not need the carer) or show frustration and anger towards resistant patterns of relating (the child demonstrates clingy, angry behaviour towards the carer). The foster carer therefore perpetuates a model for the child of carers as unavailable and rejecting (Stovall & Dozier, 2000).

The attachment and biobehavioural catch-up intervention focuses on helping carers to provide stable, consistent and nurturing care. This intervention has four components (see Lewis et al., in press):

1. *Reinterpreting the child's behavioural signals.* The carers are taught to provide nurturing, responsive care regardless of the child's ability to convey their need for such care. Thus the carer provides predictable, contingent and responsive nurturing that is attuned to hidden rather than expressed needs. In this way the carer gently challenges the child.
2. *Providing nurture even when this does not come naturally.* Foster carers can find it difficult to respond sensitively to distress in the child because of their own attachment issues. Through sensitive exploration of their histories carers are helped to respond to distressed children in nurturing ways even when doing so is uncomfortable for them.
3. *Helping children to develop regulatory capabilities by providing predictable and responsive environments.* This includes helping children to feel that they have an effect on their interpersonal world. Carers are encouraged to follow the child's lead in play and to hold and touch the child on a regular basis.
4. *Behaving in a non-threatening way with the children.*

A number of studies have demonstrated the effectiveness of this intervention with carers developing a more contingent and responsive pattern of care. The children demonstrate more secure behaviours and more typical patterns of neuroendocrine regulation demonstrated by more normal levels of the stress hormone cortisol (Dozier et al., 2002; Fisher et al., 2000). Further research using larger groups and controlled designs is underway. This is needed to confirm the early, promising results.

Case Study 1

Jennifer is 18 months old. She has been moved into foster care because of the mental health difficulties of her mother. Unfortunately the nature of these difficulties meant that parenting was neglectful and physically abusive. At the time of referral she had been in placement for a few weeks. The foster carer was exhausted, and concerned about the impact of Jennifer on her own family. She was close to ending the placement. The therapist explored with the carer Jennifer's behaviour and its link to the early trauma experienced. Jennifer was preoccupied with the availability of the carer, fearing abandonment. Her behaviour was quick to dysregulate as fear overwhelmed her, resulting in severe tantrums and a preoccupation with keeping the carer close by and attending to her. Her difficulty in trusting and feeling secure with the carer was explained as stemming from an experience of carers as unreliable and frightening. The carer was helped to develop her fostering skills tailored to Jennifer's needs. She learned to provide a predictable environment with changes in routine being signalled in advance and to view Jennifer's behaviour as a need for attention rather than as wilful attention seeking. She became adept at recognizing Jennifer's increasing anxiety and stepping in and offering nurturing at an early stage. She very gradually helped Jennifer to tolerate small separations from her and to increase her trust that she would return. Within six months there were fewer and less violent tantrums. Jennifer was able to use the carer as a secure base, and could tolerate being left in a room while the carer moved into different rooms.

APPLYING ATTACHMENT THEORY TO CHILD THERAPY

When children move into alternative homes they will be strongly influenced by their early experiences within attachment relationships. This will influence their expectations of new carers as well as the way they respond to these carers. However the children's behaviour will not only reflect their early relationships but will also reflect their experience of loss and separation. When children leave their parents this is experienced as a loss, no matter how abusive this parent was. They will grieve for the lost relationship. This grief process is complicated when the parent is still alive. Children feel rejected and not good enough. They may also have experienced previous placements leading to further loss of carers and different expectations of what relationships might be like. Additionally it is likely that some of their early experience has been traumatic. They will often re-enact this experience through their play and in their relationships. Children will also be growing up and passing through all the normal developmental stages and usual transitions of childhood (moving school, becoming a teenager, etc.). However, often their early experience has led to some degree of developmental delay or difficulty. By understanding the child's current experience, together with developmental stage and early attachment history, the therapist will be able to make sense of the behaviours displayed, and find ways to help the child.

In attachment-focused therapies the aim is to help children to use their carers as a secure base from which they can explore the unhappy and painful aspects of their past and of their present (Bowlby, 1988). From this secure base, and with the experience of positive parent–child interactions, the children can be helped to develop emotional regulation and reflective function abilities – abilities that enhance flexible responding to experience instead of rigid, repetitive reactions to events.

The ability to recognize and regulate emotion is a developmentally acquired process, but it develops within the context of parent–child interactions. Children with suboptimal experience of parenting including neglect, abuse and violence can display under-controlled, ambivalent displays of emotion with high levels of dysregulated behaviour triggered by only moderate increases in arousal. Alternatively they may display over-controlled and unresponsive displays of emotion with inhibition of distress or discomfort (Maughan & Cicchetti, 2002).

Reflective function or the ability to mentalize similarly develops within parent–child relationships. Children experiencing difficult early relationships have a reduced capacity for developing these meta-cognitive skills. Growing up with abusive or neglectful parents provides for children an intolerable view of themselves as unlovable and unworthy. To cope with this they stop processing what they learn from the mind of their parent. This in turn leads to the development of inconsistent and segregated internal working models of attachment relationships leading to difficulties in developing the ability to reflect on their own or other people's mental states. Therapy provides an opportunity to safely 'find their mind' reflected in the mind of a caring, non-abusive person (Fonagy et al., 2002).

The role of the carer is critical in ensuring that therapeutic work with the child is beneficial. The carer will be continuing to support the child at home often through an increase in distressed and distressing behaviours as the child copes with intense and stressful therapeutic work. If the carer becomes unable to tolerate the worsening of behaviour there is a danger that the child will retreat from therapeutic endeavours or that the placement will break down with devastating effects on the child's capacity to recover from this and previous trauma. It is important therefore that carers are involved and informed about the work that their child is undergoing.

There is also a strong argument for actually involving the carer within the therapeutic work itself. Carers can be powerful allies for the therapist, providing they have sufficient capacity to remain regulated in the face of child distress. They can support the therapeutic process, as it is ongoing, and continue to provide safety and containment for the child between sessions. There are also concerns that working with the child in the absence of the carer can have detrimental outcomes for children with attachment difficulties. Therapy can interfere with fragile relationships that are developing between the child and carer. In fearing family intimacy the child may instead attach to the therapist. This can then hinder the development of a genuine attachment with the carer (Delaney, 1998). Even when the carer is not actively involved in the therapy, good communication is essential. The therapist and carer can easily work at cross-purposes, often leaving the carer feeling blamed while continuing to deal with problems that can even be worsening (Delaney, 1998).

A number of practitioners are developing therapies based on attachment theory and current research on the importance of the child–carer relationship for healthy development. These therapies both consider modifications to existing evidence-based practice (e.g. Pearce & Pezzot-Pearce, 2001; Hunter, 2001) and have been developed with a specific focus on the development of secure attachments (e.g. Hughes, 1997; Brisch, 2002; Delaney, 1998; Bleiberg, 2001). At present, no treatment method based on attachment theory for children has been shown to be effective in appropriately controlled treatment trials (O'Connor & Zeanah, 2003) and systematic applications of theory to intervention are described as rudimentary (Lieberman & Zeanah, 1995). However, with a growing interest in attachment theory – especially in relation to helping children in foster and adoptive homes – it is likely that research will guide the further development of interventions in time.

Crittenden et al. (2001) suggests that we should not be focusing on developing a single intervention for all children with attachment difficulties. Instead we should be focusing attention on the particular difficulties of the children. Commonly these have developed out of the strategies learned to maintain their safety within adverse environments. For example, she predicts that the child who has developed a predominantly avoidant attachment strategy and thus inhibits the expression of negative emotion will benefit from interventions that encourage focus on and expression of these feelings. The child needs help to increase emotional awareness, reduce internal distress and improve self-esteem. On the other hand, the child who has developed a predominantly ambivalent pattern of relating to others needs help to develop emotional regulation abilities so that he or she can manage and communicate feelings at a moderate level of arousal. Thus far these predictions have not been tested in practice. They provide guidance, however, for the eclectic practitioners searching for ways of helping the children referred to them. It should be borne in mind that many of the children living in foster or adoptive homes have experienced a range of insecure relationships with past carers. A child displaying a combination of avoidant and ambivalent styles of relating to others is not unusual. Interventions will need to be comprehensive and matched to the range of difficulties the child is displaying. Hughes, for example, attends to both the co-regulation of emotion and the co-construction of meaning when working with children with attachment difficulties (Hughes, 2004).

While researchers and theorists are able to offer predictions and guidance about therapeutic methods based on attachment theory, practitioners can use

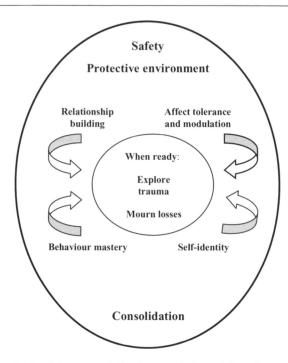

Figure 12.2 A framework for therapy (adapted from James, 1994)

theory and research to design interventions tailored specifically to the children in front of them. The responses of the children being helped can further develop these interventions into coherent treatment approaches. These include interventions designed to promote the therapeutic parenting of children (e.g. Cairns, 2002; Keck & Kupecky, 2002; Siegel & Hartzell, 2003; Schofield & Meek, 2005), as well as models of psychotherapy (e.g. Delaney, 1998). Additionally therapeutic tools are being developed to help parents to work with their children to develop different views of self and others. For example, Family Attachment Narrative Therapy guides parents in the creation of stories to tell their child, aimed at increasing the 'connection' between carer and child, facilitating the healing of past trauma and the development of new ways of behaving (Lacher et al., 2005).

James (1994) draws on theories of attachment and trauma to provide a model for intervention (see Figure 12.2). She highlights the importance first of a protective environment within which the child feels physically and emotionally safe. Next the child needs to live within a therapeutic environment. Therapeutic parenting provides support to build a sense of identity and family relationship. The child learns to regulate emotion and behaviour. Finally the child needs a therapeutic relationship within which past trauma can be explored and losses mourned.

Hughes (1997, 1998, 2004) has developed a therapy specifically for children living in adoptive or foster homes experiencing significant attachment problems. Dyadic-developmental psychotherapy is a therapy modelled on our understanding of how secure attachments develop within parent–child relationships, drawing upon both developmental, and attachment theory (Hughes, 2003). Research into early relationships and the experience of attunement (Stern, 1985) on the development of intersubjectivity (Trevarthen, 2001), mentalization (Fonagy et al., 2002), and emotional regulation (Schore, 1994) have informed the therapeutic process. This approach describes a model of parenting and a method of therapy. It not only involves but also actively uses the carer within the therapeutic sessions. For this to be successful it is important that both the therapist and the carer have an autonomous or resolved state of mind with regard to their own expectations of attachment relationships. This does not mean that they have to have experienced a secure upbringing themselves, but that they have resolved any loss or traumatic experience encountered during their own childhoods. The goal of therapy is to help the child to feel safe with their carer and to develop secure, selective attachments. This enables the child to make developmental progress in all areas of development. The therapeutic sessions are structured to replicate the attachment sequences found in healthy parent–child interactions. Thus sequences of attunement, socialization/shame, and re-attunement are repeatedly provided for the child. The child experiences the intersubjective sharing of affect that is attunement (Stern, 1985) and learns that breaks in such intersubjective experience can be repaired following conflict, and mis-attunement (Hughes, 2003).

An understanding of the role of pervasive shame in the experience of the child is important if the therapist is to support the child adequately. The emotion of shame, which is central in identity development, is initially expressed within relationships. When early parenting is provided with anger, punitive discipline and/or a lack of recognition of the child's needs, and the child experiences little attunement or interactive repair, the child develops a pervasive sense of shame that is toxic to his or her sense of self and relationships with others (Kaufman, 1996).

Hughes (2004) describes a therapist attitude of playfulness, acceptance, curiosity and empathy (which has been described in more detail in Chapter 8). This helps the child both to tolerate and enjoy positive emotional interactions and to explore the sense of shame associated with current experiences of discipline and frustration within the family, as well as that stemming from earlier experience of neglect and abuse. The therapist uses this same attitude when encountering resistance by the child. The therapist accepts the child and his or her need not to engage at that time, while being curious and playful about it. In this way the child experiences empathy for how difficult the work is and is supported and comforted as he or she gradually faces the issues.

Case Study 2

Kathryn spent her first seven years living with her mother and older brother and sister. Kathryn's mother was herself brought up in care. She was preoccupied with her own emotional needs to the extent that she could not meet the emotional needs of her children. This had become progressively more difficult for her with each successive child. Kathryn was therefore emotionally and physical neglected. In addition a series of abusive partners meant that Kathryn was exposed to a climate of domestic violence and transient relationships. Concerns about the mother's ability to care for and protect Kathryn led to her removal into foster care under the protection of a care order.

Kathryn's early experience with a mother who was emotionally unavailable led to the development of an insecure-avoidant attachment. Overt expression of emotional distress led Kathryn's mother to withdraw further. Kathryn therefore learned to minimize such expression. However living in a fearful environment also saw the development of disorganized behaviour when Kathryn was stressed. For example, Kathryn would remain sitting for long periods apparently unaware of what was going on around her. As she grew older Kathryn would at times become aggressive and non-compliant, drawing her mother into a control battle. Kathryn had developed a way of coping with the frightening aspects of being parented, by taking control of the relationship. However this strategy became ineffective quite quickly. When under sufficient stress Kathryn would again become very withdrawn or she would become overwhelmed and regress into a toddler-like tantrum state.

When Kathryn first moved into foster care she presented few problems. She did not like to be cuddled and would tend to withdraw rather than approach the foster carer when upset. Kathryn was relating to her carers in the way she had learned to relate to her mother. As they quietly supported her, Kathryn became more demanding, wanting to stay close to the foster mother and needing a lot of reassurance that she was wanted. Kathryn was now making tentative moves to relate to predictable and sensitive care in a different way. She was developing an attachment which at times was still avoidant but with the beginning of more emotional expressiveness. However, Kathryn's fear of losing this relationship was apparent in her relatively frequent episodes of sudden explosive behaviour, usually when her wishes were thwarted or when asked to comply to a request. Kathryn appeared to interpret this as a lack of love from her carer leading to dysregulated behaviour. Her anxiety that she might lose this relationship overwhelmed her.

Following a consultation the psychologist offered home visits and telephone support to help the carers further develop their fostering skills in relation to Kathryn's individual needs. Over the following months the carers learned to maintain a positive emotional atmosphere by remaining calm and clear with Kathryn. They responded quickly to inappropriate behaviour and followed this with relationship repair – reassurance for Kathryn that she was loved and wanted. A high degree of attunement and empathy provided Kathryn with the emotional support she needed to begin to learn how to regulate her emotions and how to turn to her carers for help when she was distressed.

Kathryn made progress in her placement, learning to trust and draw support from her carers. However the carers remained concerned at how quickly Kathryn could dysregulate when she felt rejected. Kathryn appeared highly sensitive to 'normal' caregiver behaviours such as requests to tidy toys away, being asked to share with other children or being told 'no'. Her behaviour quickly became confrontational and aggressive. It was decided to offer therapy sessions to Kathryn and her foster mother. These sessions were used to help Kathryn to feel more secure in her relationship with her foster mother and to help her to understand and test out her fears within the containing therapeutic setting. Early sessions were playful and engaging with opportunities for the carer to nurture Kathryn through cuddles, food and taking care of cuts and bruises. Experiences during the week were discussed with the therapist puzzling with Kathryn about her behaviour. Kathryn found this extremely difficult.

The therapist switched to talking to Kathryn about how hard this was for her. This empathic approach helped Kathryn to express her fears that the therapist wouldn't like her if she heard how bad she had been. This in turn led to Kathryn expressing to her foster mother her fear of rejection and to her receiving empathy and reassurance about this. The therapist linked this for Kathryn to her experience with her biological family using puppets, drawings and therapeutic stories to help her to process this emotionally. Over this time Kathryn became more settled in placement. While she remained quick to anger, she was better able to manage her anger and anxiety without major outbursts.

APPLYING ATTACHMENT THEORY TO ADOLESCENT THERAPY

Adolescence is a developmental stage, which, at least in western cultures involves the development of increased self-reliance and autonomy. This stage can present particular difficulties for the young person who does not have a foundation in secure relationships. These different developmental challenges need different interventions (Dozier et al., 2002).

At this stage, especially with the older adolescents, there tends to be a move towards using more adult modes of therapy. While these may continue to involve the carer, the young people will often 'vote with their feet' and prefer to work with the therapist alone. Cassidy and Mohr (2001) identify some of the difficulties in working with this age group when the young person has little previous experience of secure attachment. The therapeutic alliance becomes an essential prerequisite to helping the young person to explore and restructure working models of attachment. However there can be difficulties in creating such an alliance. For example, the authors suggest that the young people may find it alien and threatening to use therapists as a secure base. Expressions of warmth and care can lead to fear of coming to rely on a caregiver who is likely to let them down. Adolescents may therefore inhibit the attachment system by activating other behavioural systems (e.g. sexual, or caregiving system). These young people are also vulnerable to rapid shifts in the representation of self (persecutor, victim, rescuer), which can be very confusing to the therapist (e.g. see Liotti, 1999).

There is a debate concerning whether the attachment relationship is an appropriate focus for interventions at all at this developmental stage. Barth and Miller (2000) suggest that this is the time for young people and their parents to negotiate challenges that arise through growing independence rather than the time to go back and resolve historic relationship issues. For example, multi-systemic therapy provides a comprehensive and individualized treatment approach that addresses the multiple determinants of problems. Minde (2003), however, queries whether interventions aimed at social problems can be successful without first changing parent and child relationships. He suggests that age appropriate autonomy from parents is more easily negotiated when a secure attachment has been achieved. We need to help the adolescent to find a balance between attachment and autonomy. There is a danger if this is not done that substitute pseudo-secure attachment objects will be found in the form of drugs and inappropriate peer groups (Brisch, 2002). These reduce the need for genuine attachments but with devastating consequences for the young person.

Downes (1992) carried out a study of 23 adolescent foster placements. She found that many adolescents had developed difficult patterns of relating to others. Their behaviour was typically alienating, destructive to self and others, and prevented the development or maintenance of close relationships. This study emphasized the importance of an attachment for this age group to enable the young people to take responsibility for themselves and to increase their confidence. The tasks of adolescence are more achievable when they have a reliable and secure base, allowing them to shift their attachment from parents to friends, and to explore the wider world of work and sexual relationships. This is not, however, an easily achievable goal. Adolescents who found that they got inadequate or unreliable responses to attachment behaviour in infancy and childhood will find it hard to ask for help directly. Requests may be hidden in hostility or paralysis. The therapist will need to pay close attention to direct and distorted requests for help and be ready to respond. Downes (1992) emphasizes the importance of recognizing re-enactments of earlier patterns of behaviour in order to protect them from the hurt of potentially unreliable relationships. Additionally psychological interventions need to recognize the intensity of psychological support young people need, especially during transitions. As the adolescent feels confident in the availability and reliability of carers he or she is better able to leave these carers and manage in the wider world, and to function under stress. In this way the young person can be helped to have a capacity for independence and for intimacy.

Case Study 3

Paul is 16 years old and lives in a residential unit. Within the next year it is likely that Paul will have to move to an independent living arrangement. The referral was precipitated by fears that he was not going to be able to make this transition successfully.

Paul lived with his birth family until he was 3 years old. He experienced a family environment in which drug abuse and domestic violence were common. Following a series of short-term foster placements Paul was adopted along with his younger brother Mark. Initially Paul moved into the family without difficulty while Mark presented difficulties. However, over time Mark settled and Paul's underlying problems became more apparent. The adoptive parents found it difficult to relate to Paul who they compared unfavourably to his brother. Nevertheless Paul lived within this family until he was 14 years old. By this time he was excluded from school and was increasingly demonstrating aggressive behaviour within the home. This culminated in an incident when he threatened his mother with a knife. Paul was voluntarily accommodated and moved into the residential unit. Over time Paul made good progress. His behaviour continued to be up and down with periods where he appeared to be settled and able to develop relationships alternating with times of increased aggression and running away from the unit. In the six months preceding the referral, Paul's behaviour became much more difficult. He stopped attending school, hygiene and self-care became very poor, and Paul would not engage in the preparation for independence programme that had been set up for him.

The therapist initially met with Paul alone. He found these sessions difficult and was often absent from the unit for the time they were scheduled. Gradually, however, he was able to talk about his fears of the future. Paul feared independence and this related to longstanding fears of abandonment by those he cared about. Paul had developed a range of strategies to cope with these fears which all made it more difficult to move him on from the unit. The therapist worked with Paul to understand these fears, how they linked to his behaviour and related to his past experience. While Paul demonstrated some insight into this, his behaviour did not improve. It was decided that Paul needed help to develop a secure base from which he could gradually test out independence and autonomy. The therapist negotiated an extension to his placement providing Paul returned to school and worked towards a college placement. Sessions were held with Paul and his key worker. Paul was helped to verbalize his fears about losing the relationship, and not being good enough to be cared about. The key worker provided empathy and reassurance. While this proceeded well initially, extended sickness on the part of the care worker made it difficult for Paul to experience security. At this time Paul's adoptive mother was tentatively re-establishing some contact with Paul. This proceeded well and the therapist began to include her in the therapeutic work. Over the next six months they began to have regular contact and to build a more positive relationship. Paul left school successfully and began a college course. He was not able to complete this and he left the unit prior to his eighteenth birthday. He is currently living independently but visits his adoptive family at the weekends.

THE IMPORTANCE OF TOUCH

Traditional therapy discourages the use of touch between the child and therapist. More recent therapeutic approaches, especially those focused on enhancing attachment relationships, have explored the benefits of touch. This has been a controversial exploration, and guidance about the use of physical contact within therapy is currently not available. However, there are some considerations that can inform the practitioner both in supporting the carer and in providing therapy for the child.

Touch is a very natural part of the parent–child relationship. In the first few years of life touch is central to the nurturing children receive. Cuddling and physical care provide high levels of touch. Therefore touch is a central part of the attachment relationship that is forming at this time (Keck & Kupecky, 2002; Archer & Burnell, 2003). Human touch is a fundamental interpersonal need for all of us (James, 1994). When the need for physical contact fails to be understood the child experiences shame. This is damaging to the development of a sense of self (Kaufman, 1996). Touch within an abusive parent–child relationship, however, can be very different, providing pain and trauma for the developing child.

It would therefore seem that touch for children who have a history of abuse and neglect is very important. It can provide them with experiences of kind touching, missed in early childhood while demonstrating that touch does not have to be painful and traumatic. Keck and Kupecky (2002) suggest that holding a child in a nurturing and non-confrontational manner is effective at any age. The more the child is held the healthier the child will become. When the child is held and hugged, brain networks are activated and strengthened (Schore, 2003). For children with major difficulties with relationships, touch can be an important therapeutic tool.

While touching adoptive children is less controversial, within foster care more difficulties are experienced. Carers can feel uncomfortable offering normal touch and physical comfort to children who have been abused, especially when they are of the same sex as the abuser. Guidance about safe caring for foster carers can also tend to discourage touch between carer and child. Guidelines are required, but these need to encourage appropriate touch. Children should experience healthy relationships and normal parenting practices. Most importantly they need to feel loved and valued, that their early experience has not contaminated them in some way. Touch is an important component of a relationship that can offer this. When children are resistant to being held and touched there will be a conflict between following the child's wishes, and helping him or her to develop and be comfortable with a new type of relationship. Dozier et al. (2002) advises foster carers of young children to regularly hold the child but to follow the child's lead in breaking off the contact. They stress the importance of physical contact for comforting a distressed child.

Within therapy there is also a need for guidelines about the use of touch. These guidelines need to offer a balanced view, to consider the positive benefits of touch as well as discouraging its potentially damaging use.

The use of holding techniques represents the most controversial of these. Holding is used to encourage touch and eye contact. Designed to mimic the touch or holding experiences that are part of the attachment process between parents and infants the child lies across the laps of two therapists (or therapist and carer) and is strongly encouraged to maintain eye contact.

There are concerns that holding therapy can be intrusive, non-sensitive and counter-therapeutic. That it can in fact further traumatize the child (O'Conner & Zeanah, 2003; Dozier, 2003). These authors suggest that this therapy has not been adequately assessed and that it is not guided by attachment theory. Others suggest that if it is non-coercive and carried out with the consent of the child it can be an important method for emotionally recreating close proximity in order to elicit and facilitate verbal and non-verbal communication (Howe & Fearnley, 2003).

There does seem to be some confusion concerning the aims of holding therapy. Some authors suggest that this therapy aims to facilitate communication (Howe & Fearnley, 2003). Others appear to use holding therapy as a coercive method to force the child into obedience by breaking down their defences. Holding is used alongside isolation, excessive chores, deprivation of privileges, sarcasm and shaming until the child becomes dependent on the adult, and compliant with their authority (as described by Hughes, 2003). Alternatively, holding therapy has been described as a method to help the unattached child who is angry at the world. The holding represents a method of rage reduction during which children are encouraged to release their anger. After the therapists have provoked and aroused the children to the point where they cease resisting and surrender, they are handed to their carers to foster attachment (as described by Minde, 2003). These latter forms of holding therapy probably represent the most controversial of all techniques. The authors suggest that they are potentially retraumatizing and not based on principles either derived from attachment theory or from research (Hughes, 2003; Minde, 2003). Additionally James (1994) suggests that such techniques foster the development of trauma bonds. The child does attach, but this is not a healthy attachment.

While it is hard to see any potential benefit of using coercive physical contact with children whose trust in the adult world is already severely compromised, interventions are needed to help children to develop emotional regulation skills. Physical contact might be an important therapeutic tool to achieve this goal. The therapeutic challenge is to find non-coercive ways of doing this that also help children to rebuild trust. Research is needed to explore the ethical use of touch and holding with children who have given consent, to see whether it leads to benefits over and above other aspects of the therapeutic interventions.

ATTACHMENT AND CULTURE

Attachment theory is a theory of human adaptation. The carer–infant relationship is the first relationship within which mutual adaptation occurs. The success of this adaptation impacts on later relationships and the ability to adapt to changing circumstances. When viewed in this way it becomes clear that culture will have an influence on the attachment process. Culture will influence parental expectations, values and norms and this will influence their care of and response to the infant. The infant in turn adapts to the parenting practice within this cultural context. The child therefore survives within a 'cultural niche', and this can affect the attachment pattern that is normative within a culture (Van Ijzendoorn & Sagi, 1999). The authors give the example of cultural expectations that emotions should be suppressed leading to the development of an avoidant attachment pattern (not dissimilar to our UK culture of 'stiff upper lip'). Crittenden (2000) describes the assessment of attachment patterns in infants in a range of western and non-western cultures highlighting differences in what is normative and what is viewed as pathological from culture to culture.

A range of studies has explored attachment theory across cultures (see Van Ijzendoorn & Sagi, 1999). These studies point to the universality of the three basic patterns of attachment (avoidant, secure and ambivalent). Similarly, the secure attachment pattern is found in the majority of children across cultures. Some caution is needed however, preliminary studies point to normative differences in the assessment of secure attachment between cultures. Thus using the same criteria a group of researchers can rate the same behaviours as secure while a culturally different group can rate them as insecure (Crittenden, 2000).

What is missing from research exploring universality is increased understanding of differences between cultures – differences that lead to dissimilarities between groups of people in how they think about and engage in close relationships. Intervention needs to be mindful of such cultural and ethnic differences (Rothbaum et al., 2000). For example, Rothbaum and his colleagues explored the differences between the American and Japanese cultures. Attachment theory, the authors suggest, is laden with western values of achievement, autonomy and exploration. When this theory is applied to the Japanese values of dependence, emotional restraint and self-criticism, it is easy to view the child–carer relationships as insecure or even disordered. Interventions need to be tailored to the differences between cultures and social contexts respecting the outcomes that different cultures value.

What then is the implication for the practitioner? A foster carer once told me that she was fearful for her foster child who would be returning home. She was worried that offering this child a different, and a more secure experience of parenting would not help the child in the transition to home. That it might in fact cause difficulties if the child related to her parents in the way she was learning to relate to her carer. This would indeed be a danger if the intervention was designed to teach the child a culturally determined secure attachment pattern. If, however, substitute care was seen as a way of helping the child to develop a range of ways of relating to others, then this danger is diminished. We need to be cautious of overvaluing secure attachment as a treatment goal and viewing patterns of relating outside of this narrow range as pathological. Crittenden (2000) suggests that variation and diversity in patterns of attachment are adaptive. The ability to select patterns of relating to others flexibly and consciously allows for adaptability to a range of situations and circumstances. Interventions that encourage diversity are much more likely to be respectful of cultural differences.

CONCLUDING COMMENTS

Bowlby (1988, p. 140) likens the therapist to a parent 'who provides her child with a secure base from which to explore'. There is ongoing debate about how best to help the child to recover from early adverse parenting and controversy about the efficacy and even safety of so-called attachment interventions (O'Connor & Zeanah, 2003). Within substitute care children display a range of attachment difficulties and will need a range of interventions. These might be directed at the carer, the environment or the child or young person. This chapter has explored interventions that are currently being developed and evaluated for children and young people across the age range. Therapists and researchers need to work together to develop these further, being mindful of the theory that has spawned them and developing evaluations to validate them. We are working with children and young people whose miseries can be both forgotten and current. Attachment theory provides us with a framework within which to understand these miseries and the continuing impact they are having on the child. Attachment interventions hold out promise that we can help the children to move on positively and hopefully. Bowlby himself gives us a useful yardstick by which we can judge such interventions:

> This means, first and foremost, that he accepts and respects his patient, warts and all, as a fellow human being in trouble and that his over-riding concern is to promote his patient's welfare by all means at his disposal. To this end the therapist strives to be reliable, attentive, empathic, and sympathetically responsive, and also to encourage his patient to explore the world of his thoughts, feelings, and actions not only in the present but also in the past.
>
> (Bowlby, 1988, p. 152)

REFERENCES

Ainsworth, M.D.S., Blehar, M.C., Waters, E. & Wall, S. (1978) *Patterns of Attachment: A Psychological Study of the Strange Situation.* Hillsdale, NJ: Erlbaum.

Archer, C. & Burnell, A. (2003) *Trauma, Attachment and Family Permanence. Fear can Stop you Loving.* London: Jessica Kingsley Publishers.

Bakermans-Kranenburg, M.J., Juffer, F. & Van Ijzendoorn, M.H. (1998) Interventions with video feedback and attachment discussions: Does type of maternal insecurity make a difference? *Infant Mental Health Journal,* **19**(2), 202–219.

Bakermans-Kranenburg, M. J. & Van Ijzendoorn, M.H. (2003) Less is more: Meta-analyses of sensitivity and attachment interventions in early childhood. *Psychological Bulletin*, **129**(2), 195–215.

Barth, R.P. & Miller, J.M. (2000) Building effective post-adoption services: What is the empirical foundation? *Family Relations*, **49**(4), 447–456.

Bleiberg, E. (2001) *Treating Personality Disorders in Children and Adolescents*. New York: Guilford Press.

Bowlby, J. (1969) *Attachment and Loss, Vol. I: Attachment* (2nd edn, 1982). London: Hogarth Press; New York: Basic Books.

Bowlby, J. (1973) *Attachment and Loss, Vol. II: Separation, Anxiety and Anger*. New York: Basic Books (1975, Harmondsworth: Penguin).

Bowlby, J. (1980) *Attachment and Loss. Vol. III: Loss: Sadness and Depression*. New York: Basic Books (1981, Harmondsworth: Penguin).

Bowlby, J. (1988) *A Secure Base. Clinical Applications of Attachment Theory* (2nd edn, 1998). London: Routledge.

Brisch, K.H. (2002) *Treating Attachment Disorders from Theory to Therapy* (English edition). New York: Guilford Press.

Cairns, K. (2002) *Attachment, Trauma and Resilience*. London: BAAF.

Cassidy, J. & Mohr, J.J. (2001) Unsolvable fear, trauma and psychopathology: Theory, research, and clinical considerations related to disorganized attachment across the life span. *Clinical Psychology: Science and Practice*, **8**(3), 275–298.

Crittenden, P.M. (1988) Relationships at risk. In J. Belsky & T. Nezworski (Eds), *The Clinical Implications of Attachment* (pp. 136–174). Hillsdale, NJ: Lawrence Erlbaum.

Crittenden, P.M. (2000) A dynamic-maturational exploration of the meaning of security and adaptation: Empirical, cultural, and theoretical considerations. In P.M. Crittenden & A.H. Claussen (Eds), *The Organization of Attachment Relationships: Maturation, Culture and Context* (pp. 358–384). New York: Cambridge University Press.

Crittenden, P.M., Landini, A. & Claussen, A.H. (2001) A dynamic-maturational approach to treatment of maltreated children. In J.N. Hughes, A.M. La Greca & J.C. Conoley (Eds), *Handbook of Psychological Services for Children and Adolescents*. Oxford: Oxford University Press.

Delaney, R.J. (1998) *Fostering Changes. Treating Attachment-disordered Foster Children*. Oklahoma City, Oklahoma: Wood & Barnes Publishing.

Downes, C. (1992) *Separation Revisited. Adolescents in Foster Family Care*. Brookfield, VT: Ashgate.

Dozier, M. (2003) Attachment-based treatment for vulnerable children. *Attachment and Human Development*, **5**(3), 253–257.

Dozier, M., Albus, K., Fisher, A. & Sepulveda, S. (2002) Interventions for foster parents: Implications for developmental theory. *Development and Psychopathology*, **14**, 843–860.

Dozier, M. (2005) Challenges of foster care. *Attachment and Human Development*, **7**(1), 27–30.

Fisher, P.A., Gunner, M.R., Chamberlain, P. & Reid, J.B. (2000) Preventive intervention for maltreated preschoolers: Impact on children's behaviour, neuroendocrine activity and foster parent functioning. *Journal of the American Academy of Child and Adolescent Psychiatry*, **39**, 1356–1364.

Fonagy, P., Gergely, G., Jurist, E.L. & Target, M. (2002) *Affect Regulation, Mentalization, and the Development of the Self*. New York: Other Press.

Fraiberg, S. (1980) *Clinical Studies in Infant Mental Health: the First Year of Life.* New York: Basic Books.

Hart, A. & Luckock, B. (2004) *Developing Adoption Support and Therapy.* London/ Philadelphia: Jessica Kingsley Publishers.

Howe, D. (in press) Developmental attachment psychotherapy with fostered and adopted children. *Child and Adolescent Mental Health.*

Howe, D. & Fearnley, S. (2003) Disorders of attachment in adopted and fostered children: Recognition and treatment. *Clinical Child Psychology and Psychiatry,* **8**(3), 369–387.

Hughes, D.A. (1997) *Facilitating Developmental Attachment. The Road to Emotional Recovery and Behavioural Change in Foster and Adopted Children.* Northvale, NJ: Aronson.

Hughes, D.A. (1998) *Building the Bonds of Attachment. Awakening Love in Deeply Troubled Children.* Northvale, NJ: Aronson.

Hughes, D.A. (2003) Psychological interventions for the spectrum of attachment disorders and intrafamilial trauma. *Attachment and Human Development,* **5**(3), 271–277.

Hughes, D.A. (2004) An attachment-based treatment of maltreated children and young people. *Attachment and Human Development,* **6**(3), 263–278.

Hunter, M. (2001) *Psychotherapy with Young People in Care.* Hove: Brunner–Routledge.

James, B. (1994) *Handbook for Treatment of Attachment-trauma Problems in Children.* New York: Free Press.

Kaufman, G. (1996) *The Psychology of Shame. Theory and Treatment of Shame-based Syndromes* (2nd edn). New York: Springer Publ. Co.

Keck, G.C. &. Kupecky, R.M. (2002) *Parenting the Hurt Child. Helping Adoptive Families Heal and Grow.* Colorado: Pinon Press.

Kretchmer, M.D., Worsham, L. & Swanson, N. (2005) Anna's story: A qualitative analysis of an at-risk mother's experience in an attachment-based foster care program. *Attachment and Human Development,* **7**(1), 31–49.

Lacher, D.B., Nichols, T. & May, J.C. (2005) *Connecting with Kids through Stories. Using Narratives to Facilitate Attachment in Adopted Children.* London/Philadelphia: Jessica Kingsley Publishers.

Lewis, E., Dozier, M., Knights, M. & Maier, M. (in press) Intervening with foster infants' caregivers: Attachment and biobehavioural catch-up. In R.E. Lee (Ed.), *Handbook of Relational Therapy for Foster Children and their Families.* Washington, DC: Child Welfare League of America.

Lieberman, A.F. & Zeanah, C.H. (1995) Disorders of attachment in infancy. *Child and Adolescent Psychiatric Clinics of North America,* **4**, 571–687.

Lieberman, A.F. & Zeanah, C.H. (1999) Contributions of attachment theory to infant–parent psychotherapy and other interventions with infants and young children. In J. Cassidy & P.R. Shaver (Eds), *Handbook of Attachment. Theory, Research and Clinical Application* (pp. 555–574). New York/London: Guilford Press.

Liotti, G. (1999) Understanding the dissociative process: The contribution of attachment theory. *Psychoanalytic Enquiry,* **19**, 757–783.

Main, M. & Solomon, J. (1986) Discovery of a new, insecure disorganized/disorientated attachment pattern. In T.B. Brazelton & M. Yogman (Eds), *Affective Development in Infancy* (pp. 95–124). Norwood, NJ: Ablex.

Marvin, R., Cooper, G., Hoffman, K. & Powell, B. (2002) The circle of security project: Attachment-based intervention with caregiver–preschool child dyads. *Attachment and Human Development,* **4**(1), 107–124.

Maughan, A. & Cicchetti, D. (2002) Impact of child maltreatment and interadult violence on children's emotion regulation abilities and socioemotional adjustment. *Child Development*, **73**(5), 1525–1542.

Minde, K. (2003) Assessment and treatment of attachment disorders. *Current Opinions in Psychiatry*, **16**, 377–381.

O'Connor, T., Rutter, M., Beckett, C., Brophy, M., Castle, J., Colvert, E., Gregory, A., Groothues, C. & Kreppner, J. (2001) Early deprivation and later attachment-related behaviour: Lessons from the English and Romanian adoptee study. In W. Yule & O. Udwin, *Occasional Papers No. 18. Parenting: Applications in Clinical Practice* (pp. 51–59). ACPP.

O'Connor, T. & Zeanah, C. (2003) Attachment disorders: Assessment strategies and treatment approaches. *Attachment and Human Development*, **5**(3), 223–244.

Pearce, J.W. & Pezzot-Pearce, T.D. (2001) Psychotherapeutic approaches to children in foster care: Guidance from attachment theory. *Child Psychiatry and Human Development*, **32**(1), 19–44.

Rothbaum, F., Weisz, J., Pott, M., Miyake, K. & Morelli, G. (2000) Attachment and culture. Security in the United States and Japan. *American Psychologist*, **55**(10), 1093–1104.

Rutter, M. (1995) Clinical implications of attachment concepts: Retrospect and prospect. *Journal of Child Psychology and Psychiatry*, **36**(4), 549–571.

Schofield, G. & Meek, M. (2005) Providing a secure base: Parenting children in long-term foster care. *Attachment and Human Development*, **7**(1), 3–25.

Schore, A.N. (1994) *Affect Regulation and the Origin of Self: The Neurobiology of Emotional Development*. Mahwah, NJ: Erlbaum.

Schore, A.N. (2003) Early relational trauma, disorganized attachment and the development of a predisposition to violence. In M.F. Solomon & D.J. Siegel (Eds), *Healing Trauma. Attachment, Mind, Body and Brain* (pp. 107–167). London: W.W. Norton & Co.

Siegel, D.J. & Hartzell, M. (2003) *Parenting from the Inside Out*. New York: Tarcher/Putnam.

Stams, G.J.M., Juffer, F., Van Ijzendoorn, M.H. & Hoksbergen, R.A.C. (2001) Attachment-based intervention in adoptive families in infancy and children's development at age 7: Two follow-up studies. *British Journal of Developmental Psychology*, **19**, 159–180.

Stern, D.N. (1985) *The Interpersonal World of the Infant*. New York: Basic Books.

Stovall, K.C. & Dozier, M. (2000) The development of attachment in new relationships: Single subject analyses for 10 foster infants. *Development and Psychopathology*, **12**, 133–156.

Svanberg, P.O. (in preparation) Promoting attachment security in primary prevention using video feed-back: The Sunderland Infant Programme. Submitted for publication, April 2005.

Svanberg, P.O. & Jennings, T. (2001) The Sunderland Infant Programme (UK): Reflections on the first year. *The Signal, Newsletter of the World Association for Infant Mental Health*, **9** (Oct–Dec.), 1–4.

Taylor, E. & Rogers, J.W. (2005) Practitioner review: Early adversity and developmental disorders. *Journal of Child Psychology and Psychiatry*, **46**(5), 451–467.

Trevarthen, C. (2001) Intrinsic motives for companionship in understanding: Their origin, development, and significance for infant mental health. *Infant Mental Health Journal*, **22**(1–2), 95–131.

Van Ijzendoorn, M.H. & Sagi, A. (1999) Cross-cultural patterns of attachment: Universal and contextual dimensions. In J. Cassidy & P.R. Shaver (Eds), *Handbook of Attachment. Theory, Research and Clinical Application* (pp. 713–734). New York/London: Guilford Press.

Verrier, N.N. (1993) *The Primal Wound. Understanding the Adopted Child.* Baltimore, Maryland: Gateway Press Inc.

Weinfield, N.S., Sroufe, A., Egeland, B. & Carlson, E.A. (1999) The nature of individual differences in infant–caregiver attachment. In J. Cassidy & P.R. Shaver (Eds), *Handbook of Attachment. Theory, Research and Clinical Application.* New York/London: Guilford Press.

CONCLUSION

TRAVELLING HOPEFULLY — THE JOURNEY CONTINUES

Liz Stott, Ruth Nissim, Helen R. Dent and Kim S. Golding

To travel hopefully is a better thing than to arrive...

(ROBERT LOUIS STEVENSON)

At the time of writing there is increasing recognition of the complexity and ongoing needs of looked after and adopted children. We are aware that the backdrop to this is continually changing as services are reorganized. Services to children are undergoing radical transformation with increased focus on working together, early interventions and preventative work, targeted outcomes, and the involvement of service users in developing and evaluating services. Throughout this book we have contributed to this changing climate, as we comprehensively consider the role of psychological thinking for children who are looked after and adopted.

We have come to experience the writing of this book as a journey. In this process we have thought about the most valuable souvenirs from our journey. They remind us of the primacy of listening to the children themselves, their carers and the other professionals involved in their care. By listening we hear much that is different in the experience of the children and the families and in the response to this from professionals compared with more traditional child and family work.

We discover that much more can be heard when listening in the spirit of acceptance of the difference rather than in selectively hearing the same. At times the many layers of difference can lead to confusion, despair, intense emotion and hope. The different experience of the child can be unsettling,

Thinking Psychologically About Children Who Are Looked After and Adopted
Edited by K.S. Golding, H.R. Dent, R. Nissim and L. Stott.
Copyright © 2006 John Wiley & Sons, Ltd.

grotesque and terrifying. Without full acceptance a space cannot be created within which a difference can be offered in return. Many of the children's experiences are distressing even to the distanced worker. If, as professionals or carers, we stay hidden behind the defence of thinking we know best, we remain distanced from and less helpful to the very children we need to reach. This area of work challenges those who distance themselves. It demands that we use all of ourselves in connecting and attuning to, not only the children, but also their parents and carers. Working together we can make a difference in this terrain of multiple families, institutions and organizations. Acceptance of and interest in the differences leads to the creation of a potentially unique and exciting landscape. We suggest that psychological thinking, which is theory driven and well researched, can help to shape this landscape. It can help to create a strong secure foundation upon which to build and create new ways of thinking.

This book illustrates how psychological thinking can be used to create spaces within which to reflect. It is founded on the assumption that many looked after or adopted children have had experiences that have led them not to trust adults and to be easily overwhelmed with intense emotion. These children appear on the surface to be as able as their peers living within their families of origin. Their dis-ability is often invisible. They evoke strong feelings of compassion and the desire to right the wrongs of the past. Many well-meaning parents, carers and professionals believe these unthinkable early experiences can be forgotten with stability, love and good parenting. It is deeply painful for the children, the adults parenting them and those closely involved in their care to acknowledge the depth of the damage and its impact on the child's everyday life. These children demand and deserve enormous amounts of thought from all those involved with their care. They challenge individuals and agencies that believe they can succeed in isolation and confront carers and professionals with the importance of joining together to create space to reflect. In the writing of this book we have come to believe that it is only when the voices of all those concerned are heard and space is created to think about them together that the next pathway can be found.

Interestingly we are writing at a time when there is more of a climate of pulling together and joining of forces. Within the field of psychology itself there is movement away from the ideas of one or two dominant theories towards a more eclectic integration of ideas. The era of the grand narrative has gone and in its place is a multitude of excited and eager voices. In this spirit of bringing together there is recognition of the importance of the narrative and a willingness to hear the many voices. Children who are fostered or adopted need to be at the forefront of this bringing together. These most disintegrated children need the most integrated thinking.

In the fields of research and theory there is an exciting coming together of minds between neuroscience, biochemistry, psychoanalysis and psychology.

What is emerging is the physical evidence for so much that has been intuitively felt over many years (e.g. Bowlby, 1988). At last we are beginning to join up our thinking and find biological evidence of the impact of social and emotional environments, both *in utero* and in the first two years of life (Gerhardt, 2004). There is great hope that this will prove to be a major turning point in political and social fields informing the care and policy around young babies and their parents, much as attachment theory radically changed the policy around hospital and institutional care. This is also happening at a time when there is rising concern over the number of child protection tragedies, most recently the death of Victoria Climbié and the murder of Holly Wells and Jessica Chapman. Disparate and diverse agencies preoccupied with their own agendas, budgets and political frameworks are particularly dangerous for children at risk. Political pressure for integration of services for children could not be happening at a better time. However, we would advocate that in this coming together it is essential that there is also a protected space within which to reflect. Without a safe space to think it is unlikely that much can change. Without a clear structure and theoretical framework the danger is that we replicate the very same experiences of the children we are intending to help. We continue acting without integrating our thinking both within and between agencies. In our haste to alleviate the distress we don't have time to hear all the voices and so lose the opportunity for a different story.

Psychological thinking has much to offer to organize the structure of this space. As the child moves between different parents, families and carers out into the worlds of education, health, and social services, a structure is needed to hold the various aspects of the child together. In most birth families it is the parents who hold the narrative or story of their child. For children who are adopted, fostered or looked after in residential care this narrative is often disjointed, incoherent and at times harrowing. It is difficult for any one carer or professional to hold. Psychological thinking can provide a containing structure within which to piece together the various disjointed aspects of the story and to develop the beginnings of a more coherent picture. This may be in the form of an assessment or snapshot in time. It may then help to inform the next stage of deciding how to best connect with the child and carers, to work therapeutically. The continual feedback from both child and those working with him or her help to inform this next step. Psychological thinking can form a secure base from which to try out new strategies, whether this is with parents, carers, care workers or in consultation with wider networks and organizations. This is a journey in itself and challenges all those involved to remain open to the process.

Psychological thinking is challenged by the needs of looked after and adopted children. Rather than blaming the children for not fitting with the theory, we have examined what psychology can offer that is both helpful and hopeful. In the process of creating this book we have discovered that this is a never-ending journey. As in systemic thinking, if you reach a conclusion then you have lost the point (Cecchin, 1987). If you stop being curious, you stop thinking. Thinking psychologically is not primarily about getting answers but about generating questions. We have learned that to travel hopefully in this terrain you have to learn to live with uncertainty, with much discomfort and to cope with failure and mistakes. The temptation to fill the role of expert with all the answers has to be resisted as it undermines the delicate balance of understanding already created by those caring and working with children and inevitably sets the expert up to fail. We hope that we have been able to illustrate what we have learned from our clinical experiences of both the successes and the failures. One thing we have learned to accept is that on this journey there is no clear and wonderful destination. In fact by creating a desirable end point we may inadvertently derail ourselves. We have found that the target-driven culture within which we work often drives us to the wrong destination, losing the richness of the experiences along the way. Pressures to obtain better GCSE results or to reduce the number of changes in placement are in danger of becoming the only benchmarks by which successful care is measured. The well-meaning desire to push up expectations for these children is in danger of missing the point. It is almost impossible to capture the essence of a change that may take many years to materialize. Who knows what the effect of a kindly word or a well-timed hug may be a generation later. The child must be understood within the context of his or her own unique landscape.

> For example, imagine one of the children whom we are trying to understand as a passionflower struggling to grow in thick undergrowth. We may begin by clearing the space to see what is there. The space is not conducive to growth and so we dig the flower up, move it to a better place. It is difficult to pull up and we inadvertently tear the roots, leaving some behind. We find rich soil and good light and give the plant lots of water. In spite of this it still seems to be struggling. We move it again and are surprised by the abundance of roots as it hardly appears to have changed on the surface, unfortunately it gets torn again and more roots are left behind.
>
> We now feel quite anxious – 'Will this plant survive? Will this stony soil suit it? And how much water and light?' We feel less confident now. Maybe we should never have moved it at all. Gradually and very slowly the plant begins to grow and we learn by watching carefully when to water it and when to enrich its soil, which plants it likes to grow near and which it hates. We realize what we don't know and discover that it is only by creating the space to try new things and learn from their effects that we can grow in our understanding of this plant. This all takes time.

Psychological thinking has much to offer in organizing the plants to maximize their potential. It is grounded in well-researched theory. These theories may inform the types of soils, the amounts of light, when to water and when to feed but cannot in themselves fully understand the plant. Each of these plants is unique and reacts to changes differently. None of these theories in isolation will grow the plant – we need to think about the whole system in order to understand how best to proceed.

We believe that psychological thinking can rise to the challenge. With adaptation and adjustments based on the unique understanding of each child and each carer, much can be offered to this area of work. For most of these children we will never know how their journey ends but by creating a space within which to think we have a better chance of travelling alongside them.

> 'I think it's a good thing that I went into care.... I don't think I'd be the person I am now really if I hadn't. It's made us stronger. I mean, it just made us more determined not to be like my parents, or to be better than, I don't know, live a better life, to have a better life than them.'
>
> (Lara: p. 195 in Skuse & Ward, 2003)

REFERENCES

Bowlby, J. (1988) *A Secure Base: Clinical Applications of Attachment Theory*. London: Routledge.

Cecchin, G. (1987) Hypothesising, circularity and neutrality revisited: An invitation to curiosity. *Family Process*, **26**, 405–413.

Gerhardt, S. (2004) *Why Love Matters. How Affection Shapes a Baby's Brain*. Hove and New York: Brunner–Routledge.

Skuse, T. & Ward, H. (2003) *Outcomes for Looked After Children: Children's Views of Care and Accommodation*. An Interim Report to the Department of Health. Loughborough University: Centre for Child and Family Research.

Stevenson, Robert Louis (1850–1894). *El Dorado* (p. 522). *Oxford Dictionary of Quotations* (3rd edn). OUP, 1979.

INDEX

Note: Page references in italics refer to Figures